Solve You

Astro

CW00553365

Solve Your Problems
Astrologically

BEPIN BEHARI

MOTILAL BANARSIDASS PUBLISHERS
PRIVATE LIMITED • DELHI

4th Reprint: Delhi, **2018**
First Edition: Bangalore, 1988

ISBN: 978-81-208-1696-1

MOTILAL BANARSIDASS

41 U.A. Bungalow Road, Jawahar Nagar, Delhi 110 007
1B, Jyoti Studio Compound, Kennedy Bridge, Nana Chowk, Mumbai 400 007
203 Royapettah High Road, Mylapore, Chennai 600 004
236, 9th Main III Block, Jayanagar, Bengaluru 560 011
8 Camac Street, Kolkata 700 017
Ashok Rajpath, Patna 800 004
Chowk, Varanasi 221 001

Printed in India

by RP Jain at NAB Printing Unit,
A-44, Naraina Industrial Area, Phase I, New Delhi–110028
and published by JP Jain for Motilal Banarsidass Publishers (P) Ltd,
41 U.A. Bungalow Road, Jawahar Nagar, Delhi-110007

This Book Serves You in Ten Ways

Five ways of making the best use of the Book

1. If you are a general reader without any knowledge of astrology, firstly prepare a rough horoscope of your own on the basis of information supplied in the appendix. Then rapidly glance through the chapters suggested for acquiring simplified rules of astrology. This would equip you to take up the next step.

2. Identify your problems which are of greatest importance to you. Take help of the suggestions made on page iii. Also consult the index and cross references. This would give guidelines for understanding the astrological implications of your problems.

3. Work out the periodicity of the planetary rulership which you should be able to do on the basis of information given in the appendix, otherwise if you have your horoscope, this information should be available there. Superimpose on it the knowledge derived from the various chapters in Part II. That would indicate the broad direction of your life-pattern.

4. Before making any serious decision with regard to educational planning either for yourself or for your children take help of the relevant chapters. Similarly with regard to vocational matters, medical treatment, and your psychological tension, a careful

study of the connected chapters might be of some help in relieving your anxiety.

5. In case, you are developing some interest in spiritual side of life, and have been interested in understanding the nature of your own personality and the various factors operating on the same, this book could be immensely helpful in opening to you greater vista of the subjects with possible lines on which further studies could be taken up. The author's *A Study in Astrological Occultism* could be very profitable as a follow up study.

PREFACE TO THE SECOND EDITION

Astrologically, the basic human problems such as vocational selection, personal relationships, social status and spiritual upliftment are not geography specific. These are universal problems. Ancient astrologers were much concerned about them and their solution but they discussed them in archaic terms. The present study presents the classical astrology in modern terminology so that astrology students all over the world may derive advantage from the ancient astrological wisdom.

During the last decade or so, popularity of Vedic astrology has increased extensively. Intellectuals, scientists, business executives and others are showing much interest in astrology and other occult subjects. In order to meet their need, brief introduction to various planets and important astrological combinations are included in this study. It also includes appendices which give preliminary information for such readers and others who are not well-acquainted with astrology. Even a novice can begin his or her study of Vedic Astrology with the help of these appendices.

The author is looking forward to receiving comments and suggestions from the readers for improvement of the study.

C-505, Yonana Vihar   **Bepin Behari**
Delhi-110 092

PREFACE

The present study is directed to those readers who wish to make use of astrological knowledge for tackling their personal problems. The ancient seers and eminent astrologers have emphasized that the knowledge of the stars was imparted to mankind so that they could harmonise their life according to stellar influences. There was a destiny for each individual. The planetary radiations were merely endeavouring to guide the individual or the nation to that destiny. Whenever there was any deviation from this goal, one experienced pain. The astrological knowledge was given to us in order to comprehend the working of the finer forces of nature and to adapt ourselves to them. Astrology was never intended to propagate fatalism.

Those who could have an insight into this esoteric science, they could harness the stellar energy for the benefit of the world as well as for themselves. Such an exercise required an understanding of the nature of forces radiating from the stars and also the ability of the individual to harmonise himself in accordance with those forces. The yogis concentrated on the second part so that they could be benefic influence to the world. But ordinary humanbeings were confronted with many kinds of sufferings as they were ignorant of their individual destiny as well as of the supra-physical forces impinging on this earth. The exoteric astrology made them aware

that there was a destiny for them. An intelligent understanding of the stellar science could enable them to trans-
mute their sorrow into equanity, their pleasure into understanding and ambition into benefic influence. Such a
goal would however require much deeper knowledge of
astrological occultism. Only at later stages of initiation
in Mystery schools, this knowledge was imparted to the
student. Before attaining this privilege one has to
gather whatever little is available through various
sources. The present author made such an effort in
compiling *A Study in Astrological Occultism*. Some
readers may find that useful.

The present study hopes to cater to the basic needs
of general readers and beginners to the science of
planetary influences. Those who have already obtained
the preliminary knowledge of various planets, signs of
the zodiac, the various house divisions of the natal
chart, and such other elementary knowledge of astrology
should be able to derive much advantage from this book.
Those who do not have a horoscope of their own and are
unable to get it readily made, if they know their time of
birth they could utilise this knowledge with a little effort
to take advantage of this book. For this purpose, they
need to know two facts. Firstly, the Sun under the
Indian system of astrological reckoning is generally in the
following signs of the zodiac during the period shown
against them : Aries (April 14—May 14), Taurus (May
15—June 14), Gemini (June 15—July 14), Cancer (July
15—August 14), Leo (August 15—September 14), Virgo
(September 15—October 14), Libra (October 15—November 14), Scorpio (November 15—December 14), Sagittarius (December 15—January 14), Capricorn (January
15—February 14), Aquarius (February 15—March 14) and
Pisces (March 15—April 13).

The second rule they have to know is that the sun-sign of the zodiac rises in the morning at the eastern horizon which is approximately the middle of the first house or the ascendant, at the sunset time that sun-sign is in the seventh house, at noon it is in the tenth house and mid-night in the fourth house. Knowing one's birth time, it could be possible to roughly determine the ascendant and the sun-sign. Following it, the ephemeris of the year of one's birth would indicate planetary positions for the date of birth. This could be a working horoscope for pursuing further the study of the book before an accurate horoscope is cast by an expert astrologer.

Some of the basic problems in one's life which can be effectively answered by astrology are the purpose for which one is born, the profession of the person, his financial status, marital happiness and other problems relating to marriage, wife and children, various tensions and accident proneness, and the question of death and so on. An attempt has been made in this study to deal with these subjects primarily with a view to giving the reader an insight into the basic circumstances of his life. In dealing with these problems, an attempt has been made to indicate the changeability of these conditions. That which is inevitable cannot be altered but many of the unhappy conditions of our life are susceptible to change. It is hoped that the readers would be able to modify their painful events much effectively if they could know how much change is possible.

Having once aroused the desire to know one's future, the reader may make use of this book to understand the basic principles of astrology. Care has been taken here to present abstruse astrological principles in such a way that one does not have to go through rigid mathematical and technical concepts. One can read what interests him, and skip over what is incomprehensible or does not interest. This would not create any difficulty in taking up the subsequent topics.

In this book, mention has also been of modern philosophical approach to astrology. It is so done primarily to show that the approach of some psuedo-scientists to this occult science is not only irrelevant but also unscientific. Specially the chapter on *Astrology, Cosmic Ideation and Modern Philosophy* attempts to show that the fundamental thinkers like Carl C. Jung and J. Krishnamurti did not decry astrology or consider it a fraud rather they showed the rationale behind such predictions. What we cannot explain need not be illogical or a fraud. Patanjali showed the various steps which could be taken up in order to comprehend the future. On the path of self-unfoldment which is the goal of yogic exercises, it is natural to possess the knowledge of stellar influences.

Those who wish to take up the practice of yoga would find astrology useful in determining the special course to follow. The two chapters, namely *Aid to Self-Realisation*, and *Which Yoga Suits You ?* should give the reader preliminary information on the subject. He would find greater details on it in *A Study in Astrological Occultism*. Here we are attempting only to arouse the interest of the reader in such possibilities on the basis of astrological self-knowledge.

The author has tried to cover a very wide area of astrology in this study. But the subject is still much more extensive. In this book, the author has been concerned with showing the practical use of astrology in tackling one's personal problem. How far he has succeeded in this task could be decided only by the readers. If they find that the publication has enabled them to understand their personal problems a little better and are able to grapple them a little more effectively, the author would consider that his efforts have been amply rewarded. Only under that condition, probably the reader would also feel that his efforts were useful.

Many persons have helped and encouraged the author in the preparation of this book. He feels greatly indebted to all of them. He would however like to acknowledge special gratitude to Shri M. M. Mistry who took special care in preparing the diagram on lunar mansions and gave unflinching support and encourage-ment. I would also like to record my deepest apprecia-tion for Ms. Ida O'Neil of California and my wife Smt. Madhuri Behari who discussed with me the various subjects at different stages of the preparion of the book and encouraged and assisted me in completing it.

C–505, Yojana Vihar   **Bepin Behari**
New Delhi–110 092

CONTENTS

PART II

I

PLANETS AND THE INDIVIDUAL

The stars attract from us to themselves, and we again from them to us. The body is wood and the life is fire, which comes like the light from the stars and from heaven....Everything pertaining to the spiritual world must come to us through the stars, and if we are in friendship with them, we may attain the greatest *magical* effects.

Paracelsus (1493–1541)
Quoted by H. P. Blavatsky in
Isis Unveiled, Vol. I., p. xxvi

PLANETS AND THE INDIVIDUAL

STARS RULE THE UNIVERSE

Every student of occultism interested in personal as well as social progress would like to understand the relationship existing between the human individual and the cosmic life, the bond of affinity between the temporal and the eternal. Such a student is interested to know for himself, whether there is any visible or invisible power influencing the emerging social and human patterns. In fact, what the occultists endeavour to understand is the relationship between the human individual and the One Universal Life. From the inner point of view, All is One Law, and as one occult teacher mentioned, "Nature follows the same groove from the creation of a universe down to that of a mosquito". The astrological student is thrilled to find that the mysterious relationship in which every specific event of the world appears as an expression of Cosmic Ideation beginning with the creation of the Imperishable, the Svayambhu Narayana, of which the Hindus speak of in their scriptures, whilst the esotericists consider the perpetual motion, "the *universal perpetual motion* which never ceases, never slackens nor increases its speed not even during the interludes between the pralayas or "nights of Brahmas" but goes on like a mill set in motion", is beautifully explained by astrological philosophy. The triple duty of a Mason is said to study whence he comes, what he is, and whither he goes, which in essence is a study of God, of himself and of the future transformation. Such a study of Cosmic Ideation beginning with *universal perpetual motion*, which generates its own electricity, magnetism, force, will, and the sense of direction which in their summation comprise LIFE seems difficult to explain the fact that unintelligent forces can give rise to highly intelligent beings like ourselves but the astrological approach enlightens the subject well by describing the eternal progression of cycles, and the process of evolution ever perfecting its work as it goes along. The esotericists insist that it would be folly to consider it a chance 'coincidence' to learn of ''the degree of the solar heat, light, and nature of the planets by simply studying their symbolic representations in the Olympic gods, and the twelve signs of the zodiac, to each of which in astrology is attributed a particular quality''.[1] For a truer comprehension of the astrological forces, one will have to transcend the realm of physical planets to go to the world of Planetary Spirits functioning as Creative Intelligences in aid of the Ultimate Cause, or God.

The ancient sacred scriptures of the East, not giving credence to the voice of the skeptics, treated astrology as a 'limb-of-the-Vedas' whose knowledge had to be acquired before learning the Divine Wisdom, 'by knowing which everything else of this world is understood'. The teachings of this subject had remained esoteric and was imparted only to the select few in the mystery schools. Many temples of the ancients, as those of the Templars and the Assassins, were surrounded with pillars recording the numbers of the constellations, the signs of the zodiac, or the cycles of the planets, which, in a way, were thought to represent a symbol or a microcosm of the

---

1. H. P. Blavatsky, *Isis Unveiled*, Theosophical University Press, California, Vol. I, p. 267.

Temple of the Universe. Till today, the mysterious purpose for the erection of the Stonehenge and other places of Druid worship has remained speculative for the simple reason that the significance of astrology in ancient Initiatory rites has been unknown. Ignorance of the ritual and of the mystery schools today, does not indicate that the esotericism of astrology has been unknown. Even now the occultists and seers are fully aware of the tremendous significance of astrology and they do act in accordance with astrological forces taking advantage of harmonious planetary radiations.

The knowledge of planetary radiations and their esoteric influence was imparted to the students only at a very advanced stage. When the students were ready for such a training they were informed of the mystery of the emergence of *seven* divine Law-givers with their *seven* Prophets and *twelve* Apostles was explained in astrological terms indicating them to represent the planets and the zodiac. One of the causes of the disrepute of the astrologers following the spread of knowledge among the profane has been "the fraud of those who wanted to make money by means of that which as part and parcel of the sacred Science of the Mysteries, and, ignorant of the latter, evolved a system based entirely upon mathematics, instead of on transcendental metaphysics and having the physical celestial bodies as its *upadhi* or material basis".[2] Such disrepute, however, could not discourage eminent men and scientists such as Kepler, Camille Flammarion, Sir Isaac Newton, Bhishops Jeremy and Hall, Archbishop Usher, Dryden, Flamstead, John Milton and others from trying to understand the occult nature of astrology and to re-establish some of its

2. H. P. Blavatsky, *Theosophical Glossary*, Theosophy Co., California, p. 39.

lost glory. In India, atleast from the Vedic times the importance of astrology is on record which was with a view to co-operating with Celestial Powers in discharge of their divine functions. Every Hindu ritual, from birth to death, and even in after death rites, astrology was assigned an honoured status. Among the modern western world, H. P. Blavatsky also attempted to rein-state the rightful place to this occult science in its esoteric splendour and mystery. She stated that "astro-logy is a science *as infallible* as astronomy itself, with the condition, however, that its interpreters must be equally infallible".[3]

Such infallibility pertains to all branches of astro-logical interpretations. The science of horoscopy is studied chiefly under four heads, namely, mundane, state or civic, horary and genethliacal. Mundane astrology deals with problems relating to meteorology, seismology, agriculture, etc., whereas the fate of nations, kings and rulers comes in the second category. Horary astrology is concerned with spontaneous questions and doubts upon any subject arising in the mind of the questioner. Genethliacal astrology, which in fact is the most popular branch of the subject, is related to the fate of the indivi-dual from the moment of his birth to his death. All these four branches of horoscopy depend upon the study of the constellations, the stars, the zodiac, and the planets located in the sky at the time of the occurrence of the event. It would be an ostrich policy to consider all such predictions as merely "curious coincidence", as some skeptics have a tendency to consider. This is so, specially in view of the prevalence of such predictions and guidances practically in all ages and in all civilisa-

---

3. H. P. Blavatsky, *Isis Unveiled*, op. cit p. 259.

tions. Despite this, the materialistic world does not feel like accepting the occult basis of astrology, which must inevitably follow as day follows night. The materialistic forces would sustain a tremendous set-back, if human beings begin looking for non-physical dimensions of causation of the phenomenal world which they would have to do if the soundness of astrological predictions could be demonstrated. Probably it is for this reason that H. P. Blavatsky stressed the fact that "in astrology... one has to step beyond the visible world of matter, and enter into the domain of transcendent spirit".[4] It has been rightly stated that "astrology must be recognised as the soul of astronomy unless the latter is to produce nothing beyond materiality". The present day problem with most of the people is, that they refuse to accept the validity of any transcendental Spirit or to look for any reward which is of non-physical character. Evidently in a materialism-centered society, the slightest ripple of interest in astrology as a valid scientific subject is likely to create much opposition and resentment.

During the recent years, however, the progress in the study of astronomy and other allied social studies has demonstrated the influence of the sun and the moon on affairs of the world. The relationship between the tides and the phases of the Moon has long been established. The lunar influence on the emotional life of an individual has already become a scientific subject for study among the psychologists. Rudolf Thiel in his book *And There Was Light* has already given several recorded instances of various relationships between the starry heaven and the terrestrial phenomena. He has mentioned that the menstrual period in a womon is in some way under the

4. Ibid. p. 259.

influence of the heavenly body that divides time into months for us. In the animal world also there are periodic rhythms, all of a sexual nature, which is linked with the Moon. Dr. Thiel further stated that the relationship between the cosmic order and the life rhythm of terrestrial beings brings to our notice a great deal of attention which was suddenly focussed upon Schwabe's sunspot periods when the correlation between them and the cycles of magnetic storms and northern lights was recognised. On the basis of such evidence, Thiel concluded that "Here was a new tie, mysteriously linking us to the Sun, which nourishes all life on Earth".

Empirical studies of the type mentioned above does not indicate the mechanism, the process, by which a distant star situated at a distance of several million light years could affect even the thoughts and aspirations of a tiny human being, or indicate the nature of a question or the doubt and the answer to the fleeting doubt in the questioner's mind. Reasons for such phenomena must be sought at a deeper level. The occultists have already established the presence Astral Fluid or a kind of magnetic link between all parts of the universe as a result of which the radiations from even the farthest star could be registered and received on the earth. Within the very constitution of man and the different levels of existence at which he dwells, there is inbuilt mechanism by which astral radiations are received in a differentiated manner. The human body and the different planes on which he dwells are so constituted that the celestial planets have a predominant role to play for which they are well tuned. The relationship between the physical world, the human body and the planetary hierarchy has been allegorically suggested when a reference is made to God convening a meeting of the celestial planets who

promised to invest human nature with various qualities,
intellectual and emotional, good and bad, peculiarly
appertaining to the nature of the donor".[5] The influence
of the planets flowing through the seven "principles"
of man and activating his various force-centres, the
chakras, affects the very core of the human being; this
type of interplay of the divine energy on the different
forms of sentient and insentient beings is fundamentally
different from that which the modern astronomers are so
far contemplating.

It would be unscientific, if not foolish, to dogmatise
about the influence of the planets on the "principles"
of man and the various force-centres, or the *chakras.*
These subjects are beyond the reach of physical sciences
or speculative knowlegde ; those who know are very
reluctant to give out the knowledge. About the
septenary human principles very fragmentary information has been available based on any direct or
occult authority. Under such circumstances, any
discussions on this subject could be merely tentative.
C. W. Leadbeater discussed the vital functioning of the
force-centres in his monograph on the subject wherein
he stated that "into the hub or open mouth of each
(chakra) a force from the higher world is always flowing
—a manifestation of the life-stream issuing from the
Second Aspect of the Solar Logos—which we call the
primary force. That force is sevenfold in nature, and all
its forms operate in each of these centres, although one
of them in each case usually predominates over the

_____
    5. T. Subba Row, *Esoteric Writings,* Theosophical Publishing
House, Adyar, p. 234.

others. Without this inrush of energy the physical body
could not exist".[6]

The author did not relate the planets with the various
force-centres in the human body, but he quoted the
well-known German mystic, Johann George Gichtel, a
pupil of Jakob Boehme, who in his *Theosophia Practica*
assigned planets "to the chakras, giving the Moon to the
basic, Mercury to the splenic, Venus to the umbilical,
the Sun to the heart,...Mars to the laryngeal, Jupiter to
the frontal, and Saturn to the coronal".[7] T. Subba Rao,
an initiated Adwaitee Brahmin, gave a very different
correspondence. He stated in his *Esoteric Writings* that
the seven chakras are connected with the seven planets
in the following order, beginning with Muladharam
which is connected with Saturn; then Jupiter, Mars,
Venus, Mercury, Moon, and Sun.

Similar difficulties arise even with regard to establishing the correspondence between the *chakras* and
the principles of man. Since the days of A. P. Sinnett,
who began drawing attention of the Himalayan Mahatmas
to this subject and began explaining it in his *Esoteric
Buddhism*, the subject has remained quite unclear in
spite of various clarifications given by H. P. Blavatsky
and Annie Besant. Dr. Annie Besant gave three sets of
classification of these principles in her *The Seven
Principles of Man.* Any correspondence between
the principles and the planets would depend upon
which set of correspondence we take into account.
C. W. Leadbeater has attempted to indicate a relationship between the two in his book on *The Chakras,*
but finality cannot be assumed in this regard. The

6. C. W. Leadbeater, *The Chakras*, Theosophical Publishing
House, Adyar, p. 15.
7. Ib. p. 24.

only safe conclusion that can be drawn from these discussions is that there is a relationship between the
planets, the chakras and the principles of the human
being. Any categorization of these may be misleading,
and merely speculative.

Similar correspondences have been attempted even
between the planets and the races which have so far
peopled this globe. Based on the characteristics of the
various planets in classical Hindu astrology, it has been
shown that there is relationship between the planets, the
driving impulses in man, the seven basic human tempera
ments, the planes of solar manifestation and the Root
Races. It has been suggested that the ancient Polarian
and Hyperborean races were chiefly influenced by the
Moon ; when the Lemurian civilisation flourished, the
world was inhabited by impulsive persons with fiery
enthusiasm under the sway of Mars. The Atlantean
civilisation, with its great heights of scientific achievements, has been mentioned as the civilisation inhabited
mainly by the people with developed lower *Manas* ruled
by Mercury ; whereas, the Aryan Race with the predominant characteristics of synthesis, harmony, and philanthropy reveals some of the traits of Jupiter. The future
race of the new humanity, with intuitive faculties trans-
cending sectarian barriers with a tremendous urge to
unite and to create, will have the strong Venusian
influence. Obviously, these subjects are so much of
deeper nature that no definite assertion can be made.
However, based on whatever fragmentary information is
available, one may begin investigating possible explanations of such phenomena.

These studies have clearly shown that there is an
intimate relationship between the planets and the various
aspects of our living. It is obvious that the exact details

of the mechanism of this interaction are not available in exoteric literature, nonetheless the impact of the planets on terrestrial life is acknowledged. The next problem then arises as to the source of energy from which these planets derive their force. What is the fountainhead from which these planets derive their energy to activate the various force-centres or *chakras* in the human beings and regulate the affairs of men. *The Secret Doctrine* suggests that the "the Septenary Hierarchy of conscious Divine Powers, who are the active manifestations of the One Supreme Energy" resulted from the differentiation of the 'Germ' of the Universe. These Divine Powers "are the framers, shapers, and ultimately the creators of all the manifested Universe, in the only sense in which the name of 'Creator' is intelligible ; they inform and guide it ; they are the intelligent Beings who adjust and control evolution, embodying in themselves those manifestation of the One Law which we know as the "Laws of Nature".[8]

Everything in manifestation comprises 'spirit' and 'matter', so it is but natural that the Seven Celestial Beings or the Seven Planetary Logoi should also have a body and a soul. T. Subba Rao, conforming to this view, has stated that : "The Logos itself has a soul and a spirit as everything else has which is manifested".[9] Looked at from this point of view, it is logical to expect an objective as well as a subjective reality of these Great Hierarchies. Elucidating the process of cosmogenesis, H. P. Blavatsky stated : "In the ancient cosmogenesis, the visible and the invisible worlds are the double links of one and the same chain. As the

---

8. H. P. Blavatsky, *The Secret Doctrine*, Theosophical Publishing House, Adyar, Vol. I., p. 86.

9. T. Subba Rao, *Esoteric Writings*, op. cit. p. 238.

Invisible Logos, with its Seven Hierarchies— each represented or personified by its chief Angel or Rector— form one Power, the inner and the invisible ; so, in the world of Forms, the Sun and the seven chief planets constitute the visible and active potency; the latter "Hierarchy" being, so to speak, the visible and objective Logos of the invisible and – except in the lowest grades- ever-subjective Angels".[10]

Thus, considering these divine planets as sentient "Celestial Agencies" for carrying out the plan of the Logos, one would neither label worshipping of stars as superstition, nor the cyclical fluctuations in world events as figments of imagination. Madame Blavatsky has very rightly stated that "Saturn", 'the Father of Gods', must not be confused with his namesake – the planet of the same name with its eight moons and three rings. The two—though in one sense identical, as are, for instance, physical man and his soul—must be separated in the question of worship. This has to be done the more carefully in the case of the seven planets and their Spirits, as the whole formation of the universe is attri- buted to them in the Secret Teachings".[11]

Explaining the impact of the planets, H. P. Blavatsky stated : "Thus—to anticipate a little by way of illustra- tion—every Race in its evolution is said to be born under the direct influence of one of the planets ; the Race the First receiving its breath of life from the Sun...; while the Third Humanity—those who fell into generation, or from androgynes became separate entities, one male and the other female—is said to be under the direct influence

10. H. P. Blavatsky, *The Secret Doctrine*, op. cit., Vol. III, p. 36
11. Ib. Vol. V., p. 324.

of Venus, *"the 'little Sun' in which the solar orb stores high light"*.[12]

Madame Blavatsky has further stated that : "Every student of Occultism knows that the heavenly bodies are closely related during each Manvantara with the mankind of that special cycle ; and there are some who believe that each great character born during that period has—as every other mortal has, only in a far stronger degree—his destiny outlined within his proper constellation or star, traced as a self-prophecy, an anticipated autobiography, by the indwelling Spirit of that particular star".[13]

In this way, astrology only confirms the view that each being is linked with the Absolute in a very real though mysterious way. Elucidating this relationship, H. P. Blavatsky has stated that : "The human Monad in its first beginning is that Spirit, or the Soul of that star (planet) itself. As our Sun radiates its light and beams on every body in space within the boundaries of its system, so the Regent of every Planet-star, the Parent-monad. shoots out from itself the Monad of every 'pilgrim' Soul born under its house within its own group. The Regents are esoterically seven, whether in the Sephiroth, the 'Angels of the Presence', the Rishis, or the Amshaspends".[14]

In the philosophy of *Advaita Vedanta,* it is often stressed that the microcosm does not only reflect the Macrocosm, but also that the two, in fact, are one. This relationship between the world of manifestation and the Absolute is expressed in very many ways. Not a sparrow falls without a shiver in the lord. Astrologically speaking also, there is a mysterious link between every atom

12.   Ib. Vol. III., p. 37.
13.   Ib. Vol. V. p. 333.
14.   Ib

of manifestation at all levels and the Absolute—the Macrocosmic Person. In the *Mundaka Upanishad,* the Imperishable, the source and the goal of all beings is described as :

> "Fire is His head ; His eyes, the Moon and the Sun; the regions of space His ears ; His voice, the revealed Vedas ; Wind, His breath ; His heart, the Whole World. Out of His feet, the earth. Truly He is the Inner Soul of all. From Him (proceeds) fire, whose fuel is the Sun ; From the Moon, rain ; herbs, on the earth. The male pours seed in the female. Many creatures are produced from the Person".

The above is the same cosmic vision shown by the Lord Krishna to Arjuna. Instead of describing the roots of One Universal Life in all forms of creation, and the Great Breath pulsating through every event of the phenomenal world, the ancient seers of astrology presented the vision in the symbology of *Kala Purusha*—the transcendental Man and described him living in Day and Night and having the various planets as his force-centres, the *chakras*, through which the Divine Energy pours out into everything and thus sustains it.

A belief in astrology, however, should not make the human being fatalistic. Astrology gives a new vision of truth and opens out many hitherto dark recesses of knowledge for greater enlightenment. It does not shut out the possibility of human endeavour for accelerating evolution and "awakening the soul". Mr. N. Sri Ram has rightly stressed that "The stars may be an indication of certain influences which work, but how far these influences determine events may depend on ourselves. We have ultimately to fall back on ourselves. Our attitude should be an attitude not of resignation but of responsibility".

WHO DOES NOT BELIEVE ?

Presently there is a popular trend throughout the world to know more about astrology and its capabilities in assisting human beings in various ways. This is so particularly in the industrialised west where the strain for eking out a livelihood has not been as severe as in the traditionally old underdeveloped countries. In many countries of ancient civilisations, astrological predictions have already been interwoven in their everyday life. The advent of technological innovations and breakdown of the established values in life have however aroused a wave of dissatisfaction with life. The life of the individual is not very happy and satisfying in any part of the world. Many persons who are ordinarily considered very well-off from the material standpoint have been deeply concerned with the question of understanding the importance of the supernatural in human affairs. The great interest in meditational practices, classes in yogic exercises and knowledge, and the growing interest in astrology have been phenomenal. There have been instances when the general public in the west have been eagerly waiting for weekly and monthly predictions published in their journals without which there have been a feeling that they have missed their breakfast. Even the morning television broadcast in several western countries have been relaying astrological predictions for different zodiacs. When the journals or the televisions have, for some reasons or the other, failed to publish or announce the predictions concerning any particular sign, the editors have been flooded with letters from the readers and the viewers. Even the business executives are becoming increasingly interested in astrological support for their selection of the personnel. The growing interest in the occult is one of the many pointers of the growing interest in the subject.

On the other hand, at places there have been some negative trends. In countries like India and in other countries with predominating communistic faith, there has been some uneasiness about astrology. Some of the well-to-do persons are frequently visiting astrologers, professionals and amateurs, whereas there have been others who make it a principle to decry this subject in the public. There would be a large number of persons who would put on gems studded rings on their different fingers in order to gain favour from planetary deities, but questioned upon the subject, they would decry the occult. There is some kind of reluctance even in the believers to accept the validity of astrology. The contradiction in the private faith and public denouncement is often very pronounced. Fairly highly educated persons with reasonably high levels of academic degrees and recognitions, have sometimes been noted to be vehemently criticising rather crudely the astrological prognostications. Thus we find that there is a current of growing popularity of the subject on the one hand, whilst on the other some persons have been making a tirade against astrology and other occult subjects. One has also come across such persons who shout from the house-tops against astrology but have been secretly paying special attention to astrologers. This contradictory trend naturally reveals some deep-rooted imbalance of the psychological type.

One need not be seriously disturbed by such inconsistencies. Whenever some new ideas gain ground or whenever the settled habits are broken, there is a kind of reaction. By the type of the stone one wears, or the way one changes one's office table after acquiring a new position, or by consultations with the astrologers at the time of the marriage of their daughters (or their own), one is likely to infer the real attitude of the persons concerned. During the last few decades, marital disharmony has become one of the main causes for visiting the astrologers.

It is interesting to know why any individual believes in such occult subjects while others refute the rationale of the same established on the basis of even scientific investigations and on the testimony of eminent scientists and thinkers. For the last few decades, I have been watching individuals with differences in their approach to astrology. It has been a very fascinating study and I have been greatly encouraged by my observations. As a result of these observations, I am confident of the great future for the subject. I also feel that those who accept astrological guidance with judicious consideration and intelligence are adopting a wise course of action. The study made by the writer has given him considerable strength and insight into the role of astrology in our everyday life and also into the types of persons who decry it for one reason or the other. He wishes to share his experiences in order to make the readers emboldened and to cheer them up in their approach.

The first thing to watch in the present context is not to be glamourised by the worldly status of the individual who is decrying importance and efficacy of astrology.

Actually it does not matter what the individual is in the worldly life, unless he has reasons to know the subject, his opinion should not matter. When my child is sick even with common cold, I do not seek the advice of great engineers or painters or art critics : what I do is to approach the nearest physician. This is so because Rubens and Shakespeares are not expected to be omni-scient ; they may be proficient in their limited field of specialisation but not in all subjects. On this analogy, it is quite irrelevant to consider the views of a Prime Minister or a Chancellor, if the person is ignorant of the subject. That is what Sir Isaac Newton had advised the astrologers and the laymen. Unless the other person knows of the subject, it is useless to attach importance in his pronouncements. No scientist would do that. He would give credence to others only if the other person has specialised knowledge of the subject.

In matters like astrology, the second point to enquire is whether the individual criticising astrology has a horoscope of his own. This is important. Often those individuals who do not think they can make any use of astrology generally rate this science very low. I know of several vehement critics of the subject being so because they do not have any correct birth data. It is surprising how the individual considerations of this type make the person opposed to such things and take up rigid attitudes. But my personal feeling has been that this is primarily a supplementary cause ; by itself, it is not the main reason for decrying astrology.

The most important factor making one disbelieve in astrology is the communistic philosophy of the individual. It is not the profession of the cause of the poor that provides the main springs for communistic activities.

2

Even a deeply religious person does great service for the poor and the underprivileged. The central bases of the communistic opposition to religion, God, and the occult sciences rest on the fundamental philosophy of their activities. Communism does not believe in evolution : it emphasizes revolution which implies turning the wheel of karma in the opposite direction. That is the crux of the matter. Evolution implies that the forces in nature are ever balancing the distortions caused by other forces ; this in human life is expressed by the suffering of the sinful and the reward for the virtuous. Astrology is based on this law. The Laws of Karma and of Reincarnation are expressions of this natural justice. They are the fundamental planks of astrology. But, communism lays stress on appropriation of other man's property, on transgressing the social code of behaviour, and on disobeying the rules of morality. In short, communism is anti-theistic. Obviously, therefore, astrology provides the greatest proof and demonstration against the very postulates of communist faith. A belief in astrology, or even scientific consideration of the various facets of astrology would lead the communists to the very basic weakness of their philosophy. Almost every individual who subscribes to the communistic faith does so because of some psychological derangement or imbalance in his personality. As such, unless the life of such individuals is rehabilitated and they are made to see the things in right perspective, they would not have a rational approach to astrologers and astrology. But, astrology does not have to fear much from the communists because in nature, disease and distortions do not servive in the long run.

There is another group of aggressive and undeserving persons who somehow have acquired high positions in life but are not sure that they would be in a position to hold those privilages for ever. This group can be divided into two sections. The first one consists of those individuals who want more. Knowing that such achievements cannot be possible without some divine help, the individuals in this section often visit the astrologers so that they could know the ways and means to propitiate the gods and the devas for greater boons. Such persons are, generally speaking, the largest number of the patrons of astrologers, but they are not the main support on which everlasting edifice of occult sciences can be built. They often give plenty of temptations. Life being as it is, astrologers often lose their objectivity and thereby the scientific character of their work.

The second section of this group fears divine dispensation : the individuals belonging to this section think that undeserving favour somehow acquired by them may not be lasting. Astrologers may be able to know the duration of this bright period in their life. Knowledge of their forthcoming dark period will be devastating for them. The best thing for them, they think, is not so much to argue against astrology but to positively disuade others from approaching the astrologers. They create problems for those who still feel like consulting the soothsayers. They fabricate many types of arguments for the same. Their advocacies are not always effective. But, they are not very much concerned with this. What they are actually afraid of is the prediction relating to their impending misfortune. Such persons are a little difficult to handle.

There is another section of population which does not attach any significant importance to astrological predictions. It is so not because of their opposition to

astrology, but because the fundamentals of astrological
predictions have become a part of-universal psychological
structure.   They assume that there is a destiny for each
individual.   They believe that the inevitable things
would happen whether you know them or not. The most
important thing according to them is not the knowledge
of the future but the preparation for the same.   They are
interested in doing pious deeds ; they believe in living an
ethical life.   After all, these are the noble aims of life.
If the belief in astrological principles has given them the
faith and strength for braving the odds with fortitude, it
is a greater boon than acquiring the knowledge of the
future.   But these are the persons who, though supporting astrology in their own way, cannot be of positive
assistance in its further progress and growth. Astrology
also must grow and be of greater use in revealing the
secrets of the esoteric knowledge it aims at discovering.

The greatest strength of astrology lies in the enlightened support from educated masses. Those persons who
are interested in the subject objectively and are making
studies and propagating their views for the growth and
expansion of the science have to contribute much.   In
this regard, one has to acknowledge with gratitude the
service rendered to this occult science by the illustrous
B. Suryanarain Rao, and the erudite editor of *The
Astrological Magazine* Dr. B. V. Raman in India ; the
services rendered to astrology by Alan Leo, and A.E.O
Carter of the United Kingdom have been laudable. This
science needs revival. In doing so, certain tendencies
have to be resisted, and certain others encouraged. One
dangerous trend that is being propagated presently under
the impact of advancing technological innovation is the
increasing zeal for computerisation of predictions.   One
of the basic principles of computerisation is that it sorts

out the fed data in surprisingly less time. But it is always from the known to the unknown. Astrology, like other occult sciences, depends on revealing something hitherto unknown. Therefore, this kind of scientific instrumentalisation will not be very helpful in this branch of learning. Second tendency to be guarded against is the degradation of this sublime science merely for pre-diction of auspicious marriage dates, time of child-birth and favourable periods of material gains etcetera. Astrology, in fact, aims at something sublimer and nobler. It aims at revealing the divine plan for man, and the astrologer has to assist the individuals in co-operating actively with the divine scheme of things. It becomes, indeed, a very exhilarating subject, when we begin trying to discover the esoteric aspects of astrology and the long-term significance of astrological prognostications. Astrology is that aspect of Vedantic philosophy which is essential for progressing successively to higher ideals of yoga. Therefore it must be approached with veneration.

PERSONAL GUIDANCE

Quoting the *Key to Hebrew-Egyptian Mystery*, H. P. Blavatsky, the greatest occultist of the nineteenth century, once stated that "astronomy and physiology are the bodies, astrology and psychology their informing souls ; the former being studied by the eye of sensual perception, the latter by the inner or 'soul-eye' ; and both are exact sciences". The growing interest in such occult sciences as astrology, yoga, psychometry, psychic perceptions, dream analysis, and so on, almost in all parts of the world, specially in the so called materialistically advanced countries, proves that the teeming billions of the present time have been eagerly trying to develop their 'soul-eye'. Almost stagnant has been the growth and development of physical senses and organs of the human being, but during recent decades much evidence has been collected by the scientists to show that the consciousness of the man is limitless and immense scope exists for its development. Psychology has been accepted as a science which is expected to open vast panorama of human psyche. This science is enabling the modern man to take a radically different view of life. In many ways, the psychological knowledge has begun to help the human individual in understanding himself, his fellow beings and the environment in which they live. About astrology and such other occult subjects, however, there is yet abundant skepticism. Occasionally there occur outbursts from ill-informed scientists against astrology. But astrology reveals certain universal forces operating on the growth and development of our world whose true knowledge and understanding could alter our life and relationships. The ancient nature of this science has been accepted; it has been recognised that in all ancient civilisations astrology in various forms had seriously and deeply affected those societies, but the modern man is still learning to appreciate the wider ramifications of this science. He has still to know how much useful this subject could be. But, here and there, we find persons, who are led by their inner voice or by their intellectual understanding to feel that astrology has a legitimate place in our life, and for personal guidance in many areas of our existence it is very effective. It is on such enlightened rational human individuals that the progress of our society to a great extent depends.

The classical texts have given very abstruse and difficult principles for the prognostication of intricate and complex occurrences in our daily life. The horary and the mundane astrology have been practised by many astrologers to such an exactitude that the historians and the police have often been baffled. The special areas of the experts cannot be usurped by the novice. However there are many other ways in which the common man could take advantage of astrological knowledge. Most important, the human individual is primarily interested in knowing his basic attributes on the basis of which he could decide his course of life's journey such as his vocational choice, his financial possibilities, his proneness to different malignant diseases and accidents, and above all, the quality of his inner urges on the basis of which he could decide the line of yogic disciplines he could follow. All these are necessary and helpful to

him, but in order to assess the nature and grade of his
horoscope on the working of which he would be able to
evaluate the occurrences of personal events indicated
above, it is necessary that he is aware of certain intri-
casies of planetary influences. In this connection, he
should know certain inherent characteristics of his
Ascendant, Moon, and the Sun, Jupiter, Saturn, Rahu
and Ketu apart from astrological phenomena called
combustion, retrogression and so on. Without some
idea of the lunar mansions, or *nakshatras*, which exercise
immense power and were very well recognised for their
importance even by the Vedic seers, finer appreciation of
one's horoscope could not be possible. The exposition
of directional astrology is necessary and that could be
easily found by working out the degree of the Moon in
different signs of the zodiac and then relating the result
to any good ephemeris. More important than this however is the influence of transits which very easily mar or
help the effects of the ruling planets worked out as
earlier. These technical details would be helpful for the
reader in order to evaluate the astrological effects on his
life, but he may not remain contented merely by such
knowledge. He would like to see the working of God
in his special case : how the Supreme is shaping him
towards his archetype. This would require the individual
to have a knowledge of his Ray and how developed are
his various "principles" these are very complex subjects
but the common man should atleast *try* to grasp this
knowledge which would reduce much of his frustrations.
The soul enlightens the consciousness of the individual
by gradually energising and vitalising his various
"principles" and "Rays".

Every individual progresses on his individual ray, which has much deeper implications than one superficially appreciates this subject. Astrologically we are told that the Sun is the soul of this universe and it sends several specialised rays. These are seven in number and have been named as Sushumna, Harikesh, Visvakarman, Visvatryachas, Sannaddha, Sarvavasu, and Svaraj. The Sushumna is said to energise the Moon. One does not know the detailed working of these rays, but Varaha-mihira has been very clear in enunciating that all the planets, the *nakshatras* and the signs of the zodiac are produced by the Sun. Limiting ourselves only to the Sun's seven rays and linking them to the planets, when we analyse further, we find that the seven rays of the Sun produce special psychological conditions for the human individuals. At early stages of soul's growth, the characteristics of these rays are not very specialised and much mixed up effects are present, but gradually these are differentiated. Finally, the Sun would produce the ray of power working on Atmic level and expressing itself in highly specialised administrative skill on which the individual could be great emperors of Suryabansi kings type ; it is on this ray that Manus are incarnated. The Second ray is that of the Moon on which greatly developed *Buddhic* principle leads the individual to reflect Divine Wisdom and propound them for human goodness and their salvation. The Lord Buddha and Jesus Christ exemplify the incarnations at the apex of this ray. This is the ray of wisdom. The third is that of Intellect ; the great thinkers whose mind or *manas* is highly energised ; they are the logical persons who work in a specific way because they have been intellectually satisfied with that course of action. They are under the influence of Mercury. The Sun, Moon and Mercury thus considered function on the Consciousness side of life. They are very active in the realm of subjective or the inner side of life. Mars is the scientist ; the temperament concerned with this planet is engaged in physical side of life, but it is eagerly concerned with working with it in order to find out its inner *elan* but to utilise it on the external plane. The scientist discovering the latent principles in any thing tries to manipulate them for external or physical advantage. Such persons are generally skilled in their handiwork. The Sixth Ray is associated with Jupiter and exoteric religions consisting of much ritualism and externalisation of religious activity. The Seventh Ray under the influence of Saturn specialises in concretising the grand ideas and thus they are highly skilled in arts, architecture and that type of activities. Venus which is a unique planet in many ways and which is much misunderstood as well, produces harmony among different types. They are individuals who *apparently* do not contribute anything special from their own side but synthesise the ways of living thoughts, and differences expressed in different departments of life, such synthetic approach to life is the special gift of Venusian harmony. These specialised rays go so much deeper to the very core of individual's life that his mode of shopping, type of subjects he reads, the nature of people he associates with and the vocations he adopts are influenced by these rays. One has however to note that even when the individual has begun to be differentiated, at early stages, two or more rays get suffused and it is only gradually that the primary and secondary rays emerge. Any professional astrologer would find it difficult to identify the special ray of the individual because it requires much inward search in the mental state of one's being. It is an exploration in one's psychology, which none else, not even a psychologist can do effectively, but once the individual is able to establish a rapport with one's inner being, with one's inner working of the mind, he could be able to relate that with different planets, which would give immense power in his hand for building his own life and shaping it towards the destined direction.

On this path of exploration, the individual can be able even to identify the nature of his various sheaths or *koshas* of which various occult literature has spoken of. Adi Guru Shri Sankaracharya has described the various human sheaths in great detail. An identification of these sheaths with different planets has not so far been possible. Based on scatterred hints, one speculates that the physical or the *Annamaya Kosha* is linked with Saturn. Jupiter is connected with that aspect of one's body which absorbs solar globules and imparts health and vitality to the human constitution. On the effective circulation of this health aura depends the physical well-being of the person. It provides a great and effective shield against invasion from different maladies. Mars is connected with Astral or emotional nature of the person. How much of the instinctive reaction or involuntary impulses control the person is indicated by this planet. The capacity to sympathetic vibration and the power to identity one's feelings with others result from the nature and development of this sheath. Selfishness, self centredness, cravings of different kinds and the ruthlessness are the expression of this body when not very purified, but once impurities are purged out of it, philanthropy, martyrdom, susceptibility to other person's sorrows become its qualities. The healthy growth of the integrated personality also depends upon well formed emotional body ; personality defects specially of the psychological kind arise when there is some kind of impediment in the free flow of pure energy in this sheath. Mind is divided in two parts : the lower might be concerned with logical and rational intellectual perception, whereas the higher levels of it are concerned with abstract, intuitional, and spiritual perceptions. The lower mind is linked with Mercury and the higher one with Venus. Then comes Buddhic level linked with the Moon and the highest principle known as Atmic level connected with the Sun. The triad consisting of Atma-Buddhi-Manas represented by the Sun, Moon and Venus contains within itself the eternal component of the individuality which in essence is the quintessence of all experiences and all understanding of life. That is what one ordinarily calls the soul. This triad is linked with the lower quaternary consisting of Mercury, Mars, Jupiter and the Saturn. They are the progenitors of the material counterpart of the being, which dissolves and incarnates at each birth. The relationship between these seven planets to one another would give the clue regarding the harmony prevailing at various levels of the individual. By understanding this harmony, it would also be possible to know the health or otherwise of the specific sheath which could enable combing up operation leading to cleansing the sheath so that the hints and suggestions coming from the Atmic level could flow smoothly.

Often one comes across many inexplicable problems confronting every individual in his everyday struggle for existence. Some traits of character or some happenings are not of the usual type based on the rule of normalcy. These are the occurrences about which the individual enquires as to why such things happen to him. In a general way, all the planets influence the

individual which is according to the *law of karma* but
there are two planets in the Hindu astrology which
are important particulary in this r e g a r d. They
are Rahu and Ketu. Some illnesses, misfortune,
temperamental difficulties, marital unhappiness, vocational upsettings and great psychological sorrows result
from the impact of these two planets. Sometimes other
planets like Mars and Saturn come into play in this
regard as well, but they are mainly the acting agents
while the basic karmic causes arise from Rahu and Ketu.
Their placement in the horoscope indicates the areas
which are liable to karmic afflictions. A knowledge of
this situation would enable the native to take proper care
to counteract the tendency so that the final harmony is
achieved in his life and the karmic impediment eliminated
for ever. Without a knowledge of these conditions and
the direction in which countervailing efforts are needed,
the individual would be buffetted by the circumstances
occurring in his life for which he has no explanation and
which trouble him immensely. Rahu and Ketu show the
areas where special care is needed for the permanent
evolutionary change in the individual.

Equipped with such knowledge as yielded by the
planets, the individual could study his horoscope to
assess whether his particular life is important or not. In
this regard, one has to consider whether affluence is the
most important aspect of his life or other the so-called
unhappy events have greater value in orienting his life
to his soul-ward direction. This assessment could impart
a sense of fulfilment and would also instil confidence in
himself. Illness and misfortune coming to his life would
also change their significance. The choice of profession
and adjustment problems in service and employment
situations may become easier with this kind of

information. But the most important contribution of astrological knowledge is the discovery of the path of return generally known as *yoga* which the individual could practice for achieving his end-result.

One of the special outcome of astrological studies, apart from knowledge of the self, is an insight into the philosophy of cosmogenesis. Generally, questions relating to the origin of the universe, the beginning of the earth cycle and the advent of man on this earth and the course of spiral growth of human civilisation are all speculative when one studies them as a part of philosophy. But when astrology is studied in its deeper aspect, the knowledge about God, evolution, creative intelligences, the septenary principles in life, the trials of crucifixion and the stories relating to Mystery Schools prevalent in almost all ancient esoteric religions become more real. What is still more important is the advance indications of the future course of events, whether for the individual, society, or the world. With this kind of knowledge one could consider them rationally and if found justified, the intelligent men of the world could take up those hints and suggestions and begin working for either their own regeneration and orientation, or for working towards the new society. What more useful subject could there be than that which helps unfoldment of one's latent potentialities, forewarns the coming events and reveals the future towards which one could work for a better and happier society? As a matter of fact, the astrological approach to life leads us to a radically different orientation to life. The resulting balanced astrological psychology would usher in a new social relationship and expectation from life. The quality of human beings with the new mental make-up may lay the foundation of an entirely different but more satisfying kind of human society.

GOOD OR AFFLUENT LIFE

Often judgement of a horoscope is made on the criterion of its enjoying several combinations of affluence, ordinarily known as *Raja Yogas*, the kingly combinations. So far as the life of an ordinary individual is concerned, this may be a valid approach. On occasion, one comes across cases where special standards of judgement are required. As long as the human beings have physical bodies and their various necessities, money and health are basic features which would continue to interest them. It is therefore quite natural for them to enquire about their physical welfare. The success of astrological predictions would continue to be therefore assessed on their ability to predict possibilities to achieve success in such matters. Naturally, therefore, the importance of these kingly combinations is considerable. On the basis of such indications, it could be possible for individuals to regulate their life-pattern in a satisfying manner so as to avoid any impending danger and adapt one's needs according to the expected level of available resources.

The ancient sages have however in many scriptures stated that material affluence is a temptation, and any involvement in materiality is not always good for the sojourn of the ego. In that case, what could be the possible role of astrology for such persons who want to progress on the path of spirituality? In case poverty and austerity are basic needs for spiritual unfoldment, the significance of *Raja Yogas* becomes minor. Those combinations which enable the individual to move on the path of spirituality, namely, the *Sanyasa Yogas* or the combinations for renunciation, those conditions could be more appropriate for him. Such *Sanyasa Yogas* however negate the very possibility of acquiring kingly positions : wealth, social status, personal happiness, all these have to be sacrificed in order to gain spiritual heights. Spirituality and material affluence both cannot be attained simultaneously. Those who wish to enjoy the status of Emperor Janaka, who was blessed equally with supreme spiritual enlightenment and abundance of material affluence, will fail in whatever sphere they endeavour to achieve superior position. Astrological predictions to indicate their wish fulfilment would be misleading.

A difficult question often put before the astrologer is when the enquirer asks him as to the "goodness" or otherwise of his chart. Is my chart good ? Is my life going to be successful ? To such questions the reply would depend upon the assessment of the relative importance of affluence and the needs of the soul. Only on the right appraisal of the requirements of Eternal Ego, it could be possible for the astrologer either to indicate the "goodness" of the chart, that is, the effect of the trying conditions in evolving the permanent qualities of the soul, or to indicate the various restrictive events such as political status, material affluence and so on, inhibiting his faculties and thus retard the progress of his soul.

The birth chart of an individual is a peep-hole in the eternal life of the individual. In several scriptures many

characteristics have been suggested to reveal the condi
tions of the past incarnations of a person. An able astrologer with proficiency in esotericism may be able to
indicate various aspects of the life of the individual which
could be miraculous predictions.   While charting the
course of his future life, the astrologer could reveal to
the individual not only physical events, but even the
psychological impact they could make on his psyche. Even
concentrating on the happenings in one incarnation of
the individual, the astrologer may be able to indicate the
manifold dimensions of the individual's life and the
course of his evolution. Study on these lines would
give the astrological predictions a different orientation
that has hitherto been very insignificant. It has been
attempted in *A Study in Astrological Occultism*[1] ; it has
been shown there that every event of the individual's
life is eternally vibrating the archetypal message and as
such astrological guidance in revelations with this
archetypal message is of supreme value to well-meaning
serious aspirants. Day-to-day events of the world
impinging on the life of the individual are not necessarily
pleasant and joyous from the popular standpoint. In
that case, it could be rational to distinguish between the
pleasant and a good life, which implies that the individuals enquiring about the nature of their charts must
approach astrological predictons from a different standpoint. It is not enough to know that a certain event
will take place, either in the life of the individual or in
the course of evolution of a society, but it is also
necessary to know, for the right assessment of the
quality of the chart, the significance of the events in the
eternal drama of the soul's life.

---

1. *A Study in Astrological Occultism*, Bepin Behari,
IBH Prakashana, Bangalore, 1983

We are living in a cosmos. It means that the world around us is guided by rules and forces which operate in an orderly manner. Explaining the guiding priciples of the cosmos, H. P. Blavatsky, acclaimed by many as the greatest occultist of the 19th century, considered periodicity as a fundamental proposition explaining the various phenomena in nature. This proposition, she stated, affirmed ''The Eternity of the Universe *in toto* as a boundless plane periodically 'the playground of numberless Universes incessantly manifesting and disappearing', called the 'Manifesting Stars' and the 'Sparks of Eternity', 'the Eternity of the Pilgrim' is like a wink of the Eye of Self-Existence'. 'The appearance and disappearance of Worlds is like a regular tidal ebb of flux and reflux'.'' She amplified this proposition by saying that ''the second assertion of the Secret Doctrine is the absolute universality of the law of periodicity, of flux and reflux, ebb and flow, which physical science has observed and recorded in all departments of nature. An alternation such as that of Day and Night, Life and Death, Sleeping and Waking, is a fact so perfectly universal and without exception, that it is easy to comprehend that in it we see one of the absolutely fundamental Laws of the Universe''.[2] Application of this law of periodicity in everyday life is demonstratably accentuated in astrological cycles. In a very meaningful article, Y. Keshava Menon stated that the periodicity of events presently being discovered by the scientists of the advanced countries could be well forecast by astrological cycles''.[3] In this article he mentioned that the scientists were discovering

---

2. *The Secret Doctrine*, H. P. Blavatsky, Theosophical Publishing House, Madras, 1971, Vol. I p. 82,

3. *Planets and Tides of Life*, Y. Keshava Menon, *The Astrological Magazine*, Bangalore, October. 1963.

periodicity of $2\frac{1}{2}$ years, 28 days, and 33 days in various human behaviours and also the characteristic of certain industrial locations in attracting special types of mechanics, engineers and others which are possibly certain planetary characteristics. After stating these glaring characteristics of the modern society, Keshava Menon concluded by emphasizing the need for empirical studies on this subject. But his article clearly showed to every unprejudiced mind that individuals are guided and moved into this world by some harmonious universal intelligence. Leslie-Smith in his monumental monograph entitled *Intelligence Came First* stated that "Intelligence is distinct from the physical organism; it is associated with consciousness and exists free in its own domain. There is some evidence that it survives death and that a general ocean of intelligence exists. It is rational to suppose that intelligence is primal and cosmic, the original cause of evolution and not its product".[4] The Universal Intelligence does not interfere with our thinking and feeling aspect of life in the ordinary way of our everyday life : its impact is subtle and sweetly guiding the life-wave rather than life-incidents. When our actions, responses and behaviour are in harmony with this Universal Intelligence, we feel that life is good. Not affluence but harmony with Universal Intelligence is the basis on which goodness of the individual's life can be established.

This law of universal harmony in religious parlance is known as the Law of Karma. It is a difficult law to comprehend in all its aspects but it is very simple for the layman. N. Sri Ram, one of the most abstract philosophers among the past Presidents of the Theosophical

---

4. *Intelligence Came First*, Leslie-Smith, Theosophical Publishing House, London, p. 19.

Society, stated that "Karma is a Law which reflects the unity of the Spirit in the manifoldness of matter, the unity of a Being who is alone in the universe but recreates Himself through every continuing centre in the medium of the material matrix".[5] Apart from suggesting the unity of the temporal individual with the eternal Heavenly Man, Sri Ram also stated that "Karma, however bad it may appear, is always beneficient because it rectifies. It is an inexorable Law which no one can avoid. It exists wherever Nature exists. We are acted upon by Nature, the same time that we act, in a manner which corresponds to our action, though the effect be delayed by the nature of material medium in which the operation takes place, the shock-absorber of time. But it is open to us to generate and we are generating new forces all the time, by means of which the old forces are to some extent neutralized or deflected and modified. The effect of Karma is always a restitution, the restoration of disturbed balance".[6] The manner in which the restitution takes place and the time as shock-absorber functions are hidden from the sight of the common man which explains many of his anxieties and perplexities. Dr. B. V. Raman mentioned that "All the qualities we now possess in body, mind and soul result from our use of ancient opportunities. We are, indeed, the heirs of all the ages. For these conditions accrue from distant causes engendered by our older selves, and the future flows by the divine law of cause and effect (Karma), from the gathered momentum of our past impetuses. There is no favouritism in the universe, but all have the

---

5. *The Human Interest*, N. Sri Ram, Theosophical Publishing House, Madras, p. 42

6. Ib.

same everlasting facilities for growth. Those who are now elevated in worldly station may be sunk in humble surroundings in the future. Only the inner traits of the soul are permanent companions. The wealthy sluggard may be the beggar of the next life, and the industrious worker of the present is sowing the seeds of greatness".[7] The real benefic therefore would be the circumstances which induce the individual to sow the seeds of greatness which ultimately create harmony for him with the Eternal One Being.

Some of the anomalies in astrology arise precisely for such reasons of karmic retribution. One often comes across very powerful planetary combinations but often the horoscope defies the normal rules of predictions. For example, generally the exaltation and placement of planets in their own houses are considered conducive to the strength of the planets. But one remembers that the strength and weaknesses of a planet are assessed to find out the efficacy of the same towards producing certain effects.[8] If a planet is strong it is generally said that the detrimental effects of the same would be considerably reduced. But there could be another way of looking at the problem. Such questions arise when there is the possibility of some really strong person becoming thoroughly weak or ineffective under certain conditions. For example, if the king of a certain land has been imprisoned under some circumstances for certain specified duration, what could be the state of his mind ? Often a powerful soul finds himself enchained under such conditions.

---

7. B. V. Raman, *The Astrological Magazine*, Bangalore, October, 1949

8. Kindly see, B. V. Raman, *Graha and Bhāva Balas*, Raman Publications, Bangalore

Such conditions can be illustrated astrologically
from the following three charts.[9] In Chart (i), Saturn,
Mercury, and Jupiter are exalted and the two planets,
namely Venus and Sun, are in their own houses ; the
lord of the Ascendant is powerful : the Sun in his own
house flanked by two exalted benefic planets namely
Jupiter and Mercury. Still the horoscopee, in spite of
being placed in very good academic institutions could
not have any satisfactory academic qualifications ; was
not married till 25 years of age and for his living he had
to take up the profession of a tempo driver, which in the
Indian conditions is not considered very honourable. We
do not wish to discuss the rationale of this situation,
but the point we are labouring is to show that the
native has defied the *natural* expectations from such
a chart. Take the second chart (Chart–ii) where Mars
gives *Ruchaka Yoga* and Saturn *Sasa Yoga,* two of
the *Pancha Maha Purusha Yogas*—the Five Combinations
of Greatness—besides, his Sun is powerfully placed in
his own house in the fifth. Rahu is in the third house
which is considered a powerful placement. Jupiter is
retrograde in debilitation in the tenth house. With such
powerful combinations, we find that the native is very
ordinary in several ways : he is only a school teacher in
a small town, which is not a respectable position and
academically he somehow obtained a graduate's degree.
Undoubtedly, he has plenty of children and is deaf to

9. *Chart (i)* :   Date of Birth 10th September 1954, 28. 39 N, 77.
13 E, 5-40 A.M. IST. Ketu 2s 19°. 18'; Jupiter 3s. 0. 5. ; Ascendant 4s.
4° ; Sun 4s 23° 31' ; Mercury 5s 9° 29' ; Venus 6s 9° 39' ; Saturn 6s
12° 40' ; Mars 8s 13° 15' ; Rahu 8s 19° 18' and Moon 9s 16° 5'.

Chart (ii) :   Date of Birth 9th September 1926, 26. 38 N 84. 54 E,
9-30 P.M. Ascendant, Aries 23° 53' ; Rahu, 2s, 20° 6' ; Sun 4s 23°
12' Mercury 4s 14° 6' ; Venus 4s 4° 42' ; Moon 5s 19° 56' ; Saturn
6s 28° 29' ; Ketus 8s 20° 6' ; Jupiter (R) 9s 26° 25 ; Mars 0s 25° 8'.

some extent, and he is not very handsome either. We do not wish to discuss the several good points of these horoscopes but may point out that in the former case, the native has much life yet to live so there may be some uncertainty as to how his future life would shape, nonetheless he is earning much more money than a person of his qualification and status though academically and socially he is not well off. If we give importance to money in life, he is certainly doing exceedingly well for his age. But is that what we mean by affluence? Is that what is signified by such powerful combinations? In the second case, the native has been a support to his family, and people flock around him for astrological predictions but he has to depend upon favours from all and sundry for making some money. That by no means can be considered an affluent or good life though the basic strength of the planetary positions has given him some kind of unusual importance in the society he is born though it is not of very honourable type.

The third chart (Chart iii) is more interesting. The person was born in 1926 having Ruchaka and Sasa Yoga besides having exalted Mercury and Moon. He had been in good government service but had remained unmarried for a long time, had to support an old mother and almost a blind father. He did not have a good relationship with his boss. He did not have even the basic comforts in his life. One need not endeavour to examine the causes of his trying life, because certainly they are there, otherwise such incidents could not have happened. But the point that is being made is that such an important

---

Chart (iii): Date of Birth 26th September 1926 30. 12 N, 71. 28 E 10, 10 A. M. (Appx) Mars 0s 26° 32'; Moon 1s 8° 20'; Rahu 2s 19° 12'; Venus 4s 25° 5'; Sun 5s 9° 28'; Mercury 5s 14° 44'; Ascdt. 10s 21° 7'; Satarn 6s 29° 40'; Ketu 8s 19° 13'; Jupiter (R) 9s 25° 1'

chart need not, as ordinarily understood, give such
unsatisfactory results.   It is worth studying the
quality of these charts. Can one consider them good in
the ordinary sense ? As far as affluence is concerned, we
have already indicated the position and have noted
that they do not suffer any privation of any extreme kind
and some of them may even be considered comparatively
well off, but in no case they can be called kingly or
affluent. But, can we consider them 'good' ?

Coming to the goodness versus affluence of charts,
which is the central point of consideration here, we wish
to draw the attention of the readers to a famous sloka
of Adi Guru Shankaracharya in the present context. In
his *Viveka Chudamani*, he says that there are three
conditions difficult of attainment which are acquired
only by the kindness of gods, and these conditions are :
(i) Humanity, *manushyatwam* as he called it, (ii) desire
for emancipation, or *mumukshutwam*, and (iii) the
guidance from spiritually advanced persons, *Maha-
purushashrayah*. Never in Indian philosophy, or as a
matter of fact in any occult doctrine, affluence has been
considered as an indication of God's benediction. In
such cases, the strength and benefic influences of various
planets should not be considered merely in terms of
their ability to bestow money, social status or worldly
luxury. Considered on the basis of this kind of reasoning
the various planetary combinations suggesting *Raja
Yogas* should be carefully studied. *Raja Yoga* or even
the benefic influences of such helpful planetary combinations are thought of as desirable combinations because
they reveal some other deep-rooted, eternal, characteristics of the ego. They are important not for themselves
but for what they are capable of. Jesus Christ was not
a rich man   Guru Nanak had very little of personal

comfort ; Galileo, Hypatia, and Socrates were killed or persecuted for no valid misdemeanour. But verily they were powerful egos. They could not do what they did without powerful divine power working on them. So, the relationship between *Raja Yoga* and affluence should be taken with a pinch of salt. To avoid any misunderstanding, I wish to emphasize that the point I am highlighting is that the *Raja Yogas* may bring affluence and in many cases they will, but it is not necessary that they should be interpreted only in this sense because in some cases, depending upon the state of the person's evolution, they may not do so but help the ego to progress much differently and more effectively. On this line of enquiry, there is some possibility of orienting our interpretation of astrological predictions in a different manner. We may begin to examine the possible combinations under which the three conditions of godly favour of which Adi Guru Shankaracharya spoke could be identified. In fact, the first and the most important signs of a "good" chart should incorporate these combinations of Divine Blessings.

The Sanskrit word *manushyatwam* when translated as humanity is not as suggestive as the *quality* of being a human being. The most basic quality of a human being is his ability to take positive action. Animals and angels work more or less on instinct or according to the natural impulses, whereas it is only man who can, either for destruction or for creation, take positive action. He has a will of his own. Astrologically, this will of one's own is revealed in a very interesting manner. A general review of the various houses in a chart would show that only the ascendant, the fifth house or the house of learning and progeny, and the tenth or the house or Karma, would show the quality of positive action of the human

individual. As far as other houses are concerned, the
individual reaps the consequences of his past actions—
purva-punya as the Hindu metaphysicians would call
them. Whether the individual is having wealth, property,
status, renown, etc or not would be dependent upon
what he has done in lives before. What would be given
to him in future would depend upon what he does today,
in this life. The quality of being a humankind lies in his
ability to forge his future with foresight, confidence, and
rationality. How the individual uses the sum total of
his life's opportunities during the given incarnation is
characterised by the ascendant. How is he going to
utilise his creative faculties at different planes of his
existence, specially his physical, emotional and intellectual ones, which would decide his future opportunities and possibilities of his rapid evolution, is characterised by the fifth house. The tenth house or the house
of Karma which is a mysterious house though much
emphasized in astrological texts represents the aggregate of opportunities offered to the individual for the
exercise of his faculties. These three houses must be
favourably disposed in order to suggest that the present
incarnation of the individual is significant.

Secondly, *mumukshatwam* or the desire for Liberation
should be the basic consideration of a chart. Only when
the individual feels the urge for wider life, his eternal
life, he could concentrate on leading a meaningful life
making complete use of all his faculties in the most
desirable manner. The urge for emancipation is indeed
very rare among the human beings. The attraction
towards the occult and the metaphysical itself is very
singular ; many persons have however shown their
interest in yoga and such other occult subjects but

for attaining material success which is the very antithesis of the purpose of Liberation for which the occult *siddhies* are meant. Under widespread materialism, it is very rare to find someone who is really interested in life beyond, or in questions relating to soul —the eternal dimensions of man and the acquisition of this eternal life's splendour. The urge for emancipation comes from materialistic constriction of the divine spirit in man represented by his psyche and the realisation of the divine counterpart or the essence in one's individuality and the fiery enthusiasm inducing the individual to explore the limitless expansion of human consciousness. The word *Sanyasa*, meaning renunciation, has been purposefully avoided here. The emancipation of spirit is a difficult enterprise which requires complete annihilation of the personality, the little 'I'. Therefore one who desires Liberation will have to bear the cross cheerfully. The affliction of the Moon and the Ascendant, as well as of its lord, by Saturn will impose the necessary constriction and the individual would change under its torture. His life would seem melting away to meaninglessness ; his social and family relative will humiliate him ; he will feel as if imprisoned. This is not a happy experience. Tears will roll down the eyes, and there may not appear even an illusion or a mirage to give temporary solace. This kind of Divine Discontent would be further reinforced by the Moon aspected by fiery Mars which would stop the mind from settling on any illusory palliative. Exploration in Divine Dimensions of Man would be an eternal journey to him with no jay-walking or halt for any temporary respite. The charts of Gautam Buddha, or that of Adi Guru Sankaracharya clearly show these points. Gautam Buddha's Ascendant Lord, the Moon, is fully aspected by Saturn, and fiery Mars aspected his Ascendant, its lord and the Moon. In the case of Sankaracharya also, the Ascendant Lord is aspected by Saturn and Mars. From the material standpoint, these are not happy combinations. The worldly lives of these two flowers of humanity could not be considered happy, but who would deny their being favourites of God ?

The third condition of godly benediction postulated above relates to Divine Grace. In astrological books, Jupiter is acclaimed to represent God's Grace. This point need not be laboured much because it is widely recognized that the benefic influence of Jupiter is essential for every goodness in life. Even when the individual is interested in material advancement, Jupiter helps the person but his contribution in inducing the individual to Mysterious Initiations whereby the individual is brought is close association with Great Beings is greater. The favourable ninth house and the benefic influence of Jupiter must be looked for the goodness of a chart.

Thus the affluence as we find in everyday life is not necessarily an indicator of the goodness of a horoscope, specially from the basic consideration of the soul's growth. When the individual attains a particular stature in his soul's journey, he is enabled to lead a more meaningful life, though from material standpoint it may not be a satisfying one. The first three symptoms of this goodness are the astrological indications of positive qualities of individuality represented by the first, fifth, and tenth houses ; the Divine Discontent represented by the affliction of Ascendant, and the Moon by Saturn and fiery Mars ; and the benefic influences of Jupiter and spiritual qualities of the ninth house enabling Mysterious Initiations and association with Great Adepts of the White Brotherhood. There are other characteristics of goodness of a chart but they are subsidiary to these three basic considerations.

THE URGE FOR CREATIVITY

The urge for creativity is an expression of man as a part of nature. In nature, nothing stays put ; everything is ever expressing its inner qualities. In that process, the universe progresses towards the fulfilment of its destiny. To perpetuate himself is a fundamental urge of man, and therefore his desire to see his family tree flowering. This in fact was recognised in ancient India when every individual was exhorted to procreate in order to fulfil his social and spiritual obligations. To watch one's child grow itself is a great thrill. The Hindu scriptures stressed that no soul can be redeemed of its material entanglements unless his own son offered the oblation at his death. Apparently this simple mundane injunction is based on deep-rooted natural necessity and human psychology.

Astrologically, progeny is connected with the Fifth House in a natal chart. But, many other aspects of life are also linked with this house which suggests that there are more to this house than we ordinarily acknowledge Dr B. V. Raman very succintly stated this house to represent "intelligence, father, *atman*, discriminating power, children, fame and position". From this it could be seen that the prognostication of offspring from this house is only a very restricted consideration. It is considered to be one of the most auspicious trines in a horoscope. To examine its deeper meanings one could see in

classical astrological treatises various other significance
of this house. Mantreswara connected the Fifth House
with the future birth of the native and that could lead
us to one of the inner significance of this aspect of life.
According to Mantreswara, the lord of the Ninth House
signified all about the native's past birth, while the
information about his future birth is revealed by the
ruler of the Fifth House. Unless there is some relationship between the Fifth House results and the future life,
this statement would seem empty but the relationship
between one's progeny, intelligence, fame and position,
and the future of one's life is very interesting, as we
shall presently observe.

Uttara Kalamrita throws some light in the present
context. The items signified by this house as given in
this work classified properly would indicate the extensive
framework of the operation of man's creativa impulses
which would pave his way to the future. When properly
comprehended the field of these creative impulses would
reveal that the man does not work only on the physical
level of his existence. On the activisation of these
impulses, the individual earns intelligence, power,
children, name and fame of which Dr. Raman has spoken.
The fruits of these activities link the individual with
his Universal Self playing its cosmic drama on this globe.
On the rightful acting of this drama depends the future
happiness of the individual concerned. In order to
examine the implication of this drama, we may study the
details of this house of creativity which according to
Kalidasa signified "progeny, garments, ways of earning
money, mechanical art, humility, firmness, good morals,
affection, real wellbeing, liaison with courtesans,
writing of events, production of great actions, writing of
epics, attaining the position of advisers and ministers,

discrimination, farsightedness, and attainment of wealth
and inheritance from father". He further states that
higher learning, profundity of virtue and vice, contentment, prayer by incantation, offering of food, chanting
of Vedic hymns as well as extreme happiness and a
festive occasion when drums or tabor is played are also
signified by the Fifth House. This long list apparently
includes many incongruous and contradictory attributes
such as mechanical art and authorship of epics, prayer
by incantation and engagement in money earning activities, festive occasions with music and profound
contemplation, liaison with courtesans and discrimination between virtue and vice. But these contradictions
can be effectively reconciled, if we could go behind these
activities and try to comprehend the central motivation
of this house. This can be done by taking into account
the various emanations of different human activities at
varied levels of his existence. We are aware that a human
being functions at physical, emotional, mental, and
several other higher planes. The same impulse generated
at these different levels would have markedly dissimilar
responses. The different planetary intelligences would
also be generating distinctly different category of influences. Therefore the impact of intelligence on physical
plane may result in mechanical art whereas on the mental
plane it would lead to discrimination between the right
and the wrong. Similarly with other impulses. In this
way, one could find out that the various attributes
mentioned above are primarily suggestive of the
situation where the multifarious impulses generated at
various planes of human existence *fructify*. The Fifth
House actually represents the *realm of creativity* irrespective of the form of creation. Whenever we are interested
to explore the quality and possibility of creativity, we

should attend to this house. The birth of a baby, the progeny, is merely the symbolic expression to indicate the result of the creative impulse.

Four very meaningful attributes to the Fifth House given in *Uttara Kalamrita* deserve special recognition in the present context. These are *Garbha* (Womb), *Chatra* (Protection), *Rahasya* (Mystery), and *Sukatha* (Renown). Being the left hand trine located at the base of the spiritual triangle comprising the Ascendant, the Fifth House and the Ninth House, it contains the Eternal Root Matter which during the manifestative process spreads itself out to create the Great Illusion known as Life. Because of this inherent quality of fructification, whenever any impulse of any kind is imparted to this realm of manifestation it enables it regenerate itself at different realms of existence to result in different manner. Anyone wishing to know the possibility of his karmas to fructify must examine this house. It is that realm in which all individual efforts fructify. As the womb is the organ where the human seed germinates and fructifies, this also forms a link between the present efforts of the individual and the possibility of reaping their rewards or fruits in future. When the individual does some creative work, he sows the seeds of some activity which following the law of nature would germinate and frutify in its due course in future. The metaphysicians call that portion of karma as *Kriyamana* which is yet in the process of incubation whose final results would ripen only later on whilst *Sanchita Karma* is that which has natured and its fruits are stored for the ego to experience later and *Prarabdha* signifies the portion allotted out of the total for experiencing in the specified incarnation. The Fifth House is the area where one could fruitfully hope to sow seeds whose results could be enjoyed only at a later period. In this way, the appellation 'womb' is very appropriate for this house. Furthermore, the reaping of the results of some action already done is so inescapable, karma being an expression of Absolute All, that one who has already generated helpful deeds would find them as his protection whatever his existing situation. For this reason, the name given to it as 'umbrella' which functions to protect the individual from adverse rains or heat is very expressive. It has also been indicated in various occult literature that the human individual during the course of his higher levels of existence passes through many mysterious circumstances resulting from his meritorious deeds. Mention has been made of mysterious initiations whose garbled versions have been given in several esoteric religions and it has been indicated that on such great occasions, the entire nature rejoices; the angels and fairies dance; Kinnaras and Gandharvas dance and sing to rejoice the occasion. The reference to festive occasions mentioned in connection with the Fifth House is indicative of this rejoicing which results in unusual expansion of consciousness. Higher levels of such Initiations, which depends exclusively on the efforts of the individual himself, may even enable him to expand his consciousness to the very edge of the cosmic veil. On attaining such an evolved status, naturally the individual earns a right to good name and fame, as signified by this house.

From this, it is clear that the examination of the quality and the level of creativity must be examined in relation to the Fifth House. It represents that dimension of one's being wherefrom one could gauge the possibility of one's creative potential. It is the field where the right kind of seed can be sown to obtain auspicious fruits. The nature of the fruit depends upon the level upon which the human being is functioning. In case, the individual is primarily operating on the physical level, his creativity would be evident by the offspring he would beget. On the emotional plane, the result would be perceived by his affection, compassion, sympathy and to some extent, in the negative way, through his sensuous and lusty urges. When his field of operation is transferred to mental plane, intellectual activities, scientific thought, philosophical ideas, and literary talents become possible. On higher levels of existence, the consciousness is engaged in an entirely different kind of operation whereby the individual is enabled to work with the angellic hosts and Adept Brotherhood and thereby earn the right to *Prajna*—higher esoteric wisdom—and thereby give him the opportunity to enjoy real bliss. The functioning of the human individual at 'different levels of his existence does not only demonstrate the possibility of his perpetuating himself only on the physical plane, rather it shows that the creative efforts, depending upon their nature and intensity, could give him the right to perpetuate himself on various levels of higher existence as well.

The creative impulses are also of different kinds. As the quality of seed is no' less important than the right kind of field, so the type of creative impulses is also of great significance for achieving the right kind of results on different levels of one's existence. The quality of the seed or the type of creative impulse can be examined in relation to the Ascendant, as well as the nature of the Sun. They reveal the Status of the Ego, the Soul, or the Being incarnated in the present life. Jupiter and the Moon provide the protective cover to this Being. The adverse forces like the blasts, drought, pests, and viruses which could completely or partially destroy the

growing plants are assessed through the malefics such
as Saturn, Rahu, and Ketu. Mars plays a special role.
Often expediting the growth of the seed, it may be that
accidently or otherwise, it may damage the growth
process. Mars is impulsive, therefore it becomes restless when the incubation period is long, but for some
line of activities this nature of Mars may be very useful
as in the case of sports, surgical operation, emergency
first aid, but at times this may be an impediment. But
in those activities where courage is at premium than
cool thinking, the Martian impulse is desirable. In
assessing the fructification of self-perpetuating efforts
of the individual expressed as the birth of offspring,
literary efforts, radiation of affectionate and helpful feelings, acquisition of higher wisdom, and co-operation in
various ways with the occult hierarchy, having considered the maturity of the Ego, one should consider the
planetary disposition of Saturn, Rahu and Ketu to identify
the restricting influences, and Ascendant, Jupiter, and
the Moon to find out the planetary support for the
various lines of creativity the individual may find productive and easily fructifying.

In assessing the creative process, the classical texts
lay down a principle which apparently according to the
superficial astrological dicta seems contradictory but a
careful analysis of it shows an exceptional result under
that combination. The placement of the Seventh lord in
the Fifth House is said to deny the issues. This suggests
a denial of the general auspicious combination between
Trine and angle lords together. Here the Seventh House
is an angle, and the Fifth a trine, therefore the association of the Seventh lord in the Fifth House should have
been considered very lucky but it is not so. An important
reason for this adverse result lies in the fact that the

Fifth House is certainly a base of the Spiritual Triangle, and therefore a very auspicious house giving impulse for all kinds of spiritual growth, but the Seventh is the apex of the Material Triangle whose base angles are formed by joining the Third and the Eleventh Houses which would encourage material-ward journey of the Ego. The imposition of the Seventh lord on the Fifth would greatly disturb the spiritual efforts of the person. In that situation of the churning of the ocean, the creativity cannot flow smoothly. But the association of the Fifth lord with the Seventh lord in the Seventh, or the placement of the Fifth lord in the Seventh would be on the other hand, helpful for the latter.

The houses which create trouble in one's life by thwarting his creative impulses are the Third, Sixth, Eighth and the Twelfth. Dr. B. V. Raman has mentioned that the occupation of the lord of the Fifth in the Third, Sixth or the Twelfth and aspected by malefics would make the person's child die early. As these are the destructive houses in the sense that they are primarily linked with the Immutable Shoreless Sea of Eternity, the *Bythos*, from which everything has come out and to which everything would return, any link of these with the impulse of creativity would impede the onward movement of it but, for those activities which are on the superphysical planes, such a combination may even in some cases prove to be exceptionally fructifying. The progeny may be adversely affected by such combinations, but the procreative energy on other non-physical levels may have a different story to tell. It is not necessary that a person bereft of any child on this material plane to do his last rites is unable to soar very high on great spiritual planes or to create much covetted literary or philosophical work or to generate universal love and compassion. The association of Fifth lord with these houses of impediments are merely warning signals for physical procreative activities ; such persons taking heed of this precautionary indication if could engage themselves on higher physical levels of activities, their life could be very satisfying and fruitful.

The impact of benefics and malefics on creative urges is very complicated. The simple rules indicated above do not always lead to correct appraisal of such impulses. Though the human beings are capable of functioning on several layers of his existence, yet for the majority of the population, the importance of begetting progeny is great. Even otherwise, the human body is the most perfect model of God's creation and the opportunity of giving birth to a noble being is the greatest blessing that a person may aspire for. It is probably for this reason that every god in the Hindu mythology is a married god with several children of his own. There is much significance in the Vedic hymns praying for 'their seeds to multiply'. But in this process, the benefic and malefic planets have very mixed role to play, which is also due to the innumerable variety of egos required to be born each of whom would need special type of vehicles to function in this world. Keeping this in one's view, there may not be much surprise to find many different dicta pertaining to the birth of children though the texts do not provide adequate explanations for apparently contradictory indications.

The association or aspect of a malefic on the Fifth House is, generally, considered unhelpful for the birth of children. Jataka Parijatam has mentioned that a malefic planet in the Fifth Bhava while its lord is depressed and without benefic aspect would lead to childlessness. Again, when malefic planets occupy the fifth place from

The Urge for Creativity

Jupiter, Ascendant and the Moon and are neither associated with nor aspected by benefic planets, childlessness must be pronounced. Giving other combinations, it lays down that a malefic planet occupying the fifth bhava and its lord being hemmed between two malefic planets and neither being aspected nor associated with a benefic planet would lead to childlessness. This approach was supported by Dr. B. V. Raman, who stated that if the Fifth as well as its lord are placed between evil planets and Jupiter is in company with malefics, there will be loss of children. On the other hand, Mantreswara, the author of *Phala Deepika*, gives somewhat opposite theory. According to him, if a malefic planet owning the Fifth House is posited in that house, the person concerned will have sons in plenty. Contrary to it however, if a benefic planet occupies the Fifth House and at the same time owns that house or is in exaltation there, there would be loss of children.

The implications of these combinations become clear if we understand the very nature of the malefic and benefic planets. The benefic planets have the inherent quality of providing the satisfactory conditions for the growth of the inner man. Among them, the Jupiter is the first rate benefic implying thereby that the untoward events likely to impede the flowering of the man would be eliminated and the individual would be encouraged to grow luxuriantly. But this growth has to be towards the spiritual upliftment of the person. The immersion of the soul in materialism is not much encouraged by Jupiter. For this reason, Jupiter's placement in the Fifth House specially when it is in exaltation or when it rules the house is not very helpful for the birth of children. Under these conditions Jupiter would be strengthening the higher principles of the person concerned. His philosophic output would be substantial : whether he publishes those ideas or not is not so significant, his psychological make-up would be tuned up spiritually. While aspecting the Fifth House, Jupiter is only becoming sympathetic to the individual under which influence it would endeavour to help advanced souls to take birth at the person's family. The Moon is helpful but it is primarily only an influence : it borrows its life-energy from the Sun and distributes it over the earth. It activates the Buddhic principle in man. It enables the person to sustain himself, become healthy; it is the womb implying that the 'germ' or 'seed' has to be implanted in it for fructification; left by itself it cannot germinate anything. Therefore when the Moon in ownership or in exaltation is placed in the Fifth House, its capacity to help in impregnating the physical womb is very much restricted. The mind of the person however could be very sharp and any subject which the person desires to study would be extremely easy for him to grasp. Mercury and Venus are benefics of a different kind. Mercury is connected with Mind, Thought, which can be led to refusing to procreate on the physical level. If there is any other planet assisting in the procreative process, Mercury would make the child intelligent, but as far its own influence in this area is concerned, it is an eunuch, incapable of producing any physical being. Venus is extremely ease loving centering all its energy on the satisfaction of its own senses. On higher levels, it becomes so sensitive that it cannot tolerate any pain or sorrow to others. From a higher standpoint, the birth of a baby is a process by which an enfranchised soul is put to restrictions. A sensitive Venus knowing all the sufferings the soul in materialisation has to suffer would not like to assist in it. But when Venus is not functioning on higher levels by rulership or exaltation, it may encourage the self-centredness of the person and therefore in order to provide some degree of (material) pleasure, it could assist in begetting children. It would not, as a benefic, either by its aspect or by its placement without being its ruler or in exaltation, be averse to the birth of offspring. It would rather be helpful in this regard.

Among the malefics, Rahu and Ketu do not have either ownership or exaltation, in the ordinary sense of the term. Therefore they will be treated like any other malefic. Saturn and Mars are the two malefics which become very important in the present context. The Sun will have to be treated differently. Rahu is very undesirable in the Fifth House. It represents the great karmic retribution. Its main influence lies in intensifying the gross materialism and producing the feeling of depression. Under the impact of Rahu, it is not the childlessness that disturbs the native, but the feeling of depression of not having the same. The urge to creativity itself is so much depressed that the individual is left with no urge to engage himself in fruitful activities. In difference to it, Ketu makes the person very philosophic. He dwells in the realm of ideas and thoughts which do not always have their bases on the ground. Such a person acquires wisdom much beyond his age and consequently finds himself out of tune with the society in which he lives. On the physical plane, his not having a child is not irremediable. But generally speaking, there occur chances of miscarriage which if controlled could let the individual have a thoughtful child.

The impact of Saturn is typical of the characteristics mentioned earlier. It is the most dreaded malefic. Saturn restricts, wherever its influence could be observed. One

must expect the planet to considerably restrict the
function of that house. The Fifth House is related to
procreativity. The inner urges of the native under the
impulse of this house is towards building beautiful
and useful images on whatever plane or level of living it
manifests. On the physical plane, this creativity takes
the form of bringing together the *panch bhutas*, the five
basic creative elements in nature, for giving shape to a
new entity. On other planes also, similar building activities are carried out. As the creation of the human body
is the most important function of the creative genius
in man, the malefics in general and Saturn in particular
want to strangulate this faculty. The influence of Saturn
is devastating on this house unless its bad influence is
modulated either by some benefic aspect or by conjunction of some with it, none the less the planet would
somehow or the other show its result. The only protection against Saturn exists in those cases when saturn is
posited in the house itself while being the ruler of it or
in exaltation there. This situation totally alters the
nature of the planet. Under such a situation, the individual becomes much interested in discovering the natural
laws of nature. Accepting the supremacy of Divine
Power, any hardship on the physical plane is of the least
significance to him. If such a psychological orientation
is present in the psyche of the person, Saturn does not
function as a restrictive influence rather it begins to
support the efforts of the person. So the fructification
of the person even on the physical plane by way of
having a child becomes a possibility.

Mars is an impulsive planet which is very intolerant to
the slowness of any process. It wants to dissolve everything under its impact into energy-potential. Matter is the
very anti-thesis of energy and as the material content in

child-birth is predominantly high, the influence of Mars generally results in abortion, caesarean births, and if other factors are exerting some favourable influence, the planet would simply lead to conditions where the pro-creative process at some stage or the other would require the assistance of such instruments which are needed for expediting the process. In the state of exaltation or when Mars owns the house and is posited there its effect would be very different. It would give enormous amount of courage and enthusiasm to the native. The flow of energy would be very much augmented. The number of children may be many or few, which under this condition becomes less significant, but there will be no sadness and the person would be ever engaged in creative activity at some level of his existence or the other.

As far as Sun is concerned, it stands on an entirely different level. Whether it should be considered a malefic or a benefic may be debatable, but its nullifying impact can never be denied as far physical progeny is concerned. Whatever the other situations, the Sun must create its impact. In the Fifth House, the results of the Sun are certainly significant because if it succeeds in giving any physical offspring, the child would be extremely bright, but if it's creativity is on super-physical planes, the impact would be of a high order. Under the influence of Sun, the entire creative urge of the individual is drawn towards the central vortex of regal splendour. The central point from which the various dimensions of the individual has been reeled off, the central cause from which the successive lives of the person have been incarnated, that cause will always attract the creative impulses of the individual so that his successive lives are gradually directed to that central direction. As a result of this propensity, the native would not be interested in merely sowing wild oats ; he would be very selective in his sexual relationships ; he would prefer to have a few children of merit rather than a number of them produced without much thought ; his children will carve out a place in this world either by their intellect or by their political power. Such results relating to the progeny do not necessarily destroy the faculty of the person of acting on the higher echelons of life and to be creative on intellectual and spiritual planes. The total energy contained in Sun is so great that even when distributed over different aspects of one's life enough of it remains for fructification on almost all levels according to the disposition of the chart.

Generally speaking, one would like to see planets in the Fifth House. Whether they are malefic or benefic is of secondary significance. Many saints have had Ketu and Jupiter in the Fifth House which are said to be harmful for progeny. But these sages raised their creative urges to such a heights that the spiritualising forces of these planets could forcefully flow down through their efforts not for perpetuating themselves through their physical 'seeds' but for spiritualising the cosmos which almost made them immortal. Unless there are planets in the Fifth House, and this *bhava* is greatly energised, the life of the individual is colourless, he is a powerless entity, and his creative urges are so weak that he does not arouse sufficient forces to vitally influence his future lives. Even if they are malefics, they could be there only as a result of the past *karmas* which if dissolved with understanding and transmuted to better purpose, it could ultimately prove advantageous for the Soul. A man could consider his birth useful only if he gets plenty of opportunities for activities in diverse areas. This can happen when he involves himself in multifarious activities. If they happen to be 'creative' they could pave the way for a happier future life by fulfilling the obligations of a human birth. A fuller and powerful Fifth House, whether it is harmful for the issues, or for the attainment of great spiritual initiations is not that significant. It would in reality show that nature is favourable to him. Nature abhores the lukewarm, and a powerful and fuller Fifth House shows that the individual is not a lukewarm entity; he is powerful and he is going to be more powerful in future for which Nature has been preparing him in this life.

EDUCATION, EXAMINATION AND SUCCESS

When infancy begins to merge into childhood, an important problem confronting every individual is the training for fitting him in the human society. It has several aspects concerning, the individual, parents and the society. Almost in every civilised government, rules have been framed for the regulation of the education of the children. Almost all over the world there have been serious concern regarding the educational system, curriculum, school leaving age and so on. In all these, many interests have to be synthesized. Nowhere the experiment has succeeded in providing complete satisfaction. The crux lies in differing objeetives of the educational system which often overlook the basic needs of the child and the students by over emphasizing the politico-social considerations. Unless the student is satisfied with his education and gets the full satisfaction, the system in the long run would only breed friction and dissatisfaction between the individual and the society.

Often the individual is not aware of his own requirements. The child has the natural proclivity for pursuing one line of study, whilst the parents are keen on imparting another kind of training for the child whereas the society either because of its social policy or its technological requirements endeavours to guide the young population to a different direction. These goals require to be appropriately synthesized in order to work out a system which meets the needs of everybody. But in all this the interest and the natural inclination of the student is of supreme importance. Each individual brings with him from his very birth certain faculties based on which he wishes to pursue certain line of studies to which goal he arranges his toy brick-blocks. The natural aptitude tests are very helpful for the growth and development of the child's latent faculties. But it is also observed that the child has talents in one line of studies whereas he wishes to work in diametrically opposite direction. When such conflicts confront the child or his educator, a dilemma arises which needs solution. Even the parents either on account of their superior experience or to fulfil their own aspirations wish the child to adopt a course of studies not-liked by him or unsuited to his aptitude. To resolve such conflicts, astrological counselling may sometimes be very helpful.

Apart from the inner urge of the child and his latent faculties, another consideration from the practical standpoint is to explore the possibilities for their fructification. The non-availability of training institutions or the lack of financial support for undergoing those training courses may sometimes impede the development of those faculties. Thus the conflict between the latent interests, the past acquisition of expertness and the interests are not decreed by the Lords of Karmas to be encouraged in the present incarnation often becomes acute. These in some cases could be highly pronounced. The interests of the individual may be deeply entrenched in some lime of studies, or he may have some underdeveloped association with some subjects in which he may be superficially interested, but whatever the reason, there is a possibility that the Lords of Karmas, in their

wisdom have thought that the person should devote his
energy and time in the present life in the pursuit of some
new subjects. His profession or his contribution to the
society would reveal the course of studies the individual
would finally pursue. While deciding the educational
programme for a child, it is useful to be aware of all
these conditions. But, it should be kept in view that the
application of the student, his proficiency in any subject
and the result in examinations are not necessarily well
connected. Within these seemingly unco-ordinated
situations one has to decipher the hands of destiny and
that is what the astrology aims to reveal.

There are four factors very important in educational
planning : these are the level of educational or intellectual capacity of the individual ; the different subjects
of his interest ; the possibility of success in examination
pertaining to the various courses of study and the likely
subject which could be the basis of his avocation
Astrologically there are clear indications regarding these
considerations. The ancient seers were also aware of
the two main goals of learning, namely *Paraa* and
Aparaa Vidya as signifying the occult wisdom and material
learning. For the acquisition of different kinds of
knowledge, there were various requirements and these
were well identified. Three main stages involved in the
process were the disire or the determination to know,
capacity to know and the absorption of knowledge. The
last is also known as the ability to express the comprehended knowledge. With regard to *Aparaa Vidya*, that
is the knowledge pertaining to the material world, the
third, fourth and the fifth houses in a natal chart indicate
the possibilities. The Third House represents the
Prakrama or valour of *Kala Purusha*, the Heavenly Man,
referring to that stage of manifestation when the

subjective spirit decides or *wills* to manifests on the lower planes of existence. That is the phase when the *Universal Mind* becomes aware of itself in the Shoreless Waters of Eternity or in the everlasting Darkness of the Spirit. In individual human beings, the strength and vitality of the Third House would signify the urge to enquire, which is an essential precondition for every educational activity. Unless the child wishes to study, no amount of external coaching could help him. Then follows the capacity to comprehend. The Fourth House signifies that power in man which could link him to the natural state of the things and the relationships enquired into. The power to observe, analyse, compare, and to feel the significance of the object of enquiry lies in the Fourth House. In the case of J. Krishnamurti, the famous philosopher of the twentieth century, exalted Sun in the Fourth aspected by the Ascendant lord Saturn from its exalted position in the Tenth House has made his comprehension very acute : he easily goes to the very root of the things which is the very quality of Sun and of Krittika star in which the same is posited. In the case of Albert Einstein the Fourth House lord Mercury placed in the Tenth House along with Sun, Venus and Saturn in the house of Jupiter gives him one of the finest power of comprehension in the present era. The Fourth House is the determinant of the power of comprehension.

But, for the fructification of the mental power, the involvement of the mind, one has to examine the Fifth House. The various appellations given to the fifth *bhava*, or aspect, of the *Kala Purusha* such as *Vichara* (deep pondering), *Panditya* (wisdom), *Viveka* (discrimination), and *Gambhirya* (profundity) suggest the special nature of this house in relation to educational activities. Besides learning, mentation, lengthy discourses, and production

5

of epics, this house is said to be the womb, signifying the capacity to absorb, preserve, and produce in a new form the 'germ' assimilated. The fifth is the personal crucible in which all the experiences gathered by the individual are objectified in a totally new form. Without it all the studies, evidences collected, case histories taken, and lectures attended would be futile to fructify in a meaningful way. In the chart of Professor Einstein, we find that the fifth house with Libra as the sign of the zodiac aspected by Jupiter from a mysterious sign which is also the lord of the tenth house, has given it special strength which is greatly recognised by his achievements in the field of science, his interest in occult philosophy, proficiency in music and tremendous interest in humanitarian activities. Again, in the case of H. G. Wells, one can see the fifth house lord Venus, his ascendant being Capricorn, placed in his Tenth House along with Saturn giving him immense insight into world history, scientific fiction, was greatly strengthened by the Jovian aspect from the Ascendant. The power of comprehension and the capacity to concretise the assimilated ideas and information depend on the strength and nature of the Fifth House. Educational expectation must be realistically assessed on the basis of the Fifth House.

The subject of specialisation is the most difficult decision in educational planning. On the basis of nine planets it is extremely speculative to identify the specific line which the individual should be advised to pursue ; these days the courses of studies are so numerous requiring so many different talents that the simple astrological texts are almost helpless. But, the planets which act in one manner in order to arouse the interest and fructification of material studies act differently when occult studies are pursued. Therefore, before the nature of studies harmonious to the Egoic goal is examined, it would be of interest to find out whether the three houses which we have mentioned above would guide this line of enquiry or some other astrological considerations would become important in this context. The ancient seers have established that the material knowledge are the earlier stages of the higher learning, that is, the study of occult subjects including those under *Paraa Vidya*. The three houses important in this respect are the Sixth, Eighth and the Ninth House. The Sixth House represent the six primary forces in nature over which the individual could if the factors are favourable achieve control. These forces are given, according to one set of nomenclature, the following names : *Parasakti*, which is connected with, light and heat ; *Jnanasakti*, the power of intellect, knowledge or real wisdom. When placed under the influence or control of material conditions, it could manifest in the power of the mind in interpreting human sensations, in recalling past memories and raising future expectations, its power in forming persisting connections between various groups of sensations and thus generating notions or ideas of an external object, and its power in connecting our ideas together by the mysterious link of memory and thus generating the notion of Self or Individuality. When intellect is freed from the bondage of matter it could lead to clairvoyance and psychometry. *Ichchasakti* is the power of will whose most ordinary manifestatian is the generation of certain nervecurrents which set in motion such muscles as are required for the accomplishment of desired object. *Kriyasakti* is the mysterious power of thought which enables it to produce external, perceptible phenomenal result by its own inherent energy.

Kundalinisakti, popularly known as the Serpent Fire is the force said to be located in man at the base of his spine; it is the power which moves in a serpentine or curved path. This force is the universal life-principle and includes in itself the two kinds of great forces of attraction and repulsion whose manifestations are electricity and magnetism. *Matrksakti* is the force on which basis *mantras*, words of speech and musical notes influence the human beings.

In developed beings, these powers, could take the aspirant to great heights, but even for common and ordinary individuals, one could see that many of these in some degre or the other manifest unconsciously. In the chart of J. Krishnamurti, one could see that the placement of Mars, Jupiter and Venus in the Sixth House fully aspected by the Moon from the twelfth bestowed on him considerable degree of control over these primary forces in nature. In this regard, the exchange between the lords of the Fifth and the Sixth Houses have also been helpful. Raman Maharshi had Libra as his Ascendant and Saturn in Pisces and Jupiter, the lord of the Sixth House in Aquarius thus giving the exchange between the Fifth and the Sixth Houses providing to Maharshi supreme control over such primary forces of nature. Jesus Christ, with Virgo Ascendant, had Mars in Saturnine sign of Aquarius which was his Sixth House. Thus, one could find that the sixth house accomplishments do not depend upon scholastic training but due to some kind of inherent inborn faculty or occult training under some Adept teacher, such powers could be developed or controlled and regulated.

The Eighth House is another indicator of occcult attainments. The mysterious nature of this house is well known but its implications have not yet been fully revealed. Sun in Scorpio, in relation to *Kala Purusha,* is said to represent Vishnu which implied that which has expanded. This has reference to the Germ which expanded into the Universe. From the Eighth House, one could get an idea of the possibility of the expansion of the spiritual power of the person, which indicated the levels of Initiations in the Mystery School that could be possible for the individual. It leads not only to the supernormal expansion of consciousness as a result of which the aspirant comprehends the inner working of the nature at various higher levels of the world, but also to the accomplishment of eight perfections which have been talked in yogic literature. These eight accomplishments are *Anima*, the power of becoming as small as an atom ; *Lughima*, the power of assuming excessive lightness at will ; *Prapti*, the power of obtaining anything ; *Prakrayam* which bestows irresistable will ; *Mahima*, which is the power of increasing size at will ; *Ishitwam*, superiority ; *Vashitwam*, to subjugate anyone under one's control ; and *Kamayasayita* which is the power to terminate the sway of passion. As a result of these attainments, the understanding and capacity of the individual to function consciously in this world are completely changed and have become superhuman. Perfection of these qualities makes an individual an Adept, who has gone beyond the trammels of life and death. Sri Adi Sankaracharya, whose biography recorded his use of these powers while engaged in discussions with Mundan Mishra, had Jupiter in the sign of Aquarius placed in his Eighth House which was receiving full aspect of its owner Saturn from Scorpio, another occult sign ; there was exchange between Sixth and Eighth Lords which supported this yoga, and Mars in the house of Jupiter strengthened it furthermore. The wisdom attained by

Sankaracharya was not so much based on his Fourth and Fifth Houses but on the strength of his Eighth and Sixth Houses because these houses provide *Paraa Vidya*, the transcendental wisdom which is much superior to material worldly learning. In everyday common life also, one comes across persons with Ketu and Moon located in the eighth house supported by the zodiac like Scorpio or Leo linked with supernatural powers having considerable expansion of consciousness on these lines.

While on this subject, one could refer to Ninth House which is mainly the house connected with exoteric religion. Those who are inclined towards religious observances would find the effect of this house very helpful. But even .otherwise, those who are interested in philosophic studies will have to get support from this house. Being a house which indicates the acquisitions of the individual in his earlier incarnations, the latent talents, natural inclinations of the student should be examined in relation to this house. Jupiter in this house is very auspicious for the reason that this planet is concerned with exoterism and his aspect on any house is helpful for the growth and expansion of that house. From the Ninth House, Jupiter could bestow immense power of comprehension as a result of its fifth aspect on Ascendant, its Seventh aspect on the Third House could increase the determination to pursue studies diligently, and its ninth aspect on the Fifth House could greatly help the comprehension and fructification of the knowledge acquired.

The specific subject with which the individual would be concerned in his life would be decided by the disposition of the planets which basically radiate certain force-currents which according to the existing circumstances express themselves in different forms. On this line of enquiry, one will have to analyse the possibility of the individual pursuing various kinds of studies in the contemporary society.   The Sun has a special importance because it bestows power of comprehension as well as interest in certain line of erudition.   Being intimately linked with the Soul of the person whatever is the direction and quality of the Sun that would be decisive for the nature and content of the educational progression.   The planet being the universal energiser cannot assume any restriction on itself consequently the influence of this planet on the Third House would be tremendous in energising the individual in actively participating in experience gaining activities in this world which would imply desire to pursue different lines of study. The person in that situation would not be negative to educational activities no matter whatever is the line of study.   In the Fourth, it would certainly bestow immense intelligene but it would be so because of the special sense of detachment leading to clarity of vision and impersonality of approach.   When the individual has excessive attachment to anything, whether material or spiritual, the presence of crystalline nature in which the true image of the things could be reflected is not possible ; when the mind is purged of all attachments, there is immediate identity between the knower and the known resulting in true understanding of the thing.   The Sun in the Fourth House enables that deep incisive approach but the impersonality growing under the situation often makes the person look like stony heart.   Because of the special influence of the solar radiation, it arouses deep interest and understanding of subjects like science, esoteric philosophy, Vedantic philosophy which all lead to the vision of the unifying principles in life.   It would, on the same consideration, associate the student with mathematics, logic, psychology, mental diseases, space science, origin of the earth, electronics and electricals, computer science. Wherever clarity of approach is needed, the support of the Sun is extremely desirable ; for successful legal profession along with Mercury, the Sun would raise the person to great heights ; in association with Saturn, it would increase the capacity of engineering skill ; when in conjunction with Mars, the Sun may make the person highly proficient surgeon.

The Moon is the life sustaining planet and under its radiation, the student could hope to be efficient medicine man specialising in life-saving drugs. Psychological analysts, mental disease speciality, herb specialists, cardiologists, naturopath, neurologist, and gynocologists would be born under the special influence of the Moon. In conjunction with Mercury, there could be specialisation in children diseases. Otherwise, navigators, fishery experts, marin product scientists, businessmen and economists specially those who specialise in international trade and balance of payments problems would be influenced by the Moon, but the aspect or association with Mercury would greatly assist it in this regard. In order to influence literary faculties, poetry writing, cultivation of fine arts, and market counselling, the Moon would be very helpful. Wherever one is required to understand the reactions of others, in those activities, as well as in those areas where the person is involved in prolonging the life of other persons, and in areas of activities which are intimately connected with moving water, the association of the Moon either in the Fourth or in the Fifth House is greatly helpful. One should however note that the effect of the Moon is greatly increased when it is in association of any other planet.

Mercury has special significance in the determination

of educational interests.   In the special field of transportation, communication, and journalistic enterprise,
the contribution of Mercury is fundamental.   Unless
Mercury is favourable, the quality of speech or the capacity to communicate with others would be inefficient. For
this reason, a good teacher, an eminent writer, a
successful journalist, a proficient lawyer would need the
blessings of Mercury.   Even for astrology, it is necessary
that the student has got good Mercurial benediction.
When Mercury is associated with any other planet, it
has the special gift of augmenting the capacity of the
other planet immensely.   In association with Jupiter,
Mercury could give birth of efficient teacher, professor
and educationists.

   Saturn is time, and consequently old age.   Its influence on concretisation of Universal Mind thus enabling
the origin and growth of this universe is very marked.
Every subject of study which is related to this basic
characteristic would be related to Saturn.   In this category, we may find anthropologists, orhopaedists, archi-
tects with old style designs, engineers with tremendously
big structural work-programme, ancient historical exca-
vators, ethnologists and the like. It would be connected
with such efforts in which much intensive work is
required to externally produce very little at the tip.   For
occult studies, austere yogic practices it is very helpful.
For questions dealing with labour relations, one may
look to it.

   Mars is a planet in many ways opposed to Saturn :
wherever quick (impulsive ?) results are needed, wherever
efforts are needed to bring things from within to without
that is wherever externalisation of action is imperative,
wherever constructive courage is wanted, Mars would
be there to assist. Mars is also fire, activity, speed (but

in a different sense from Mercury). Following from such characteristics of Mars, one finds that the support of this planet could make a surgeon successful specially on emergency duty, Mars wages wars, whereas Saturn defends. The defence science should be mainly the concern of Saturn but because it cannot be effectively done so without understanding the war strategies, it is generally the influence of Mars which makes one efficient in defence strategy; a successful general who is primarily a combatant would be a protege of Mars whilst the strategist at the base camp should have the support of Sun, Saturn and Mercury. A surgeon specialising in malignant ailments like cancer, should have the combination of Mars with Saturn. As a transport engineer dealing with locomotives, automobile (for which Mercurial support could be helpful) or thermal power stations, the contribution of Mars would be substantial. Mars finds itself impatient in implementing its objectives, for which reason the Jovian support could make it sustain its tempo.

Jupiter is highly auspicious for educational activities. By profession, Jupiter itself is a teacher, adviser, always giving good spiritual counselling and protecting the kings and royalties from spiritual downfall. These characteristics would be present even in ordinary mundane conditions. A favourable disposition of Jupiter would make a person amply suited for teaching profession; ethical counselling would also be in his jurisdiction. Education, jurisprudence, ethics, and personal counselling are special areas where Jovian influence would be helpful. As Mars is connected with agriculture and agronomy, if it gets the support from Jupiter, there would be great possibility of the person becoming an agricultural or rural economy expert. Ancient Indian history, history of ancient civilisations, philosophy, culture, and religious performances are some of the subjects with which Jupiter would be closely linked.

Venus representing the creative positive fluid from the latent passive potential Germ symbolised as semen ever seeking the procreative base for the generation of the primeval bliss is expressed in very many ways in the actual life of a person. Venus is an adviser of the No-Gods, *Asuras* suggesting that those who endeavour for material splendour and happiness would get assistance and guidance from this planet. The primary aim of Venus is to make the everyday life of the human individual happy, so sociology, civics, fine arts, lyrical language, poetry, and the new scientific innovations to make one's home life comfortable come within the purview of this planet. Hotel management, interior decoration, tourism, perfumery and fashion garments would come within the jurisdiction of Venus. In association with Mercury, it would support economic studies, in conjunction with Mars it may be impulsively (immorally?) associated with marriage counselling, venereal diseases, sexology, and sex related psychological disorders. Business management, behavioural sciences, personnel management, dance and music teachers would have strong Venusian influence.

Ketu arouses strong occult interests and it could bestow extremely astute understanding of human psychology whilst Rahu is concerned with industrial labour relations. In conjunction with Saturn, it could often lead to problems of jail management but with Jupiter it might give an insight into (prisoners' and criminals') reform problems.

On the basis of these indications and their placements in a horoscope, one will decide the various

avenues open before the individual but the proficiency
in a subject which would be decided on the basis of the
above is different from academic recognition as evident
from success in examinations. The latter would be
examined in relation to the Tenth House. Unless any
planet has benefic aspect of the Moon or of Jupiter,
generally speaking, recognition of merit in any direction
is difficult. Even if a planet has bestowed talents and
comprehension for any specific line of studies, unless
Jovian or Lunar influence enables it to flower, it could
only remain largely as a hobby. If it related to the Tenth
House there is a possibility that the study could affect
the vocation of the person. But the full advantage of it
can be secured only if it is well integrated with the
Tenth House. Recognition of merit in that subject would
depend upon the rulership of the planet at the specific
period when such success results are expected. Adverse
planetary rulership when the examination results are
expected would not lead to happy ending. This makes
the student often very depressed and lose confidence in
himself. It can be warded off by a careful analysis of
the periodicity of the planetary rulership in order to
examine whether the favourable influences are present
when the results are expected. Co-ordination of the
period analysis could avoid much psychological strain.
In case the particular talent is to be utilised for the
vocational selection, one should lay much greater
emphasis on the Tenth House disposition in this regard,
and if the subject in view is not in consonance with
vocational choice, such lines of studies should better
be relegated as hobby. Many administrators succeeding
in their professional examination on the basis of proficiency in certain subjects like classical literature, history

and languages, with strong interest in painting and horticulture have succeeded well after their joining service in beautifying their city on the basis of their this knowledge. The distinction in the studies required for vocational selection, and success or satisfaction in other lines of interest must be made clear and carefully related to the planetary rulership at the required time.

COMBINATIONS FOR FINANCIAL SUCCESS

It has been rightly stated that ''poverty is a horrible spectre more grim-like than even death. A poor man leads a wretched life. He will be compelled to live in squalid houses and unhealthy environment. The children will have no facilities for education, health and decent existence''. These characteristics of poverty clearly indicate the intense pain and deprivation the poor suffers ; not only personally but his entire family has to reap the consequences of the same. The wealth and personality have their own significance not only for affluence and convenience and luxurious living but also for providing better opportunities for the self and others so that the inner possibilities are fruitfully and effectively evolved. Search for financial success is therefore not an expression of parasitism, rather it is an essential requirement for a good and happy social life.

But there are many avenues for acquiring money, wealth and riches. Some people have steady sources of income like those who are in well positioned services, generally signified by prominant Raja Yogas in astrology, while there are others who receive huge annual returns from their investments, or from conditions resulting from steller influences on the Seventh House in the chart. There would be basic differences between the flows of income in these ways ; in one case, the receipt may be highly fluctating often with a sense of great uncertainty;

much of the results of investment resources depend upon partners, companies and other financial institutions on which the individual concerned is having no or very little control. Even those persons who are engaged in business, private medical, legal, consultancy and such other professions, mainly guided by the specific planets connected with profession and financial gains, they also are vulnerable to income fluctuations but in a different manner. Fluctuating financial gains do not necessarily signify inadequate receipt, the quantum of which depends upon the planetary strength, while the nature of gains is signified by various planetary combinations. Those who depend upon black marketing, smuggling and bribes, symptomatic of Moon's affliction by Mars, Rahu, Saturn and such other malefics, they also derive substantial financial gain but the nature of their receipts is of a different category. Gain from theft, robbery, and dacoity, result from cruel planets impinging upon the Moon ; these also yield much money to the miscreants but the dishonesty and anti-social element of the act affects the nature of the gain in an important manner. In the same way, one has also to discover the quality of the professional beggary, which does not necessarily indicate poverty in the present age ; flesh trade, the job of a hangman and such other means of acquiring money have different astrological implications. And so has the money received by way of legacy and lotteries, which to a great extent is linked with the disposition of the Eighth House, in which unexpectedness and no effort on the part of the individual concerned are the main characteristics. These conditions very much affect the human individual involved in the money earning trade with ambition for acquiring wealth and riches. Astrologically, factors influencing all these sectors of financial

activities require distinct considerations. They may
be kept clearly in the mind while prognosticating
financial success or otherwise of an individual.

The basic principle to remember in the case of
financial prognostication is that all kinds of gains are
connected with the lord of the Second House, the lord
of the Eleventh House, the lord of the Tenth House, the
Moon, the relationships between the lords of the Trines
and Quadrant that is, between the lords of the Fifth
and the Ninth Houses and those of the First, Fourth,
Seventh, and the Tenth Houses. The disposition of the
Eighth House is also important. The association or
affliction by the lords of the Sixth, Eighth and the
Tweifth Houses destorys the auspicious effects of wealth
providing combinations. *Kemdruma* and *Sakata Yogas,*
the former formed by the absence of planets on the
either side of the Moon while the latter (that is, the
Moon) itself is not in a Quadrant; the *Sakata Yoga*
formed when the Moon and Jupiter are placed in Sixth-
Eighth relationship from each other and none of them
specially the Moon is in a Quadrant, considerably
dampen the financial prospect of the person concerned,
but there are also the combinations connected with
Moon as well as with Ascendant, and their presence or
absence must be taken note of while prognosticating
financial prospects of a person.

The *Pancha Maha Purusha Yoga* which is formed by
the ownership or exaltation of any one or more of the
planets excluding the Sun and the Moon. Each of these
five causative planets are bestowed with special
characteristics as far as their financial gifts are concerned and these combinations can also be considered
along with a set of auspicious yogas formed by the
exaltation or strength of the lords of the Quadrants.

The *Sasa Yoga* formed by the ownership or exaltation of Saturn in a Quadrants makes the native rich but licentious in nature. He may even employ unscrupulous means to gain other's money unless there is some benefic influence in the planet. The *Ruchaka Yoga* formed by Mars placed in similar situation makes the person rich but makes him arrogant with a touch of aggressiveness and destructiveness. Jupiter in such a position causing *Hamsa Yoga* bestows riches while producing a man of sterling character and immense moral fibre, which are basic features of Jupiter. When Venus causes *Malavya Yoga*. the native gets wealth and riches but also are given the basic conditions where one could enjoy those gifts such as beautiful wife, luxurious house, good conveyance and sensuous atmosphere around him. When *Bhadra Yoga* is formed by exaltation or ownership of a Quadrant by Mercury, the combination bestows wealth but it also adds its special gift of intellect to the individual. These five special combinations have been assigned great importance in classical treatises. The essential feature of these combinations is the supreme vitality—exaltation or ownership—of the planets in a Quadrant. Powerful planets indeed give powerful yogas and generally of auspicious nature.

The association of the lords of *trikonas* (trines) and *Kendras* (quadrants) specially when they are different from one another is auspicious for wealth. Such associations can be of different kinds such as combination, aspect, interchange and so on, but all of these are conducive to auspicious results. The lord of Ascendant or of the Second House in Ninth, Tenth, or in the Eleventh Houses, or the *vice-versa*, that is, the lord of Eleventh, Tenth, or of the Ninth Houses in Ascendant or in the Second House is an important producer of financial

gain. *Neecha Bhanga Raja Yoga* which occurs when
a planet is in its debilitation, but either the lord of
that house itself where the planet is debilitated, or of the
house where it becomes exalted, occupies a Quadrant
position from the Ascendant or the Moon, specially if
that planet is exalted or otherwise strong, is also considered auspicious. A singularly important combination
in the present context occurs due to the location of the
Sixth, Eighth, and the Twelfth House lords either singly
or together, whether partially or completely, in these
houses. This is one of the important combinations for
wealth which is produced without any reference to the
Ascendant, Moon, *Dhanesh* (lord of the Second House),
Labhesh (lord of the Eleventh House), *Karmesh* (lord
of the Tenth House), *Konas* (trines) or *Kendras* (Quadrants), but it is very powerful in its effect.

In fact, there are many combinations for financial
success given in astrological treatises but here, we wish
to highlight a few of the important combinations which,
besides the above, should be taken into account in
deciding the financial success of an individual :

1. A strong Second House, specially if its lord is
   exalted or otherwise strong and unafflicted while
   placed in a Quadrant or trine having an aspect of
   benefics will give wealth.
2. Mutual exchange between the lords of the First,
   Second and the Eleventh Houses.
3. The lords of the Second, Sixth and the Eleventh, or
   of the Second, Tenth and Eleventh Houses in a
   Quadrant or a trine.
4. Sun in Sagittarius, Gemini or in Leo should make an
   individual rich.
5. Mercury in Cancer, and Saturn in Aquarius make one
   rich.

6. Jupiter in Cancer, Sagittarius, Pisces, Aries, or in Scorpio ; Saturn in Sagittarius, or in Pisces.

7. Jupiter conjoined with Venus makes the native rich.

8. Mars in the Eleventh or the Second House even in depression gives wealth.

9. Venus in Gemini conjoined with Mercury gives wealth.

10. *Lakshmi Yoga*, caused by powerful Ascendant while the lord of the Ninth is in the Ninth House or in exaltation sign identical with a trine or a quadrant bestows much wealth and riches.

11. The Moon and the Ascendant lord together, the lord of the Moon sign in a quadrant or a friendly house aspecting the Ascendant and a powerful planet posited in Ascendant is conducive to financial gains.

12. Planets on either side of the Sun.

13. Benefics in Quadrants, and the Sixth and the Eighth Houses either not occupied by any planet or occupied by benefics.

14. Benefics in the Third, Sixth, Tenth, and Eleventh Houses either from Ascendant or the Moon.

15. Lords of the Ninth House from the Eleventh House occupying the Eleventh House in conjunction with Moon, and the lord of the Eleventh House aspecting the House.

16. Venus owning the Fifth House from Ascendant and posited in the same house while Saturn is posited in the Eleventh House.

17. If the seven planets contiguously occupied the houses it beginning with First, Second, or the Third Houses or it gives much money and wealth.

18. If the Navamsa lord in which the Ninth Lord is placed, along with the Tenth lord posited in the Second House in conjunction with the Ninth lord,

Vishnu Yoga is formed which bestows immense wealth to the native.

19. The Sun, Moon, and Mars in trine with one another is extremely auspicious for giving property, wealth and riches.

20. The Ascendant lord placed in the Second House, the Second lord in the Eleventh House, and the Eleventh lord in the Ascendant, if they are strong planets, will bestow good financial fortune.

These combinations will have to be considered very carefully and the amount of money and the sources of income flowing from these combinations will have to be assessed taking the horoscope in its entirety.

The practical influence of these combinations can be tested on the basis of a few illustrative horoscopes to see how the interpersonal variations affect the results. *Chart I*[1] belongs to an United Nations Official who having put in several years of work in the Government of India joined the World Bank at Washington, D. C. where he worked for about fifteen years. The prestige, money, and social status enjoyed at the world's highest organisation gave a tremendous boost to the individual and he began to move in the highest echelon of the Indian society. That was the influence of Saturn leading to *Sasa Yoga* while the lord of the Ascendant was posited in the Ninth House. The influence of Saturn was further reinforced by the *Punya Kartari Yoga* caused by the flanking of two benefics on the either side of the Ascendant. As a result of such a long period of assignment with the World Bank, he not only earned millions of rupees during the period of his service abroad, he

---

1. *Chart I* : Ascendant and Saturn (R) in Libra ; Jupiter (R) in Scorpio ; Mars in Capricorn : Ketu in Aquarius ; Mercury (R) in Aries : Sun in Taurus ; Venus in Gemini ; Rahu in Leo ; Moon in Virgo.

even successfully invested them (one may note Mercury in the Seventh House) whereby he multiplied them several times, and after the completion of the assignment, he earned a sufficiently substantial amount of pension which could have been impossible if he did not get this special opportunity. As a result of efficient financial management, he has become a multi-millionaire. It is worth noting that the two of the *Pancha Maha Purusha Yogas* are powerfully applicable in this case ; actually the period of Saturn was responsible for making him rich and wealthy. In the present case, Ascendant lord is in the Ninth house ; two planets namely Saturn and Mars are exalted, and in Quadrant ; benefics are on the either side of Sun—Mercury and Venus—both intimately connected with the individual making an economist, specially in the field of balance of payments problems. Strong Second House lord is in a Quadrant (No. 1 combination tabulated above) and that planet also causes Ruchaka Yoga ; Jupiter is in Scorpio (No. 7 of the above combinations), Venus is in Gemini (No. 9 combination) and Sun, Moon and Mars are trine to one another (No. 19 combination) which is one of the special combinations for financial gain. As a result of these combinations for wealth and income, it is quite natural to explain the riches and wealth accruing to the individual, specially when the entire money is "white".

Chart II also belongs to an United Nations official but his financial position has made him richer both on account of official position as well as from family relationships. The number of combinations and the quality of financial status enjoyed by these two horoscopes are distinctly different from one another. In the second case, there is no *Pancha Maha purusha Yoga*, but there are many other combinations which make the

individual acquire much money, and that also money for
the money's sake. He himself does not enjoy the fruits
of his income. One should note that the Fourth house is
afflicted by *Papa Kartri Yoga* formed by the placement of
malefics on either side of the house, and powerfully
aspected by Mars, a yoga Karaka for the horoscopee, as
a result of which he has all the conveniences but psychologically is unable to enjoy them.   The native of *Chart I*
has earned to live a comfortable life and to become
charitable, whereas the Chart II[2] is primarily centred to
oneself and his family members which is also apparent
from the fact that the four planets of Chart II are concentrated in the First (self) and Second (family relationships)
Houses.   The Ascendant lord in Chart II is strong and
associated with lords of Tenth and Eleventh and
Second Houses.   The Ninth lord is also in a trine
house.   The Second House lord—Mercury—placed
with Sun (Ascendant lord) causes powerful *Budha
Aditya Yoga*, that is, the combination formed by the
association together of Sun and Mercury ; Tenth lord is
also in the Ascendant.   The Second House is well
aspected by Jupiter, who is himself causing to a little
extent, *Veepareeta Raja Yoga* formed by the lord of the
Eighth House placed in the Sixth House. The lord of
First (Sun), Second (Mercury), Tenth (Venus), and
Eleventh (Mercury) are together in a Quadrant (No. 3 of
the above mentioned combinations). There is also powerful *Laxmi Yoga* (No. 10 combination) caused by powerful
Sun and Mars in a Quadrant.   It can also be seen that
the horoscope is free from the afflictions of *Kemdrum,
Sakata,* and *Kala Sarpa Yogas.*

---

   2. *Chart II* :   Ascendant Leo with Mercury, Venus and Sun ;
Moon in Virgo ; Saturn in Libra ; Ketu in Sagittarius ; Jupiter in Capricorn ; Mars in Sagittarius ; and Rahu in Gemini.

Quite different from the two charts given above, it would be interesting to examine *Chart III*[3] which is also exceptional in many ways. The native was not even thirty years of age when he became highly rich earning several thousands of rupees a month but his social status is not commensurate with the amount of riches at his commmand. The lords of Ninth (Mars) and Tenth (Venus) Houses are both afflicted as a result of which good social status is not expected. The individual could not even complete successfully school leaving examination which also results from badly placed Fourth and Fifth Houses. But he is an owner-cum-driver of a tempo and very successful at that. His personality is powerful and he has many powerful contacts at different levels of governmental and political levels. He is married to a beautiful girl and has two issues. Born in an humble amily, his financial achievements specially when he could not even complete his basic educational training in spite of his best efforts and facilities on the part of parents is certainly remarkable. The horoscope has three exalted planets though none of them has given *Panch-Maha Purusha Yoga* though the exalted planets, namely, Jupiter and Mercury, have produced *Punya Kartri Yoga* flanking the Ascendant on either side giving much strength to the Ascendant. Thus Ascendant is well fortified which is an important consideration for successful financial gains. The lords of Eleventh House is placed in the Second House in exaltation. There is neither *Kemdrum Yoga* nor *Sakata Yoga*, and to some extent the effect of *Gaja Keshari Yoga* is applicable. This chart shows combinations of financial gain but

---

3. Chart III: Ascendant and Sun in Leo ; Mercury in Virgo ; Saturn and Venus in Libra ; Mars and Rahu in Sagittarius ; Moon in Capricorn ; Ketu in Gemini ; Jupiter in Cancer.

the finer qualities of life which goes with wealth and riches are absent. Jupiter is aspected by Saturn and Mars, both malefics; Mars which is a *Yoga Karaka* for this horoscope is malefically aspected by Saturn. Thus the distinction between "whiteness" and "blackness" of wealth seems blurred. The association of Tenth lord in his own house with exalted Saturn connected with mechanical engineering skill and such other qualities of Saturn has influenced the capacity of the individual to earn much money. It would be interesting to go into details of these horoscopes for discovering fine nuances of astrological principles.

The above examples show that the various indications for affluence must be carefully considered and no hasty decisions made. Nevertheless, the general and several special combinations given for the financial success cannot be ignored. But it should be emphasized that the gain in terms of money, wealth and riches does not necessarily lead to mental peace, domestic harmony or social status.

VOCATIONAL GUIDANCE

Since astrology is increasingly recognised as a valid scientific pursuit, the astrologers have an added responsibility of assisting those who seek their advice in orienting their life pattern according to the stellar direction. In this regard, vocational guidance has great importance. The significance of marital compatibility has increasingly led the concerned parties to seek the advice of astrologers, and the Indian astrology has established its credibility in this sphere. The ancient seers have already formulated basic principles on the basis of which married happiness of the couples can be very reliably predicted. As far as vocational guidance is concerned, it is still an unchartered area. The job requirements of various professions are extremely varied. The social and institutional framework within which the individual has to seek his or her profession differs radically from one society to another. The stellar influences will show the basic forces operating on the individual which will have to be applied intelligently, not in a routine manner, in order to suggest the line of vocation in which the chances of success are greater which depended upon the basic urges of the individual, his physical and mental capacities as well as the preordained destiny of the individual incarnation. For this purpose, it is necessary that the horoscope of the person should be discussed with him in order to find out the areas of his interest and the available possibilities, and then, to examine the practicability of the planetary tendencies. An attempt is made here to give some of the basic rules for the consideration of astrologers as well as the enquirer some important aspects of vocational guidance.

The classical text states that the Tenth Bhava represents occupation, rank, temporal honours, self respect, religious knowledge and dignity. On the basis of such formulations the profession of an individual is predicted. As a matter of fact, these treatises while describing the avocation of a person, or the significance of the Tenth House have described so many things that an amateur astrologer will find himself at a loss to conclude the nature of any one's profession with certainty. For example, *Uttara Kalamrita* indicates the Tenth House to point out besides other traits, the nature of trade, 'riding on a horse' (*ashwagamanam*), government work, service, agriculture, doctor, fame, preeminence, elders, talisman, mother, magnitude of moral merits, accomplishments of a spell, honour, honourable living, supremacy, etc. This citation is just to show that mere routine predictions would be neither scientific nor would they satisfy the requirements of the present day society. Many of the indications of the house as indicated by *Ashwa-Gamanam*, going away on a horse, are even symbolic and the astrologer has to go deeper in their significance in order to be helpful to the modern mind.

The Tenth House, as acknowledged by most of the astrologers, is certainly basic for the determination of one's avocation. A rational view of this house is that it indicates the way the individual would spend most of his time, the way he would involve himself in the world of activities, it would indicate his '*karma*'. How the qualities and the Root-Destiny of the individual Soul imprinted on its Fate, its archetype, decided at the time of its Initial Fragmentation from the Divine Flame would be worked out in each successive incarnations is reflected by this house. That is why this is the most important house in the horoscope. All other houses indicate the influence of the past (or, of the stars) which would operate on him whereas the Tenth House indicates the manner of activities of *his* physical involvement; the most important of these activities being the manner of earning the livelihood which occupies most of the waking time of the individual. But from this house, other forms of activities such as hobbies, subsidiary interests in life, philanthropic work, and such other pursuits will also be inferred. The astrologers ascertain the level of income and wealth from other indicators; the satisfaction or otherwise which is concerned with mental peace and happiness is also indicated by other significators. It is therefore necessary to emphasize that the decision about the vocation should be connected with the basic factors which are related to the various inherent forces inducing the individual to pursue different lines of activities whether for earning money or for other interests. Undoubtedly, the Tenth House is the most important house in the present context.

While counselling the individual regarding vocational selection, the Tenth House must be related to the Ascendant or the First House. The Ascendant signifies basic urges, potential, marching order for the present incarnation. On a sympathetic vibration of these two houses depends the sense of fulfilment, which may be different from the sense of peace. Often people do express that their life had been full of troubles and storms, full of agony and pain, but they are happy that they fulfilled their destiny, the purpose which they held

high.   The latter is the result of synchronization of the
Ascendant and the Tenth House effects.

The vocation is also dependant upon the inherent
qualities of the individual. This requires that the
basic disposition of the planets irrespective of their
placements, that is, whether they are in the Tenth House
or not, as well as the basic features of the Sixth and the
Second Houses are carefully examined. The Sixth House
represents the latent faculties, the perfections, which
the individual is capable of ; the Tenth House being fifth
from the Sixth House should be rightly considered its
basic significator. The Second House is the fifth from
the Tenth House which would indicate the nature of the
outcome of the Tenth House efforts specially with regard
to riches and family relations. The planetary disposition
is important because they would impart various qualities
to the individual according to their capabilities. The
Ascendant would signify the basic urges, the potential,
the marching order for the present incarnation. On a
sympathetic vibration of the two houses, namely the First
and the Tenth, depends the sense of direction, and the
other factors, namely, the planets in different houses
would indicate the strength and capabilities provided by
these planets specially in order to externalize the latent
faculties, whilst one's the Second House would suggest
the level of riches and family satisfaction resulting from
his vocational achievements.

In vocational counselling on the basis of all these
factors an integrated view should be taken for suggesting concrete action. An individual who is intensely
physical, material, and down to earth should not be
advised to take up such activities which require fine
sensitivity, a fine logical analysis, an imaginative flight
and a deeper understanding of the forces of nature. A

person whose life revolves round sensual pleasure, acquisitive tendencies, material splendour should not be expected to feel happy in pursuits which require involvement with traditional values, exhuming the past to reconstruct the splendour of past civilisations. The mind and the heart of the individual, linked with the Moon, Mercury, and the Sun are specially important for vocational guidance but other planets such as Saturn, Mars, and Jupiter also play an important role. So, there is need for having a well informed knowledge of the various possibilities regarding different kinds of job opportunities on the background of which the individual capabilities according to astorogical directions have to be considered.

The success and impediments in one's profession depend to a great extent on the support it derives from various other characteristics and the difficulties the individual has to encounter in his life. The fifth from the Tenth House, that is, the Second House, and the Ninth from the Thenth House that is the Sixth House, as we have mentioned earlier, are important in many ways ; they determine the support to activities of the individual. The Second House indicates *inter alia* speech, tongue, eyes, determination, family relationship, trade, effort in the acquisition of wealth, clear oratorial ability, nose, firmness of mind, living power etc. Actually the Second House is the creative potential. Unless the efforts towards the acquisition (of anything) and trade (purchase and sale—*krayavikraya*), are favourably disposed towards the profession, the necessary support for it would be missing. The ninth from the Tenth House which is the Sixth House shows the past accumulation, the latent propensities and capabilities for the success of the vocation. The Sixth House itself has been considered affluence (*vibhawa*), fortune (*bhagyam*), circulation of money etc. Esoterically, the Sixth House represents the different kinds of natural forces which go to build the world. An understanding of the forces developed in the past which go to affect the present activities of the individual is necessary. The Sixth House even otherwise is intimately connected with service conditions of the individual.

The limitations, impediments, or the restrictions acting on the avocation could be predicted on the basis of the Sixth and the Eighth Houses from the Tenth House, which implies that the vocational guidance should be given keeping in view the influences generated from the Third and the Fifth Houses. The third represents 'courage'. *Uttara Kalamrita* has amplifed it by saying that the Third House is connected with courage, capabilities (*samartham*), valour (*vikrama*), power (*sakti*), bodily strength, large undertakings (*urukaryam*), and one's own religious duty. In short, the Third House represents personal initiative. Unless the person has adequate personal initiative for the work in hand, much progress in the same cannot be expected. Similarly, the Eighth House from the Tenth House is the Fifth House, which represented discrimination, great action desirable in many ways, creative activities and profound learning, and so on. Unless the individual functions creatively on different levels of his existence, his involvement in the physical world is bound to go to the rocks, bound to perish. Without a favourable disposition of Fifth House, the individual should not be expected to make a mark in any specific line of activity.

So far it is common knowledge, which every astrologer knows but the integrated view to be taken in specific cases will not be an easy task. All the factors which have been indicated above should be discussed

with the person for whom the assistance is sought from
the astrologer. Only on the basic of intimate discussions
with the individuals concerned, the line of vocation
should be decided. The exploratory discussion could
investigate the various directions of forces operating on
the individual as suggested above, and then the concrete
lines of possibilities should be identified to examine
the best suitability for the person concerned. The
illustrative charts given below would give some indications of the difficulties confronting vocational guidance
and the possible course that could be adopted. In
Chart I, the Ascendant being Gemini portends an
extremely sensitive, imaginative nature, always eager to
express oneself with something physical, desirous of
producing sensation, pleasure and synthesis. B. V.
Raman once indicated that the intellectual sign Gemini
rising gives a sympathetic and sensitive nature, mental
restlessness and inherent intuitional ability. Discussing
the chart of Albert Einstein, he further stated that the
Ascendant was aspected by *Gnanakaraka* (the significator of wisdom) Jupiter from the mystic sign Aquarius
(which is true also in the case of the chart cited here)
suggesting the Einstein gave to the world *gnana*
(wisdom) not merely of an abstract conception like
Euclid's space but knowledge of the real medium—space
—time—in which physical processes operate and are
observed. In the present case, Chart I, Jupiter happens
to be the lord of the Tenth House and it is fully aspecting

Chart I (Rasi) :   Ascendant : Gemini ; Rahu in Cancer ; Mars in
Leo ; Venus in Libra ; Sun, Moon, Mercury in Sagittarius ; Saturn and
Ketu in Capricorn, and Jupiter in Aquarius.

Amsa :   Ascendant in Taurus ; Venus and Saturn in Gemini ; Sun
in Cancer ; Rahu in Leo ; Moon in Virgo ; Mercury in Sagittarius ;
Jupiter and Ketu in Aquarius ; Mars in Aries.

the Ascendant which clearly lays down that the native's restlessness for attaining intellectual synthesis in a concrete way would persist throughout her life. This intellectual quest for harmonisation with one's inner being is also reflected by the fact that the Ascendant lord in placed in the Seventh House along with the Sun and the Moon and is not combust. Her quest for intellectual fulfilment would be considerably quenched by partnership with diverse type of research investigators. The combination of the Sun and Mercury together forming *Budha-Aditya Yoga* shows that the person would be highly intelligent, skillful in all works, good reputation, personal respect and surrounded by all comforts and happiness. This combination is not very rare but the yoga certainly bestows sharp intellect, penetrative insight, logical mind, capability for understanding deeper and hidden meanings of seemingly simple objects in life. There is no adverse aspect or restricting influence on it. Mercury is in the Navamsa of Jupiter which by itself is Vargottama. Mercury is Eleventh from Jupiter which shows that the planet of intellect would be very productive and fruitful for the Jovian efforts. Jupiter, the lord of the Tenth House placed in the Ninth House, in a mysterious sign which to be effective must be outward turned, and fully aspected by Mars from the Third House will be highly productive and auspicious for the individual. Even in determining the vocation of the person, the influence of Jupiter aspected by Mars, an earthly planet, must be decisive.

Among the various qualities attributed to Jupiter, one is inclined to highlight the following in order to discover the particular line of profession that may be suggested : Brahmin, astrology, philosophy, mansion, gem, jewel, a beautiful mansion facing north, moving in villages, an used garment, a new house, happiness, *mantras*, a house bestowing full happiness, throne, vessels, lapis lazuli, fruits arising from an *agnisthoma* rite, guessing the thoughts of others, ornamentation, and travelling in a carriage borded on all sides. These guiding items are apt to suggest that the vocation must take the individual to the past with huge mansions, jewels, ritualistic way of life leading to a happy social organization. One is inclined to feel that serious research investigations in past civilisations, either carrying out excavations or restructuring the broken glass and pottery to suggest the past splendour may be a very fruitful line of avocation. Mars in strength should also make the person able to concretise the traditional wisdom ; Mars may help to construct and create majestic edifices. From this angle, it is possible to suggest that the person could develop very well as an architect of new style of mansions, which could be based on ancient royal designs. The most important lines on which the professional excellence could be explored would be serious historical researches leading to excavations, unearthing of old manuscripts, scripts, philosophy, or of new styles of classical architect.

As Jupiter is wisdom, education, advice whereas Mercury in strength would be logical reasoning, law and draftsmanship, it is also possible that legal profession, counselling (legal) and teaching profession (without much success as an orator) may be possible.

While looking for the supporting features for these professions, one finds that Rahu in the Second House is not conducive to good speech ; Saturn is also aspecting this house. Therefore the profession where speech is an essential requirement for success should not be attempted. This rules out school teaching where much

7

depends upon the efficiency of the vocal chord. But Saturn is aspecting the Tenth House, and so is Mars. As a result of these aspects, one is inclined to suggest that the person would feel happy only when she could concretise something, create something tangible. From this consideration, the profession of archivist, historical restructuring of the past glory as well as of architect is still more plausible. The Sixth House is ruled by Mars which is connected with the Tenth House, so the profession must be down the earth, where intense activity is needed.

The profession of the individual would be greatly restricted by Venus which is also very powerful but in Navamsa with Saturn, in the radical chart aspected by Saturn (as well as by Jupiter). Sloth, desire for comfort and ease would often retard the progress. There would be serious conflict in the mind of the person when the self is not engaged in fruitful activity. The aspect of Mercury in Navamsa, Venus's placement in Mercury's Navamsa and such other characteristics would always arouse a feeling of guilt that the person is not fulfilling the mission of her life. But the strong influence of Mars and the position of Mercury in Jupiter Navamsa and in Vargottama position (while Jupiter also is in a Vargottama position) strongly emphasize that the stellar influences would inevitably drive the individual to whatever is her destiny through the spirit of restlessness, the desire to achieve higher and higher goals would always persist.

The clue to the discovery of real vocation also lies in finding out the ruling planets over different phases of life. The native was born in Venus Mahadasa which lasted for 11 years, 4 months and 25 days. It implied that the early life of the person was spent under the conflicting influences of Jupiter and Saturn though the personal urge must have been for self-expression which was not given adequate opportunities for fruition. The adolescence, from the age of 12 years to 18 years was ruled by the Sun when the great sense of loneliness must have eaten the largest portion of the quest of the new world. The lack of companionship also destroyed much of the creative power. But the Moon's period started from the middle of 1979 which must have been a strong turning point in her career. During this period, when the phases of different planets pass, new vistas of opportunities and ambitions would be revealed. The planet would provide sustenance for the germ lying deep in her psyche. When Mars comes to rule the life some time in 1989, at the age of 27 years or so, the real stature of the person would begin to unfold. The seven years intense activity in research, study, investigations, meeting people would completely change her life pattern. There would be much splendour, glory and creativity. But once the taste of quick success is realisd, the urge for easy and cheap achievements will be given up. Rahu Mahadasa would make the person a little quiet, secluded and entrenched in deep research whose results would take much time to come out. By the time the girl becomes a middle–aged women with grey hair and repute for her serious contributions to the ancient civilasations, or by establishing herself as a creative architect, her abilities would come to public view. Then, there would be no frustration and the life would be for others, for the good of the society, advising and helping others in many ways which would be the benediction of Jupiter.

The above exercise attempts to show that the vocational guidance on the basis of astrological indica-itons could at best be vocational counselling, implying

that the astrological tendencies should be discussed
with the persons concerned so that on the available
astrological characteristics, the various alternatives and
opportunities are discussed and explored. The aptitude
of the person, the basic urges which only the self could
well understand, and the changing requirements of the
society should be synthesized in making the suggestions.
While considering the various possibilities not only the
Tenth House, but the Ascendant, the Second, the
Sixth, the Third and the Fifth Houses should be properly
blended with the influences of the Tenth House and
with the planets concerned, and the strength of the
horoscope should also be properly considered. This is
an area in which the astrologers are increasingly required
to play an important part, and if properly done this aspect
of astrological counselling is likely to be much more
effective and helpful.

JOURNALISM

Journalistic profession is very complicated requiring careful consideration of several combinations. Those who rush headlong to this profession without serious consideration of its long-term prospects as well tribulations, do sometime get into serious troubles and their promising career is dashed against rocks. Many individuals who can write clearly only small pieces of news items often consider themselves adequately qualified for this profession. Publication of a few articles or a few correspondences in a daily newspaper often arouses among budding writers a thirst for joining the galaxy of successful columnists. On the other hand, there are instances of persons, who in the beginning joined the profession as a matter of course by merely gliding to it unconsciously, in the long run attained eminent positions. Obviously, therefore, it is not the early prognostications which qualify for reputed and successful journalistic career. For a sustained satisfactory journalism, several factors must contribute to yield satisfying results.

In the modern age, the thrill and the excitement associated with risks and adventures as well as professional hazards have aroused tremendous attraction among the youth to join the rank and file of journalistic profession. In order to avoid frustration, however, suitable professional guidance is helpful. But the

difficulty in this kind of vocational advice arises from
the fact that the ancient texts on the subject have been
silent about its exact requirements. For those who
endeavour to instal themselves in this exciting profession
with a great possibility of even moulding the public
opinion, it may be helpful to find out whether they are
astrologically carved out for this profession.

In the present context, a difficulty of considerable
dimension arises due to the fact that there are many
professions like those of publishers, editors, authors,
proof-readers, and journalists which are seemingly alike
and interrelated, but require quite distinct and specialised
characteristics and natural aptitude. All these are
interconnected professions often merging in one another
but any astrological guidance in their regard would
require fine balance and deeper insight in special
features of all these activities.

Publishers are also connected with educational and
intellectual activities ; they would have significant
differences with those of machine fabricators, business
entrepreneurs, doctors or defence personnel. A journalist
is also connected with educational activities. As such,
both of them should have strong Jupiter. But the
publishers are primarily concerned with commercial aspect
of the activity while the journalist is a creative artist.
For the former, Jupiter could be related to the Tenth
House whilst for the latter it should be linked with the
Fifth House.

The difference between an author and a journalist is
subtler. An author writes his own personal ideas,
generally to expound a viewpoint. He is also a creative
artist. In his creativity, there is an emphasis on his
own ideas, opinions, viewpoints, arrangemnts of
sequence of events and the structure of the same ; he

superimposes his personality on the readers. These qualities require a strong Ascendant and Fifth House. A journalist, on the contrary, tries to pierce through the apparent confusion or the concealment of events and present a new spectacle to the public. In doing so, he also cannot avoid involving his own personality with the events he describes but the important point to consider in this regard is the externality of the described events and things. These qualities require a literary Mercury to help him.

The requirements of an editor and a journalist are also quite distinct. It is true that eminent editors have been renowned and competent journalists as well, but both the professions do not have identical specifications. The journalists collect, review, and coordinate the various aspects of the subject under consideration which may be a fleeting news item or a serious topic of universal interest. The editor on the other hand, is concerned with streamlining the stuff presented for publication ; he judges the suitablility of a write-up for its inclusion or otherwise in the journal or in other forms of publication ; he corrects, improves and assigns appropriate weightage to various arguments and viewpoints. Thus, the editor assumes to a great extent the role of an educator, teacher, director of an artistic performance whilst the journalist is an actor, a student, a worker struggling on his own. The journalist in this way is more an active agent whilst the editor has to be receptive, understanding and guiding. These are distinctly two different types of attributes which are not substitutable though may be complimentary in some ways. A combined influence of Jupiter and Mercury is helpful for an editor, while Mercury with Venus will be helpful for a journalist.

When we examine the difference between an author, editor, and a journalist we have to be much more careful. An author is always concerned with discussing deeper aspects of the subject-matter whilst the journalist as a columnist is involved with fleeting events. The difference does not refer to the social value or political significance of the topic discussed. The Watergate Scandal is an example of journalistic venture in revealing some event of far-reaching consequence, but when the implications of this episode in its political, social, historical, national and international dimensions were examined in depth, it became appropriately a subject of an author's study. The serialisation of a write-up in a periodical does not make the writer a journalist, but the profundity or otherwise of the analysis which has lasting significance would be the deciding factor is such regard. The difference between an author and a journalist is therefore not of quality but of profundity.

Many journalists at the early phase of their career have to do some proof-reading; even authors are not free from this ordeal ; yet the act of proof-reading is definitely a subordinate, routine type of work which cannot be considered the function of a creative artist. The journlist has certainly to have much imagination, quick intelligence, sociability, diplomacy, power of expression, ability to see deeper in the superficial appearance of things, events and relationships ; they should also have power of discrimination so that they could pick up that which has news value. These are certainly qualities which are not common and astrological guidance in discovering whether the individual has innate competence in this line would be basic in this vocational decision.

We have also to consider whether the individual has luck and money. This is important because in several other vocations, there is regularity, constancy, security, and promotion prospects based on seniority. This rule does not always apply in the case of journalists. Presently, there is an all India body under which some sort of security of professional promotion exists, but that is not in the spirit of free-lance journalism or in the line of those journalists who make their name because of their dash, their quality to make scoops, their ability to make something of public interest patent, which otherwise would not have seen the light of the day. In this way, whether there is a regular service or not, whether the individual is a free lancer or is in an organised service, his success lies in making successful stories of public interest. On such lucky factors his success depends and also on such break-through his standing in the profession.

Approaching this profession of journalism in this way, we find the need for certain astrological combinations essential for such a career. Unless the Fourth and the Fifth Houses are very special, the inherent requirements of the job would not be fulfilled. The Fifth and the Fourth Houses are related to intelligence. *Uttara Kalamrita*, for example, indicates learning, pure intellect, the art of giving clues to the places where stolen property is kept some of the characteristics of the Fourth House, while for the Fifth House, it lays down mind, learning, discretion, moral stories, auspicious letters, great actions desirable in various ways, foresightedness, profundity, secret, writing of news, wisdom, profound learning as some of the main features. These are the qualities which provide the very basis for journalistic career. The disposition of these two houses must indicate agility, quickness, intellectual penetration and intuitive understanding of the events and relationships. For such qualifications, their intimate link with Mercury is desirable. No successful journalist can rise without favourable benediction from the planet of writers, intellectuals and of quick mobility. The core of the profession is Mercury related to the Fourth and the Fifth Houses. The linkage between these cannot but be laid down very broadly : only the placement of Mercury in either of these houses may not provide the required qualifications. Assuming the lords of the Fourth or the Fifth Houses have intimate relationship either by way of association or aspect with Jupiter, Mercury and the Sun, one could expect remarkable journalistic career. If the lord has connections with Mars there would be dash, ability for scoop, etcetera.

One has also to take into account the fact that the journalists have their own specialisations as well. Some journalists are preoccupied with political affairs ; others are specially related to social affairs ; some are art critics ; some deal with sports ; some are concerned with scientific development ; many specialise in industrial problems ; a large number of them write on financial and commercial matters. These areas of specializations also must show themselves in the planetary disposition connected with the Fourth and the Fifth Houses and with Mercury. In association with Venus, the journalist would do well in restricting his sphere of writing to ladies' affairs, social problems, chemistry related to pharmaceuticals and so on. In case there is a touch of Jupiter either by association, aspect or ownership of these houses or with the houses where their owners are located, there would be some kind of ethical judgement or an ethical aura surrounding his writings. With a touch of Saturn, one may expect reactionary or historical overtones. Such writers may either delve deep in the mysteries of occultism, esotericism, and historical excavations, or they would be encouraging trade union activities, covering lobour troubles, and would be dealing with social discrations. Under the influence of Mars, one may acquire specialisation of military affairs, agricultural situation or surgical perfections. Thus, the areas of specialisation will have to be decided according to the influence of other planets on these two most concerned houses and Mercury, the most concerned planet.

To sum up, the basic qualifications for a successful journalistic career require (i) a good disposition of the Fourth and the Fifth Houses ; (ii) favourable Mercury, Moon and Jupiter ; (iii) presence of good Raja Yogas and Saraswati Yoga ; (iv) lucky Tenth House ; and (v) sociability of Venus, courage of Mars, and prestige of Jupiter. This is one of the most complicated professions in which an integral view of the chart is more required than in other professions. One must distinguish between the possibility of becoming a successful and renowned author and a journalist ; the influence of Jupiter is more important in the former than in the latter though a good and powerful Jupiter is necessary for the both. In the latter, however, one should look for a powerful Mercury to play a powerful role.

MEDICAL PROFESSION

Even when the modern medical system is radically different from the one pratised in ancient times, some of the astrological hints for making a successful physician still hold good. These hints do not necessarily refer to successfully qualifying for admission in medical colleges, or to obtain medical degrees. They refer to successfully acquiring and expertly practising the healing art. This skill depends upon an understanding of the mechanism by which energy of the Logos enlivens the individual ego to give light to his eyes and breath to his lungs so that he could discharge his worldly obligations assigned to him during the present incarnation. A successful physician has also to acquire the ability by which this divine energy could be manipulated to rectify the distortions of the body mechanism of the individual so that his natural health and balance of energy are restored. Such an ability does not depend upon the rigours of any certification process evolved by any medical association testifying the candidate's knowledge of the researches made during the period under a system of medicine. This understanding and skill cannot be related merely to the period of apprentice over a number of years under any renowned medical practitioner either. To be a successful doctor, one must have an intuitive perception of the life-giving force in its multifarious forms and he should also possess the divine gift to set the distortions right. The successful physician is like a chalice of divine down pouring intended for soothing the numerous ailments afflicting the different individuals. That is why in ancient times, almost all over the world, the saints and the sages miraculously healed the diseases and made the dead alive. The successful medical men were often trained in occult sciences like astrology, ethics, yogas, on the basis of which they could divine the karmic causes of the ailments and apply the right remedial curatives. The contemporary case of Edgar Cassey exemplifies the efficacy of this approach.

But, presently, the medical profession has become very specialised. The degree of specialisation has gone to such an extent that some physicians deal only with a few organs of the body whilst others concern themselves with only certain special functions of the same. In the first-category we have such specialisations which deal only with eyes, nose, throat, and ears or that kind of specialists who call themselves dentists, heart specialists, specialists in skin diseases and so on. In the second category, we could include the pediatrists, gynacologists, those concerned with midwifery and the like. Another category of doctors deal with special methods of clinical examinations such as X-ray, blood examination, urine and stool tests. The fourth category may refer to the degree of specialisation. It is in such categories that highly skilled surgeons who have gained renown in heart and brain surgery could be included. The fifth category of doctors are concerned with investigations of the impact of chemical substances on various diseases and human parts. Those medical men who are engaged in funda-mental researches like cancerous growth, functions of tumours, prevention of leukemia with use of viral antigen and antiserum administration, genetic manipulations and such other highly complex medical investigations could be considered as the sixth category of doctors. In a different category, one can place those doctors whose main function is to dispense the medical prescriptions. Even the manufacture of drugs is a responsibility from which qualified doctors cannot completely absolve themselves.

The practising physicians can also be classified according to different systems of medicines they practise. The medical practitioners in India can be classified as those who are practising either the modern allopathic system of medicine or the ancient traditional system, the latter category doctors being called the *Vaidyas*. Those medical men who are following the system of medication obtained from the ancient Greeks are called the *Hakims*. Then, we also have the magic-men who indulge in curing diseases according to superstitious beliefs, non-recognised methods of treatment and with herbs and the like. The astrologers have also been helping to cure the physical and psychological troubles by prescribing appropriate gems, *mantras*, and *tantras*. There are also the psychiatrists and psychoanalysts whose way of handling human ills is entirely different and their area of treatment is highly specialised. Some doctors cure many diseases, such as bone dislocations, tummy upset, and the like by physical manipulations whilst the spiritual healers make an impact by prayers, passes, and several such other unconventional methods. All these methods of curing human troubles cannot be lumped together in a single category of doctors for determining astrologically whether a particular individual could be a doctor or not. In astrology, we must find out details of all these categories of the medical men.

One also finds that there are some doctors irrespective of the system they follow, making very high grade whilst others in the same category are making poor grade. Even otherwise, there are different levels of these physicians. Some are deans in highly respected medical institutes and others are efficient practitioners. Some doctors set up their own clinics in sophisticated areas having social elites as their patients whilst others are sent to rural areas under compulsion in order to eke out some living for themselves and their family members. Some people are considered doctors, some are compounders, prescription dispensers, nurses and the like. So even in the same system of medicine, there are different orders or grades of medical men and the individual may like to know the grade he is likely to make if he took up medicine as his profession.

In order to go to the root of astrological support for such fine distinctions between one category of medical practitioners and others, one will have to study the problem in a radically different manner. The classical astrological texts have given several combinations about becoming doctors but merely by traditional methods of interpretation one cannot apply those rules to predict the success or otherwise of an aspirant to this profession. In tackling this problem one will have to approach the texts differently. For it, it would be necessary to synthesize the various combinations indicated in different scriptures. In doing so, it would be necessary to enter into the spirit of what B. V. Raman advised when he stated that "Configuration of planets in the heavens in certain angular portions emanate certain forces or energies, which when they are not in harmony with the energies of an individual, bring about certain disturbances in his physical and mental dispositions. To avert the evil influences of planets, the ancient seers contemplated upon discovering remedies, and the science of medicine was gradually founded and developed in this manner".

From this it can be seen that the successful doctor must have a comprehension of the universal principle which energises the universe. Cosmic energy links every individual with the source which sustains every form. The universal life-force is modified by the individual life-force. This life-force is an aspect of Vishnu. Mercury is intimately connected with Vishnu and in a way Jupiter has that expansive universalism which is an expression of this life-force. Life itself is the Sun, so that the influence of the Sun, Mercury and Jupiter must be significant in any horoscope to make the influence important for making the individual a successful medical practitioner. Unless the benefic influence of Jupiter is there, the nature of the Universal Life Force may not be easily comprehended by the individual. Moreover, a teacher is also the Spiritual Healer. Whatever the other planetary combinations in a horoscope, unless the chart shows good influence of Jupiter, the native cannot be that skillful which makes the person specially gifted as a doctor. A doctor has to know much of the spiritual side of life. He has to know the functioning of the physical body. All types of knowledge of unseen things with a view to helping the mankind come from Jupiter. So the doctor must have good disposition of Jupiter.

Mercury and the Sun are very vital for making a person successful doctor. This is because the mind of the doctor must be very quick and sharp in taking immediate decisions. Such sharpness can be possible only when these planets are favourably inclined to the person. Even in classical texts these planets have been assigned considerable importance in enabling the native acquire skill and proficiency in medical science. Even for admission in medical colleges these days it is necessary that the student has done well in his examination which can be possible only as a result of the good Sun and Mercury.

In *Jataka Parijata*, it is stated that the togetherness of Mars and Mercury will make the native eloquent and clever in medicine and fine arts. Mercury is intelligence and Mars is the creative energy which takes the inside out. When these two planets are placed together, the intellect of the doctor would be activised to take the disease which has entered the body-system of the patient out and thus relieve the person of his ailments. Such a doctor will be a skilled surgeon because the function of the surgeon is to take the ailment out. In certain medicinal systems such as homeopathy the administration of medicine is to aggravate the disease before it is cured. This kind of treatment would be well administered under the influence of Mars.

In *Brihat Jataka* it has been stated that the lord of the Tenth Navamsa from the Ascendant, Moon or the Sun would give the profession of medicine. But every astrologer worth his salt would corroborate that able civil servants and administrators are also born under that influence. The important point to note here is that the function of the Sun is to give life and light to the world. Through the solar rays comes to us the life-giving *Prana* —the very energy which makes all the things living. Placed in the above situation, it makes the native a partner in the life-giving activities. Under this impulse, therefore, the native has a special gift whereby his touch would be healing and his treatment assuring because he could be contacting the very root of the life-giving energy. The Sun in Sagittarius makes the person

8

skilled in medicine. Here also the same principle applies. Sagittarius is the sign which transforms the beast into a man and animality into human qualities. The essential nature of medicine is also to transform the degenerating body functions or the animality of the human individual into creative positive functions, that is, into human qualities. The association of Sun with Sagittarius, therefore, implies that the basic life-giving energy would be set in right motion so that the positive functions of animality in man could be activised.

Similarly one has to take care of Rahu, Saturn, Ketu, and Venus. All of these Planets have to make an impact on making the person a good physician. Those doctors who specialise in malignant diseases will be skilled under the influence of Rahu. Those who treat chronic patients gain their efficiency due to Saturn. Ketu is connected with deadly poisonous drugs. Venus is pharmacologist. Thus the planetary influence in deciding the area of specialisation is very important. To put all doctors in the same category of the Sun–Mercury, or Mercury–Mars combination would be erroneous in the present era of extreme degree of specialisation.

Those who want to branch off in that special field of psychotherapy will have to take another set of considerations. Psychiatry, psycho-analysis, and psycho-therapy are distinctly different modes of operations and the methodology adopted in one is not applicable to the other. In all these however the influence of Moon is great. The doctor has to perceive the psychic structure of the patient before the patient could be helped. If it is a matter of analysis, he has to be carefully examined and the doctor has to be extremely careful about his words in conveying his observations, he has to be most considerate in expressing his emotions and feelings. In psycho-analysis the doctor has to be very careful about his words, and has to show extreme consideration to the feelings and emotions of the patients. In all these the influence of the Moon is predominant. When electrical appliances have to be used, and shock treatment has to be administered, the influence of the Sun and Mars along with the Moon becomes important.

When the system of medicine is the traditional Indian Ayurveda, the association of Jupiter is important but if it is Unani, that is, the Greek system, association of Saturn has to be looked for.

A very important point for consideration is the house from which the skill and proficiency in medical science could be divined. Mention has been made in astrological treatises that medicinal drugs are connected with the Ninth House, the renown of doctor with the Tenth House and medicines of great supernatural efficiency is connected with the Fourth House. These are again the houses which are multifaced. They signify so many things that to predict the emergence of a doctor's skill based only on these characteristics would be fallacious. One must go a little more deeply into the matter.

The connection of the above mentioned planets with the Eighth and the Twelfth Houses is more meaningful in the present context. Undoubtedly, the Eighth is the hidden house, which indicates several connected aspects of the individual. But it is also the hidden power, ordinarily considered as the Serpent Fire. When properly activised it could rejuvenate the person. All healing power comes from this source. Unless the doctor is able to establish the faintest connection with this house in proper perspective, he cannot be a doctor of any eminence. Again, the Twelfth is the house of life beyond. One of the functions of the doctor is to prolong the life span of his patients. Unless he has been bestowed special power from the unseen entities dwelling on the threshold of life-beyond, miraculous healing under which the doctor gives the patients another span of life would not be there. It is therefore necessary, though it is an unorthodox approach, to see whether special combinations exist for the person connecting his Eighth and the Twelfth Houses with the special planets which make skillful doctors.

The above description will open the subject in a very expansive way but one may illustrate some points with the help of a few charts. In this context, it must be recognised that the renown and the money earning capacity of the doctor would depend upon the presence or otherwise of Raja Yogas. The skill and natural aptitude of medical profession may have nothing much to do with this aspect of the individual.

In order to illustrate some of the points suggested above, one could examine a few horoscopes of eminent physicians in India. The *Chart I* belongs to an eminent physician of the country who had been a Principal of Patna Medical College one of the premier medical colleges in India. His skill and renown as a physician earned him much renown and money. In his chart it could be seen that the Eighth House is tenanted by Saturn with Rahu along with the Moon which is in its own house thus providing immense strength and special aptitude for the medical profession. Consequently these planets bestowed him with a touch that many patients with complicated chronic ailments being cured by him

---

Chart I: Ascendant and Jupiter in Sagittarius ; Sun, Mercury, and Ketu in Capricorn ; Mars and Venus in Pisces ; Moon, Saturn and Rahu in Cancer

had been considering him almost divine. It was generally believed that only those patients which were
ordained to die were not cured by him. Furthermore,
his personal success was also due to the presence of the
Ninth House lord in the Second House, and the association of the lord of a trine (Sun) and of an angle
(Mercury) together in the Second aspected by the
Eighth house lord and specially the Moon bestowed
unaccountable quantity of wealth to him resulting
from his healing power. The strong Jupiter as the
Ascendant lord made him rise very high even in his
social status.

   Chart II is that of a doctor of the All India Institute
of Medical Sciences, New Delhi where he acquired fame
for his work on lead poisoning. He is a pharmacologist.
Association of the Ninth lord (Mars) with Saturn, the
lord of the Twelfth House in the Fifth House, the house
of creativity and deep thinking, while the Ninth House
itself is posited by Ketu, the planet dealing with poison,
has rightly given him natural aptitude for handling
difficult drugs. In this connection, the Eighth House is
also significant. The Moon, Mercury, and Venus all in
Eighth House would certainly give him the healing touch.
He has indeed much greater heights to attain in this
specialised field into which very few medical men have
delved. This is a case of extreme degree of specialisation though not of as much money and popular renown
as in the previous case.

   Chart II :   Ascendant in Pisces ; Rahu in Taurus ; Saturn and Mars
in Cancer ; Sun in Virgo ; Moon. Mercury and Venus in Libra ; Jupiter
and Ketu in Scorpio.

Chart III is again of a doctor from the All India Institute of Medical Sciences, New Delhi who has had the privilege of working for the World Health Organisation. He is a paediatrist. Jupiter, the lord of the Tenth House and Ascendant lord gives him the natural empathy with children and teaching. Lords of the Twelfth House and of the Ninth House have exchanged places. The horoscopee is exceptionally skilled in smoothing the disturbed feelings and physical balance of the children and other patients. The combination of Jupiter, the lord of Ascendant and the Tenth House, Mercury and the Sun have made him tremendously equipped to deal with a kind of superhuman touch in alleviating the malignant diseases. This aspect is also strengthened due to the presence of Saturn and Ketu in the Ninth House. All kinds of malignant and complex diseases of children are so effectively treated by him that It looks as if from an unknown source he gets his healing power. He is an embodiment of balance, insight and helpfulness. It is said of him that he knows the diseases of children even better than the patients themselves and in many cases, though he does not assume so, he is considered the last word on children diseases.

To sum up, we have seen that the decision to take up medical profession these days is very complex and difficult. The astrological suggestions in this regard have to be carefully applied. All the planets will impart their special characteristics in the area of their specialisation. The healing touch however would be there if the planets have some special connections with

---

Chart III : Ascendant in Pisces ; Rahu in Taurus ; Saturn and Ketu in Scorpio ; Moon in Sagittarius ; Mars in Aquarius ; and Sun, Mercury, Venus and Jupiter in Aquarius.

the Eighth, Ninth, and the Twelfth Houses. The match-
ing of horoscopes of the doctors as well of the patient
would also be significant in deciding whether the
particular doctor could be effective in dealing with the
malady of the patient and whether the flow of forces
between them is harmonious. The houses mentioned
here go to the fundamental process of healing and life-
giving energies and activities. They relate the patients,
doctors, and the unknown life-force in such a way that
the distortions are easily cured. Healing, after all, is the
result of the life-force flowing through the doctor to the
distortions in the life-force of the individual patient
through the benefic forces coming through the planets.

INDIAN ECONOMIC SERVICE

Many conflicting characteristics have to be taken into account in deciding the native's potential for joining the Indian Economic Service. Essential requirements for this service are a good knowledge of economics, commerce and international trade relations, all under the control of Mercury ; good command over language and a basic degree in economic subjects requiring powerful Fifth House and a permanent conflict with other organised all-India services under whose humiliating subordination these personnel have to suffer despite the fact that they will have to work harder and on more important subjects. With the basic qualifications that qualify the native for this service, they could be eligible for many other avenues of employment. Many business organizations welcome such bright professionals with lucrative emoluments and attractive service conditions. Even for the Indian Administrative and the Indian Foreign Services the basic requirements for entry is not so rigorous. Academic institutions provide much helpful opportunities for the development of intellectual qualities and specialised knowledge of the subject which are essential for the Indian Economic Service. Such varying conditions would make the task of the astrologer very difficult. How can one advise the suitability of an individual for this all India service which has such rigorous and important basic conditions for a long-life job where the constituents feel miserable as the years roll by ?

Despite the prospect of service which could enable the personnel to reach the highest echelon of the Government of India, may be at a much younger age than other administrative services, and in many cases international organisations are more inclined to recruit members of this service than other generalists, it is one of the most disliked services both by its constituents and by those whom it serves : the affliction of the Third, Sixth, and the Tenth Houses therefore must be an essential feature of it.

An affliction of the Tenth House is also emphasized by other conditions. It has been noted that a special feature of this service has been the unhelpful attitude of the cadre authorities. Those who manage the day to day affairs of the service belong to another cadre which looks to this service very unfavourably. Recently some improvements in this cadre management has been attempted yet the basic hostility or unhelpful attitude of those who are managing the service continues. As a rule, they try to approach each individual case of the Indian Economic Service personnel with a feeling of animosity. Even the fate of senior officers are decided by junior officers who take their responsibilities not in a spirit of helpfulness. Despite these handicaps, the duties of Indian Economic Service officers are very hard. The assignment to them is very specialised but such specialisation which could help them rendering the service effectively go against their own promotions and placements. Some of the officers have, however, fairly light work. Out of turn promotions are quite possible which gave the cadre authorities much hand in humiliating those who are unable to curry favours with them. At each level, these officers have to appear before promotion committees and be subjected to several rigorous tests of academic nature at times unconnected with the work they are performing, answer technical questions which they have never handled, and prepare for several other ordeals. Rules of seniority are often changed to suit some of the candidates without any reference to others. Those officers who have capacity to pull strings and have effective "connections", they have better chances for promotions and preferments. There is no time bound scale of promotions. These clearly indicate that the Tenth House and the Ascendant should not well harmonise. The affliction of the Tenth House should be prominent. Planets for intrigue as against the combinations of righteousness should be more prominent. On these factors one will require to take an overall judgement before evaluating the possibility of someone joining this service.

The conditions of the service must be reflected in the horoscope of the individual aspiring to enter it. The rigid technical qualifications require that final examination for taking the requisite academic degree for completing the necessary formality should be successfully completed : the same must be done at the right age; it implies that there must be good Mercury connected with economics and commerce. It should be related to the Fifth House in an important way. The individual should also have good combinations for the power of written and vocal expressions which assume the relation of Mercury with Jupiter and with the Second House. And above all, *Raja Yogas* are also to be assumed without which entry into such an all-India Service could not be possible. All these indicate that Mercury, the Fourth, the Fifth, and the Tenth Houses, must be powerful.

Astrological texts have already emphasized the rules for assessing the power of a house and a planet. These rules will have to be applied in the present context. But, it should be borne in mind that these are very general conditions and are applicable to many other professions as well where intelligence and good general education are required.

The real crux of Indian Economic Service lies in the presence of Raja Yogas and affliction of the Tenth House. Unless good Raja yogas are present, the possibility of such appointments is meagre. Only on the basis of inherent strength of the chart, the status enjoined to this service can be possible. But what is very important is the examination of the future course of the life. Invariably, every Indian Economic Service officers meets serious blocks sometime in his career. So far one is aware, there are very few officers of this service who have risen satisfactorily to high positions, but in there cases they enjoyed satisfactory number of combinations and strength in their chart for becoming even the Administrative officer, but for them the chances of such rapid promotions in the Indian Administrative Service did not occur so they joined the Indian Economic Service to reach the high position but with delay and some difficulties. Such difficulties and handicaps which arise in the career of an Indian Economic Service Officer could be seen by the planetary directions, *mahadasa*, which should indicate that during the course of the life some serious difficult periods must occur. It is important to note that in the case of Indian Economic Service personnel, there must be some period in their working life which show difficult service conditions.

As indicated above, there should also be some combinations of *Raja Droha*—Enmity with the King, i.

the present case implying unsatisfactory relationship
with the boss or the cadre authorities. This is generally
concluded from the afflicted Sun or disturbed and discordant relationship between the Ascendant lord and
the Tenth House lord ; or the Ascendant lord and the
Sun, or there should be some affliction to the Sun by
bad placement in the Sixth, Eighth or the Twelfth House
or due to its association with Saturn, Ketu, or due to its
debilitation. Presence of *Raja Droha* is a necessary
condition at least for personnel entering the Indian
Economic Service as it is presently constituted. In case
the Ascendant or the Tenth lord is stronger than the
afflicted Sun, there would be the possibility of the
individual resigning from the service and taking up other
assignments.

It is surprising that the position of Saturn has been
very significant in all cases of important members of this
Service. It is not necessarily a question of exalted
Saturn which could be very rare and found only in
persons of certain age groups. The strength of Saturn
should be assessed according to various astrological
criteria already laid down by the seers for this purpose.
When powerful Saturn is present, the opportunities for
foreign assignments, international contacts and recognition of merit abroad are available which open up many
fruitful avenues for professional betterments.

The position can be summed up as follows : the
planetary positions for Indian Economic Service must
indicate : (i) powerful Raja Yoga, (ii) strong position of
the Sun and Mercury, (iii) powerful combinations for
wealth and official (governmental) status, (iv) affliction
of the Tenth House, and its lord in some way, (v) Raja
Droha and the afflicted Sun, (vi) powerful Saturn, and
(vii) uneven planetary directions (the periods ruled by

different planets extending over the working duration of the individual). If the Tenth House and the Sun are not significantly afflicted, and the Ascendant is strong, the individual even if he initially joined the Indian Economic Service would either have meteoric rise therein or will resign to take up other brighter and more lucrative profession. Generally, the chances are that he would resign to take up some other assignment, but in Indian Economic Service, there has to be some combination for subordination to inferior and humiliating boss, or bad service conditions in spite of fairly strong combinations for high official status.

SOCIABILITY, FRIENDSHIP AND LOVE

Desire for sociability is innate in every individual. Something abnormal exists in those who want to remain isolated. The degree of sociability which depends upon various factors is a measure of psychological happiness one enjoys. Some of the characteristics of this quality are fitness for companionship, ready willingness to converse with others, not averse to society, communicativeness, desire for companionship, not stiff or formal. From these one could clearly see that these are not all cultivated qualities but astrologically one could decipher many of them.

One who has an amiable disposition would have a very pleasant Ascendant, as well as fourth and the seventh houses. The eleventh house also must be supporting. The nature of the first house is very misleading in the sense that a strong Ascendant is not necessarily an indicator of amiability. Leo, Scorpio, Capricorn and Aquarius signs are powerful signs which give a personality of their own to the native, but their sociability is not their strong point. In their case, the personal pride about their being special is so great that the equality required in companionship or the abnegation of their personality in social intercourse could not be cultivated by them. For these Ascendants, sociability appears to be belittling their self because there is the sense of pride and superiority which creates impediment in right communication. As far as Aries, Virgo Sagittarius are concerned, they are not unsocial but they would like the other group to sustain the relationship. To them, there is another world which absorbs them more effectively though they have sympathetic regard for their companions. But the best group for sociability is that which has Taurus, Gemini or Pisces as the Ascendant. They are genuinely social creatures.

Among the planets, Venus is the best which gives the greatest support for sociability. In Ascendant, Venus gives a very amiable disposition but if placed in the seventh, the personality becomes very charming so much so that the sexual attraction of the person increases tremendously. It becomes difficult for him or her to maintain balanced married relationship with the spouse. The association of Venus and Mercury either alone or together would make the person very sociable. The Moon and Jupiter also have very strong influence on the sociability of the person but in this case there is more of respectful distance though remaining sympathetic with the companions.

Benefics in fourth, seventh and eleventh are very favourable for the sociability of the person. When the favourable aspect of Jupiter or Venus falls on these houses, the sociability of the person increases. But, the ascendant lord and those houses connected with sociability should be free from the restrictive influence of Saturn. Mars does not create adverse disposition, but its impulsiveness sometimes makes the reaction inconsistent. In such a case, when the personality traits of the person become familiar to any group, he becomes likeable. As a matter of fact, such persons are more liked as a friend than as mere companion. It is primarily so because of their intrinsic honesty and integrity of character.

Friendship is markedly different from the quality of sociability. It is based on mutual respect and sympathy. Though Leo, and Sagittarius are not very good mixers, yet as friends they are superb. Once they give a promise, they would keep it in thick and thin. They would not necessarily wait for their friends to inform them of their requirements, once they come to know that their friend is in need of any specific assistance, they would try to fulfil it. Their sincerity is of the highest order and their capacity to help is also effective. They do not like demonstration of their friendship ; their approach is to help effectively. This is also one of the reasons why they are averse of superficial social relationships which appear as sociability. Aries ascendant as a friend has many qualities of Leo, but not the capacity of doing the same. Such persons are very eager to help but their psychological limitations sometimes make them ineffective. They are well meaning and always sure support. Gemini and Libra are more superficial and not always sacrificing which is essential for friendly relationship. Such persons are also not basically sympathetic ; they are calculative in their social relations. If other persons are likely to help then the Gemini or Libra persons would stick to them. The phrase "fair weather friendship" is apt in their cases. There is marked difference between Scorpio and Aries. Both can be effective provided their emotional maturity is achieved and both of them, can be dependable as far as they are capable. A marked difference between the two is that the Aries ascendant would become reckless thus at times become a bull in the china-shop whilst the Scorpio ascendant may become so self-centred and cautious that the opportunity to help may slip away. Consequently, much misunderstanding could arise among such friends.

When the friendship becomes intense among the two sexes, it need not always result in marriages. But the level of friendship could become so intense that the relationship between the persons concerned is more intimate than among the married partners. Such friendships have been well studied in Indian astrology and special indicators have been suggested for them. As a matter of fact, the Indian marriages as mentioned in ancient scriptures were of several types all prognosticated on the basis of the Seventh House and its lord, but the possibility of friendship developing into sexual intimacy is signified by the Elevenths House. For other kinds of such relationships, however, the Third, Second, as well as Fifth Houses are also considered relevant in some cases. This kind of intimate relationship which in modren times has been gaining much significance requires very cautious approach.

It is certainly difficult to say when friendship between two sexes could assume the phase of personal intimacy but if there is some contact between the planets in the Eleventh House and Ascendant, having some kind of relationship with the lords of the Seventh and the Eighth Houses, depending upon the nature of the planets involved, there is every likelihood of some kind of extra-marital relationship developing between two sexes. Jataka Parijatam stated the possibility of sex relations outside the married bond occurring in the horoscope provided the planets in the Eleventh Bhava are strong and predominantly friendly with the Ascendant. In this context, association of Eighth lord or the placement of Venus or the Seventh House lord in Eighth House could make the relationship clandestine. The same situation

9

in relationship with the Twelfth House could make it quite open and providing comfortable situation, specially for the convenience of comfortable bed pleasure. Under such conditions the fellows may even live together without entering into any formal marriage relationship.

In the case of a woman with Taurus Ascendant, in spite of the Jovian lordship of the Eleventh House which was posited in the Tenth House, and Rahu placed in Eleventh itself having the aspect of Saturn, a malefic, and of Mars another malefic and lord of the Twelfth House, with Mercury and Venus in the Seventh, she had been living in close friendly intimacy with various individuals. In another case, a male born with Gemini Ascendant and Saturn the lord of the Eighth House, along with Ketu placed in the Eleventh having fourth house aspect of Mars from its exalted position in the Eighth House enabled the person to have intimate friendship with very many girls of high class families. In another case of Aquarius Ascendant female whose Ascendant lord Saturn who also happened to be the lord of the Twelfth House, placed in the Fifth House fully aspected Jupiter placed in the Seventh House which happened to be the lord of the Eleventh House and it also aspected the Eleventh House fully under which condition the girl lived in friendly intimacy with a person for whom she had tremendous love and affection and continued the relationship for more than a decade. In another case of a girl, who came from a very respectable family, having Scorpio as the Ascendant with lord of the Eleventh (Mercury), the lord of the Twelfth (Venus) which also happened to be the lord of the Seventh, and the lord of Ascendant Mars together in the Third House having ninth aspect from Jupiter from the Seventh House made the girl live with a man like a husband and wife for a large number of years when their friendship broke away and they separated. Then she started to live in such a relationship with several persons together. These examples should be able to show that there would be great possibility of friendly love-relations under certain situations in which the Eleventh House and its lord played an important role.

The astrological texts have given various other combinations of sex relationship between intimate friends. If the lord of the Eleventh House is in conjunction with Venus occupying a malefic sign, the person would not hesitate having sexual partnership without formal marriage. Similar conditions may arise when the lords of Second, Sixth, and the Seventh Houses occupy the Ascendant and are associated with a malefic planet. The association of the First and the Sixth Houses with a malefic planet gives rise to similar tendency. If the lords of the Tenth, Second, and Seventh occupy Tenth House, then also the person concerned may have intimate relation with the other sex. The number of friends from the opposite sex is quite large if the person gets the combination of Jupiter, Mercury or the Moon and Venus in the Seventh House.

The sociability, friendship and love life of a person can be determined by taking into account the Ascendant as the prime mover and the disposition of its lord and the sign belonging to this house. In association with Fourth, Seventh, Eleventh, and the Second House, the intensity of the friendship may transcend physical limit and it may develop into sexual intimacy. When the friendship between two sexes transcends the physical limit and results in intimacy without marriage, the touch of the Seventh, Sixth, Eighth, Twelfth, and the Second with association or aspect from malefics and some short of connection with Venus may be expected. In case such astrological combinations exist, the individual should examine the total nature of his life to ascertain whether such combinations are present in order to trap him in some kind of social or moral difficulties or they are inconsequential. Often, their long-term implications are not good specially because all these houses linked with this question are related with general prosperity of the person and fructification of the yoga on such lower levels of manifestation denies him lasting prosperity and comfortable living.

MARRIED HAPPINESS

Married happiness is essential both for personal as well as social harmony. The relationship between man and woman is fundamental for the balanced personal development, the elimination of physico-psychological tension, and for the provision of amiable milieu for the birth and growth of healthy children. The availability of such an environment does not depend upon the efforts of a single individual ; the *prarabdhas* of the individual, the future progeny, as well as of the human society in which the individuals are born, determine the conditions to a great extent. The physical health, the psychological make-up, the social traditions, family expectations, and the group of taboos conjointly create the situation in which the man and the woman have to play their role for fusing in one another. The biological needs of the male and the female are no less important than the emotional cravings, intellectual aspirations and the spiritual thirsts of the persons concerned. Obviously such complex forces cannot be identical in any two persons. Such an identity is not even conducive to the growth and development of the persons concerned. When different types of personalities come in contact with one another, there is the possibility of clash between them but it is only in such fusions of different personalities that their angularities are rubbed off and new aspects of growth potential aroused. Among married partners, the relationship being very intimate, there is always the possibility of larger areas of one's life to come in contrast, and therefore greater likelihood of differences. In order to strike the fine balance between identity and differences, understanding of one's make-up, the points of differences, the challenges of social adjustment, the need for personal compromises, and the necessity of discharging one's personal, family, and social obligations, the individuals concerned have to exercise their greatest ingenuity ; the adjustment and achievement of mutual harmony without any feeling of subordination depends upon immense understanding and effort. The planetary forces have tremendous influence on this aspect of life, probably much more than it is usually recognised. Given the urge to achieve harmony, the astrological knowledge and assistance in this regard, could be of great help for personal growth and fulfillment of one's destiny.

Each individual has in him the male and female counterparts : biologically the composition of male and female harmones determines the various sex impulses in an individual. But the balance of sex-harmones itself does not decide the active or passive nature of the person. The psychological complexities and sexual abnormalities of the modern society complicate the problem of mutual adjustment. But the task becomes more difficult due to several other factors. For example, deterioration in the health of the partner might impede their satisfaction of the biological urge ; even if the upsetting of the health is not permanent, duration of it may be sufficiently long to cause the pain. It is also sometimes noticed that the biological satisfaction is not the villain of the piece, but inability to view life in a mutually satisfactory manner causes serious friction between the partners. With many persons, marriage is solemnised with some other end view, not necessarily for the purpose of living and enjoying life together. Occasionally persons of sheltered existence without appreciating the full responsibilities of marriage enter into the relationship unprepared to experience disappointment later on. As there is no substitute for actual living together, no prudential considerations generally attempted in the contemporary (westernised) society can protect the married relationship from going to rocks.

The astrological counselling, provided the counselling is accepted with understanding and seriousness, to a great extent throw light on the problems of marriage, the possibility of achieving happiness, the kind of pitfalls to be avoided and so on. Having considered the essential features of a "fulfilling" married relationship, the ancient Indian seers laid down several criteria which they suggested should be examined before the relationship was solemnised. They thought the compatibility between the *nakshatras* in which the Moon of both the partners was located determined to a great extent the chances of a mutually satisfying married life. It was in essence this purpose for which the horoscopes of the prospective marriage partners were compared and "tallied". The degree of compatibility indicated the level of happiness or "fulfillment" expected from the relationship. A study of the characteristics of the *nakshatras* or the lunar mansions could indicate the importance of tallying of the horoscope. The quality of life currents flowing through the various sheaths of the personality between the man and the woman is not merely of sexual nature, and the sexual satisfaction being merely biological in nature is not all that requires harmonisation. The disposition of *nakshatras* in which the various planets in a chart are located to a great extent indicated the life of the individual as it is going to be unfolded. Unless the two charts had complementary or mutual strengthening potential, the initial infatuation requires to be curbed. The married relationship requires to be considered over a long duration consisting of many rough and tumbles of life through which the partners should have adequate strength to stick together for mutual advantage from the soul's standpoint.

The second main consideration is to examine the Ascendants of the two partners. The best relationship is obtained if the two ascendants and specially their lords are in angular relationships. The relationship between Aries, Leo, Sagittarius, or between Taurus, Virgo and Capricorn, or between Gemini, Libra, and Aquarius, or between Cancer, Scorpio and Pisces could be mutually supporting. It is no use delivering sermon on non-violence when the husband is preparing to wage a war against the enemy. Those who are possessed of intense biological urge may not give much heed to deep esoteric philosophy on chastity and celibacy. A person who is deeply entrenched in materialistic aspirations would find happiness and strength only from those who can assist him in that sphere. The square relationships are conducive to tension, whilst the *Trikons i.e.*, the fifth and ninth positions are strength giving. If the ascendant signs or the ascendant lords are in sixth-eighth relationship, the relationship between the persons should best be avoided. The same rule applies in relation to the Moon and the Sun. The Moon represents the emotional force and the Sun the power of the Soul. In case these are not in harmony, the long enduring relationship becomes difficult.

Since marriage is conceived as a life-long journey, an important aspect of the horoscopes to be considered relates to the course of planetary phases in the life of the two persons with a view to discovering the curve of life to see that the misfortune of both the partners does not occur at the same time. In case the charts of the man and the woman are very well matched, but they are such that at the same time both of them are going to experience misfortune, such occurences would merely intensify the trials of their life without any relieving feature. The wife or the husband is generally considered as support during the periods of unhappiness. If both of them are suffering their own ill luck, there would be no one to console, encourage and guide the other. If both of them fall ill together, who would give them the medicine ? In the first flush of cupid's arrow, this warning seems non-consequential and the young dreamy youngmen and women think that the two weary travellers might sympathetically share one another's plight, but wisdom forewarns that the avoidance of such an eventuality is prudential. Generally speaking, however, it is suggested that the prospective partners should have their periods of misfortune, if at all such have to be confronted, spread out in such a way that they cancel one another.

When two persons want to get married, their chief objective is to provide pleasure and happiness to the other person. This can be possible when they are able to work together and be creative which give them a sense of satisfaction. As the ancient house-holders thought chiefly of the physical plane existence, they attached greatest importance to progeny. But in modern times, the couples have many diverse avenues of creative activities. One should endeavour to see that the impediments to creativity in one sphere is counteracted by support to the same in an another area. If the ascending node of the Moon is located in the fifth house of the one and Mars aspects the same house in the other, there is very little likelihood that they would mutually succeed in having a creative life. The cruel disposition of Saturn to the same house should be counteracted by the favourable Jovian support in the other. Unless the creative activities, whether intellectual or physical (by way of begetting children) are indicated, there is always some apprehension of the marriage going to barren land.

The greatest precaution in the Indian society is with regard to longevity. Widowhood is considered a severe curse. All attempts are made to avoid the possibility of this occurrence. Generally, when such a combination which forebodes widowhood is present in the horoscope of a girl, stronger widower combination is looked for in the chart of the boy before the marriage is decided. This is on the assumption that it would enfeeble the effect of the combination of the planets in the girl's horoscope. Three main factors are avoided in this regard. Any combination or association between the lord of the seventh house and the eighth house, specially the placement of the seventh lord in the eighth house, is considered inauspicious. There is also a possibility that the position of the week seventh lord in the cruel eighth house would result in pre-or extra-marital relationship under some mysterious (unhappy) circumstances which would taint the psyche of the girl so adversely that happiness in married life would be denied to a considerable extent. Secondly, the association either by location or by aspect of Mars with the Seventh or the Eighth House in the girl's horoscope would endanger the life of her partner or would create such situations that marital act under harmonious circumstances would be denied to the girl. Generally speaking, the girl would suffer sorrow on this account for a long time. Thirdly, the association of Sun, Saturn, or Rahu, with or without the Moon and Venus, in the Seventh House would lead to marital unhappiness.

These are some of the general conditions which must be avoided but it may not be possible to avoid such occurrences in all the cases. If some one has to select a girl or a boy for marriage purpose, this kind of selection could be attempted, but if the chart belongs to oneself, then one cannot do much about it excepting meeting the situation with stoicism. There are certain conditions whose knowledge however might enable the person concerned to fence oneself against any untoward event. In this regard, there are a few combinations which could warn the girl to take extra precaution.

For example, when there is any association of Mars with Venus specially if the latter is connected with the Seventh House or its lord, there is every likelihood that the female would be taken up by surprise and seduced. This can happen prior to actual wedlock or even afterwards. Such a situation does not necessarily destory the marriage but even if the person seducing the girl becomes the husband he does not enjoy her respect, though the girl might still enjoy the relationship. Similarly, if the Moon in a girl's horoscope is aspected by Saturn, the love between the husband and the wife does not remain lasting. Either there could be widowhood, or divorce, or merely living together and even accepting the responsibilities of married life but the love between the wife and the husband does not exist for long. The wife either becomes frigid or is incapable of providing sexual warmth to her husband as a result of which the husband either functions merely dutifully or look aside for sexual warmth. There is a very unusual combination which usually is expected to give much marital pleasure, but in actual life it gives entirely a different result. If in the case of a female, the Seventh House is connected with Venus, and Jupiter is associated with Venus, then the husband and the wife have strong antagonistic feelings towards one another. There is ordinarily something lacking in their married relationship. A kind of disillusionment grows among them ; this either leads to divorce or to complete detachment from one another though from the world's viewpoint the both may look "respectful". The placement of Jupiter or of the Sun in the Seventh House is also not considered very desirable for a girl. But the *aspect* of Jupiter on the Seventh House or on its lord is always very auspicious ; as the touch of Saturn with the Seventh House or with its lord always brings about some unconventionality in the marriage. Similarly the aspect of Jupiter always protects and gives respectability to the marriage.

The astrological factors have to be recognised. If they cannot be avoided or one should be prepared to face them stoically as 'karmic' situations. In order to exhaust their restricting influence, it is better for the individuals to go through the trying experiences and harmonise themselves with the inevitable. In this way, they could pave the way for a more harmonious future and a healthy life in present without introducing much bitterness in the existing relationships.

MARRIAGE AND MOTHERHOOD

Those who are familiar with *Stri Jataka* by eminent late B. Suryanarain Rao, would recall his famous statement : "The highest appointments in religion are given to the ladies in preference to males. Brahma, Vishnu and Maheswara, came after their spouses for respect and worship".

The sublime position we give to the ladies because they conceived future generations and made the course of human evolution progress according to the stipulated course of the stars, "the operation of the orbs from whom we do exist and cease to be". To consider men and women as equal partners is the Indian way of life ; woe to the persons who consider that the Indian females are fetterred to domestic chores of childbirth and family maintenance and as such they are unable to discharge their legitimate responsibilities in social affair.

In the life of a woman, love making and bringing forth life, either in the shape of monthly menstrual flow of blood or living human entities in the form of children, are very important. Venus and Mars, connected with marriage, sex relations and the like are therefore very vital in the life of a female. The importance of Venus and Mars in the present context has been well emphasized by Dr. B. V. Raman as follows :

"The inter-relations between the planetary and stellar positions and the sentiments of men and women are very intimate. Apart from the other astrological considerations, Mars and Venus are to be carefully considered. It cannot be a coincidence that divorce, separation and crimes of passion increase whenever there is a conjunction of Venus and Mars in the heavens, especially when the constellations involved are those of malefic planets. The Venus–Mars configuration could of course be one of the contributing factors. Children born when there is a Venus–Mars conjunction should be brought up in a disciplined manner and should be made to avoid dissipating habits of immediate pleasure. The adverse effects of the conjunction could be made to express through constructive channels if Jupiter aspects the combination or is in quadrant therefrom".[1]

The above quotation shows to a great extent the essential features of a women, the functions of married partner and the possibility of avoiding the adverse planetary influences by properly generating the countervailing forces.

The first question which arises in the case of female horoscopy is therefore related to the feminine nature of the person. It is said that even signs are feminine and the odd signs are masculine. "If the birth Moon or *Chandra* falls in even signs, the girl will have feminine characteristics. If they have beneficial aspects or conjunctions, the female will be beautiful, will have ornaments, and will be respected. If the Lagna, or the Ascendant, and the Moon fall in odd signs, the female would be masculine in character, appearance and temperament, would have bad character and would be sinful ; if these

---

1. *The Astrological Magazine* Bangalore, July, 1974.

two, the Ascendant and the Moon are combined with or aspected by cruel planets, her character would be bad and sinful''. Examining these pointers in detail, one finds that Scorpio and Capricorn, though being even signs yet would not be helpful in generating beneficial feminine qualities, whilst Libra and Sagittarius in spite of being odd signs could be very desirable for females. Furthermore, the touch of positive planets such as the Sun, Mars, and the concretising self-centred planet Saturn, or of the karmic planets such as Rahu and Ketu which specialise in bringing out the forces of karmic retribution, are not conducive to the tender sensitivity of a lady-like personality. In feminine horoscopes, the impact of *Thrimsamsa*, which means 1/30th of a sign or one degree, is great but this is only another method of assessing the quality of a planet or a sign as such, and thus the basic problem remains to find out the temperament of the individual concerned. Even if born in a female body, if the temperament of the person and the physical sex difference are not in harmony with each other, that is, if the individual has got a female body but male temperament, then there would be much disharmony in her life. When born in a female body, if the nature is different, that is, if it is un-female-like, the person would suffer from inner contradictions and the whole life of the person would suffer from the condition of doing or wanting to do something for which the body is not given the necessary vitality. For discharging the responsibilities entrusted to a female by her *dharma*, it is necessary to have the planets like the Moon and the signs which are passive so that the positive male planets are harmoniously, without any psycho-physical distortions, reflected on it their forces for generating fresh life. As a result of this contradiction of psyche being at variance with the body constitution, we often find that the so-called positive or male qualities in a person born in a female body succeed in obtaining professional opportunities requiring such temperament and intellectual appropriateness, but the lack of passive or feminine virtues in them which are unlikely to exist may make their family or domestic life unhappy and ill-adjusted unless their life partners are also such as to have male body with female temperament.

The second question to ask in the present context is the state of happiness or harmony in married life. This is the area of investigation in which the Indian astrological system has special contributions to make. Marriage is a necessary step, rather an important step in making the individual socially happy and well adjusted by making the concerned persons maritally happy. Those who are maritally well adjusted and happy often make themselves socially useful citizens. In married relations, it should be recognised that any two individuals specially when meet together as marriage partners evolve their own life patterns though some areas of their life events have to be coincident. The coinciding portions are not necessarily identical, rather they have to be mutually supplementing and satisfying, apart from sexual compatibility and adjustment. The horoscopic tallying of the prospective marriage partners is intended to show whether both the partners would be matually helpful to each other and as such whether there is any possibility of both of them having their life journies together. In this sojourn it is not merely the sexual compatibility that counts though it may be at the initial stages a major factor. The youthful infatuation does not last long and other facets of personality come into fore for development and these can be better comprehended on the basis of astrological prognostications. The basic nature of the partners, namely, *daivic* that is, those who have angellic or divine nature, *manushic*, that is, those who have human qualities, and *rakshasic*, that is, devilish in nature ; *Yoni Kuta* which reveal sexual compatibility ; and the health compatibility as revealed by *vata* (windy), *pitta* (billious) and *sleshma* (phlegmatic) constitutions are merely external characteristics on the basis of which the future current of events has to be imposed. The various methods and considerations needed for tallying the horoscopes are attempts to evaluate the future possibilities of *soul's evolution in togetherness.*

The ability of the person to carry on relationship with the other person depends upon the nature and disposition of the Seventh House. The famous *Kuja dosha* under which the placement of Mars in several houses such as Twelfth, Ascendant, Fourth, Seventh and the Eighth, under certain special circumstances merely shows that the person would not be able to have positive-negative, or active-passive harmony with anyone. The disruption could occur because of ill-health, separation, death, or any other such causes of the spouse. These are merely milestones which are specially important for traditional women. In those cases where begetting children and raising of the family and looking after its welfare are the ideal, the above mentioned considerations are important, but for those who want to relinquish their traditional ideals or chastity, family welfare. But want to jump in political or politicalised social service lines, the approach to marriage partnership has to be quite different.

The third important question often enquired in the present context is related to progeny. In the Indian society, begetting children is still considered the

10

greatest responsibility and the highest fulfillment of one's life's mission. The Fifth House is connected with progeny. The type of children one would get and whether happiness could be derived from them should be determined on the disposition of this house. This aspect of female horoscopy is very important because it is the central direction of the woman's life. Unless they are able to beget children, the very purpose of their female incarnation is unfulfilled. Association in any form with malefics is conducive to destruction of progeny. Here the general rule is beset with many difficulties. Only on the realisation of the goal of one's life the significance and nature of children can be determined. Moreover, the basic difficulty in this regard arises from the fact that the fifth is also the house of creativity. Only when the female is functioning on the physical plane that the birth of a baby or its destruction could be signified by the disposition of this house. In case the lady is operating more on intellectual level, as is generally the caset in modern age, or when she is more interested in her own sensual gratification, instead of fulfilling her social or divine obligations, the birth of a physical child is generally avoided, and it does not have the same importance. Even for the politically motivated women, often though not always, birth of a baby is more a drawback than a help. Unless the astrologer could assess the general psychological make-up of the female concerned, her role as a mother and a wife could not be rightly assessed and fruitful guidance provided.

For divining the rightful obligations of a mother, the astrologer can very well begin by considering the disposition of the Ascendant, the Fourth House and the Seventh House. It is not without much significance that the Indian goddesses are also mothers. They are also portrayed as full-bodied beautiful forms of females. Their breasts are well developed signifying that they are full of motherly milk in order to nourish and sustain their (numerous) children. Their general appearance is fleshy, fair, graceful (not exotic and voluptuous) which signified that their body did not suffer any karmic drawback and they were given such bodies which could be aspired by any one for imparting motherly love and affection; no child could feel a sense of shame in being begotten by such graceful goddesses. The female incarnation requires that their buttocks should be well developed in order to carry the child in the womb successfully without any difficulty. The Ascendant's disposition would be concerned with general physiological make up of the person, and the Fourth House would indicate the capacity of the mother to provide nourishing milk and caressing love and affection to the child. The Seventh House, apart from indicating the conjugal relationship with the husband could also reveal the physical capability of bearing the child.

The most important planets connected with motherhood are Jupiter and Moon. When the Ascendant is occupied by Jupiter and the Fourth House by the Moon while Mercury is in the Fifth House, the combination would show good effect as far as progeny is concerned. The relationship between the mother and the child would be strengthening to each other : the home life would be peaceful, mother would be extremely generous and sensitive to the requirements of the child and the child himself would be very intelligent. When the Fifth House is afflicted, that is the most unhappy experience for the mother. If there is an aspect of weak Mars on the Fifth House, there would be either an abortion, or a Caesarean birth. Rahu in the Fifth House often mystifies the birth ;

often for months the mother feels that she is carrying a baby which later on turns out to be something else. With Ketu there, the possibility of still birth is great. The aspect of Saturn leads to some kind of pathological symptoms, often creating some structural deficiency whereby the childbearing capacity of the mother is seriously affected. It is important to note that the placement of Jupiter in the Fifth House is not considered very auspicious.

When the lord of the Fifth House is placed in the Sixth House, there would not be any pleasure derived from the children. The lord of the Sixth in the Fifth House also is not very desirable. When the lord of the Fifth House is placed in the Eighth House, the health of the children would be in jeopardy. The lord of the Fifth in the Tenth House would cause the mother to struggle very hard for establishing the child well in life and the success achieved in this regard would not be commensurate with the effort.

The above considerations however would very much get modified if certain special combinations are present. For example, if for the Libra ascendant, there is Mars in the Fifth House and its lord is in the Fourth leading to Sasa Yoga while Moon aspects Mars from the Eleventh House; under these conditions, there would be no death, abortion or Cesaerian birth, rather the Motherhood would be blessed with tremendous energy and there would be many issues. In another case, for example, with Aries Ascendant, retrograde Saturn in the Fifth House aspected by Jupiter from the Sagittarius sign placed along with Sun, (the lord of the Fifth House) and with Venus, (the lord of the Seventh House but not combust with the Sun) did not give any birth-time difficulties. The lady got two baby boys without any difficulty. This kind of Jupitarian protective aspect is of immense value. However, Jupiter can sometime be ineffective if by itself it is not strong and other adverse factors are very strong. Take another example : the Ascendant Libra, the Fifth House posited by Sun, Venus (which is combust), and Mercury, the Lord of the Fifth House Saturn posited in the Sixth House and powerfully aspected by Mars, the retrograde Jupiter which also happens to be the lord of the Sixth House aspects the Fifth House. As the Ascendant lord Venus is combust, the lord of the Fifth House is in the Sixth House, and the Seventh House suffers from *Papa-Kartri* by being flanked by Saturn in the Sixth and Rahu in the Eighth House, the lady has been singularly unhappy as far as her domestic life and issues are concerned. People have even expressed serious doubt whether she had the necessary physical ability to conceive which was further reinforced by the fact that Mercury is in the Saturn's House (both not very conducive for child birth), Jupiter is in Sun's House when the Sun itself is in Saturn's House having burnt Venus, the lord of ladies' affairs, and Mars decapacitated by the full aspect of Saturn which is much strengthened in its negative aspect by the aspect of Mars, thereby bestowing much adverse effect to the lady. This type of planetary combinations, every woman would like to avoid. This shows that Jupiter, unless well disposed of, becomes ineffective in protective the progeny. As a matter of fact, such combinations do not show the capacity to produce. Unless the lady has the capacity to produce, and adverse aspect of negative planets are not very powerful, then only the protective cover of Jupiter can be beneficial and effective.

The above shows that there cannot be any general rule as far as the question of motherhood and progeny are concerned. In this connection, apart from the general configuration of the planets, the significance of different yogas and their relative importance must be carefully assessed before pronouncing any final conclusion. In this regard, it is necessary at first to distinguish between male-female and female-female type of women. The category with male-female characteristics includes those women who are born in the body of a female but they function like a male, their approach to life and station therein induce them to take those functions which are generally discharged by a male. These are the ladies who take male professions, temperamentally adapted to administrative, police, diplomatic and out-of-door social works at the neglect of their own family life. In the modern world the number of such women are increasing. These women have predominantly male characteristics and more appropriately they should be treated differently, more like males rather than as females.

But even in their cases, there could be certain physical considerations. These factors arise from the fact that their physical organs are different from male organs. The most important consideration in this regard relates to menstrual flow, about which the classical texts have indicated various combinations signifying the state of their future marital life. Professor B. Suryanarain Rao stated that

"For a woman, we have to take into consideration three important Lagnas, namely, Janma Lagna or the ascendant at birth, the Lagna for the first appearance of the menses in her and the Lagna or the sign in which she had the first sexual contact with the man, be he, her husband or lover or raper. All the astrological writers in Sanskrit have attached the greatest importance to the appearance of the first menses in

a girl, so much so that not only have they explained
the influences of the constellations, signs, planets,
lunar and solar days, special occasions and appearance of phenomena, eclipses, omens, but they have
also elaborately explained about the direction, the
place, the cloth, the time, the number of drops of
menstrual fluid which has come out, and also about
weekdays, yoga, karanas and other peculiarities
connected with the appearance of the first menses".[2]
This and other considerations relating to diseases
pertaining to female internal and external organs would
be common to both types of women. But the female-
female would have the prime importance of the Seventh,
the Fifth, and the Eighth Houses which should be
examined in this context. If these houses are well
fortified, happiness could be prophesied; otherwise,
they should turn their gaze to the special planetary
disposition and try to propitiate those planets. Only on
such a reorientation in their mental attitude the women
cursed by planets could expect their happiness and peace;
peace and consolation more than happiness in their life.
Care and affection for their children are the prime
concern of female-female women, whereas for other
categories, care and affection of children do not take
primary importance; they have other values and targets
in life. Their happiness depends on the fulfillment of
those objectives.

CONCERNING PSYCHOLOGICAL TENSION

Mental affliction is a preserve of specialized medical students ; the astrologers are not very much welcome in this precinct. Only when the victim finds that the doctor has been dodging him for sometime that he desires to know whether there is an end to his impasse. The disease has such a wide spectrum of affliction that the modern astrologers if they are unaware of the dichotomy used by medical practitioners would find themselves in *cul-de-sac* : the ancient seers did not give details of such disorders. Compared to the vast amount of literature available on other aspects of human problems, the ancient astrological savants gave very little attention to this subject ; probably because the people in ancient times lived a more healthy life, in obedience to the laws of nature, that only occasionally karmic influences- influences which were due to their past abnormal and unethical lapses — created such difficulties as insanity, insomnia and the like. But in modern times, the psychologists do not concern themselves only with these two mental afflictions but with many more. The stress of living has increased so much that the individuals, almost of all ages, suffer from a wide variety of mental diseases whose genesis even eludes trained neurologists or psychopaths.

A basic understanding of astrological principles might even establish a closer rapport between the astrologer and the psychopath which could be of immense value to the patients but the common ground between the two has not yet been established. The interest shown by Carl Jung in this context has been exemplary but others have shied away. In some countries a few psychologists have been showing interest in this approach but they do not possess the basic requisite for this kind of synthesis. The Transpersonal School of Astrologers have been attempting to work out some kind of common ground between the two but these efforts are yet at very initial stages. Unless much more ground-work is done, a synthetic approach between the two, of which Carl Jung could be considered a precursor in a practical way, would take much time. But when it takes place it would be an immensely fruitful approach to life and its varied complex psychological problems.

It is a pity that the modern scientists of several disciplines very glibly desire to test the authenticity of astrological predictions without subjecting themselves to such critical scrutiny. To discredit astrology is their aim because they themselves are very shaky about their method of approach. Now, even the scientific laws so called, are considered merely hypotheses without claiming absolute certainty about them. In several areas of consideration, astrology has in the modern times, demonstrated its surprising accuracy. As a result of these accurate predictions, there is however arising now some, though still very little, openness to astrological principles.

In modern times, there are many psychologists of international repute who have testified to the accuracy of astrological predictions and the possibility of mobilising the astrological assistance in diagnosing and treating mental ailments. Astrologers have claimed that astrology is a fact in nature because it is based on two fundamental natural laws, namely, the law of action and reaction known as the Law of Karma, and the Law of Reincarnation which emphasized the ego taking various births after the decay of its physical body known as death. Many difficulties during the course of human life specially of fundamental nature are related to karmic problems and unless they are so recognised, their cure is not permanent. Some psychologists have recognised that but not all of them have done so. I remember late Mrs Phoebe Bendit, a famous British clairvoyant psychopath once telling us that she was questioned by Dr. Carl C. Jung at the time of her admission as an apprentice under him as to her belief in reincarnation. On her indicating that she did not believe it but *knew*, as she was herself a clairvoyant, that to be a fact in life, she was readily accepted by the great psychopath.

This approach to mental disorder relating the present of affliction to events in previous lives, which is mirrored in one's natal chart, is generally neglected by the modern psychologists which to a great extent, has thwarted the progress towards a better mental health cure. It would be an interesting study to find out as to how many of the modern psychologists and neurologists believe in the two fundamental laws of nature dealing with human life basically ; if they did not do so, how do they expect that the illness originating in previous births and so much intricately woven in the lifestyle of the present incarnation could be cured by a few pills ! Astrological assistance in this regard could be of great help, and that is why Edgar Cassey proved so marvellous in his approaches to curing physical and mental illnesses of his patients.

Before the relationship between astrological disposition of natal chart and mental illness is established, it is necessary to understand the nature and scope of mental disorder. Astrological diagnosis is based upon symptoms of the malady, and without a clear comprehension of these characteristics of the disease it would be unscientific to provide astrological support to the patient. At present, there are so many diseases included under the broad category of mental disorder that the psychologists would find it rather impossible to find out a single sane individual. Astrologically, every individual is bestowed with his individual uniqueness, as such no abnormal insanity is associated with a common man. Psychologically, mental deficiencies or retardation may imply lack of powers associated with normal intellectual development resulting in inability of the individual to function adequately in everyday life. This has reference to inadequacy in normal growth and development of the mind principle. In fact, the full and perfect development of the mind principle in an individual can take place when he is extremely and ruthlessly crystalline in nature, but in actual practice every human being has his deficiencies.

So when we want to enquire into the abnormality of the person, we do not wish to discover the degree of intelligence of the person ; what we want to know is the knots, mal-functioning of this aspect of his life. Such mal-functionings can be of various kinds ; they can manifest in the form of insanity where the symptoms are acute ; they can express themselves in severe neurosis as well. Psycho–neurosis is an emotional disorder in which feelings of anxiety, obessional thoughts, compulsive acts, and physical complaints without objective evidence of disease in various patients dominate the personality. Such mal-functioning of the emotional-mental structure of the human personality may emphasize the emotional character of the neurotic illness. The absence of physical or objective evidence suggests that the illness is caused at first in the invisible dimensions of the personality which later on descends to the physical or objective conditions of life. From it one could clearly see that the astrological houses such as the Eighth and the Twelfth must be related to this kind of illness. Because this kind of illness is connected with the psyche of the person leading ultimately to the physical conditions, such ailments are known as psycho-somatic which for astrological diagnostic purposes must be related to the Moon and the Fourth House. Insanity is a condition very difficult to describe ; brain disorder which is a physical symptom of the disease is merely one aspect of it ; the others are lunacy, craziness, maniacal behaviour ; such outword expressions are generally considered foolish, irrational, mad, etc., and for assessing their relationship with the various planets one has to consider the intelligence of the person as evident from the Fifth House disposition and the position of the Sun. To go deeper into their causation, one has to understand that insanity may have a physical origin arising from damages in the brain cells, or it may have a psychological cause due to mal-functioning of the psyche of the person. In the former case, it is the First House representing head, brain and thinking portion of the body which has to be considered ; Mars connected with blood circulation and nerves may be enquired into in the present context. In the latter case, it is the condition of the Moon which is significant.

Various other kinds of mental afflictions like phobias, fear complexes and obsessions which are milder forms of personality imbalances are also included in this category of illness ; they are mainly mental in origin. Under the impact of Sigmund Freud, most of the mental disorders have been argued to be sexual in origin ; he stresses the importance of sexual imbalance, perversions and other shortcomings. These sexual characteristics under certain conditions express themselves in difficult mental aberrations. Several psychologists have not accepted the Freudian theory, but that is not the point we are discussing ; it is sufficient to indicate that many mental disorders are sexual in origin. Freud meticulously inquired into mental aberrations and showed that many of them definitely had sex disorders as the basis. Thus in astrological predictions, importance of sex draws attention to Venus, and afflictions of this planet should warn the astrologer to look for intensity of the affliction to predict serious mental disorder or just tolerable sexual digression.

From the above, it is apparent that the mental disorder have relations with brain and head, emotional nature of the person and general sensitivity, mental make-up and the thinking principle of the individual, nervous system, and sexual urges and distortions in the same. Many mental disorders arise from unknown causes, and what some psychologists have considered as invasion from external mental stuff should also be acknowledged. These suggest that in predicting mental disorders, one must carefully examine the First House and Mars, the Fourth House and the Moon, the Sixth House for general susceptibility to diseases, the Sun for mental make-up and the general disposition of the Fifth House ; Venus and the Seventh House also are important ; for invasion from the world of the invisibles one must direct one's attention to the Eighth House and the Twelfth House.

The classical texts have not specified the planets in this way but they have very ably emphasized the importance of these planets and houses in predicting mental disorders. Afflictions are either due to inherent weaknesses of the planets, or due to their adverse placements as in the Sixth, Eighth, or in the Twelfth House, or due to aspects or associations of malefics like Rahu, Ketu, Saturn and the weak Moon. The planets like Rahu, Ketu, and Saturn are so much related to karmic diseases that for serious malignant nature of the malady, one has to look into their position. Other planets could give the temporary afflictions.

Among the various classical texts, many combinations have been given to indicate mental disorder but the most direct reference one gets is from Dr. B. V. Raman which could be applied to differing conditions. He clearly lays down that Aries, the Sun and the Ascendant are connected intimately with brain disorders ; he also emphasized that the weak Moon in the Twelfth Bhava specially in conjunction with Saturn would lead one to insanity. For this kind of disorder one has to look to the disposition of the Moon. As far as the nervous basis of the disease is concerned, there has to be some relation of the adverse type with Ascendant and Mercury. While indicating these, Dr. B. V. Raman has also stressed that each sign of the zodiac represents a certain part of the human body and the diseases peculiar to it and each planet also indicates certain types of diseases. On the basis of this general principle, one superimposes what has been stated earlier. In that case, diseases of the brain must relate to Aries, Ascendant, and the Sun with the Sixth House ; nervous disorder is related to Ascendant, Mercury and the Sixth House. The views enunciated by Dr. B. V. Raman lead us to think that brain disorder must be clearly specified as well as its causation identified with the basic principles and planets connected with such maladies.

On this line of enquiry, one finds that one of the ancient astrological texts, namely *Brihat Jataka*, has laid down that the placement of Moon in Ascendant would cause insanity ; if the Ascendant is afflicted with weak Moon, then the emotional nature of the individual becomes psychopathic and there could be instability in the personality make-up of the person. Any other weakness could affect him under such conditions very easily. The relationship between the Moon and Rahu while malefics are present in the Fifth and the Ninth Bhavas makes the person very susceptible to influences from the invisible regions ; the sensitivity to goblins and such other entities have been stated to be possible under such conditions. In the Eighth House, the Moon could make the person fickle-minded. From these it is apparent that the mind is intimately connected with the Moon and its association with malefics and in inauspicious houses such as the Sixth, Eighth and the Twelfth would create mental unhappiness for the person, *Uttara Kalamrita* very much emphasized the importance of houses like the Sixth, the Seventh and the Twelfth but the significance of Rahu in creating sexual abnormality has also been pointed out.

An exhaustive treatment of mental disorder has been made in *Jataka Parijata*. It is important to note that the combinations indicating the importance of three planets in depression only suggest the general instability of the personality. Three planets or as a matter of fact, large number of planets in weaknesses should forewarn the astrologer to look for indications of a psychopathic personality. This does not necessarily lead to mental aberrations but it only suggests that the native might be susceptible to such afflictions. Several other combinations have also been mentioned in this text, which any reader can conveniently refer to, but the essential feature of these combinations is to suggest that mental instability or abnormality is primarily a function of the weak Moon, Saturn, Mars, the Sun and Rahu specially due to their association with the Twelfth, Eighth, Seventh, Sixth, Fifth and the Fourth Houses. Obviously, these Bhavas are the repositories of those principles which go to influence the creative aspects of the individual as well as the influences on him from the non-physical realm of existence. In order to understand the propensity to mental affliction one has to go deeper in the very constitution of the personality of the native and the basic strength or weakness of the horoscope. It would be only on the basis of the totality of the horoscopic influence and composition that the questions relating to mental disorders should be tackled. Much sure predictions are possible only by working out the detailed relationship in any specific horoscope.

In the end, a word of caution. On occasion, one comes across very powerful personalities finding themselves on the psychiatric chair. The writer has come across an individual with a brilliant international record of scholarship often finding himself on the psychiatric chair for the astrological reason that his Sun was very strong but with some affliction of Saturn. In another case, affliction of Moon with Rahu made the person maniac and suicidal. On several occasions, one would find presence of Rahu in the Twelfth House making the person lonely and depressive. Whenever a person has serious affliction of Ascendant, that is of the First House, specially when Mercury is involved in it, the person is not susceptible to any friendly advice ; he would do exactly what he thinks right and this feeling of his being right is sometimes so much off the mark that the lunatic asylum seems to be the right place for him. But, as a general rule, it should be stated that the mental disorder is that aspect of human personality and his inner life which has deep karmic relationship with earlier incarnations.

INDICATIONS OF PHYSICAL ILLNESS

Unless the cosmic forces energising the human individual is harmoniously absorbed and rightly disseminated, it is extremely difficult to maintain a healthy body. But the stress and strain of modern life is not very helpful for such a natural life-style. Apart from problems arising in everyday common existence, the demand of professional hazards, psychological insecurity aroused due to emotional, economical, and law and order problems is so great that an ordinary human individual often finds himself much less than the challenge facing him. Some of the sufferings are results of the modern civilisation which every one will have to bear collectively, but there are many maladies whose germs were implanted in the past the fruition of which one experienced in the present incarnation. Many of the diseases to which an individual is exposed at different periods of his life are enduring, some of them leave when they have sufficiently tried the afflicted person, others become part of his self itself. Some diseases are contacted during the course of one's life whilst there are others which accompany the ego at the time of his birth itself. Whatever the nature of ailment, the planetary disposition as revealed by the horoscope of the person should throw considerable light enabling the individual to cope with the situation effectively. The ancient rules of forecasting human diseases will have in the modern times to be considerably adjusted in the light of the contemporary conditions.

The growing number of patients at the psychological clinics clearly demonstrates that the life-style of the modern man has moved from the physical level to the psychic or the psychological level. Presently, the modern man is more concerned about his emotional or psychological welfare than the physical one. The progress in medical science has almost controlled most of the physical maladies. Management of such diseases is quite easy and within the reach of most of the persons, but the psychological ailments are varied and still in the exploratory stage. Psycho-somatic diseases discussed by Sigmund Freud, Alfred Adler, Carl C. Jung, and more recently by Abraham Maslow, and the spiritual factors in health and diseases investigated clairvoyantly by Edgar Cassey, Phoebe Bendit, and Geoffrey Hodson have shown that the modern medical science has much to learn from so far unrecognised systems of treatment. Apart from unravelling the past memories and psychological traumas, these investigators and their work have begun to emphasize the importance of astrological readings in assessing the nature and significance of contemporary human sufferings.

Undoubtedly, illness is a necessary aspect of human birth. But, all diseases are not equally important. Some maladies are congenital. Colour blindness, discovered primarily as a result of psychological aptitude tests, has so far does not yield to any treatment; it is congenital. There are many such diseases which have to be endured without any hope of redressal. Such diseases are *karmic*, they have to be borne with fortitude while attempting to mould one's mental and physical attitude so that the deeper roots of the ailment are completely eradicated. Edgar Cassey's work in this area has been pioneering. He mentioned that the Ego did not always suffer consequences of its present wrong action : sometimes certain wrong acts of past lives react in the present incarnation. He has identified several of these causes and helped his enquirers by suggesting the different adjustment forces to be applied to attain the natural harmony. His studies show that the diseases are sent to the individuals in order to incapacitate them in some ways so that they, apart from endeavouring to counterbalance the distortions in natural harmony could begin to appreciate the gifts of God and thereby reorient their lives to make the same beneficient divine force directed towards alleviating in whatever measure it is possible the universal sorrow. The identification of karmic ailments will require an integral approach towards understanding the horoscopic influence on the life of the person concerned, nonetheless the planetary disposition of Rahu, Saturn and Ketu could show the direction. The tackling of karmic diseases and their management cannot be done merely with the aid of medical therapy ; some kind of spiritual and philosophical orientation in the life-pattern is essential.

Among such karmic diseases like cancer and others which are related to special abnormality of gens itself thereby showing inbuilt characteristic of the body-mechanism, there are very few which can be controlled totally though they can be managed to some extent depending upon their intensity and nature. Most of them have to be borne for the life. They appear at a particular age without any apparent cause. Such diseases are also karmic and they cannot be cured at all. These diseases occur in order to impress certain special divine message. Unless that lesson is learnt *completely*, there is every likelihood of such troubles arising oft and on. Some of these diseases are curable but they may leave a permanent scar either physically or psychically.

The astrological chart has a quality of indicating the chances of the occurrences of such maladies which could arise if proper precautions are not taken. Due to apparent carelessness with regard to hygienic rules and disregard of healthy conditions of living, one is likely to contact several diseases. Venereal infection, tuberculosis, epilepsy, stomach disorder, food poisoning and the like fall under this category. Such maladies can be predicted astrologically. In order to do so, the immediate or the inciting planet should be examined along with the strength of the Ascendant specially because the primary objective of such an exploration is to assess the intensity of the damage. If the Ascendant is strong enough, either to thwart the affliction of the planet by providing appropriate life-giving energy, or by arousing sufficient will-force so that the fore knowledge of the impending misfortune could enable the individual to muster up adequate determination to avoid the anticipated situation, the warning could be worth its while. This is possible because sufferings of this kind are not the carry overs of the previous incarnations. They only indicate the storm under which his ship of life is likely to pass and as captain of his ship he could take suitable precautions taking the planetary disposition as weather reports. For example, a weak Moon with Rahu in the Fourth House, specially if it is aspected by malefic Saturn and Mars, would arouse in the person suicidal proclivities. Depression, sudden loss of control over oneself, mental derangement, murderous feelings, and unpredictability of his behaviour are some of the results of this combination. A strong Ascendant however would provide such strong inner strength to the person that these tendencies cannot assume pathological proportion. The knowledge of planetary disposition should also enable him to take precautionary measures so that he does not get entangled in such a morass. And if caught, he should not let his psyche be seriously affected by such occurrences. The individuals concerned who could have aroused such reactions or physical conditions are saved by their fore knowledge. Their astrological knowledge should act like a teacher giving them a width of vision wherein such episodes of life seem insignificant ; the real cause could be considered the planets, a factor beyond him as well as beyond the control of others. Therefore, they could either not allow the situation to develop to that extent that such unhealthy situation had to be confronted, and if at all the same could not be avoided they are able to contain it.

Then, there are accidents which are caused by many different factors. Any sudden trouble must have some association with Mars. This planet must expose the hidden troubles ; it must expose the weaknesses of the self. Mars also spills blood. Most of the road accidents, surgical operations, murderous attacks, and amputations result from some or the other association of Mars. In case, the danger is apprehended from this planet, it is better to pitch one's activities at a low keel. Once such an accident or trouble is apprehended, it is better to avoid outdoor activities or restrict involving oneself in such situations where the same might occur. By doing so, the astrological knowledge might protect the individual from any serious mishap though one cannot vouch that the total escape is always possible : the fatality of the accident could however be considerably minimised. The actual escape depends upon the intensity of the Martian affliction and the amount of precautions taken.

Psycho-somatic diseases like mental aberrations, insomnia, obsessions, phobias and such mental derangements have immense scope for astrological diagnosis and possible rectification. During modern times, a large number of persons suffer from these diseases. Their astrological investigations cannot be supported much on the basis of ancient texts and the rules suggested therein yet the broad lines of approach made there will have to be kept in view. The astrological investigations in these diseases would take us to the very root of life energies. The life-force radiating from the Moon is the very basis of one's psychic life and of one's psychological well being. But the Moon derives its energy from the solar radiation. Thus the Moon and the Sun, both are very important in such a study. But the importance of Ascendant cannot be minimised. This house is the very bedrock on which all problems of psychic and psychological mal-functioning, apart from problems relating to physical health, must be examined. In studying the extent and consequences of psycho-somatic diseases, therefore, the Moon, Sun, and the Ascendant in that order of importance must be carefully considered. It is important to consider the possibility of the disintegration of mind, body and soul of the person on a careful study of these three. If they are not well harmonised, the psychopathic nature of the personality of the individual can be apprehended. These three must be in disequilibrium to give these diseases. The nature of the specific diseases could be found on the basis of the weakest of the three. If the Sun is the weakest planet, the man might suffer from madness; if it is Moon, the disease would be insomnia, phobia, or some kind of obsession ; and in the case of weak Ascendant, epilepsy, nervous disorder, or schizophrenia might occur. The presence or aspect of strong Mars on the Ascendant would however mitigate the likelihood of such an occurrence provided Mars is a friendly planet and is in a benefic disposition.

Furthermore, there are diseases caused by stress and strains of daily life. They are the ailments such as cold and cough, fatigue, body ache, and such other inconveniences caused by over work, fatigue, lack of proper exercise and rest, and absence of mental and physical diversion. These ailments are indicated by the weaknesses of planets like Mercury, and Venus, but mostly they could result from adverse transits. These are not important problems requiring astrological consideration. They occur like the transient wind ; they come and go like the passing winds causing some inconveniences but their effect is not lasting. These should not be given much thought. And, happily, very few persons attach much importance to them though they would feel the troublesome nature of these visitations.

The human diseases can be viewed differently also. Some diseases are mental related to the head, heart, and the thinking apparatus of the person concerned while there are other diseases which are connected with the functioning of the heart. One can, in this group, put emotional disturbances, cardiac arrests, nervous disorders, palpitation and the like. The third category may be considered as those which are connected with intestines, urinary tract, pelvis region, and the connected organs of the body. The other kind may refer to localised ailments like eye troubles, ear problems, skin afflictions, and so on. This sort of classification has the advantage of relating the different planets with various diseases.

Even if the trouble thus identified is a new one and whose details are yet in the exploratory stages, this relationship can yield some astrological causes of the same. By connecting these diseases with glands of their origin or specific organs of the body, the planets associated with them could reveal the intensity, durability, and significance from longer point of view.

In order to find out the curability or otherwise of the diseases, one has to establish the deep-rooted karmic significance of the problem. Some ailments are karmic and the individual must suffer their consequences on physical, psychological and mental planes. Such afflictions find their roots in Saturn, Rahu and Ketu. These three planets are primarily the significators of karmic diseases. The most distinguishing feature of Saturn is its power to atrophy the part affected. Rahu is malignant. Ketu creates aberrations. Their influences are however modulated according to the positional strength and aspects on them. An exalted Saturn with benefic aspects of Jupiter will not give very restrictive diseases. But, even exalted, such a Saturn for Aries ascendants cannot be helpful because of the inherent hostility between the two. Moreover, Saturn is a *badhaka*, or the obstructing planet for this ascendant. The past sins of omissions and commissions will always deter the smooth flow of life whatever the enthusiam and potential strength for carrying on the same.

Placed in Ascendant, Saturn will restrict the personality and impose physical fetters. The individual may like to do many things but will be physically handicapped. Adequate energy will not flow through his veins for fulfilling this task. In the second house, his words will be foul, his tongue tied and speech defective. In the third, he will suffer at the hands of his brothers and co-equals. In the fourth, he may have heart ailments. In the fifth, his procreative urges will be fossilised and paralysed. In sixth, he has to be careful about his pancreas. In the seventh house, he will suffer from sexual disorders mainly arising from impotency, either physical or psychological. In the eighth house, he will have difficulties relating to the rectum regions. In the following houses also, Saturn's capacity to inflict disabilities will be localised to the various connected parts of the body. Similarly, the results of other planetary afflictions will have to be examined.

In ancient times, the Sixth, Seventh, and the Eighth Houses were considered very important in order to predict the impending diseases. In modern times, the situation is vitally changed. It is more significant now to consider, the First, Fourth, Seventh, and Tenth Houses even for identifying the source of the trouble from which the individual can suffer. These cardinal houses can be related to the various places of origin of the diseases which we have mentioned above.

Ascendant is the whole of one's life. It is also the mind and the general approach to life. Most of the diseases of modern life arise due to the psychological factors. The disposition of the First House is very important from karmic standpoint. If the First House is afflicted the disease would be surely the result of past karmas. It is caused in order to impart important lessons in life. Whatever the planet causing the affliction, the effect would be permanent. Only a careful understanding of the object of such afflictions and a careful adjustment of oneself to the effect likely to be produced by those ailments could help in the redressal of the affliction. In cases of such mind-born diseases as confusion, mental aberrations, and psychological complexities of the personality, one has to safeguard permanent scar on the psyche which can take place with clarity of view. With such mental discipline the problems and pangs of such diseases could be considerably reduced. In such diseases, one has to examine the conditions of the Sun and Mercury carefully. If these planets are strong, there will be clarity of thought and sharpness of intellect which will enable the individual to overcome his mental difficulties very effectively.

The increasing impact of heart ailments, nervous disorders and psycho-somatic diseases arises from the affliction of the Fourth House. The Moon is the psyche of the person and connected with these diseases. An affliction of the Fourth House and the Moon will result in heart disorders and psychological problems ; the disease or the disorder will either arise from the weakness of the physical heart or it may be connected with the emotional nature of the person, some set-backs in matters relating to heart. If the affliction is caused by malignant Rahu, the disease will not only elude detection, it will even cause its lasting impact even after its cure. Generally speaking, such diseases end only with the final end of the individual's life. Cancer of the heart is a typical example of this kind of affliction. Heart is a vital organ and the *Anahata Chakra* located near it should not be damaged for a healthy functioning of the body. Most of the human individuals are living in an atmosphere of psychological pollution. Jealousy, hatred, malice, gossip, and similar daily habits of the individual are daily outpouring much of psychological pollution, and the emotional atmosphere is being severely affected. They affect the easy and smooth functioning of the *Anahata Chakra*. Only by a clean life and purity of heart energising this force centre, the psychological structure of the body can remain pure and healthy. This will be an easy and effective protection against most of the maladies of the modern age generated by emotional disturbances and heart weaknesses. But, the sins of the past lives might visit the present incarnation. That explains a large number of god-men dyeing of nervous disorder, heart failure, and even Cancer.

The Tenth House is important even for considering disease because many of the diseases arise due to stress and strain of one's professional career. Suicides and nervous breakdowns have often occurred due to difficult professional conditions. A pilot dyeing of plane crash, the miners being trapped inside the mine, or a writer suffering from finger cramps must have the cause of these ailments in their Tenth House. Whether to divine such ailments merely on the basis of the Tenth House and its lord or on the basis of the total disposition of this house is a point which the astrologers has to do decide for himself depending primarily on the nature of the horoscope before him. The only point which could be emphasized here is the importance of the Tenth House in deciding some professional hazards, a factor which is ordinarily overlooked in many cases.

As far as the Seventh House is concerned, it is important because the pelvis region is the third vital locale of serious physical ailments. Sterilisation, venereal infection, urinary troubles, and impotency have their basis in the conditions of the Seventh House. But, there are many other diseases which arise in intestines, or in liver and kidney. There are diseases like piles, fistula, and others which are connected with the rectum region. Many diseases actually have their origin in the mal-functioning of the organs of this region and their results are noticeable in other parts of the body as well. Therefore, it is suggested that Fifth, Sixth, Seventh, and Eighth Houses should be taken into account together for discovering the causes and curability of many diseases which are primarily physical in nature.

The astrological guidance regarding curability or otherwise of the diseases in modern times must be approached not from the traditional standpoint. The essential astrological principles should be related to the currently identified psycho-somatic ailments and other newly identified human maladies. In this process the main characteristics of the diseases should be linked with the various planets and their basic radiations. It is to be noted that the psycho-somatic diseases are chiefly associated with Sun, Moon and the Ascendant. The cardinal houses namely, the First, Fourth, Seventh, and the Tenth are *also* very important. While discovering the reasons of any specific disease, the main consideration should be the causative factoros rather than the outward symptoms. Saturn, Rahu, and Ketu give rise to diseases which are seldom curable or are malignant in nature. Their intensity can however be reduced to some extent by palliatives, mantras, offerings, gems, and a radical reorientation of one's life style. Venus is connected with sexual disorders, but for serious ailments even in this area, it is necessary to examine the disposition of Mars, Rahu and the Seventh House. Mars will give blood diseases, and in adverse relationships with Moon and Saturn, or with Rahu it will cause serious heart failures. Diseases related with Rahu and Ketu will often elude diagnosis. That which is a karmic disease will not be easily cured and will always leave some imprint on the life of the person. Many of the diseases including the karmic ones will lose their intensity and malefic character if the spiritual or the basic causes of the same are located, identified and the life style appropriately modified.

ACCIDENTS

A clearer understanding of the various factors involved in prognosticating any impending accident requires a definite delineation of the two terms namely death and accidents. There is much confusion in this regard. Shall we call suicide an accident ? What is the position of an individual being knifed by a thief, or killed in a battlefield ? The heart failure which is also a sudden occurrence is not considered an accident while death by fire might be considered so. In order to investigate the causative factors of an accident, it is necessary to know the nature of an accident and the special ways in which it differs from illness, sucide, murder, death; devastation and such other occurrences which are alike in the sense of putting an end to life. Astrologically they are quite different from one another.

The *Concise Oxford Dictionary* defines accident as an ''event without apparent cause, unexpected (so *chapter of —s*, unforeseen course of events) ; unintentional act, chance, fortune ; mishap ; irregularity in structure ; a property not essential to our conception of a substance.'' From this, one may infer that the essential feature of accidents is their *unexpectedness*. An accident is an unforeseen course of events, un-designed ; it has irregularity in structure. Astrologically, however, there is no irregularity, or any unforeseen course in the pattern of one's life as designed by the planets. From general standpoint one may consider whether a particular act was expected or not. When a soldier goes to the battlefield, it is natural to expect that he may have to face bullets and in the process sustain injuries and he may even die. But for an ordinary individual living in a peaceful society, it is an accident if a building collapses and he dies underneath. When a person is driving a car on a road with expert knowledge of driving and with a road-worthy vehicle, then if he collides against something, a moving object or an inanimate object, it is an accident. It is specially so because no one was trying to do it *intentionally*. When we consider this problem astrologically, we are also concerned with an individual and his physical wellbeing and therefore very vitally concerned about his safety or otherwise under such unexpected, unintentional dangers.

Charles E.O. Carter, a British astrologer who published his *Astrology of Accidents* in 1932, did some pioneering work in experimental astrology. Since then, much data have been collected on the subject. Even *The Astrological Magazine*, Bangalore has been publishing from time to time details of different kinds of accidents as evident from various available charts. The importance of Carter's researches is significant for the reason that the author had compiled and analysed 168 cases of accidents from widespread areas : 100 charts were from the United Kingdom, 12 from the United States, 5 from Australia, and 2 from India. On the basis of these empirical data, he examined the operative causative factors for the different kinds of accidents. His analysis was based on the Western system of prognostication but the data furnished there could even be taken as the basic case histories for analysing them according to the traditional Hindu astrological principles.

Carter defined an accident as "a bodily mishap occassioned without intent either on the part of the sufferer or the agent (if any) inflicting it." He discussed the limitations of this definition when he stated that "we might say that a man was accidently killed by a bull or by being thrown from a horse." But in such cases the bull certainly and a horse probably did not mean to inflict injury though it may look so. Again, a street accident may be due to such gross rashness on the part of a pedestrian or a motorist as almost to make the injury intentional but it would not be proper to consider it so. Or, if a man is blown up in war on a battleship, we should not call it an accident ; but if he were fatally injured playing football, we should call it one ; yet in both cases the victim volunteers to meet certain risks, and whether he does it for sport or for glory, the choice is deliberate, hence Carter rejected all cases of death on active service or of death or injury when a clear risk is willingly incurred.

Whatever the theoretical refinements concerning the definition of an accident, there are certain general understanding about accidents, and generally people consulting astrology in this regard have a kind of general understanding about the subject. There are certain essential features of accidents which could be taken up for astrological considerations. Such accidents will have the essential ingredients of unexpectedness, irregularity in the structure, suddenness, and physical injury. Pure accidents could be unexpected, sudden and unintentional, not necessarily the result of active human agent but necessarily resulting in some degree of physical ill-being of the person, either temporarily or permanently, and in some cases the accident may even be fatal leading to death of the person concerned. In this way, a suicide will not be considered as accident because there is intentional active physical agent involved in it and so murder will be ruled out. Death of a test pilot incurring willingly the risk of undergoing difficult air-worthiness test of an aircraft is not so much an accident because the pilot risked the same intentionally, whereas the victim of an aircrash where no such probability of significant order was present is an accident. In such cases one has to distinguish between the probability and the possibility. In accidents, the chances of probability is considerably reduced, though this does not rule out the possibility of the same.

Accidents can be of many kinds and the astrological causes could be worked out on the basis of the special type of the accident. Fatality is an important consideration in the context of accidents, which will require a careful examination as the longevity of the native. In addition, an investigation will also be needed regarding the instrumentality through which the injury is inflicted and the type of injury inflicted. All accidents cannot be treated alike. Had it been only a question of death and physical injury, the general rules of longevity and diseases could have been adequate. But it is not so. Carter himself collected evidences of accidents under the following categories, namely, asphyxiation, drowning, burns, scalds, gunshots, blows, crushings, wounds and cuts, vehicular accidents, falls, machinery causing injury, railway accidents, poisons, explosions, animals and miscellaneous accidents. Even a casual examination would show that these categories could be classified differently depending upon several considerations. Carter avoided air accidents, house collapses, falling of trees, and such other accidents which are quite common in several parts of India and such other countries. One

12

finds that in some accidents, whatever the causative factors, the entire body mechanism is affected and the person gets affected either mortally or otherwise. Asphyxiation is such an example. Here the smoke surrounds the individual and he is not able to take breath satisfactorily. The same could be the result if the individual is caught in a dust storm in a desert land. Drowning is another type of the same process of death. Here, instead of smoke or dust, water surrounds the person and he is not able to breath properly. Saturn is significator for all types of suffocation but in the case of drowning the Moon will have to be afflicted. Chocking is necessarily a function of the lungs. Astrologically, the Fourth House must be related in such cases. But because smoke will also require some connection with fire but in a dormant or not in so much of an active state, it would be helpful to see the disposition of Sun, and Mars as well. When we come to explosion, blows, gunshots, vehicular accidents, crushings as well as falls, many active forces are in play. Destructive activities will have to be related to Mars in its multifarious aspects. It should be underlined by every thoughtful astrologer that the type of constellation would play a very important part in deciding the nature of the planet which is basic for astrological prognostications but here the main thrust is to show the guidelines with regard to accidents. Mars has the strange affinity with blood, suddenness and earth. In accidents leading to cuts, haemorrhages, bleeding through veins, fall on the ground and such similar events there has to be the destructive element of Mars. In crushings, in instances where the limbs are smirched, where the mechanical equipment has been instrumental in affecting the individual, it is logical to look for the affliction by Saturn.

Whenever vehicular accidents take place, it would be possible to find some relationship with Jupiter. Assuming the individual is crushed in head by a big automobile owned by a dignitary, the affliction of first house by destructive Mars, may be from the sign of Taurus or Aquarius and a weak aspect from Jupiter, could also be noticeable : if Jupiter aspects Mars, the vehicle would be of some respectable person whereas his aspect on ascendant may decrease the fatality of the accident and the individual may escape with only minor injuries. On the other hand, with bad affliction of Saturn, the vehicle could be some truck driven by drunken type of low class employee and the chances of survival could be very much decreased.

Some case of poisoning, either by accidental taking of poisonous drugs or laboratory chemicals, could be traced to Rahu. Here one cannot even completely overlook the significance of Mercury. But in the cases of burns, scalds, gunshots, explosions, and such other instances where the element of fire is important, it would be possible to find out the impact of Sun and Mars. In accidents where mechanical devices as in the case of Industrial accidents, railway disasters, and air crashes are involved, one will have to find out the causative planets and their nature. Saturn, Rahu, Ketu, and Mars will have their due share in such occurrences depending upon the nature of the accident.

Thus, we have to examine in all cases of accidents, firstly the nature of the influences causing accidents. It is true that the nativity must display some basic weakness to provide the structure of planetary combination making the accidents possible. Secondly, the type of accidents must be related to the planets functioning as the causative factor. Thirdly, the parts affected must be correlated to the different limbs of the *Kala Purusha*, the Heavenly Man, and the different houses in the horoscope afflicted. Fourthly, the age at which the accident could occur should be ascertained. Lastly, the fatality or otherwise of the accident which is of supreme importance in this context must also be examined.

Carter showed that the highest number of accidents took place when Sagittarius was the rising sign followed by Leo. The possible significance of Sagittarius sign is noticeable because Venus in this sign as well as Saturn in Capricorn have caused much damage. Mars in Virgo and Mercury in Aries have also caused much accidents. It is surprising that Jupiter in Pisces has not diminished the number of accidents but it is not known as to how many of the accidents under the influence of Jupiter have been fatal. One could argue that these accidents but for the influence of Jupiter could have been fatal. The signs which contained the highest number of accidents were Sagittarius, Scorpio, Pisces, Libra, Leo and Cancer in descending order and these signs had above the average number of accidents.

The data presented by Carter are inadequate for any generalisation. Nonetheless they do indicate the areas of sensitive points where the trouble could be looked for. On the basis of these empirical data, one could very well infer that there is no *one* planet as such which should be considered causative ; it is the whole conjuncture of planetary relationships along with the house and sign position which should be taken as the basis of astrological prediction. In order to assess the value of planetary juxtapositions, one needs a carefully disciplined mind. For this very reason, B. V. Raman has very rightly stated that the traditional astrology forms the warp and woof of genuine astrological knowledge and we would not be vain enough to think that our findings could ever surpass those of ancient masters. Omniscience in astrology cannot be monopolised by any individual however loud his protestations to the effect that he is the 'Messiah' sent from heaven to pull out astrology from the depths of tradition. This is a very apt warning to those who wish to superimpose empirical data on traditional and classical principles enunciated by the ancient seers. In fact, with humility one should approach the entire juxtaposition of the planets and try intuitively and with passivity of mind to find out the mode of expression of these planets in modern times. One may always keep one's feet on the ground thinking that the ancient seers have given sufficient hints and clues on the basis of which the planetary disposition could be worked out in the modern context and for that purpose, the contemporary empirical data should be considered merely as the starting point in this discovery.

Once the Mahatma K. H. stated that ''accidents occur under the most various circumstances ; and men are not only killed accidently, or die as suicides but are also murdered—something we have not even touched upon—Bear always in mind that there are exceptions to every rule, and to these again and other side of exceptions and be always prepared to learn something new.'' The problem of accidents, obviously, is very complicated and it would not be easy to apply simple astrological principles in dealing with this aspect of the life process. Of the various perplexities related to the problem of accidents, there are two aspects which have often eluded the astrologers. The ancient seers did not devote special chapters on this aspect of astrology. Probably life then was very peaceful and untimely deaths by whatever means were considered the result of the sin of

the king as well as of the subjects. There was something unnatural about accidents which according to the
ancient seers was not helpful to discuss in open. Hints
are available in classical texts for finding out the possibility of accidents either resulting in death or in physical
injury. In *Brihat Jatak*, for example, unnatural deaths by
drowning, by being a prey to wild animals, by fire,
torture, suicide by hanging or falling, decapitation ow-
ing to royal displeasure have been related to the Eighth
House. Mention has also been made of accidental
deaths including deaths by cholera and plague to be
related to Mars and such deaths connected with water
to Moon and with fire to Sun. The position of Sun in
the Tenth House while Mars is in the Fourth is supposed
to lead to death caused by a fall of a stone from the top
of a mountain. When Saturn, Moon and Mars are in the
Fourth, Seventh, and Tenth Houses respectively, the
person could die by falling into a well. If the rising Sun
be a dual sign, and the Sun and the Moon occupy it, the
death occurs by drowning in water ; it has also been
stated that Moon in a sign owned by Saturn, under
certain conditions would lead to death by accidents
connected with a fall from a high place. If the Sun is
in the Fourth House, and Mars in the Tenth aspected by
Saturn, the person may die from the effects of a collision
with a piece of timber or death may occur due to being
beaten with wood. Many similar combinations have
been given in *Jatak Parijatam*, *Brihat Jatak* and other
astrological works but they all are considered along with
the topic of death and the instrumentality of death. The
point that can be emphasized here is that the old school
of Eastern astrology did not give any special attention
to accidents in considering it as a way of exit from this
world. As such we could consider all types of accidents

with the Eighth, Second, and Seventh Houses in the consideration of this important question. We can even put the question differently, if we enquire accidents merely as another form of death. It is also important to decide whether there are other implications of the problem which also should be taken into account in prognostications relating to accidents. Can the different types of accidents be considered as a variant of death, or are there other lessons for the native to learn from such events ? These are some of the wider implications of the subject which every serious student of astrology will have to keep in mind.

Before discussing the wider implications of accidents, we may dwell a little longer on traditional methods of investigations relating to the subject. In this context we find that some interesting things are mentioned in *Uttara Kalamrita*. It has been stated there that the Twelfth House is connected with awakening from sleep (*nidrabhanga*), ascension to heaven (*swargarohana*), and mutilation of a limb (*angavaikalypita*). The Eighth House is also connected with the mutilation of a limb but the word used here is *angahinata* which means the lack of a limb. This house is also connected with an afflicted face (*sakleshavaktram*), decapitation (*sarchhedanam*), and longevity. The Sixth House has been related to a fall from a boat, and to poison. The longevity of a person has been related to many houses such as First, Second, Eighth, Eleventh, and Twelfth. The Sixth House is generally connected with diseases but again, almost all the houses are connected with different parts of the body and the diseases connected with those related limbs are related to the strength and afflictions of these houses· Of the signs, Scorpio and Virgo have been prominantly mentioned as causing various physical mishaps, and different kinds of physical injuries. From such indications, one may infer that the goodness or evil nature of a planet is as important a factor for the examination as the deeper import of different houses. The most significant conclusion from the underlying principles of astrological rendering of accidents as under *Uttara Kalamrita* would be a clearer understanding of the significance of death and accident from the Soul's standpoint. Whether an accident, mutilation or disfiguring of a limb or death occurs at a specific age would depend upon the task undertaken by the *Atman* or soul during the life-span of a specific incarnation. Whether an accident will result in death or would result in mere minor injury would be a consideration which will open out certain very fascinating aspects of the subject. For the time being, we shall defer this consideration to examine the relationship of certain accident-prone age in the life history of an individual so that we can later on examine the reasons of accidents occuring at a particular age of the person.

Generally speaking, the Sixth House is related to diseases, Eighth House with unexpected and serious accidents, and twelfth House to dangers to life, hospitalization and the end of life. These are subservient to the strength of the Ascendant. But the investigation into the general conditions of health and longevity has to be related to causative factors for a specific malady at a specified age. In this regard the death inflicting and accident causing planets become important.

From the empirical case studies given by Carter, it is significant to note that the accidents takes place primarily during the early years of one's life : 74 per cent of the accidents recorded by Carter occurred before the age of 30 years and 90 per cent before the age of 40 years. Again, it is observed that the accidents due to fall, crushings, blows, burns, scalds and drowning which generally represented the types of accidents over which human control is minimal, accounted for about two fifths of the total. About 43 per cent of the accidents occurred to persons below 10 years of age ; only marginally larger percentage, that is, 45 per cent of the persons involved belonged to the age-group 15 years to 40 years. About 36.9 per cent of the accidents occurred during the first ten years of life, 20.3 per cent during the age group 10–20 years ; 16.6 per cent during each of the second and third decade of one's life and less than five per cent of accidents occurred during the fourth and subsequent decades. From this, it is noted that the children are most prone to accidents. This being so, it would be necessary, in the present context, to assess whether the person, rather the child, is susceptible to *Balarishta,* that is, whether the chart shows weakness during the early years of its life span.

On the question of misfortune during childhood, or *Balarishta,* the ancient astrologers devoted considerable thought. Unless the child is destined to live, astrological prognostications are of no avail to him· In the chain of incarnations of the *Atman,* all life stories are not expected to be unfolded to the full : some lives are meant to be intensive, some extensive, and some are merely time marking incidents. In the last case, certain egos take birth to counterbalance some karmic forces meanwhile providing an opportunity for the *Atman* to equip itself on higher planes of existence so that when the next full intensive life histories have to be lived, it has acquired adequate strength to confront it and to give a full account of itself. Such child deaths should be predicted and examined on the basis of planetary combinations given in *Balarishta* yogas. Such an assessment could even forewarn the parents to be careful about their children and not to neglect any of their ailments. If the child fatally succumbs to such a mishap, the incident could be taken philosophically. It may to a little extent reduce the sorrow of the family.

In deciding the consequences and implications of an accident, the first task before the astrologer is to determine the longevity of the individual. Unless the die is cast against the individual, no amount of murderous assaults can destroy him. When the life force pulsating the veins of the native is weak and ego has planned only a short stay in this coil, even a minor mishap could be the cause of the fatal end. So the determination of the span of life is of the foremost importance. In this connection, there are certain houses which are very important : the Eighth House from the Ascendant, the Eighth House from the Eighth House itself, that is, the Third House from the Ascendant are termed the Houses of Life. The energy flowing through the child is expressed by the disposition of these houses, namely, the Ascendant, the Eighth, and the Third Houses. The vitality, courage, activity and the output of action and the way the total sum of energy is ultimately merged in the cosmic aggregate, that is, First, Eighth, Third, Tenth, Fifth and the Twelfth Houses, are all connected and must be examined carefully to determine the life force in the child. The Seventh and the Second are called the Houses of Death. These are the negative houses which show the danger points for the efficient flow of the Life Force. These dangers occur due to the disposition of Second, Sixth and the Eleventh Houses. On the basis of the positive and the negative considerations of the quantum and the free flow of the energy discharge, it is possible to realistically determine the danger points. These houses have to be related to the different planets in order to arrive at the final result. The lords of the Second, Seventh and their occupants and the planets which are in conjunction with them are the death inflicting planets. These points could be summarised as follows :

Death will be caused by (i) planets occupying the Second and the Seventh Houses, (ii) planets which are the lords of these houses, (iii) planets which join the lords of these houses, (iv) it may occur during the period of a planet not *yoga karaka*, that is, the planet which are not very auspicious but which become evil and conjoin the lords of the Houses of Death, (v) lords of the Third and the Eighth Houses also cause death, and (vi) death may occur even during the period of the most malicious planet. In the case of *Balarishta*, infant mortality, the importance of Moon is given in almost all the combinations. The affliction of Moon either by position, malefic aspect or association, besides the affliction of Sun and birth time—the time just before the sunrise or just after the sunset being considered very inauspicious—are conducive to infant mortality. This affliction could, to a great extent, be counteracted by a favourable aspect or association of Moon by Jupiter, or other benefics. In determining the life span of a child during his infancy, the positions of Sun and Moon are of great significance. It is only after determining the accident prone age, or the period when the individual is likely to be physically affected that the next question of the type of accident could be undertaken. The fatality of these planets will have to be related to the degree of injury or the physical damage that is likely to take place at the specific age under consideration. Unless the time for death has arrived, nothing can kill a person.   Only at the specified time of death, sudden accident or long drawn illness can be the causative factor.

In order to relate the different planets with various types of accident, one will have to go into details of the latter.   The nature of the accident changes according to the change of time.   Death by gunshot, injury by the operation of a mechanical equipment, burns in laboratory experimentation, asphyxiation due to gas, and air crashes could not be thought of in ancient pastoral civilisations.   The degree of vehicular accidents has been much more severe in sophisticated countries whereas in a primitive society, there could be death due to thirst, animal attacks, fall in a deep well, or by drowning.   Therefore the characteristics of accidents must be clearly defined in order to relate them to the different planets because the basic nature of the planets does not alter over a period of time though their repercussions and the quality of damage done may change according to the differences in society and culture.

Accident due to vehicular mode of transportation is one of the commonest kind of accident during recent days.   The age at which the accident occurs is important in order to determine whether the accident would be fatal or otherwise. While examining the nature of accident, one could investigate whether the accident would take place due to the fault of others or of the native himself.   Many a time the affected person may be accompanying some one else and the death or the injury may be purely accidental to him.   It often happens that the individual was going by a public transport system to some place such as by bus, railways, airplanes and the accident meets him.   On other occasions, the accident may occur when the individual had been going by his own bicycle, and another van or truck dashed against him. It is also possible that the railway accident took place because some one had removed the fish-plate and it was not detected in time to save the accident. The accident could also occur due to mechanical contraption not functioning satisfactorily or due to misplacement of the human limb at wrong locations thus causing cuts and loss of blood or even the death. All these finer differences will have to be properly reflected in the planetary conjunction if the planetary association with the accident has to be established.

The exact prediction of the nature of the accident is a very fine point. Such decisions can be taken only when the individual chart is examined. The above dis-cussion however would make one think that the prognostication of an accident is a very complicated decision. The determination of longevity is the most important point in this regard, but no less significant is the discovery of accident sensitive points in life. Each accident occurs to impart some specific lesson to the Ego and as such they are adequately reflected in planetary juxtaposition. Those accidents which are of deep significance are connected with Saturn, Rahu and Mars. Their imprint on the psyche of the person is deep-rooted. In case the Ego is able to learn the lesson quickly and is able to counterbalance the retributive karmic impulses effectively, the accident could be a minor one. But it is difficult to know what the Ego has to learn. Sometimes the loss of limb is necessary to arouse sympathy for those who are similarly affected; on another occasion, long-drawn suffering with physical limitations generates perseverance and fortitude. If the lessons could be learnt otherwise and easily, the accident could be avoided. For this very reason, the ancient seers advised the human beings to concentrate on cultivation of virtues and to lead a righteous life so that he could be prepared to cooperate with his Higher-Self without any untoward incident. This injunction indicated the necessity of cooperating with God's plan for the mankind in which every individual has got an assigned role to play. Every event, accidents as well as other happy turns of life, occur for the growth and development of the psyche, the *Jiva*, for which purpose physical events occur to lead the individual to psychological modifications. There is certainly a scheme of things not generally recognised by us. The purpose of astrology is to unveil that scheme for the human individuals ; astrology unveils the nature of the mysterious power surrounding us and it shows the relevance of birth in the cosmic drama in which the Soul is merely an actor on the arena of Eternity. Considered this way, accidents are not accidental but they are meaningful and they teach, guide and act with nature as a coutervailing force intended to balance the life events so that ultimately the individual is able to cooperate with nature in the task of realising one's real nature and one's latent powers.

MALIGNANT CANCER

Among the various maladies likely to afflict a human being, cancer is one of the most malignant. The common cancer of man is not generally inherited, although some families show an incidence of a particular cancer beyond the normal level of expectation. Some familial tendencies have been observed for cancer for the breast, prostate, stomach, colon-rectum, and lung, although the heredity effect regarding these also is not strong. Even when multiple cases of childhood cancer is observed in a family, or when leukemia develops in one of a pair of identical twins, the other is also likely to develop it, but these tendencies are not linked to genetic factors. It is often felt that these tendencies reflected some common environmental relationship along with a genetic factor if any. The factors causing cancer are so complex that the modern medical science itself is still exploring the various causative and assisting factors. Under such circumstances, it may be an useful exercise to explore the possibility of establishing some basic principles to indicate the susceptibility of an individual to this disease.

The first point in the present study is to consider the nature of cancer which is still an enigma in many ways. Its process of development and origin are much different from other kinds of maladies. It can be considered as a processs of physical growth but not of the ordinary natural type. Cancer may arise in any of the body's tissues and is characterised by the uncontrolled and disorderly multiplication of abnormal cells. The cells are said to undergo some abnormal kind of mutation and their natural course of growth and development is radically altered. The disease causes a progressive, unrestricted division of abnormal cells. As a process of physical growth (as distinguished from psychological) it is known in all groups of animals, and many plants also develop cancer-like growths. Such changes have been found in million-year-old fossil dinosaur bones ; in man, the phenomenon has been recognized since earliest time and occurs in all human population. These facts indicate that the malady is neither of recent origin, nor is it restricted only to human individuals; it is coexistent with physical forms of living entities—vegetables and animals as well. As such the basic principles of terrestrial growth and evolution expressed through planetary disposition should be generally applicable to explain the occurrence of cancer in human beings. As a matter of fact, the astrological study of cancer reveals one of the most abstruse principles of human growth, namely the fight between life and anti-life energies expressed allegorically in the churning of the ocean between gods (life energies) and *asuras* or no-gods (representing anti-life principles or energies).

The important point to note in the study of cancer is its malignant character. Pathologically the malignancy or an affliction is related to its being fatal, tending to produce death. But in all cases of cancer, death is not an inevitable result. In certain forms of cancer, depending upon the place of affliction and the stage of its growth, it is possible to eliminate the cancerous growth and save the individual though with some sacrifice of the damaged tissues or the organ. This leads us to think that cancer is not necessarily the cause of death, but a disease in the sense that it afflicts certain organs which arrests the growth process in the human being and by arresting the function of these organs the disease indirectly strangulates the normal functioning of the body which leads to the death of the person. If we focus our attention on cancer as an affliction of the specific body cells whose mutation leads to other complications rather than a disease by itself causing death, there is likelihood of approaching the subject a little differently.

The way cancerous growth develops is interesting from the astrological standpoint. In ordinary bodily afflictions, whenever any disease takes place, the bodily functions are incapacitated, but in cancer, it is not merely incapacitating of some body cells, tissues and organs, but a struggle between two different kinds of growth cells occurs. It is stated that the malignant process begins as a progressive and unrestrained division of abnormal cells initially maintaining some degree of differentiation, that is, their specialised structure and function, so that they resemble those cells from which they arise, or some development stage of tissues of origin. As the disease progresses, the cells usually become increasingly abnormal in appearance, structure and function until they may not be recognizable as an offshoot of the tissue of the origin. If their growth is not checked, these cells infiltrate and destroy adjacent tissues ; often they are transplanted to different parts of the body where they grow as colonies which in medical terminology are called metastases. With increasing degree of morbidity, these ultimately strangulate the normal funtioning of the afflicted cells, tissues or the organs in order to provide avenues for the growth as an outcome of the afflicting 'cause'. In this way, one could visualise the normal bodily growth as an outcome of some life-giving 'energy' which in the cancerous affliction is gradually overcome and overpowered by some kind of 'anti-life' growth process. A deeper understanding of astrology distinguishes *Daivic* or Divine planetary forces, such as, for example, the Sun, the Moon, and Jupiter, which provide the impetus to growth in the positive manner, whilst the *Asuric* or non-God-like forcess, for example, Saturn and Rahu, which arouse negative growth process, specially when their disposition is 'perverse'. When the latter have completely thwarted the benign forces of the former and begin to sway the various body organs, death occurs because the positive life-energy for whose growth and expression the vehicle was provided with the afflicted organs has been completely suffocated. A proper understanding of the alignment of planetary forces between *Daivic* and *Asuric* groups in a particular horoscope and their relationships would lead to right prognostication. Merely a consideration of the Sixth, Eighth and the Twelfth, or even of the Second and the Seventh Houses by themselves may not become conclusive in the present context.

A clearer view is obtained by examining the process of the cancerous growth. The medical science has described the process in terms of cancer causing agents known as carcinogens, agents which do not by themselves cause the affliction but assist the affliction as cocarcinogenic and those agents which inhibit the carconogenic effect known as anti-carcinogens. The cancer-causing agents are the most important ones which we have to look for at the first instance. Although the precise mechanism of the malignant cancerous growth process is not yet medically established, various factors singly or in combination with others are recognised as being able to initiate the process. Chemicals, radiation, genetic factors, repeated trauma and most recently, viruses have been considered by pathologists to cause or to be strongly associated with certain forms of cancer. Even geographic variations in the incidence of cancer have been observed. Some metals, minerals and other chemicals in the general environment and in industry, and other occupational settings have also been shown to cause human cancer or has been suspected of causing it.

A closer scrutiny of various carcinogens would indicate an interesting astrological similarity. For example, it is stated that industries concerned with coal-tar and its derivatives such as pitch, tar oil, or creosote, account for the largest known group of occupational cancer. Skin cancer was observed in several workers engaged in those industries that use benzo, a chemical connected with coal, oil, shale, lignite and petroleum. Coal tar fumes inhaled by workers in coke-oven operations have been associated with lung cancer. Benzine, a petro-chemical and a product of coal-tar distillation has been stated to affect the blood-forming tissues and produce leukemia. One could observe the interply of Mars and Saturn in such occurrences. Arsenic has been implicated in cancer of the lung ; Rahu has special connection with poisons of this kind and as such it has an important role in such cases.

The risk of cancer is greater in those who smoke. Polycyclic hydrocarbons that result from incomplete combustion of automobile fuels make the environment very cancerous. Certain ingredients in widely used birth-control pills have been shown to produce high risks to cause breast cancer. Radiation, specially X-rays, radium salts and such exposures which decompose the body cells of the affected region initiate the cancerous growth process. These are strongly linked with Saturn.

Spreading of cancer occurs by one of the two processes : either it may progress from one area to adjoining ones by infiltration of surrounding tissue, or a cancer cell, or a group of cells may separate from the main mass and travel in the blood, in the lymph system, or through body tracts to another parts of the body. If not destroyed in transit, the cells may become implanted at the new location and start growing there. Either of the processes shows that the basic cause of cancer carried by various carcinogens somehow get mixed up with positive life force and begin to search out its usual channels of growth such as the blood vessels, lymphatic system or the digestive system and make the life giving energy unable to strengthen those channels, and while doing so, it injects the negative life energy to those channels thus gradually increases the malignancy of the disease. The location where it begins its negative growth process, or its perverseness becomes the seat of cancer. In astrological prognostication, the first task is to investigate the possibility or the susceptibility of the negative-life growth as evident from the perversity of Saturn, Mars and Rahu. The second task is to determine the growth points of this perverse process. Because the channels of life-sustaining power pervade throughout the body, and the cancerous agents take recourse to those channels they can find their seat of localisation anywhere in the body: kidney, prostate, liver, pancreas, blood, muscles, cartilage, breast, lung, cervix, ovary, rectum, intenstine. Cancer often establishes itself at one location and after attaining considerable size at that site, it spreads to distant areas but certain organs do not harbour cancer from other sites. Examples of such organs are the prostate, breast, thyroid, spleen, kidney, heart, and skeletal muscle. Based on the type of tissue and the type of cell in which cancer arises, various categories of the same have been recognized. From astrological standpoint, it would be necessary to identify the possibility of cancer affliction, and then the specific organs or the part of the body which can be affected may be determined. In this regard, the Indian astrology is well developed. On the basis of the natal chart and the association of various planets with different parts o the human body, the astrologer can fairly accurately pinpoint the area of the physical body which is likely to be attacked.

In astrology, the different countries are assigned to different signs of the zodiac and different planets. Details of this classification are available in several texts. For ready reference one could even find this classification indicated in B. V. Raman's much popular study entitled *Hindu Predictive Astrology*. Statistically it is suggested that Scotland has the highest overall cancer mortality rate among men and Portugal the lowest. Among women, Chile has the highest reported cancer mortality rate and Portugal the lowest. Pisces is said to be related to Portugal which has the lowest incidence of cancer both for male and female. If the individual has strong Pisces sign, the susceptibility of cancer is certainly greatly reduced. Scotland having the highest cancer incidence comes under the sign Cancer ruled by the Moon as well as under Libra ruled by Venus. These two planets should indeed be carefully watched for perversity ; and affliction of the Sun, the Moon, Jupiter

and the Ascendant specially for individuals hailing from
Scotland make them very liable to attack from cancerous
growth process. Several constellations, planets, and
the signs of the zodiac have in ancient astrological
scriptures been associated with different countries which
require to be kept in the background while assessing the
susceptibility of the individual to this kind of afflictions.

The general principles of cancerous growth as indicated above make any prognostication of cancer a
difficult task and it is advised that the astrologers should
not rush hastily in attempting such prognostications.
There are many pitfalls in the same. It is so even for
the simple obvious reason that the malady if detected
timely could be surgically eliminated making the individual permanently free from the trouble. Thus Mars
which could cause the disease may even show the way
to its cure.

Much empirical work has been done by way of
collecting charts of different persons who have had
cancer affliction. In this regard it may be indicated that
Surendra Pai did a pioneering work in collecting 173
cases of cancer and published his findings in the annual
number of *The Astrological Magazine*, 1982. A careful
study of these charts could be highly beneficial to the
students of the subject, but here I would take up for
illustrative purpose only a few. *Chart I*[1] is for February
18, 1959 with Virgo Ascendant. Virgo ascendant in the
present context is very relevant in several ways. The
sign symbolises the various *siddhis* or the latent powers
of the individual which if properly activated could give
immense power over natural forces. It is the store house

    1. *Chart I:* Ascendant and Rahu in Virgo ; Jupiter in Scorpio ;
Saturn in Sagittarius ; Sun, Mercury, and Venus in Aquarius ; Ketu in
Pisces ; Mars in Aries, Moon in Gemini.

of one's possibilities.   One therefrom can conclude that
the native's strongest point should have been his latent
possibilities, that is, the store house of positive life-
energies which he could develop to attain his full stature.
But he was destined not to do so. The placement of Rahu
in the First House made his personal life bitter ; his
latent energies were stragulated.   There was no benefic
influence to mitigate this tendency.   The Sun which is
the core of one's being, from which all the soul's directions flow is also severely afflicted, specially by the
Saturn's aspect on it which reduced all the goodness
whatever possible of Mercury and Venus.   Venus is also
not giving him any opportunity for making his life-
energy grow favourably.   Perversity of Saturn is
enhanced also due to its aspect on Ascendant, thus
sapping out the energy essential for his sustenance. The
Moon, another life-giving planet, is contaminated by
Saturn by its seventh house aspect whilst the Moon in
Tenth House should have given some saving grace otherwise.   Furthermore, the horoscope has been additionally
weakened by the presence of Sakata Yoga.   In this
horoscope one finds the positive life-giving planets
seriously afflicted by Saturn and Rahu, the two deadly
planets, and both of them of deeply malignant nature.
The position of the Ascendant lord, that is, Mercury, is
also not favourable.   Mars in the Eighth House as lord
of the Eighth and the Third Houses also cannot be by
any way considered helpful.

Let us examine another chart given in the same
collection. *Chart II* is for August 11, 1943[2] with Leo
Ascendant.   In the present case one finds that the

2. *Chart II* : Leo as Ascendant with Venus and Mercury ; Moon
in Scorpio ; Ketu in Capricorn ; Mars in Pisces ; Saturn in Gemini and
Sun, Rahu and Jupiter in Cancer.

Ascendant lord the Sun is placed in the Twelfth House along with Rahu and exalted Jupiter. Saturn aspects the Ascendant and Venus. The strangulation effect of Saturn is very powerful in the present case also. The quantum of life-energy with which the individual is born had been very much restricted and its power of growth circumscribed. The Ascendant lord placed in the Twelfth House along with poisonous Rahu could not be considered very helpful. The Moon closely associated with the life-giving impulse, the planet which helps the growth and blossoming of the life-giving energy, is debilitated. Thus we find that the Ascendant lord, the Moon, the Sun and Jupiter are all in very adverse situation, whilst Mars, Saturn and Rahu are free to do the harm.

Another *Chart III* given for January 23, 1923[3] shows that Aries Ascendant has Mars in the Twelfth House fully aspected by Saturn from the Sixth House, and also Venus already placed in adverse Eighth House is aspected by it. Sun is also in enemy's house. Ketu is also in the Twelfth House along with the Moon. This conjunction of planetary positions emphatically indicates that the positive life-energy is greatly handicapped in its effective and nourishing operation whilst the negative life-energy impulses are quite strong.

In conclusion, one is led to state that the prognosis of cancer whether medically or astrologically is not easy. One has to distinguish it from leprosy which is entirely a different kind of disease but it also involves decomposition of certain organs of the body but its germ has been isolated. Cancer is still a mysterious affliction.

----

3. *Chart III* : Ascendant is Aries ; Saturn and Rahu in Virgo ; Jupiter in Libra ; Venus in Scorpio ; Sun and Mercury in Capricorn ; Moon, Mars and Ketu in Pisces.

The occult philosophy has already begun postulating Life and Anti-Life energies both circulating in the cosmos and astrologically, it is possible to identify the role of the both in everyday life. The allegorical reference to the Churning of the Ocean, astrologically made evident by the disposition of the malefics and benefics in constellations with their mysterious powers, can have much to say in the present context. But investigations on this line could open many new aspects of life. A pinpointing of the affliction may not be possible so easily, but one could only find out whether an individual chart has the tendency to harbour such possibilities ; the responsibilities of the astrologer like that of a doctor, is great in warning the individual so that he could defend himself. In this kind of susceptibilities, a careful and alert watchfulness and spiritually oriented life could be of great help. It is not without significance that several great sages had suffered from this disease and they had borne it cheerfully. It might be revealing to go deeper in their charts to work out the spiritual significance of this causation and its astrological relationship with the evolving Soul.

REMEDIAL MEASURES

Much confusion persists regarding the role of astrology in alleviating human sufferings. To a great extent, rational human individuals who have been endeavouring to comprehend the unexplained laws of nature have begun to accept the validity of astrology. It is no longer, in the circle of scientists, dubbed as prejudice and blind belief. The number of individuals who has been attending astrological schools and teaching lessons is certainly amazingly large, specially so in westren industrialised countries. But the validity of remedial aid in astrology is still not very well recognized and it is often questioned in learned circles. Even the astrologers are not unanimous on the efficacy of gems, stones, *mantras* and such other methods of thwarting the occurrences of many unpleasant situations or in eliminating or reducing several unhappy afflictions. This, happens primarily due to differences in the basic under-standing of astrological influences. An understanding of the occult nature of the astrological science will enable us to see clearly that the study of the tendencies of various physical and supra-physical forces does not lead us to fatalism. The forces of gravitation operating on every individual do not preclude the humanbeings from flying in the sky and to send rockets beyond the realm of solar influence. When one understands the real nature of these laws, one inevitably comes to accept

them but one may, having accepted their validity try to
mobilise them for one's advantage. It is with this object
that the seers have stated that ''Those who know astrology can only indicate in a way what will take place in
future. Who else, except the Creator Brahma, can say
with certainty what will definitely happen''. As an
astrologer can only study the tendencies likely to manifest under certian situations, it may be logical, as an
extension of this approach, to find out the additional
forces that can be generated in order to deflect any
unhappy influences likely to manifest as a result of the
given planetary configuration.

As a matter of fact, the scientists and modern
thinkers have begun to explore on this line the possibility of utilising astrological knowledge to caution
individuals against impending dangers and to take
remedial measures. It could be helpful if in India the
various empirical results of practising astrologers are
collected in order to evolve a synthetic approach to this
subject of remedial measures to enable others to try
them and verify the results. The scientific method in
astrological researches would help us to greatly expand
the scope of Hindu astrology which has a wide and
useful role to play in the modern world and useful contributions to make in the realm of occult science. Occult
science does not obligate us not to take aid of natural
recourse in alleviating one's troubles and tribulations.

The need for studying the significance of planetary
afflictions and remedial measures is important also from
another standpoint. The interest in astrology in purely
objective form is not very useful unless this knowledge is
gathered for some higher study or for some practical
use. International predictions made by various astrological savants, both Indians as well as international, ones

have been with the object of cautioning world politicians of the impeding dangers so that they could take appropriate steps to ward off the afflictions or atleast reduce the intensity of their impact. The ancient method of Ayurvedic system of medicine linking the *pranic* forces afflicting the individual with the three basic flows of energy, namely, phlegm (*kapha*), bile (*pitta*), and wind (*vayu*) which in turn were related to planetary radiations had required the ancient medical practitioners to have a deeper understanding of astrological principles on the basis of which they examined the natal chart of the patient prior to commencing treatment. Those who are aware of the basic Ayurvedic system of treatment would indicate that the linkages between various herbs, minerals, gems, and the time for beginning the treatment with planetary radiations were based on an occult understanding of cosmic forces affecting the human individual. Even the yogic teachers who taught their disciples in various schools of occult perfections had deep knowledge of the relationship between the planets, the *chakras*, and the functioning of the human organism. When they required their students to follow a particular dietary regulation, they did so because all these are intimately related subjects. The efficacy of yogic practices in remedying many physical ailments and in enabling the maintenance of physical welfare which was also achieved by the ancient Indian medical practitioners, is open to every research student to verify. On the same analogy, one can affirm that the understanding of planetary influences could be very useful in helping the individual to lead a confident and meaningful life.

I once knew a practising clairvoyant psychopath in London who also administerd homeopathic medicines to her patients. Her method of selecting the specific medicine for her patient was to examine the aura of the individual patient and that of the specific medicine and to examine the harmonising possibilities between the two in order to set right the lost balance. She was very effective. I feel that this is the basic approach required of an astrologer as well. While examining the horoscope of an individual, the astrologer should attempt to find out the purpose and the basic reason for the disturbance in the life of the individual. The planetary radiation is a way of harmonising the disturbance : the individual disturbance and the cosmic harmony cannot exist together for long. They must, in order to maintain the balance in nature, get harmonised which is the goal of all planetary afflictions. There are many ways of harmonising the two. If the astrologer could extend his understanding of the supra-physical or the occult dimension of astrological forces, it is possible for him to link the present affliction with the past omissions and commissions of the individual and to suggest various steps whereby the afflictions can be remedied or minimised.

Every astrologer knows that all the planets have special radiations. Many of the afflictions are caused primarily by three planets namely, Saturn, Mars and Rahu. But before discussing their special radiations, it may be useful to expose one's personal experiences relevant to the topic to indicate how the astrological knowledge can be helpful if linked with common-sense and some other systems of tackling human problems. For example, let me mention here the case of an elderly lady with several children living in a middle class family in Tamil Nadu. For several years she had been suffering from pathological symptoms of high blood pressure but she was not reacting to any treatment. The doctors were perplexed : the misery increased, the malady remained uncontrolled, the family atmosphere became much depressed, and the disease remained elusive. On an examination of her chart, it appeared that she was running Rahu's main period, according to Vimshottri System of Direction, and the planet was afflicted by Mars and her Sun was weak. A general understanding of her chart and the family history showed that the lady was at cross-road ; her self-centredness had to be turned outwards so that she could begin to appreciate the reality of the spiritual world. Connected with Rahu, there are several stones and many rituals but I was not sure that all these would be effective. Selection of the most effective remedial measure. was difficult. Stones could help to some extent but it would have been unable to activise her mental body which required reorientation. As she belonged to an orthodox Brahmin family with many relations knowing the sacred texts of *mantras* and *japas* in which they were adepts, I casually suggested to her that she could consider having the Rahu *japam* done while she also regularly attended the Shiva Temple specially where the idol contained many black serpents carved around the idol. While this continued, she could continue the medical treatment without neglecting the same. Surprisingly, during the period when the pandits were performing the Rahu japam, the medicine started showing positive results and the doctors began getting clear symptoms of the disease for effective treatment of the malady. During the course of the *japam* and the improvement in her physical conditions, the lady showed increased interest in religious observances and her psychological conditions greatly improved This event subsequenty was quite effective in such a way that the disease did not recur in any great intensity or complexity for a very long time.

Much categorical inferences cannot be drawn from the above incident, but it does show that there is the possibility of radically reorienting the individual to the conditions surrounding himself. After all, it was felt in the above case that Rahu had the primary influence in making the individual dissatisfied with the existing physical (material) conditions which if administered with the celestial nectar (of spiritualism) may enable him (Rahu) to attain a state of permanence (eternity or harmonization). The vibrations of the *japam* and the involvement of the lady in the ritual and the attuning of herself to the serpent *naga* imperceptibly affected the aura and the response of the physical to the higher influences made the physical symptoms of the disease more specific which the doctors could easily treat. In this process of helping the patient, one had to approach the problem at first by determining the general nature of the personality pattern as shown by the natal chart, the specific forces affecting the person at the moment by calculating the directions, the orientation, that is the expectation by the occult forces, and the various alternatives by which the result could be achieved. As a result of such a combined integrated approach, the remedial methods of astrological afflictions can certainly be helpful.

As indicated earlier, there are three planets, namely Saturn, Mars and Rahu which are greatly dreaded for their afflictions. Much of the remedial methods are sought for them. As it is, Rahu makes the symptoms confused, the disease difficult to diagnose, and the individual is greatly depressed and self-centred. The most important task for an astrologer confronting such individuals is to arouse in him the desire to shake off the malady. In spite of all pretensions and vocal statements,

the individuals with Rahu's afflictions, to a great
extent, enjoy their malady because of the accentuation
of the identification of their psyche with the self.
In this psychological framework, the individual
moves in circles without any urge to move out.
But once the urge to get the nectar is aroused, and
he somehow contrives to approach the gods (devas), he
would get rid of the malady (of death and the temporal
existence) and attain the higher levels of existence of
deva-hood which would absolve him of his personal
concern and as such he would have no anxiety about his
own existence and welfare. One has to seek right aid
for such a transformation.

In the case of Mars, the conditions are very different.
This planet is full of activity. The individual under its
influence would be restless and anxious to be dynamic.
The affliction under Mars takes place because the various
sheaths of the human personality are not adequately
harmonised to one another. Thought, emotion and the
physical sheaths pull themselves in different directions.
As a result of such fulls in different directions, there
may be carelessness resulting in accidents, there may be
imbalances between emotion and the physical body
leading to physical disease and malfunctioning; similarly,
other disharmonies may lead to other afflictions. The
nature of these imbalances can be understood by the
planetary disposition and the astrologer will have to
find out the means for setting the incongruities right.
Sometimes wearing of a specific type of ring will enable
the emotions to calm down and to set the vibrations
around him right. The same result can even be achieved
in another case by right *japam*. The idea is to set right
the imbalance among the various sheaths of which Sri
Sankaracharya has spoken very elaborately in *Viveka*

Chudamani, which would calm down the individual and eliminate the affliction or reduce it greatly.

Saturn is one of the most difficult planets to tackle and also the most dreaded one. He creates a ring round the individual who under the influence of it feels stifled, caged, imprisoned and put to servitude. The ego in the individual is crushed. This being a very disturbing experience, which manifests in many ways by the planetary combinations expressing themselves at different periods of life, one feels greatly disheartened. No one can control Saturn for this planet is an aspect of Lord Shiva whose domain extends to the cremation ground where every physical constituent of the physical body is completely annihilated. Any malady arising as a result of Saturnine affliction will have the result of breaking the ego of the individual. This planet, like the Lord Shiva, is easily propitiated provided the right attempt is made. It is very simple : the individual has to surrender himself completely to the Almighty. This is easily said than done. There are various degrees of surrender and many methods for it depending upon the individual circumstances.

An interesting experiment in this regard may be mentioned here. The chart of an individual who was an engineer by profession and had earned much money showed an affliction of Saturn and Rahu. During the period when these planets had their main and sub-periods, the individual came under clouds and began to be persecuted for various kinds of financial irregularities. When the litigation started, he began to lose much money, social prestige, and peace of mind. In such a predicament, he did not have any trust in traditional pandits who usually performed *japam.* He felt that they would ask for much money without performing the right

14

performance of the right kind of *japam*. It was also felt
that stones would not have the right psycholagical impact
because he was an intellectual with whom one did not
wish to enter into theoretical discussions on the efficacy
of gem therapy ; the amount of money required for the
purchase of gem also would have meant a big sum for
him. So it was suggested to him that he should go to
a Shiva temple on Mondays and pour milk on the idol
having taken his morning bath and on an empty
stomach. Reluctantly he agreed to do the same because
he thought that one did not have any other interest in
him except of helping him. At that time, the strain of
litigation was also showing on him. So when he began
going to the temple; he began to feel relieved, and as he
began to surrender to God his psychology changed ; his
aura got gradually rearranged, and the personality began
to take a happier frame. The flow of the higher force
made him more harmonised. The influence of Saturn
began to change him. He became adjusted in his
limitations. Surprisingly, with such a change, he began
to get favourable results in court cases as well, and
other proceedings began to turn in his favour. While his
personality was becoming reoriented to a new way of
life linking him to cosmic forces in a more harmonious
manner, the results of the various complaints against
him began to manifest in his favour. There is no way
known to us so far to establish any causal relationship
between the two, but it appears that the Saturn–Rahu
radiation aimed at making the gentleman recognise the
Supreme Divine Power which he had so far resisted due
to his intellect. Once his intellect gave way, the result
of these planets began to express in their supra-physical
dimensions making him a more composed and happier
individual.

There are many examples of Jupiter, Venus, and Mercury causing inconvenient conditions from which the individual often desires relief. Gems have often been prescribed for these planets. The Sun and the Moon are also often propitiated and gems connected with them recommended for the redressal of their malefic influences. While recommending the gems, it is often observed that there are several orthodox astrologers who blindly adhere to the traditional rules of prescription. Undoubtedly, they are effective as far as they go but many a time side effects are also noticed. For example, once a person with afflicted sixth and the seventh houses was greatly perturbed about his professional matters. An astrologer suggested him to wear a stone which did help him in destroying the evil effects of his enemies and he was quite satisfied about it. Shortly later on, he came to inform of this result but he casually mentioned that his wife's eye-sight was getting seriously impaired and he was contemplating a trip abroad to get it set right. On enquiry it appeared that the elimination of the hostile professional influences and the intensification of the wife's eye trouble both occurred at the same time. It was suggested to him that he might remove the ring with the stone for the time being to watch the effect. It was found that the removal of the ring made the professional atmosphere slightly worse off but there was an improvement in the eye ailment of the wife. As the official situation by that time had already greatly improved, he preferred to keep away the ring and to continue with the local medical treatment. His wife reacted very favourably to the treatment by this time. From this, one could conclude that the stone which destroyed the professional hostile influences also adversely affected the wife's eyes. The astrologer who had prescribed the gem had overlooked the influence of the stone on the Seventh House which should have enabled him to warn the native of its possible consequences on wife's health.

In another case connected with Moon, some uncommon results were observed. This happened in the case of a female with weak Moon. During a particular phase of her life, she was passing through much mental agony and disturbance. The astrologer advised her to wear a Moon-stone, which greatly relieved her of the mental symptoms. But as her Moon was connected with the Twelfth House, the Moon-stone affected her monetary outflow and she began to experience considerable increase in expenditure. As she was not short of money, she did not get upset by it but it clearly showed it to be a significant instance of the simultaneous effect of a stone in several ways and at several levels.

These examples would show that there are many more dimensions of astrology than we ordinarily recognise. Nature has imbued occult powers in the entire manifest world in several ways. When sorrow and troubles arise, Nature has several remedies to counterbalance the same. If the process is unhappy and inconvenient, one can select the remedial measures very carefully so that natural harmony, both externally as well as internally, is achieved. It can be done by introducing additional occult force to the state of his existence. There are many alternatives in this regard. Careful selection of the method suited to the occasion is the essence of astrological remedial measures.

TRANSMUTING SORROW INTO KNOWLEDGE

Patanjali in his treatise on Yoga laid down rules for attaining the pristine state of one's awareness which he called *Kaivalyam*. During the period when the Divine spark gets immersed in modifications of different sorts, the man is afflicted by *Klesha*, which freely translated means trouble. Patanjali stated the nature of this affliction or the cause of all miseries in life rooted in *avidya*, the lack of awareness of reality, *asmita*, the sense of egotism, or I-am-ness, *raga-dwesha*, attractions and repulsions towards objects, and *abhinivesha*, the strong desire for life. If one analysed these causes deeply, one would find that penury, ill-health, absence of any satisfactory profession, denial of progeny, humiliation and such other troubles in life about which an ordinary man is much concerned are not the real causes of sorrow. The different circumstances through which the individual passes depending upon his *samsakara*, the innate tendencies, are caused by *klesha*. Cosmic forces impinge upon the individual to direct his future course of events and actions. Those who could appreciate this fact would acknowledge that the interaction is caused by incoming cosmic forces and the inherent karma of the individual which is related to *klesha*. As these cosmic forces are beneficient in their true nature, they present those conditions whereby the individual can modify his *samsakara* and change the course of one's life. In this general scheme of one's evolution, astrology is capable of directing the efforts of the individual in a helpful manner in which process he becomes strong enough to counteract any misfortune that could come in his way.

In astrology, different methods of counteracting the malefic influences of the planets are given. Mantra, pooja, *graha-shanti*, and several other methods have been indicated to propitiate the planet. Gems, *kawacha*, tantra, and other methods of this kind have been indicated to ward off the malefic influences. Astrologers also suggest other *upakramas* or methods such as pouring water on Lord Shiva's Linga Sharira, or getting released a long black serpent, or dedicating flags on specified temples and such other methods. It has been found empirically that these prescriptions for warding off the afflictions do have their effect. Many astrologers have related warding off of various kinds of affliction with the reading of different portions of certain scriptures but this could be included in the category of pooja. When these methods have shown their efficacy, one cannot deny that there is some validity in these relationships. They all show that the cosmic forces differentiated in nature under the influence of different planets are not rigid. They represent certain forces whose nature is explained by different astrological rules. Gravitation is a fact in nature. The law of gravitation only describes a condition. One who wants to manipulate this force according to his requirements may take measures accordingly. The result of the manipulation would be directly related to his knowledge of the law and the potency of his measures undertaken. Similarly in astrology, the steps taken to ward off the afflictions of the planetary forces would depend upon the knowledge of these forces and adoption of measures to counteract the affliction. As these are very difficult subjects to master, it is necessary to take assistance of knowledgeable astrologers in this regard.

Apart from the various methods suggested above for propitiating the afflicting planets, there is another method in line with what Patanjali had assumed. The afflictions are caused by certain forces impinging on the inherent nature of the man. In case he could comprehend the direction in which the psychological modifications or the transmutations are needed to absorb the full benefic effect of the planet, a new vista of experiences could open to the individual. In this context, it is however, necessary to understand that sorrow is not a physical phenomenon. It is primarily psychological. The immediate cause for it may be physical, as for example, the loss of one's limb, death of one's only son or some such misfortune, but the physical cause makes an impact on the psyche of the individual which arouses various reactions. These reactions are the result of one's *samskara* and following the incident this samskara is further modified. The resultant modification in the individual's samskara is what the planetary deities look for. They know that the individual at a particular stage of his evolution is liable to react in a particular manner so that the karma for him is arranged in such a manner that a particular event takes place at a particular time. So the person has the affliction ...... his reaction and consequent modification in his psyche. The special contribution of astrology lies in indicating this modified state of consciousness which the planetary deity wants for the particular individual. By a comprehension of this ultimate result, in case the individual is able to attune himself to the expected modification, that is, if he has transmuted his basic attitude to life in the expected direction, there is every likelihood that the impending misfortune itself would vanish. In case the misfortune however, occurs at all, that may be to work out certain past karmic debts, and its impact would not be so sorrowful.

Let us for example see the impact of a few planets in order to get the principle clear. The Sun is the most powerful planet. It is a planet which requires the greatest care in its propitiation. It is not considered a benefic in the ordinary sense of the term. When the Sun does a thing, or creates any specific impact, very little can deflect its powerful influence. But all the influences of the Sun enable the individual to move towards the real essence of the life-force. Patanjali has mentioned *abhinivesha*, as mentioned earlier, a cause of *klesha*, and the effect of the Sun is very intimately linked with this *abhinivesha*, the clinging to life. Under favourable confluence, the Sun will open out the inherent real essence of the person, his latent supreme qualities. But in case the conditions are not so favourable, the afflictions of the Sun will churn the life of the individual so much that the inner core of his being is ruffled. The individual suffers severe sorrow after which he is less attached to the material aspects of life. He clings less to life. It has been mentioned that the Sun under certain given conditions gives peevish temperament, on another occasion hatred of relations, on third set of conditions there could be late marriage, troubled marriage, hatred by the fair sex, wive's character questionable and so on. The most powerful planet, the Sun, which is said to be the representative of the Supreme on this globe, cannot radiate any influence which is truly unhappy for the individual.   Therefore, one should consider the solar radiation which is felt unfortunate as the guideline for transforming the individual in such a way that he realises the futility of this life. When one would learn the lesson of not to cling to material and physical life, the afflictions of the Sun could be an exhilarating influence showing the path of one's true evolution.

Let us take another example.   The affliction of Saturn is said to be very intense. The intensity of sorrow aroused by this planet is next to none. Every one is greatly apprehensive of the malefic influence of Saturn and they try all sorts of methods to propitiate this planet. It is supposed to be a representative of Yama, the Lord of Death. Before it, every achievement of mankind is turned into dust. Every astrologer can tell the various sufferings signified by the adverse situation of this Saturn. The point for consideration in this connection is the transmuting result achieved by propitiating this planet. Complete surrender to this planetary regent would imply a complete annihilation of one's egotism. The sense of I-am-ness must be thoroughly eschewed. Only in the state of utter helplessness the affliction of Saturn is over. This psychological transformation could arise as a result of serious deprivation in one's life, significant death of one's relation, or it can be any calamity depending upon the position of Saturn in the horoscope. But the truth is that the slightest affliction of Saturn would leave a deep scar on the psyche of the person. In case this transmutation could take place by wearing a horse-shoe-nail ring, or by performing pooja for the planet with a sense of awe and fear, the result is achieved. When Patanjali spoke of *klesha* rooted in egotism and I-am-ness, he was referring to one type of human affliction which took the mankind away from his ultimate goal of pure realisation of Truth. Saturn gives this realisation by demolishing everything which is not permanent and not True in the ultimate analysis. By changing the direction of one's desire and aspiration in life, the afflictions of Saturn would not create unhappiness to the individual. Those who are afflicted by Saturn could get the necessary transmutation by devoting themselves to deeper philosophy of life and by trying to make that philosophy a part of their everyday living.

Rahu is another dreaded planet. Its nature is said to be like that of Saturn. Still there is a fundamental difference between the two. One is a planet, a concrete manifestation, whilst the other is merely a shadow, a point, a node. This difference is very vital. Saturn creates a situation with some action point in it. The situation caused by Saturn is due to some action, may be related to the past, may be just a peg around which certain changes take place. Under Rahu, it is not an action that creates the situation but the law iteslf. It is like limitations imposed on the individual. When a person is put in prison, it is not the food, work, or the fellows who create the unhappiness, but the very fact that someone is in prison makes his life miserable. The same is true of Rahu. It puts the karmic ring around the person beyond which he cannot hope to move out. This karmic bond is expressed in many different ways. It is said by Kalidasa that under the influence of adverse Rahu, the person will be liable to danger from reptiles, poison, disease and trouble all over the body ; there would be danger from missiles and fire, and enmity with the mean, fall from a tree and torments from enemies. These effects of adverse Rahu could create much sorrow and unhappiness in the life of a person. These are some of the difficulties over which the individual may not have any control. But, in case, realising the inevitableness of such occurrences, if the individual begins pondering over the karmic roots of these misfortunes, there is also a possibility of undoing some of these unhappy events. For it has been said that criticism brings worry, unhelpfulness creates unhappy physical surroundings and so on. Such suggestions are ample in Jataka stories as well as in many other scriptures. By trying to relate these correspondences, the individual may get deeper knowledge of the law of karma. In case Rahu is adverse, and one preoccupies himself in understanding the nature of the downtrodden, in case he voluntarily begins to assume unpalatable responsibilities, if malignant diseases become his subject of enquiry with which others are suffering, there would be a situation when the individual would acquire the sacred knowledge; and there is also the likelihood of his getting some material reward. In fact, one has to learn the consequences of the exalted planet and the purpose for arousing of those causes which lead to any specific effect. This could be done by reversing the action of the adverse planet by preoccupying oneself with those conditions which are caused by the adverse planet. In doing so, he should consider the effects of the adverse planet as the media through which the image of the effect of the exalted planet could be created.

An example of this kind of transmutation can be given in the present context by citing the example of Sakata Yoga. This yoga is caused by the Moon in the Twelfth, Sixth, or Eighth from Jupiter. The effect of this yoga is stated to be : The native loses fortune and may regain it. He will be ordinary and insignificant. He will suffer poverty, privation, and misery. He will be stubborn and hated by relatives. In this yoga, it is important to note that the same is caused by the Moon which is the *karaka* or the causative planet of mind, psychology, peace and tranquility, and Jupiter who is connected with affluence, expansion, benediction, and philanthropy. By the placement of Jupiter in the Sixth position, the planet of affluence would itself be restricted ; secondly, it would also restrict the expansion of mind, disturb the tranquillity of the mind. Similarly, when the Moon is Sixth from Jupiter, the philanthropic and happy conditions ordinarily available to the individual may be put to difficulties by the attitude of the mind. One could work out the various implications of these positions to see the powerful effect of this combination in causing misfortune.

There have been many powerful personalities suffering from this affliction. Take for example, the horoscope of Pandit Jawaharlal Nehru. Though there is some cancellation of Sakata Yoga because of the Moon being in the Ascendant, yet the Sixth–Eighth relationship between the Moon and Jupiter would necessarily leave its scar. Panditji had his ups and downs in life. His personal bank balance, as his will showed, was not worthy of envy. But what he himself did was not to work for himself but for others. The Sixth and the Eigth Houses being also the houses of *sakti* (power), and *kundalini* (serpent fire), by his efforts in turning himself towards others, these limitations became the source of his power and strength. He went to prison, he lost his wealth, he could not develop his professional expertise, but all these endeared him to the teeming millions.

Another example of Sakata Yoga is present in the horoscope of late Y. Keshava Menon, whose recorded predictions of the martyrdom of Gandhi and Mujib are known world over. Menon had also suffered in life. For his political activities even in foreign countries he had been put to prison and had even to undergo humiliation of externment. His personal health had not been very satisfactory, but he had the ability of directing his mental power to higher realms as expressed by his philosophical writings and contacts, by his astrological erudition, by his political involvements. His Sakata Yoga had not made him an unhappy man, but he had started taking delight in those activities where the personal limitations had given him the great power for doing good to others. In this way, one could find the way out through every limitation and affliction and in this escape he could turn his misfortune into a joyous event.

In the present context, one would like to quote Dr. B. V. Raman in his rendering of the horoscope of his famous grand father Professor B. Suryanarain Rao, when he mentioned that the Moon in the horoscope was with Rahu aspected by Mars as a result of which he suffered from mental worry. But, Dr. Raman mentions, that ''it enabled him to cultivate that strength of the mind and spirit of optimism which stood him in good stead at the most critical times of his life''. This shows that hidden in many of the afflictions, there are indications which if rightly understood could take the sting out of it. Each one of us, even ordinary human being have our personal problems which have planetary causes but these planets are not interested in causing pain to us in but bringing about certain changes in the psychological structure of our being and if that transmutation could be deliberately adopted, the sting of sorrow could be greatly minimised.

AID TO SELF REALISATION

Those who have studied the Vedas would at least agree that it is a very mystic work. The hymns of this work were not intended merely as laudations for the natural deities or supplications for the grant of petty, material gifts of personal advancement. Within the veil of invocations to various nature spirits and mythological gods, the ancient seers have given clues on the understanding of which the man may attain the highest that is possible for him. The diverse approaches to the Vedas could be well realised if one studied the hymns relating to Soma and interpreted them in terms of astrological aphorisms. Many a time, the inner meanings of the astrological Moon are better understood with the help of these hymns. Similarly, when the *Atharvins* invoked the various *nakshatras* for the grant of various human gifts and welfare of their society, they were revealing one of the hidden cosmological principles concealed in these highly electro-magnetic force-centres which discharge highly powerful energies which when properly harnessed could be of immense aid to the human society. The Hindu philosophy, *Karma Kanda* or "the presciptions as how to live in this world", astrology, yoga, the science concerning physical health, emotion and intellect or the *Ayurveda*, and several such other branches of Hindu learning were all intimately connected with the primary objective of understanding the true significance of life and the role of individual in this scheme of natural evolution.

In search for happiness and in the effort to thwart the occurrences of unhappy events, one consciously or unconsciously looks to the real source of energy and benediction. Gradually this urge is converted into the ray of devotion and one begins to cooperate with Spirit. In course of time when devotion matures and the individual begins to get a glimpse of the Divine realities, his mental power develops. His intellect strengthens. But, a time comes when another dimension of life opens. He realises that the intellect is of limited use. The usual devotional practices do not satisfy him. On that lonely night when intellect has failed him, and the old devlotional outbursts do not give him solace, he feels lost and after all bafflements there dawns a faint star of inspiration. Such experiences are valid only for opening the greater portals of spiritual understanding. When the soul becomes stronger and it begins to realise the significance of the night and the day, the Moon and the Sun, he begins his spiritual journey. On this path, there is no personal sorrow, no personal happiness. Only the pilgrim on the path knows the ordeals of the journey. By the time he reaches this stage, like Tennyson, he almost repeats the words

.......all experience is an arch wherethro'
Gleams that untravelled world, whose margin fades
for ever and for ever when I move.......

The role of astrology in revealing the immeasurable extension of human personality is considerable. There are many dimensions of the human-being and astrology, which if properly understood, unveil many hidden corners of life. The ascendant on whose strength and nature depends the life's main course—if the ascendant is strong, the individual is expected to weather all the misfortunes of life, even if other planets require him to undergo those troubles. The planets might bestow a period of ease, comfort, luxury and affluence, but the ascendant's spiritualism and ascetic nature would enable him to maintain equipoise and serenity. The ascendant's strength also determines whether the injury-inflicting planets are able to destroy the personality. Whether the person would die at any age would be related to the condition of the ascendant. The life of the person is considerably dependent upon the quality and strength of his ascendant ; the other planetary influences can only be subsidiary to this main factor. This is so because the ascendant describes the nature of the personality of the individual. When an ego takes its birth, a period of life-span is given to it and it is also assigned a period of activities during which time it has to learn various lessons. Approached from this standpoint, it is necessary to examine the ascendant and its interrelationship with other houses and planets in a different manner. The fact that the astrological aphorisms assist the astrologer in predicting the future course of events is not so significant in the context as the causes which necessitate such events to be thrown in the life-flow of a person. Supposing someone is distined to face the death of his only son when the child attains maturity, this event is vitally significant for the individual concerned, and the contribution of astrology in forecasting such an eventuality may be helpful in many ways and in preparing the individual to face the misfortune. But the cause for such a misfortune is left out of the scope of astrological predictions. Astrology underlines the inevitability of certain events depending upon karmic forces, and the possibility of certain events which

by proper precautions could be avoided, but the fundamental question that has to be answered in the present
context is the why of these events. Here the science of
astrology has to be related to religion and other occult
sciences. If the individual is having the predominance
of *Rajasic* (activity connected) attributes, the events will
strike him differently from what they could be if he were
the *Tamasic* (inertia-type) or *Sattwic* (harmony-type).
The decision of the type of the personality is easier than
the working of the significance of the pattern of events.

The second question in the present context is to
find out the maturity or otherwise of the ego. At the
early phase of the journey of the soul, the events are
presented in order to teach it certain lessons. The
events occur either to show the different facets of life or
to deflect his reactions in a particular direction. When
an event of sorrowful nature takes place at the early
phase of the soul's growth, it is to make him understand
that sorrow is a fact of life. A primitive man is not
touched by the death of his only son whereas a man who
has developed sensitivity and is emotional would find
this experience very painful. A primitive man on the
other hand would find the flesh of his beloved wife
tastier than that of other beings ! This shows that the
events have a relationship with the stage of the growth
of the soul.

When the soul's journey has advanced and the ego
is nearing the goal of perfection, these events have a
different purpose. For example, the abduction of Rama's
wife, cancer of the throat for Rama Krishna, denial of
love-life to Mira and crucifixion of the Christ or the
starvation of Gautama Buddha could not be considered
ordinary events in their lives. At the same time, accepting the fact that nothing happens in life without any

cause requires one to approach these problems differently. The fact that the incarnations of gods also take place according to some law of nature which does not transcend the planetary influences, requires one to understand the significant facts in the life-history of advanced souls differently.

One fundamental consideration in such lives is that karma in their cases works out differently. Such events are not causative, rather they are balancing. What the *Jataka* stories reveal in relation to the Lord Buddha is very significant. These events are the results of the past actions done and not done. They have caused the forces which will have to be borne by the individual to counterbalance the disturbances caused by thoughtless acts. At an advanced stage, when the soul is able to make use of those disturbances in a purposeful manner, these karmic forces are presented so that the soul could react favourably and effectively. Thus, the purpose of many events in the life-story of evolved persons is to enable them to clear their past debts while giving them opportunities to make use of these so-called troubles to some better use. If the maturity of the soul could be assessed and the direction of its life determined it could be possible to find out whether the event is causative or counterbalancing, and in the latter case, the individual has to make use of these factors for the beneficient purpose in aid of nature.

When the maturity of the soul is to be assessed, one has to confront several difficulties. It is not always easy to succeed in such an evaluation. Before we come to this vital question of soul's maturity, there are many other problems concerning the personality of the ego which are important for a more useful life in the given incarnation. In this regard, it is necessary to distinguish between soul and ego or personality. When we talk of soul, we always think of the permanent portion of our being, whilst the latter is always the transitory dimension of the same. For this reason, the latter is said to be that portion of the being which takes birth and which dies. It is said that the physical body, the emotional sheath and the mental sheath all in due course after the physical death of the person dissipate one after another and there remains a portion of the essence of various experiences gained during the life-span. The essence is the element which, later on, in a subsequent incarnation, affects the *samsakaras*, the inborn tendencies, of the incarnating ego. Finally, this essence enables clearer perception of one's true nature. The perception of one's evolving essence gives a greater freedom to the soul and therefore though nothing is added to soul yet the quality of self awareness achieved during the course of several incarnations is said to be responsible for the evolution of the soul.

The quality of life that the individual expresses during a life-period does not depend upon the *years* of his existence but upon the *intensity* of his experiences. How active he is in life is very important, but this activity is not only that of physical existence. This intensity is connected with the quantity of the vital energy that is distributed throughout the network of his living relations. In this connection, the disposition of Mars is extremely important. The Sun is not so much significant as Mars. The Sun is said to be the Soul of the Universe ; it is also said to be the soul of the *Kala Purusha* or the Heavenly Man. But the importance of the Sun is there because it *is* the Soul, the direction to which all efforts are leading, it is the central force which is directing all activities. But Mars is the vitality, *Prana* which would enable the ego to express itself with greater or feebler intensity. When the ambition of the person has been aroused, it is necessary to see whether the individual has the necessary energy latent in him which could give him the necessary impetus to work for it.

In order to find out the intensity of eternal man's efforts, or the purpose of the soul's efforts in giving itself the chance of having a physical body, it is necessary to know as to the why of the ambition of a person.

To find out the possibility of succeeding in any of our ambitious projects, it is necessary to know whether the ambition is related to the spirituality of the ego, that is, whether the soul considers the ambition necessary and helpful for its Eternal Being. Or, whether the ambition is helpful for the spiritual growth of the person. If it is so, there would be greater possibility of soul adding its own force to the achievement of the same. The relationship between the ninth and the tenth houses is important for such an examination.

It is also important to find out whether the individual has the required creative urge in him. One may have the desired amount of vital energy for completing the act, he may get the necessary support from his past deeds, and the present incarnation may have well defined work target for the ego, yet if the desired level of creative urge is not there, all these would be futile. The life of the person for that birth could be considered, in all probility, a waste. That explains the classical works insisting on the relationship between the quadrants and the trines, specially the relationship between the trines and the tenth house to be auspicious for such an achievement.

There is another dimension of this problem which also should be mentioned in the present context. Apart from the physical life which we have so far been dealing there is the *chit* or the consciousness aspect of the being. The English translation of the Sanskrit word *chit* as mind is very inadequate. There is a being or the portion of the being which comprises all the psychological, psychic, and spiritual content of its existence; it is related intimately with the eternal essence of the being but it is also the transitory portion of its existence. It is the Moon which signifies all these aspects of his life. Whenever the individual desires to know the invisible countetpart of his life, he can examine the disposition of the Moon in depth and some new dimension of the person could thus be revealed. For this very reason. the Moon is considered one of the most mystical planets. The mythological origin of the Moon is related with the sage Atri who was himself born from the ears of Brahma or with the churning of the ocean. Those sages who were given birth initially by Brahma were given special assignments for arousing those forces which could enable the birth, growth and evolution of the cosmos and the human beings. As such, the Moon was a great creative energy. But he, the Moon, was the child of the sage who was born from the ear of the Highest Creative Energy. Ears are the organs through which one could hear and the act of hearing implied being in tune with the cosmic order. The invisibility of this sympathetic relationship between the cosmic order and the capabilities of the individual is truly reflected in the nature of the Moon.

Moon is said to moves on a chariot which has three wheels and is drawn by ten horses five of which turn in one direction and the other five in another. In interpreting the function of this luminary in one's daily life, this symbology is very enlightening. The three wheels of the chariot represent the three basic *gunas,* the primordial attributes, namely, the *sattwa* (harmony), *rajas* (activity) and *tamas* (inertia) ; the psyche of the individual is concerned with these three aspects of the being. The psychological or the spiritual motivations of action come from one of these attributes or from a combination of these. The ten horses are the ten organs of action and understanding. The different sheaths of the individual are directed by the different organs of the person. As long as these horses are the masters, there is no central direction in the spirit-dimension of the individual. But when the *Chit—Buddhi* or the Mind —with all its complex relationships begins to take control of the movement and reactions of the various organs, there is the central direction and greater coherance in the life of the person. A clear Moon well aspected by Jupiter, in harmonious relationship with benefics, would indicate that the Spirit-Life of the person is clearer, purer, and well directed towards the goal set out by the Soul. On the other hand, if it is seriously afflicted, the conclusions have to be drawn differently. The disposition of the Moon in this way reveals the real spiritual nature of the person which can in many cases be camouflaged by artificial culture, social good behaviour and hypocrisy.

The discovery of the status of the Soul is very important but extremely difficult. A proper understanding of the nature of the Soul working in one's life depends on an understanding of the basic human principles, that is, how the divine forces work through the several sheaths of the Eternal Man. This knowledge has to be related to the planets and their innermost nature. The in-depth examination of the Sun does not only indicate the level to which the Soul has sunk, but it also reveals what could be done to salvage it and to reinstate it in its proper place. That is the problem of yoga. Astrological aid to yoga discipline is the most fascinating topic but in pursuing that topic we shall be transgressing our present limit. Here we shall only state that the disposition of the Sun is extremely significant because like the Soul to the Man, this luminary gives the central direction to the life and it also functions like the pivot around which the entire life of the individual rotates. The Sun is the Eternal fulcrum till the man has merged himself in his Eternal Being.

One may like to know whether an individual is still deeply interested in his earthly attachments ; or his faculties are properly directed towards the pursuit of spiritual subjects, or his efforts could be directing all the energy at his command to things which are of value only for a life. One can enquire into these questions on the basis of Mercury, the messenger between the heaven and the world. Mercury reveals the quality of the mind one possesses. Mercury has the singular attribute of going heaven-ward as well as earthward. It is a link between the earth and the heaven. On this two way traffic some persons go upward, some go downward. The neutrality of Mercury has been expressed in many ways. It is said that Mercury is an eunuch. In association with positive male electro-magnetic radiation, it behaves like a male, while in company with negative female radiation, it functions like the female. On occult considerations, it implies that Mercury could assist in spiritual direction, help the mind to soar high in the realm of nymphs, fairies, gods and goddesses ; arouse deeper urges for occult knowledge. But if Mercury is entrenched in *tamasic* proclivities that is, with darkening or the intertia giving planets, it would pull the mind of the concerned person towards earthly things. Thus, Mercury which is concerned with economics, commerce, business, trade and trading associations, mercantile activities, sexual intercourse and enjoyments, and dancing which are indicators of its involvement with materiality, is also said to be related to mathematics, astrology, pilgrimage to holy places, temples, Vedantic philosophy, renunciation, devotion, worship of Vishnu, and spells of high order which show the spirituality latent in the planet. From these opposite attributes, it may be inferred that the persons whose mind is attracted towards outgoing subjects which are in tune with the Path of *Pravritti*, that is, the path of material involvement, would not be interested in spiritual subjects and in the enquiry leading to self-realisation. Those who have the pull from such subjects which are related to spiritual unfoldment would under the favourable disposition of this planet, would revolve round spirituality and the individual under the influence of Mercury would become greatly interested in spiritual subjects.

There are two other subjects in the present context which one may like to touch in passing. The first is related to the storm and stress that come in the life of the aspirant when he feels extremely baffled. On such occasions, he begins to think that the path of spirituality whose ultimate goal is Self-Realization is an illusion and not worth trying. These are the moments of trial. By knowing beforehand that such storms are likely to confront the aspirant, it is possible for him to have a clearer idea of the battle likely to take place in his psyche. When he knows that the churning of the ocean, the struggle between the good and the evil, is not something external but a part of the person's inner life, he becomes aware of another aspect of his Real Self.

Such events are related to Rahu and Ketu, the ascending and the descending nodes of the Moon. An examination of the disposition of these planets would indicate the period and the direction from which the attack on the spirituality of the person could be made. The churning of the ocean under the spell of Rahu could be so severe that the whole life of the person could be dissolved under its impact. But the process of Self Realization itself is a process of gradual unfoldment of the latent faculties and greater understanding of the occult truths. An objective approach to this unfoldment lays the foundation of true understanding of the Self, the Cosmos, and the relationship between the two.

The second is related to the final goal of the understanding in which regard the astrology has a very special contribution to make. It makes the aspirant perceive that the Eternal Man, the Absolute All, is always breathing through the mortal coil of the individual. This metaphysical philosophy, which even the great saints and sages find difficult of comprehend, could be easily demonstrated by the astrologers. The concept of the Heavenly Man, the *Kala Purusha*, which is one of the basic postulates of Hindu astrology, relates the different aspects of the individual's life with this Heavenly Man whose different urges are considered linked with different planets. On the basis of this relationship, one knows that the temporal individual is merely the tip of the iceberg submerged under the water level of the *Kala Purusha*. The cosmos is merely an expression of the individual and the individual is another aspect of the cosmos. This understanding of the true nature of the human being becomes realistic by analysing the natal chart of the person and relating it to the Cosmic Man, the Heavenly Man, the *Kala Purusha* which are the various names attributed to this Universal Self. What the Vedantists mean by the aphorism "I am God", is the same thing which is comprehended by the relationship between *Kala Purusha* and the mortal man with a life-span of only a few decades. The relationship between the individual and the Cosmic Energy known as the Universal Self is the essence of Self Realization which is more easily understood with the help of astrological principles than with the help of other austere practices.

WHICH YOGA WILL SUIT YOU?

In ancient times, the highly evolved spiritual sages were much concerned with essentials of the life-process —the origin of life, its growth, the ultimate goal and inner depths of phenomenal existence. In order to arrive at the basic truth, they did penance and got enlightenment. Born out of such spiritual *tapas*, penance, esoteric knowledge of things that matter was gained which they gave out to the masses in fragments so that the people could lead a life of righteousness and be happy. The sages were not interested so much in mundane achievements and prosperity of human individuals as much as in their spiritual growth and unfoldment. At the root of all living religions which at differnt stages of human history assisted the development of human individuals, *yoga*, meditation and astrology have been important. These three subjects have been dealt with under different names and methods having different approaches. But the strength and nourishment of all living religions are based on their basic approaches to the discovery of life-process to which these three subjects are intimately related.

While counselling human individuals on their personal problems astrologically, meditation and yoga are often overlooked as a result of which the proper place of astrology is not integrated to the inner life of the individual. Many devout Muslims, Christians and a few other religionists who would not readily accept the validity of reincarnation or of the hierarchy of Divine Beings assisting and supporting the evolutionary process of nature would readily believe in astrological predictions and even vouch their truth. They would look to astrology for guidance but in many cases even deny the existence of angellic hosts. An objective and careful understanding of the relationship between the various dimensions of astrology and deeper aspects of life and religions even paves a rightful bridge between different religions. Astrology, on the very face of it, is religious in outlook and essentially spiritual in character.

In fact, a proper study of astrology requires deeper study of yoga of which meditation is an important practical dimension. The effect of gems, *mantras*, offerings and such other palliatives for the planetary inflictions if rightly comprehended would suggest that yoga is the only way for true cooperation with nature and a surer guide for one's happiness.

For true happiness, three things are necessary. There must be the knowledge of one's own self. It includes the knowledge about the constitution of one self, the forces linking him to its past and the goal of its future course of life. In short, a comprehensive knowledge of oneself. Secondly, there must be the knowledge of the external phenomena ; how they begin; what constitute them ; how they grow ; the invisible dimensions of the external plane of existence ; the role of planetary and Divine Hierarchy, and the rest of these. In the *Bhagavadgita*, mention has been made of the Field and the Knower of the Field. This refers to these aspects of the life-process. The third essential requirement for living a fruitful life is to know the mechanism for mobilising the external forces, the forces operating on the Field, for the benefit of the Knower of the Field, the human individual.

It may be observed that meditation is the process given for the understanding of these essential require- ments of happiness. Meditation is essentially a way to understand Reality. Sri Sankaracharya called this phenomenal world an illusion, *Maya*, but to us, to be candid, it seems that this phenomenal world is the only reality and the other descriptions given of other realms are illusory. During the course of evolution, one is led from illusion to Reality. The psychological transfor- mation that takes place during the course of one's evolution is in fact the result of conscious or unconscious meditation. Done rightly and under sensible guide, meditation could be helpful in enlightening the intricacies of life. Here emphasis is not on the act of meditation, which could merely be translated as deep contemplation, but on the right method of meditation, the goal, the direction and the effect anticipated of it. This practice is like sharpening the tool for effective action. Unless the purpose for which this tool is used is clearly comprehended, the act of sharpening the tool may be useless, and in some cases even dangerous.

The direction, or the purpose of meditation is indicated by yoga. This word has been very little understood and much abused. Even the physical exercises for better health maintenance are called yoga ; the object of sexual gratification is also linked by many with this subject; attainment of various *siddhis i.e.*, capacities for doing miracles by controlling the finer forces of nature, is generally considered an important aspect of yoga. Unless the different kinds of confusion are eliminated and the concept clearly understood, it would be futile to discuss the relationship between astrology and yoga, which implies the relationship between the planetary influences and the fulfilment of the purpose of one's life.

In essence, yoga is the process by which individualization of the human individual which has enabled him to function in his self, in his separated consciousness, is assimilated in the Universal consciousness. It is the process by which the sense of saparateness is completely eliminated. This goal has been stated as the identity between the Universal and the particular self. It is said to be the process by which *Jiva*, the reincarnating self, becomes Realised Soul, or the Self, and finally becomes one with the Universal Self. It is the process by which *Atma* becomes *Paramatma* ; it is the process by which *Jiva* ultimately realises its own nature as *Para-Brahma*. In simpler language, it is stated to be the way whereby the drop merges in the ocean. The Hindus call it the stage of *Moksha,* the Buddhists understand it by the term *Nirvana*, and the common man calls it Liberation. It is not the term which is important in the present context, rather it is the act of elimination of personal self which is important. In Nirvana, which is the Buddhist conception of the ultimate goal, there is no trace of the individual flame, though the essence of all the experiences gained by the individual is present there. The Ultimate state of the being said to have attained *Samadhi,* or the deep contemplation, is not a state which can be described in words, nor is it a level of existence which can be demonstrated to others. It is an experience which is unique.

The knowledge of the self can be comprehended only when the nature of the individual is crystalline ; when it is capable of reflecting the true nature of consciousness, when the dross does not contaminate the receiving instrument. Purification of the Self is therefore essential before the individual can comprehend the true nature of his being. It is said that only Brahman within can know Brahman without. It is only when one has in himself, in his body, the same which is outside him that he can know the true relationship between the individual and the Universal. Removal of the veil, or the impediments is a process which takes lives. True meditation can be the process which takes lives. True meditation is a means for the understanding of these veils and the impediments ; in the exercise of the yogic practices, they are eliminated. Patanjali is therefore very explicit in stating that the cessation of the medifications of the consciousness is the ultimate goal of yoga for which eight preparatory practices are essential. While explaining these eight steps for meaningful meditation, he has also mentioned that the individuals would achieve perfections at the various levels of consciousness during these practices which would give them what is popularly known as *Siddhi*, the attainment of special powers. In meditation, it is comprehension rather than psychic power that is aimed at. The integration of yoga and meditation in this way is understandable.

The relationship between astrology and yoga does not seem obvious to those who are only interested in the exoteric aspect of the subject. The ancient sages were concerned with Ultimate Reality, still they have given us astrology which indicates to us the significance and possibility of material prosperity as well as of sorrow in achieving the final goal of life. There seems to be some contradiction in this approach. To study astrology in order to discover the intricate details of one's being which reflect the soul's growth through reincarnations, and to know the various karmic forces aroused in the process which have to be resolved into white or neutral potential before the Ultimate Reality is comprehended is the right approach. In the everyday course of life, the individuals are likely to think of themselves differently from what they actually are. One's hopes, ambitions, aspirations and many other desires and emotions intervene to distort the true image of the person. One of the greatest difficulties of the Divine Teacher is to make the disciple see himself as he is. Different kinds of psychological training are imparted in Mystery Schools so that the individual could see himself as in a mirror reflecting his seven-fold personality without any distortion. A knowledge of astrology is helpful in short-circuiting this process. A proper understanding of astrology reflects the true personality of the individual in his eternal aspect,

Scriptures have emphasized the seven-fold nature of man. Even Sankaracharya has described the various extensions of human personality. Before the individual could raise his consciousness to the great heights of seedless state of pure awareness, his consciousness must flow smoothly through the seven-fold levels of his existence. It must travel backward and forward without any impediment. The physical personality is the one with which most of us are familiar ; other dimensions of our personality are etheric, astral, lower or concrete mind-stuff, higher or abstract mind-stuff, intuitional or Buddhic sheath and Atmic or Universal vesture. These terms as used here are not universal but have been explained differently in different religions. These 'bodies' or the garments of the human beings are intended to function in different ways at different levels so that they could absorb the vibrations at various wave lengths. At different levels they arouse different kinds of consciousness and activities. Sensation and intuition are not the same kind of experience. Different faculties of the human beings are aroused by the interplay of different "principles". These principles energise the different "bodies" of the individual.

The various sheaths or the bodies are very well described by the astrological chart or horoscope of the person, on the basis of which many interesting predictions are made. Every astrologer bases his inferences about the physical form, physical activities and such other occurrences of the physical nature of the individual by the first house of the horoscope. Similarly, the fourth house is intimately connected with his emotional or astral nature. Mind or intellect has correspondence with the fifth house. Here we do not wish to go into the details of the various houses and their correpondences with the different sheaths of the individual. Suffice is to mention that the various sheaths or the bodies of the individual are well taken care of by the various houses in a chart. In order to know the welfare or the state of health of these sheaths, one must direct one's attention to the relevant house division of the chart.

These sheaths are connected with certain radiating impulses deriving their basic force from the Ultimate. The planetary orbs are the store-houses of these differentiated impulses. To consider the planets merely of the physical nature is misleading. They are like the power-houses which step down the power from high-voltage stations to low voltages. The process of this stepping down occurs through the planetary positions to the respective sheaths of the individual where-from it is manifest in the world of action. The planets whose nature we are trying to understand for astrological

16

predictions are in this way electrically charged and magnetically influencing the various bodies of the human personality.

In deeper contemplation when one wishes to function dynamically through one's entire personality, through one's all the seven sheaths, he has to understand the weaknesses of his various sheaths. It is like X-Ray to the entire personality. On the basis of this kind of inquiry, the aspirant could remedy the diseased body. Unless proper cure is obtained success in meditational practices and thus finally in yogic exercises will be impossible. Proximity of right teacher sometimes eliminates the need for such astrological examination but the end-result is the same : either through his psychic faculties of perception, the teacher understands and recommends remedial measures, or the disciple on his own, due to his astrological knowledge discovers the health condition of his different bodies and applies the remedial measures wherever necessary to restore them to perfect health and right functioning.

The second consideration in the present context is related to the discovery of one's Ray. This is a little complicated theme not very well appreciated by the common aspirant. Every disciple on the path of yoga is a specialised entity. Different species of animals behave differently but almost all the animals of the same species show no marked difference in their behaviour pattern. Among the human beings almost every individual acts and reacts differently. However, one can group them according to their racial, geographical and family groupings. Within these broad divisions, the individuals have been classified in seven groups primarily based on the consideration as to their functioning on the subjective or the objective planes, and whether they are primarily concerned with or are induced by the forces of Will, Wisdom or Activity ; there is one group of persons who are generally concerned with the goal of synthesis, adding force to everything like that of the activity of Mahadeva, the Great Lord of the Burning Ghat. Characteristics of these seven types of individuals are so prominent that their basic characteristics are displayed in every minor details of behaviour as well. A knowledge of one's primary Ray helps oneself to chalk out one's path effectively because the technique of performing various deeds would differ for different Rays. A knowledge of one's Ray would enable the individual to do things in such a way that success is easily achieved by organising one's activities in harmony with its characteristics. At the head of each Ray stands a Mighty Being who is magnetically, on the basis of affinity, linked with the progress and welfare of all the aspirants on his Ray. These Mighty Beings are in harmonious relationship with different planets, and they function in affinity with planetary deities connected with their Ray. Astrological knowledge reveals the Ray of the person, his natural archetype and the planetary beacon light from which he should try to derive his sustenance. This aspect of the problem is discussed in detail in *The Study of Astrological Occultism.*

In astrology, various kinds of methods, *mantras,* gems, and other propitiatory practices have been indicated for different planets. They are based on the specialised characteristics of these planets and their special influence and radiations. By properly attuning the influences of these planets to the goal in view, it is possible to tap the unlimited reservoir of spiritual power. In yogic exercises one plays a dangerous game with these spiritual powers. Unless these powers are well mastered, the end-result for the aspirant is not always happy. For this very purpose, it is necessary to have a good knowledge of the linkages of planets, *tantras, mantras*, and the propitiatory practices connected with them so that in case of need special endeavours could be made to regulate the various influences flowing to the individual so that the dangers could be avoided or the benefic influences accentuated. These planetary influences will have to be regulated according to the special Ray of the individual which could determine what planets are in harmony and which are in disharmony with him. On the basis of the knowledge of friendly and inimical planetary dispositions, one could propitiate those which are not on sympathetic wave-length with the aspirant.

The next step is to ascertain the karmic impediments with which the individual is surrounded. The various waves of sorrow and happiness arise to the individual because of his own action of omission and commission in the past. Once a deed is done, its repercussions will have to be borne. No action can go in vain. Once a good deed, in harmony with nature and in accordance with God's plan is done, it is bound to react to the good and happiness of the person. Similarly, a deed against the plan is bound to react to the person leading him to misery. These reactions have two impacts : firstly, the natural balance has to be restored, and secondly, the human individual suffering these reactions must learn the lesson to finally enable him to attune himself with the One Life Universal.

During the course of everyday life, when the planetary configurations portend the sequence of events which the individual has to bear,—these are so because the Lords of the Karma have placed the sequence in such a way that the individual is able to restore the natural balance—and learn the lesson of life and progress forward in the evolutionary process. When propitiatory rites, gems, *mantras*, and offerings are made to ward off any specific effect of the planetary disposition, they succeed only when they are able to create the same impact on the human psyche, or the universal life-element in him, as that intended by the original planetary situation. For example, if a series of physical illness is intended to teach perseverance and resignation to nature, then many other means, say the pronouncing of *mantras* several thousand times may generate the same influence. If the man is able to do so, the suffering may be avoided. This explains that the astrological predictions must be related to their wider impact in order to evaluate their relationship with yogic practices.

In yoga, as hinted above, the disciple wishes to speed up the process of evolution. This can happen only when he is able to overcome the past karmic impediments. For such an understanding of the past karmic forces, the Teacher with his deep psychic faculties could see them and suggest the practices helpful for the disciple. This need to a great extent can be fulfilled by astrological knowledge. The various astrological (planetary) combinations reflect the karmic status of the native. On that basis he could regulate his life in such a way that he is in harmony with nature. Thus, for co-operating with nature, it is necessary to know the karmic status of oneself, and thereby to regulate one's life in harmony with God's plan and be happier.

From the above, it could be inferred that the right approach to yoga, which is not just idle curiosity and which is not merely intended for acquiring abnormal psychic faculties, requires an appreciation of the poly-dimensional extension of human personality, the laws guiding and regulating life, the inner depths of phenomenal existence and above all, regulation of one's life according to laws of nature, the God's plan which is evolution and Eternal Life. In this process of self-unfoldment, one has to acquire support from Divine Beings, Planetary Hierarchy, and such other cosmic deities. For achieving any marked success, one has to know one's karmic status, the impediments one has to overcome, the shortcomings of one's personality manifest in the specific incarnation and the specific Ray on which one has to evolve and the special Ray-Deity whose benediction one has to invoke. These are some of the less talked of aspects of yoga which the modern world in some cases is approaching either in a credulous manner or is pooh-poohing it, but it has to take these seriously into account in order to attain greater degree of happiness destined for the world. For a comprehension of these aspects of life and for character building as well as for eradication of personality weaknesses, meditation is an intimately personal effort yet it is essential. Meditation depends upon personal capabilities for taking hold of one's entire life into one's hand and ruthlessly controlling it. Meditation is an intimately personal affair depending upon individual power and individual uniqueness. For all these, a good and penetrating knowledge of astrology is as much necessary as other general principles of yogic exercises, their goals and essential requirements and the performance of right meditation. The knowledge of Stars was imparted to hierophants of the ancient Mystery Schools only at very high order of accomplishments. A good astrologer has the onerous responsibility for not only guiding the physical life of the human individual but also for his own spiritual growth and soul's evolution.

MEANING OF DEATH

Astrology solves one of the greatest mysteries of life. Death has always remained a hidden chapter in the book of human evolution. This subject has been so dreadful that people have even called it the King of Terrors. On the other hand, there are many occultists who have time and again emphasized that death is just like sleep and each individual dies several times even during the course of one incarnation.

The ancient Indian philosophy of which astrology is an integral part gives a very comprehensive scheme of human evolution which solves many of the riddles baffling the modern and the so-called scientific mind. An understanding of the problem of death which was investigated in great detail by our ancient sages will not only enable us to have a balanced view on various problems of everyday existence, it will also aid a sensible prediction relating to the future of man.

There are various types of death. Apart from the fact that the experience of some intense pain which completely disintegrates the emotional life of the individual and he begins to reorganize his life on a new pattern, there are other aspects of death which astrology takes into cognizance. For example, there may be infant mortality where the incarnating ego before having entered the vast arena of life recoils and begins to live its life on supra-physical realms. There may on the other

hand be the death of a person who having lived a full
life dies after suffering for a long duration and ultimately
breathes his last in the lap of his near and dear ones. Or,
one may be shot by the enemy and/or in the prime of
one's life when the flowers of life are just beginning to
blossom, the ego may leave the physical coil. Every one
is aware of many circumstances in which the physical
death takes place. There is significance of every individual kind of death and the main guiding principle of all
these is to assist the future course of individual's evolution. Many occultists have discussed and indicated the
significance of such problems. An examination of all
these details would take us to great depths of the subject
which we do not wish to undertake here. Every experience of the ego, whether in life or in death, is intended
to impart to the ego the experience leading to the realisation of the Divine Essence of Life. Here we intend to
give some general aspects of the problem and to suggest
in brief the relationship between the natal chart and the
various facets of death.

In Indian philosophy, death has been considered
merely an event of life. It is like birth, marriage, livelihood, pilgrimage, children and the like. *Shrimad Bhagvad-
gita* clearly distinguishes between life and death. The
former is the eternal aspect of existence—the Primordial
Essence, the permanent link between the Ultimate and
the transient. Neither can weapon slay it, nor fire burn
it. Death, according to Lord Krishna, is just a chapter
in the eternal drama of life and the wise do not grieve
over it. It must be noted that astrology assigns to death
no more significance than any other aspect of existence.
It is not insignificant that the considerable importance
attached by the mortals have been watered down in

astrology. An astrologer never grieves over death ; he considers it merely as an act of divine dispensation.

There are two aspects of life ; one that is eternal, permanent and continuing during the soul's pilgrimage through diverse experiences, and second, that which differentiates between one life and another in a series of incarnations. The latter is death. But what is the purpose of incarnations ? The incarnating soul has to learn many lessons in life and he has to work out the load of karma gathered during several incarnations. There is every possibility that the individual may be given several fundamental lessons to learn in one life. In that case, though there may not be snapping of the chord connecting the transient part of the individual with his eternal counterpart each time a new lesson is given to him, but his life may be rent asunder and he may feel as if he has to begin his life a fresh each time. Should we not consider all these as different deaths the individual has to face ? The cause and circumstances of each death need not be identical.

Rev. C. W. Leadbeater in his book *On the Other Side of Death* has given various instances of the fact that the dying ego does not sever all his relationships with the physical world. He has to continue his onward journey but the arena of his activities to a considerable extent remains in this physical world of ours. Geoffrey Hodson in his *The Miracle of Birth* has recorded how the angelic hosts take special care during the birth of a child so that the miraculous phenomenon of the birth of the human body takes place in consonance with the universal forces of cosmic evolution, the karmic forces generated by the reincarnating. ego and the special requirements for his growth. Astrological charts picturing the stellar constellations, in fact, reflect this unique decision of the

Ultimate which is built-in in the soul of the reincarnating ego. Birth as well as death is the playground of great many esoteric forces.

Recently, Dr. Cassey attempted to show that every event of life connected with the historical past of the individual extends over his many past lives. Edgar Cassey had been a practising medical doctor but his clairvoyant conclusions have been extremely fascinating from the occult standpoint. He was able to establish connections with certain diseases as well as pleasants and unpleasant events of life with the past omission and commissions of the individual. Even the modern researches of the West have been suggesting that the great law of nature—of action and eternity, or the law of Karma and Reincarnation—are facts of life which must be taken into account while evaluating the course of human life.

It is said that there is not much difference between the conditions of sleep and death. At the time of death, the umbilical chord connecting the physical and the astral body is snapped, whereas during sleep the two remain linked. Other experiences of the soul during the sleep are very much the same, or at least similar.

An important feature of sleep as well as death is that the two represent something intangible. We cannot cognize either, nonetheless they exist which cannot be denied by anyone. It is because of this hidden aspect of death that the Eighth House of the natal chart representing concealed aspect of one's life is considered for predicting death. But there are several other houses which are also very meaningful for knowing the supra-physical life of the ego. For example, everyone knows that the First, Second, Seventh, and the Twelfth Houses also have much influence on this aspect of the individual.

But why are all these houses representing the very life-force, the essence of personality, wealth, speech, and the light of the eye, *kalatra* (the marriage partner) and the wasteful deeds, the realm of supra-physical entities connected with death, if death means the end of all ?

Astrologically speaking death becomes very meaningful. The general strength of the chart is assessed in relation to the First House. Even longevity, the general status of the individual, his potentialities, his *elan vital* and everything connected with life-force are examined firstly in relation to the First House. One must not forget that the First House is the fifth from the Ninth House which implies that the life of the individual is the result, progeny, offspring, of his own *punya*—the past—that is, astrology begins assuming that the present condition of the individual is always in the womb of his past. The quantum of *prana*, the life force with which a man lives and moves on this earth, is apportioned at the time of his birth as a result of his past deeds. In this way, the First House becomes meaningful. If the life-force itself has been very limited, no matter how strong other houses are, the life of the individual would not be very long.

The Seventh House is very intimately connected with the question of death. The house is also considered the house of marital happiness. One must appreciate the fact that the Hindu philosophy considers life as emerging from two poles—*purusha* and *prakriti*, the positive and the negative forces of manifestation. If the First House represents *purusha*, the element of creation, the Seventh House stands for *prakriti*, the matter for creation. Purusha is the inherent, built-in vital energy ; prakriti is energy on the move, the

expression of the Spirit in Matter. In the marital phenomenon, this cosmic principle comes into play. Man
expresses himself through his wife : Lord Shiva for
manifesting His creative potentialities required Parvati,
the World Mother. At the same time, the quantum of
life-force provided initially to the individual at the time
of his birth due to the Seventh House activities gets
dissipated. When all the energy with which the individual
was born has completed its creative functions, the
person's physical life ebbs out and he passes to the next
realm of manifestation, higher planes of creation.

The Eighth House is where the soul proceeds after
death, the plane of non-physical existence. This house
can be viewed as the First House for considering the
soul's journey in the astral world, which means the
nature of death and experiences therein.

The Twelfth House is the fifth from the Eighth
House. Occult investigations indicate that the soul's
attainments during the two intervening births do not
only depend upon the quantity and intensity of life lived
on this physical plane, but also on the experiences of
the astral world. The soul is very active on the astral
plane. We are told that the 'Invisible Helpers' meet
us at the threshold of death. Many mysterious ceremonies also take place in that region. As a result of all
these, the spiritual height attained by the ego is determined.

The Second House is also considered as a *maraka*
(death inflicting) House, but the fact that inheritance
and wealth of a person are also indicated by this
house gives the clue to this mystery. We get much
money because during our past incarnations we have
done charitable deeds and are still attached to our
physical possessions. The Second House is one of the

maya houses implying thereby the aspects of life which attaches the individual to the world of manifestation very rigidly. How much the individual is caught in the illusion of this world is shown by this house. For the liberation of the soul, it is necessary to break the bond of illusion. Life of the individual as represented by the First House. dangling between material possessions, the Second House, and the spiritual forces like Initiations, mysterious alliances with occult schools, etc represented by the Twelfth House, decides the course of the First House. For this reason, the Second and the Twelfth Houses become important for deciding the life-span of the incarnating ego.

There are many aspects of death which one would like to know. Even for the prognostication of the timing and the means of exit from this earth there are many combinations indicated in the astrological texts. Every layman is curious to know various related matters on the basis of which he could arrange his worldly and often religious affairs, but after all, death is a weapon in the hands of God for directing the human affairs in the best possible manner. No amount of astrological calculations could ever definitely establish the end of any one's life, though indications could certainly be found. The astrological meaning of death should however help the astrologer to counselling the individual so that he understands the purpose of his life and the intricacies of the binding forces. With this aim in view we have limited ourselves to only a few of the basic considerations with regard to this subject. We have attempted to indicate that (i) death is not an end for the soul. It is merely an event like any other event of life, (ii) Death results from the ebbing out of the quantum of life-force provided at the time of birth, represented by

the First House, as a result of the *punya* or the meritorious deeds done by the individual in his earlier lives as
represented by his Ninth House. (iii) After death a new
non-physical existence of the individual begins which is
indicated by the Eighth House. (vi) During the inter
vening period between the two incarnations much
creative occult activities take place which are represented
by the Twelfth House. (v) The longevity of the person and
his death depend upon the balance between his material
attachments, *maya* forces as suggested by the Second
House, and his occult attainments indicated by the
Twelfth House in his chart.

ASTROLOGY, COSMIC IDEATION,
AND MODERN PHILOSOPHY

Even J. Krishnamurti, the most outstanding though the most controversial philosopher of the twentieth century who had been held in great esteem by Albert Einstein, C. G. Jung, Bertrand Russell, Aldous Huxley and others, who has been vehemently destroying the traditional concepts of God, temples, scriptures, moral codes and the need of spiritual teachers, and has been zealosuly endeavouring to make mankind perceive how much they are imprisoned in their own thoughts and thinking apparatus that they are unable to liberate themselves from the shackles of the dead past, has however, as it is evident from the following excerpt from his talks, accepted the validity and possibility of knowing the future. On being questioned once when the questioner had drempt the dress, mode of walking, the way of his approaching and sitting on the dias, as well as the talk J. Krishnamurti delivered on the following afternoon, exactly they happened the following day, he replied as follows :

"when the mind, because you have been listenng here, has become somewhat sensitive—naturally it observes more whether of tomorrow or today. It is like looking down from an aeroplane and seeing two boats approaching from opposite directions on the same river ; one sees that they are going to meet at

> a certain point and that is future. The mind, being
> somewhat more sensitive, becomes aware of certain
> things which may happen tomorrow, as well as of
> those which are happening now. And you will find,
> if you go into this very deeply, that nothing
> happens at all : any happening is part of life.''

From this, one finds that possibility of certain occurrences likely to take place in future is not denied by
J. Krishnamurti. The knowledge of the future may be
perceived by the individual if his mind is so sensitive as
to transcend the limitations of time. On another
occasion, the occult teacher of J. Krishnamurti who
taught him during his early youth and prepared him for
the expansion of his consciousness and his philosophic
as well as other insights, once stated that

> ''I have a habit of often quoting, *minus* quotation
> marks—from the maze of what I get in the countless
> folios of our Akasic libraries, so to say—with eyes
> shut. Sometimes I may give out thoughts that will
> see light years later ; at other times what an orator,
> a Cicero may have pronounced ages earlier, and at
> other what was not only pronounced by modern
> lips but already written or printed''

Obviously, if these thoughts are recognised as valid, the
only problem remains as how to get a knowledge of the
technique of contacting the river of life. The fact that
the future is very much, not always in absolute certainty,
predetermined and reflected in Eternal Record of Life, is
not disputed by the occultists and by those who have
developed their latent psychic and other faculties
to some extent. Apparently, therefore, the ability of
prognostication depends upon the development of
those faculties or acquiring that knowledge, with
whose assistance it could be possible for the

soothsayer to contact the 'akasic' records or the library. As it would be seen from the following, the astrologer, based on his knowledge of the classical astrological scriptures, has received a knowledge of the unfoldment of life (of which the individual in respect of whom the prognostication has to be made is a part) in time dimension on the basis of which he attempts to see and calculate 'the course of the boat' in the language of J. Krishnamurti. If astrology is seen in this way, there does not remain any thing highly esoteric about it. It is very much like any other physical science.

The course of life's flow is generally described in scriptures in four symbols. Such symbols are helpful for the simple reason that finite language or similies are unfit to express the abstract and the infinite, nor can the objective ever mirror the subjective. Life is not only a flow in three dimensional world of physical senses. Therefore certain symbols are used in order to assist the student to understand the polydimensional dynamic movement of life in which myriads of entities of different forms and life-contents evolute. These four symbols are a lotus, a conch-shell, the *Ashwathama* tree, and a river. None of these symbols are able to describe the flow of life in its entirety : all of them attempt to suggest various aspects of this evolutionary course, some of these describe a little less or a little more.

The lotus which is commonly seen in the hands of most of the Hindu Gods, or on which Brahma himself is seen seated, symbolise the growth of life from ''within without'', from almost a non-descript seed passing through water rising to air and sunshine finally to wither away scattering the seed which has all the potential of regeneration. Thus from an inner level of existence, following a course in which several radical transforma-

17

tions take place in the outer coverings the lotus seed ultimately vanishes in the 'spiritual' nothingness and merges into void, waiting for the Pralaya after which once more to revive and follow the same course. The symbol primarily emphasizes the fact of growth, radical transformation, and the germ of future development lying in the bosom of the past.

The *Ashwathama* tree is slightly different because it stresses the importance of the invisible counterpart of our life. As this tree is supposed to have its root in the heaven and branches along with the leaves and fruits in the physical world downwards, it is a reverse image of a tree. Usually a tree is expected to have roots in the ground and the trunk and branches in the area above the ground and in the sky so to say. But *Ashwathama* grows in the ethereal 'upwards' and instead of growing upwards, it grows downwards. This sumbolises the fact that the root of our physical world is in the ethereal 'spiritual' world wherefrom it obtains its sustenance whereas the visible world is merely a tip of the wholeness called the tree of Life. This symbol does not describe the intermediate stages and the various heavenly forces exherted on it for its growth but it does emphasize the importance of the inner or the invisible counterpart of our known existence.

The conch-shell, which is generally found in the hands of all the gods and many of the goddesses of the Hindu pantheism, is a much more deeper and sugestive symbol. The shape of the conch-shell is not any less significant than the manner of its use. When the priest blows into the conch shell, then sound is produced having moved in the circular body of the conch-shell, which grows gradually till in the middle it is maximum and then as the wind comes out of it, there is diminution in its girth which gradually tapers out. We are told that the manifestation at the earliest stages of concretisation had the impulse of *Nada*, the Sound, in the *Mahabindu*— the primeval Central Point-which getting support of necessary *upadana*, the support of various *Tattwas* generates Life Wave which moving in its septenary spiral waves finally reaches the grossest point of material creation—the central point of the conch-shell, after which the spiritualism takes sway and gradually the physicality of the manifestation declines and everything once more vanishes in the spiritual realm. This symbol stresses the relationship between the spirit and the matter, the necessity of giving Divine Impulse for the creation, the need for *upadana*, the process of septenary cyclical waves in imparting Life Essence and gradual unfoldment of various faculties, and finally the merging of everything in Divine nothingness.

. The symbology connected with river, is the most important one because it contains many of the characteristics of cosmic ideation and similarities between this and the astrological assumption of cosmic ideation on the basis of which individual prognostications are made. In order to show the various subtlities of these two descriptions of cosmic ideation, one will have to go a little deeper and in a detailed manner in their descriptions. Some of the Hindu *Puranas* have described the various stages in manifestation but according to their special points of view they have exphasised the different stages, but all of them in fact are in agreement as far as the basic ingredients are concerned. Invariably, the creative process is described at the initial stage with Nothingness which could be called Void, Darkness or *Pralaya*—the dissolution. At that stage, even the Unmanifest Prakriti was not there ; only *SAT*–Truth prevailed. The nature of this existence is not possible to describe in any mode of expression. But the next stage is the stage of the decision by the *Supreme* to manifest. Parabramha or *that* which then existed desired to manifest as a result of which *Sadashiva* appeared. Etymologically this word means Eternal Beatitude, or Blessedness. This single generative Active Potential in order to maintain balance required a negative generative potential. Sadashiva is therefore said to let arise from himself *Swarup Bhuta Sakti* or Shivaa also known as Ambike which never separated from his body and she became the Mother of all men. Then, later on, Shiva from one of his thighs produced after rubbing nector on it Vishnu. Vishnu became the Prime Source for creating the River or the Ocean of Life.

The Lord Vishnu had been lying on for millions and billions of years on his serpent coil on the ocean of pure essence—kshira sagar—when from his naval arose a lotus on which remained seated Brahma. Vishnu built nature with twentyfour *tattwas*, but *Purusha*—the male procreative principle was separate from these as a result of which the creative manifestation could not begin. Brahma was created by Sadashiva by rubbing nector on another of his thigh and was also called *Hiranyagarbha*. Vishnu pervaded the Hiranyagarbha with his twentyfour tattwas but this pervasion was not conducive to the manifestation of the universe. Brahma had to perform further penance manifesting thereby the various lokas, creating different Kumars but they refused to undertake procreation. Shiva then appearing as Ardha-Narishwar created various Rudras at Brahma's request but they also refused to procreate. Then, Shiva finally asked Brahma to work for procreative manifestation. Then the Great Drama began on a different plane.

Brahma from one part of his body brought out

Swayambhu Manu and from another a female called *Satrupa*. There are various versions of this bifurcation of Brahma into two, but in essence they all stress the act of 'polarisation'. The marriage of these two, the positive and the negative magnetic forces symbolising sexual union or mutual attraction of the two opposing forces, produced two sons and three daughters. These daughters were in turn married to different *Prajapatis*. Daksha Prajapati was married to *Prasuti* meaning procreation and they begot sixty daughters of whom 27, the *nakshatras,* were married to Soma, the Moon. And then, the regenerative creation began.

From the above description one could easily realise the manifestation as a flow of events, very well symbolised by a river. On this flow is superimposed the forces of polarisation manifested as the centripetal and centrifugal forces which finally began as involution and evolution of mankind.: in astrology it became the dual division of each signs of the Hora division of the zodiac into that of the Sun and the Moon. The triple manifestation of Mahesh, Vishnu and Brahma represented the three *Gunas* of Tamas, Rajas, and Sattwa at different levels of manifestation. The Brahma's four faces, or his four hands and the four Vedas all suggested not only the four directions, but the qualities of Dharma, Artha, Kama, and Moksha. They also referred to the Lower Quaternary of the human personality comprising the physical body, *pranamaya kosha* or the etheric body through which the vital air circulates through the whole body, the emotional body and the thinking body. Above these are the *Atma* which could very well for the simplicity of expression be considered as the Fragment of God.

Such a description of cosmic ideation may not be readily accepted by the modern experimental scientists, but the occultists who have given the above in garbled version have also on another occasion stated the cosmic ideation more succinctly. While denying the existence of any anthropomorphic god, (and even the *Kala Purusha* of the astrologers can never be considered as anthropomorphic because that is merely a symbolic representation of the metaphysical concept) they laid down the Universal Perpetual Motion as the primordial cause ; the motion being such which never ceased never slackened nor increased its speed not even during the intervals between the various Nights of Brahmas or between pralayas of diverse duration. As all movement is polar, this motion or the force is also polar indicating thereby that it also arouses the two aspects of it viz., attraction and repulsion. The development of Spirit-Matter duality along with the third which could be the quintessence of the two known according to the Vedantists as the only Reality and everything else as *Maya,* gives rise to the trinity expressed in different ways. As a result of the motion with its resulting conflict, neutralisation, equlibration, correlation infinite variety prevails in nature. This occult view of the cosmic ideation is accepted by the Hindu astrologers but they go further and superimpose on it the operation of the various Creative Intelligences created during the ideational process which have been assigned many specialised functions to further the evolutionary impetus. In this connection, the astrologers have described the preparation of the matrix of evolution in poly-dimensions (the astrological field exceeds the three dimensional world) by the various zodiacs, and the very powerfully sensitive asterisms. On the basis of these the planetary spirits take the special charge of the incarnating egos and guide their destiny. The Hindu astrology by linking the individual with the *Kala Purusha* demonstrates the unity between the Macrocosm and the Microcosm, or between God and man. That is a unique feature of Hindu astrology.

The Appendices attempt to describe the matrix of astrological predictions. The most important point to note in this chart is that the signs of the zodiac and the lunar asterisms by themselves are the store-houses of various potentials which when activised would radiate corresponding influences. The nature of these radiations may be mysteries hidden from the profane though well known to the seers, but suggestions and fragmentary knowledge and information about them as revealed by their symbols, planetary ownership, the association of creative intelligences with them, the elements such as fire, water, air and earth, or their division according to the prominent *gunas* or the basic Attributes such as *Sattwas* (harmony), *Rajas* (activity), and *Tamas* (inertia) are all pointers to the basic characteristics of these lunar asterisms and signs of the zodiac. They are the various kinds of force currents flowing all over the cosmos and enveloping under it almost everything that consists the cosmic manifestation. The cosmos in this way is rightly a mighty flow of currents, magnetic radiations, each current having specialised influences to radiate. They continue till the existence exists ; till the solar and cosmic system of ours survive.

For exactness of prognostication, it is not only necessary to know these eternal flow of forces and magnetic radiations, but also the disposition of planets which activise different imfluences. These impacts are not meant only for the human individuals. They are universal. They influence the nature, they bring the rains and sunshine ; they provide nourishment for the plants and vegetation ; they develop the minerals and precious stones in the womb of the mother earth ; the planets send different kinds of emotional and mental impulses and they are ever engaged in creating the concrete entities which can imbide those impulses. The astrological cosmic matrix in this way could be conceived as the current of strong magnetic influences both, passive energised by the asterisms and the zodiacs while the active or the positive forces are generated by the planets, the mighty creative intelligences. In this way, even when the great occult seers denied any anthropomorphic god while postulating the universal perpetual motion as the primordial cause, the motion being such as never to slacken, nor increase, nor ceasing from its operation even during the various nights of Brahma, one need not consider them atheists. The astrological matrix of mighty flows of intensive magnetic motion of force currents of various kinds does reveal that the unending cosmos which can only be rationally inferred contains within itself such inconceivable latent potentialities that the cosmic evolution could be considered a multi-coloured splendour in which the man will have its particular role to play. The contemporary philosophy exploring to establish the relationship between the man and the universe is not confronted with cul-de-sac, rather they are breaking many new grounds which are very encouraging for the growth of astrology and increase of popular interest in the subject. Generally speaking, the modern philosophical thoughts can be classified in three broad categories, first, denying the existence of all non-material postulates concerning man and his universe ; second, approaching the vast mysterious universe revealing only the tip of its iceberg through its material content, and third, endeavouring to dig deep in the human psyche to establish that the man is a helpless creature because he does not seem to have any worthwhile rational equipment to comprehend himself and his significance in his universe.

The first category of philosophers, the so called scientific thinkers, who consider that everything for being 'rational' must be brought within the compass of physical observation and experimentation. The impact of the growth of science and technology taking up much of the functions of the human being relegating man as an automaton has been responsible for this approach to life. But the same science and technology has been revealing so much of non-material counterpart of human personality and the cosmos that its role in guiding researches for the understanding of human destiny is greatly discounted.

The second category of philosophers take the advantage of expanding frontiers of human knowledge in various directions : they recognise the technological achievements in photogrophing and recording the non-physical extension of human aura and advent of maladies before their actual occurrence on the physical body on even these non-physical counter parts of the body. The life after death and possibility of reincarnation are increasingly being accepted. The influence of heredity, which once remained merely an astrological hypothesis on lines of he Mendalian law of biological growth, in matters of psychological development of the person is being recognised. The influence of planetary disposition on psychological growth and evolution of the persons as well as on their psycho-somatic diseases is now acknowledged scientific assumptions on the basis of which human personality is being assessed. The increasing number of predictions on mundane astrology which are demonstrably proved true these days are opening the new vista of the influence of the unknown on human affairs. The philosopher astrologers who are calculating the advent of the Aquarian Age based on the precession of the earth have already received respectable hearing from the modern men. The plethora of publications relating to the transformation of the new man according to astrological principles indicating the emergence of the new age humanity based on the Aquarian characteristics of the zodiac amply shows to us the belief in the unknown *influences*. These are reminding us of the simili of the conch-shell being blown from its behind thus activating the septenary spiral of growth ultimately fading itself in spiritual nothingness.

The third category of philosophers are rather very abstruse. They approach life from a radically mystic standpoint. In a way, they uphold the view that the human individual in his present state of the being is unable to comprehend the reality about his life and himself. The human emotions comprising his fear, the sense of insecurity, agitation of the struggle for existence, the thraldom of ambition and so on are so much blinding the real view of the person that a kind of illusion pervades for the person and he is unable to see his own real self. As he cannot see correctly, he cannot discriminate between the truth and the falsehood, as he cannot so discriminate, his ethical sense is completely atrophied. The most important aspect of this line of reasoning is that the human individual cannot understand the reality and live in perpetual rejuvenation because of his thought. According to them, thought is always the past because it is sustained on memory of the past experiences.   On the projection of past experiences one cannot experience the eternal light. In order to get the real feel of the newness of life, the individual is required to abandon thought.   But this is extremely difficult. So the individual is caught in a contradiction : thought is the only means for his understanding of the reality around him but this equipment of his is fallacious and ineffective in doing the job assigned to it.   The modern mind is, according to them, in a state of bewilderment. Their solution is to give up thinking which is a kind of deep meditation in which the unknown sends its own messages and on the basis of such a relationship with the unknown, the man may live a confident life and in reality.

The philosophers of this type, many of the modern thinkers are following this line of mystic thinking, do not pass judgement on several aspects of life. They consider them unimportant and not directly related to the main subject of enquiry. To them astrology comes in this category of subjects.   But they are assuming that the Life is like the *Ashwathama* tree with its roots in the heaven and the branches and leaves in this physical world. To them the heaven is the realm of the unknown. This realm is very powerful and is supplying all the nourishment for the physical concrete world.   Only by establishing a contact with this unknown realm of exist- ence the human individual can live a fulfilling life. This approach to life based on this line of thinking which assumes life resembling this mysterious heavenly tree does not talk of astrological planets and the stellar forces but one can see a strong affirmation of their possibility. The real basis of astrology is theism. The science of stellar influences does not attach importance to merely the planets but considers them as the vestures of the real celestial deities functioning behind these outer sheaths. Any offering to the planets is an endeavour to establish a relationship with the celestial deities, not merely to the physical planets. These planets are really unknown and the forces working from behind the veil. These thoughts are not spelt by these philosophers but on the basis of their line of thinking, the validity of astrological predictions is understood. It is for this reason that they feel that by going up in the sky, as if in an aeroplane and viewing life from above, one can perceive the occurrences in the present and *in the future* more clearly. To them time is an illusion whereas from astrological standpoint time is in the womb of the great Lord who made all these planets and the stars. By knowing the functioning of the stars and relating these forces as far as the human beings are cocerned, one can transcend the veil of time. Thus, there is no contradiction between serious modern philosophies and astrological predictions.

A rational view of astrological predictions, on the lines suggested above would enable serious astrologers to link astrology with other occult sciences. The ancient Indian seers considered astrology as a part of the Ancient Wisdom. Astrology revealed the mysteries of life much more easily than other methods of yoga. The civilisation that prevailed even prior to the *Vedas* knew science of astrology extensively and practised it widely. That is why one finds profuse references to the stellar effects in the sacred books of the east. By denying the validity of this science and neglecting it, the modern generation may lose one of its best allies.

II

PLANETARY RADIATIONS

Blessed *is* he that readeth, and they that hear the words of this prophecy, and keep those things which are written therein : for the time *is* at hand.

The Revelation, I.3

ASCENDANT, MOON, AND THE SUN

The occultists have laid considerable emphasis on the eastern horizon and the forces flowing from it. It is not without any reason that the Sun always rises in the east and vitally magnetises the ascending horizon. At the time of one's birth whatever forces radiate from that direction make permanent impact on the being. The quantum and the nature of life-force imbibed at that time by him are his life-long assets. Everything else is secondary to this basic impulse. This asset is astrologically reflected by the disposition of the Ascendant, or the First House, or the First Quadrant. The astrological savants have very rightly attributed, in a way, the greatest significance to this house. For those who wish to take astrological assistance in discovering their own basic impulses, latent faculties, the pilgrimage route, and the final destiny will do well in studying their Ascendant very carefully.

The various texts have described the First House as the significator of various aspects of life which when viewed closely amply demonstrate the fact that the Ascendant portrays the amount of Life Force and the quality of the same which might fructify during the course of the unfoldment of one's life. Dr. B. V. Raman having mentioned other characteristics of the ascendant indicated it to show the personality, the physical body and character and the general strength of the horoscope. If one enquires the meaning of the last phrase, it would be obvious that the learned editor of *The Astrological Magazine* intended to convey that this house contains within itself all the possibilities of the development of the individual as revealed in detail by the several other houses. The *Jataka Parijatam*, the classical text by Vaidyanath Dikshita, suggested that apart from the body, its form, its characteristics etcetera it would indicate the fame, qualities, happiness and unhappiness, splendour, strength and weakness of the person. These are the general assessment of the person which does not depend upon the condition of any one aspect of one's life. For example, the fame, the splendour, the strength and the weakness of a person would depend upon the activities and expressions of the Life Force contained in the very constitution of the individual being which is not necessarily circumscribed by his physical sheaths. In *Uttar Kalamrita*, Kalidasa has given the following aspects of the individual as indicated by the First House: knowledge, fame, dream, strength, dignity, tranquillity, pride, honour, discontent, nature and so on. Varahamihira in his *Brihat Jataka* used a very apt appellative for the Ascendant: he described it as *Kalpa*. This *Sanskrit* word has many different connotations, some of which are as follows: practicable, duty, a day of Brahma and so on. In fact, the Lagna or the Ascendant is one of the incarnations out of the series of lives that the individual as a fragment of the Divine has to live and in each specific incarnation certain 'possibilities' are assigned to him. The fructification of this 'practicability' or the 'possibility' depends on the manner of the life lived by the individual implying the opportunities availed of and missed. Viewed in this way, the other attributes such as body, physical appearance which are related to the gross physical sheath, happiness and unhappiness, denoting the quality of the passional nature of the individual, pride and knowledge pertaining to the mental body, and fame, splendour and dignity depending upon God's Grace are all indicative of the quantum and the quality of Life Force ensouling the person and the regard the various Planetary Spirits show towards the Ego incarnate.

In order to assess the quality of the life force it is necessary to study the characteristics of the Ascendant much more deeply than ordinarily done of this house. The nature and characteristics of the sign of the zodiac and that of the Nakshatra rising at the birth time are very important. While examining the chart, only the broad exoteric attributes of these are not adequate; one should find out their Gunas—whether they are Rajas, Tamas, or Sattwa; their elements whether they are representing earth, fire, air or water; whether they are connected with Dharma, Artha, Kama, Moksha; and who are the Prajapatis or the Guardian Deities connected with these signs; these should be gone into very deeply. They would suggest the dimensions of the individual wherein he would have the scope of his activities and the areas wherein he would have opportunities for further development of his faculties.

The next exercise in this regard is related to the study of the entire planetary disposition towards this house. Beginning with the nature of the Ascendant lord and the aspects and other usual relationships of different planets one will have to cast one's glance to the disposition of other planets even if they are not directly connected with the Ascendant lord. For example, for the Aries lord Mars, no matter howsoever favourable Venus or Saturn are placed they could not be very satisfying for the simple reason that Aries is a sign very

18

sensitive to the Solar Rays and anything which is not in accordance with the powerful nature of this planet cannot be in affinity with this sign. This is the basic law of harmony but even otherwise one finds that Venus as the lord of the second and the seventh houses for Aries ascendant is considered as death inflicting planet. Even when such a native is granted the luxurious conditions signified by Venus, he would not be restful in that situation. His married life ordinarily will be a bed of thorns and many kinds of uncomfortable problems might arise. He would have very trying life with the opposite sex : he would have unusual attraction for the opposite sex but none of these relationships could provide to him the normal source of happiness and peace. The women would often create the most trying problems for him. Similarly, Saturn being the lord of the *Badhaka* house for the Aries ascendant, Saturn and Mars are radically opposed to one another. Such an individual would have the inherent inborn quality of leadership, initiative, courage and valour, he would be highly original in almost all his approaches to life problems so much so that he would utterly dislike any plagiarism and second-hand stuff, nonetheless such a person with Aries ascendant could never find his path smooth. What other persons can obtain as a matter of course'he would have to acquire after hard work and much struggle. Thus all the planetary disposition has to be reckoned in relation to the sign of the Ascendant, its lord and the underlying radiation released from that sign.

Once the Ascendant is identified, all the other *bhavas* fall in their respective positions. If it is Cancer ascendant, naturally the Tenth House would be Aries, Ninth would be Pisces, seventh would be Capricorn and eighth Aquarius and so on. The characteristics of these signs would naturally work themselves out in the respective *Bhavas* as far as the native is concerned. Capricorn and Aquarius are ruled by Saturn but apart from this they have their own special features. Cancer ascendants would as a matter of rule have unusual importance of their marriage in their life The married partners of these persons are not necessarily bad, cruel, terrifying, yet either by their goodness or on account of their coldness, philosophic temperament, or some special inherent character of their, the partners would create some situation so that the marriage of such persons could lead to some sort of squeezing out of the vital energy in some unusual direction. Some persons might indulge in regular extra-marital relationships or they might be led to austere spiritual kind of life as a result thereof. A special feature of such persons would be highly sensitive sense of social relationships specially because their fourth house would have Libra whose unique quality is balance. A perfect equilibrium between extreme qualities of life can be attainable for such persons. In this way, it becomes almost axiomatic that identification of the Ascendant would reveal the general pattern of one's life.

The next step in astrological self-discovery is related to the Moon sign. In several parts of India, the significance to this sign is assigned so much that along with the natal chart, the horoscope cast on the basis of the Moon sign as the ascendant is conjointly produced. This is based on the assumption that the astrological assessment on such considerations to a great extent affect the individual and it reveals much of his problems and the course of his pilgrimage. The very determination of the ruling planetary period is dependent upon the Moon's position with regard to the various Fixed Stars, the

Nakshatras. Even these Nakshatras are allegorically linked with the Moon as his wives, Rohini being the most favourite, are very importantly connected with astrological prognostications. In tallying the horoscopes, specially for marriage purpose, it is the placement of Moon in various Fixed Stars in the two charts that determine the degree of their compatibility or otherwise. For the beginning of any auspicious act, the position of the Moon at that auspicious time, is of vital consideration. Whether it is the beginning of a house construction, commencement of a journey, wearing of new clothes, performance of any marriage or any other religious activities, or even the purchase of any new article all are in orthodox considerations, closely linked with the Moon and no practising astrologer who wants to be the day to day guide to his clients can afford to neglect these considerations.

But even otherwise, for serious geological or human problems, the significance of the Moon is immense. Geological cataclysms from the upheaval of oceans, deluges, and shifting of continents, down to annual hurricanes, earthquakes, volcanic eruptions, tidal waves, and even the extraordinary weather and shifting of seasons are due to planetary changes amongst which the Moon plays an outstanding role. The health and longevity of an individual, to a great extent, are linked with the Moon. Special influence of Moon is noted on the functioning of the female organism and on sexual impulses of both the males and the females ; the latter are in an important manner guided and regulated by the phases and position of the Moon. As a matter of fact, in almost all religions, the Moon was intimately thought to be linked with the growth, waning, dying and re-appearance of the life process : the conception.

birth, growth and death of an individual were the special domain of the Moon. The ancient civilisations had noted the impact of Moon on coupling and conceptions. The Greek mythology connected the Moon with child birth because of its influence on women and conception whilst the connection between the Moon and fecundation, though not well recognised by our present day physiology and generally considered a part of gross superstition, was well appreciated by ancient Judaism which formed the base for Christian beliefs. Even among the Israelities there is a reference of Jehovah symbolising God connected with child-bearing. In the Hebrew Kabalah, the Moon symbolised by the Argha of the seed of all material life is still closely connected Kabalistically with Jehovah who is double-sexed as Anu in the Chaldean Trinity identical with Sin. As a matter of fact, it is observed that the impact of the Moon is so pronounced on generative functions of the terrestrial organism that the phases of the Moon has been associated with their growth so much so that the determination of time-period in many cases is linked with the same. For example, it has been observed that the lunar month of 28 days has four distinct phases well recognised in astrology which are classified first in two as the bright and dark periods which according to their waxing and waning phases have been further divided into two thus making the entire lunar month classified in four distinct stages which are very vital for astrological determination of the malefic or benefic nature of the Moon, but these four phases of the Moon denote the week which is the unit of calculation of our time duration. But this weekly time-period is very interestingly linked with several reproductive functions. It has been found that the eggs of the pigeon are hatched in

two weeks (or 14 days), those of the fowl in three ; those
of the duck in four ; those of the goose in five, and those
of the ostrich in seven. Madam H. P. Blavatsky, the
famous occultist of the nineteenth century, in her *The
Secret Doctrine* quotes from an unpublished ancient
manuscript in which certain very important lunar basis
for time determination linked with human generative
functions was given. She states that "What is known
of Chaldean Moon-Worship, of the Babylonian God, *Sin*,
called by the Greeks "Deus Lunus" is very little ; and
that little is apt to mislead the profane student, who
fails to grasp the esoteric significance of the symbols.
As popularly known to the ancient profane philosophers
and writers–for those who were initiated were pledged
to silence–the Chaldeans were the worshippers of the
Moon under *her*, and *his*, various names, just as were
the Jew, who came after them, then quoting the unpublished manuscript, Madam Blavatsky states :

> One of the first occupation among men connected
> with those of actual necessity would be the per-
> ception of time periods, marked on the vaulted arch
> of the heavens, sprung and rising over the level
> floor of the horizon, or the plain of still water. These
> would come to be marked as those of day and
> night, of the phases of the moon, of its stellar or
> synodic revolutions, and of the period of the solar
> year with recurrence of the seasons, and with the
> application to such periods of the natural measure
> of day or night, or of the day divided into the light
> and dark...—*

After describing such perceptions of time variation of which
the ancients became aware linking them with stars and

* H. P. Blavatsky, *The Secret Doctrine*, Madras, Vol. II. pp.
104–105

planets, they very closely perceived the relationship
between the Moon and the life regeneration process on
the earth. They realised that the Sun was the giver of
Life to the whole Planetary System, whilst the Moon
was the giver of life to our Globe. The relationship was
observed to such an extent that the unpublished manuscript mentioned earlier indicated much greater details.
Madam Blavatsky quoted the earlier author further as
follows :

> (a) The feminine physiological phenomena every
> lunar month of 28 days, or 4 weeks of 7 days each,
> so that 13 occurrences of the period should happen
> in 364 days, which is the solar week-year of 52
> weeks of 7 days each. (b) The quickening of the
> foetus is marked by a period of 126 days, or 18
> weeks of 7 days each. (c) That period which is
> called "the period of viability" is one of 210 days,
> or 30 weeks of 7 days each. (d) The period of
> parturition is accomplished in 280 days or a period
> of 40 weeks of 7 days each, or 10 lunar months of
> 28 days each, or of 9 calendar months of 31 days
> each, counting on the royal arch of the heavens for
> the measure of the period of traverse from the dark-
> ness of the womb to the light and glory of conscious
> existence, that continuing inscrutable mystery and
> miracle......Thus the observed period of time marking
> the workings of the birth function would naturally
> become a basis of astronomical calculation

She further states :

> ......Notoriously Osiris was the sun and the river
> Nile, the tropical year of 365 days, which number is
> the value of the word Neilos, and the bull, as he
> was also the principle of fire and of life-giving force,
> while Isis was the moon, the bed of the river Nile,

or the mother earth, for the parturient energies of which water was a necessity, the lunar year of 354–364 days, the time-maker of the periods of gestation, and the cow marked by, or with, the crescent new moon........

But the use of the cow of the Egyptians for the woman of the Hebrews was not intended as of any radical difference of significance, but a concurrence in the teaching intended, and merely as the substitution of a symbol of common import, which was this, *viz.*, the period of parturition with the cow and the woman was held to be the same, or 280 days, or ten lunar months of 4 weeks each. And in this period consisted the essential value of this animal symbol, whose mark was that of the crescent new moon...... parturient and natural periods are found to have been subjects of symbolism all over the world. They were thus used by the Hindus, and are found to be most plainly set forth by the ancient Americans, in the Richardson and Gest tablets, in the Palenque Cross and elsewhere ; and manifestly lay at the base of the formation of the calendar forms of the Mayas of Yucatan, the Hindus, the Assyrians, and the ancient Babylonians, as well as the Egyptians and old Hebrews. The natural symbols ....would be either the phallus or the phallus and yoni........*male* and *female*. Indeed, the words translated by the generalising terms male and female, in the 27th verse of the first chapter of Genesis are... *sacr* and *n'cabvah* or literally, phallus and yoni. While the representation of the phallic emblems would barely indicate the general members of the human body, when their functions and development of the seed-vesicles emanating from them were

considered, there would come into indication a
mode of measures of lunar time and through lunar,
of solar time.

Having quoted the above, H. P. Blavatsky went on to
say : "This is the physiological or anthropological key
to the Moon symbol. The key that opens the mystery
of theogony, or the evolution of the manvantaric Gods,
is more complicated, and has nothing phallic in it. There,
all is mystical and divine. But the Jews, beyond
connecting Jehovah directly with the Moon as a generative God, preferred to ignore the higher Hierarchies, and
have made their Patriarchs of some of these zodiacal
constellations and planetary gods........[1]

The above is expected to highlight the fact that the
ancient civilisations of the world attached considerable
importance to the Moon as a generative force and its
well ordered impact on various generative functions
enabled them to base their time counting in accordance
with this gestation period. The various religious practices
and symbols referring to the Moon or connected with it
have been phallic suggesting the Moon to represent the
universal female generative principle. The Hindu mythology of the Moon on the head of the Lord Shiva from
which the Ganges flowed, and the worship of phallus
and yoni also indicated the same understanding of the
Moon as the universal generative force. The question
of considering the Moon as a male or a female deity has
however remained baffling. As Soma, the Moon is
considered a male, a king, whilst as Indu, she is a female.
As Isis, Phoebe and Diana, the Moon is a female
goddess. It is observed by H. P. Blavatsky that in
religious rites, the Moon served a dual purpose. Personi-

---

1. H. P. Blavatsky, *The Secret Doctrine*, T.P.H., Adyar, Madras,
Vol. II., pp. 105–106.

fied as a female goddess for exoteric purposes, or as a male god in allegory and symbol, in occult philosophy our satellite was regarded as a sexless potency to be well studied because it was to be dreaded. Thus, we can for the time being accept that the Moon was universally worshipped as a universal generative principle, but there had not been any unanimity about its sex which could be best understood along with its function and importance in terrestrial growth.   There has not been complete unanimity regarding the benefic influence of this planet either : often its influence is considered very dangerous and harmful.   So it is necessary to plod through the mythologies, allegories and occult hints and suggestions in order to grasp the basic forces generated by this important planet with which every humanbeing is consciously and unconsciously, everyday connected, that also in a vital manner.

Among the various mythologies relating to the origin and functioning of the Moon, the two are of great significance which relate the Moon with the Churning of the Ocean by the Devas and the Non-Devas, and with the Moon's seduction of Tara, the wife of Brihaspati, Jupiter, the priest of the Devas, and the birth of Mercury over whose identity and ownership much conflict occurred between the various concerned parties.   An understanding of these two would also help us to understand the Shiva allegory better.

The Moon is said to have arisen as a result of the churning of the ocean which is an allegory of deep significance.   As a result of the churning of the Pure Essence, which was the universal perpetual motion which never ceases never slackens nor increases its speed not even during the interludes between the *pralayas*, or the nights of Brahma but goes on like a mill set in motion, whether it has anything to grind or not, many precious jewels said to be fourteen in number came out of this perpetual motion of Pure Essence which had· spread both in the subjective as well as in the objective dimensions. Amongst the various jewels that came as a result of this churning, the result of the magnetic polarities, the result of basic centripetal· and centrifugal forces in nature expressed as attraction and repulsion, or as Devas and non-Devas, poison as well as nector came out besides the Moon. It has been mentioned that this allegory is simply a representation of the unseen and unknown primeval intelligences, the atoms of occult science, Brahma himself being called Anu or the Atom, fashioning and differentiating the shoreless ocean of the primordial radiant essence. H. P. Blavatsky commenting on this cosmic process for the manifestation of different levels of existence, stated that "at the Churning of the Ocean" by the gods, the Nagas came and some stole of the Amrita—the gods and the Asuras, the no-gods and the gods were worsted. This refers to the formation of the Universe and the differentiation of the primordial primeval matter"[2]. The emergence of the Moon can therefore be well recognised as one of the primeval creative forces essential for the existence of (at least) our globe. The mythological reference to the Moon as the universal generative force is clearly in agreement with this allegory. The placement of the Moon at the forehead of the Lord Shiva who could be considered the personification of Time itself, also strengthens the Moon as the basis for the expression of Time. The tremendous motion of the Cosmic Energy, the Ganges, could have certainly devastated all efforts of Creative Intelligences

2. H. P. Blavatsky, Transactions of the Blavatsky Lodge, Theosophy Co. p. 110.

unless its speed was modulated by Time, the Moon, who absorbed much of its energy and thereby became even the progenitor of water. But as water can be generative, sustaining and destroying agency ; the Moon as the planet of all these three attributes of the Lord Mahadeva, is very truly associated with Him.

The second allegory of the Moon's enticement of Jupiter's wife Tara and impregnating her, refuging to give her back to Jupiter, the war in Heaven, her refusal to tell the real father's identity, and ultimately god's interference in getting her returned are all suggestive of another level of activities at the human level. The Moon's preference for certain types of female is well recognised in scriptures : even when he was married to 27 daughters of Daksha Prajapati (the daughters who symbolised the 27 Fixed Stars) he was more attached to Rohini which led the others complain against him which induced the Daksha to curse him but on reconsideration it was reduced to gradual decay and recuperation. The constellation of Rohini is related to the Moon which is the sign of its exaltation while the constellation itself is associated with Brahma, the god for generation and creation, it is given the symbol of a chariot which shows its affinity towards *Rajasic* movement, and the constellation is also having the attribute of Moksha bestower. Obviously, therefore, the Moon's attraction for this constellation is guided by the special qualities and radiation through this group of stars. The Moon is attracted wherever there is need for spiritual generative activities, any function which finally could give liberation, *Moksha*, with which Rohini, besides being related to Taurus, is linked. The upward, that is, Liberation-ward, propulsion of Moon is better signified by the Moon-Tara-Jupiter-Mercury allegory. Brihaspati or the planet Jupiter or Brahmansapati, as he is known in the *Rig Veda*, is a deity who is the symbol and the prototype of the *exoteric* or ritualistic worship. He is a priest, sacrificer, suppliant, and the medium through which the prayers of mortals reach the Gods. He is the *Purohita* (Family Priest, or Court Chaplain) of the Hindu Olympus and the spiritual guru of the Gods. The Moon, as the King Soma, is a Mystery God and presides over the mystic and occult nature in man and the universe. Tara, the priest's wife, who symbolises the worshipper, prefers esoteric truths to their mere shell, exotericism, hence she is shown as carried off by Soma. The appellation Soma attributed to Moon also refers to the means by which the Divine esoteric vision is got while on this earth. Soma is the sacred juice of that name, giving mystic visions and trance revelations. The partaker of Soma finds himself linked to his external body and yet away from it in his spiritual form. Freed from the former, he soars for the time being in the ethereal higher regions; becoming virtually "as one of the Gods", and yet preserving in his physical brain the memory of what he sees and learns. It is said that the Soma is the fruit of the Tree of Knowledge forbidden by the jealous Elohim to Adam and Eve, "lest man should become as one of us". H. P. Blavatsky has mentioned that the real property of the true Soma was (and *is*) to make a new *man* of the Initiate, after he is reborn namely once that he begins to live in his *Astral* Body; for, his spiritual nature overcoming the physical, he would soon snap it off and part even from that etherealed form"[3]. It is also said that the Soma-juice is self-purifying. When the moon–god pours down his ambrocial rain through the sieve of heaven, he is addressed and worshipped as

3. H. P. Blavatsky, *The Secret Doctrine*, Adyar, Vol IV, p. 67

Pavamana, which is one of the sacred fires and is considered self-purifying.   Represented by the soma-juice, it
undergoes purification by flowing through the Moon
which is used as a filter or a strainer.   The Moon, as
Soma, the means by which esoteric wisdom could be
envisioned which could be self purifying and through
which one could be a reborn 'Initiate', would be attractive
to anyone who is well regulated, disciplined, and ear-
nestly seeking True Enlightenment. Tara had been a pious
wife to *Brihaspati,* who could guide her in all exoteric
religious rituals but they could not make her life fruitful
(she did not beget any offspring from Jupiter), but with
the first call from Soma at dawn when Jupiter could be
induced to engage himself in exoteric ritualistic practices,
Tara without any sense of moral guilt (she did not even
wish to return to her husband after her copulation with
Soma) went ahead to unite with Soma and her life
became 'full'; she was impregnated.   She saw the
possibility of fulfilment of her life.   When the passional
nature of an individual vegetating in ritualistic everyday
life gets the call from *Buddhi* or Spiritual Soul, it cannot
resist the urge to mingle with it, nevertheless the
conflict aroused due to the necessity of breaking the
thread linking the physical with the universal or the
pure spiritual consciousness is so severe that a major
crisis is created at such moments.   That is the Churning
of the Ocean or the War in Heaven for the individual.
One does not wish to leave the state of Bliss, but the
pressure on it, the *karmic* responsibilities, and the work
to be done (for the humanity) require the individual to
return to the earthly life.

But how to identify the cause of the radical transformation? Is it the past scriptural studies and religious
discipline which make the life of a person satisfying, or

is it the union with Buddhi, the Intuition, which is a part of the Universal, Eternal, and Duration that the individual changed? No one other than the individual concerned can identify the cause of Divine Awakening, Tara herself had ultimately to indicate how she got her fulfilment in life. That fulfilment came after the birth of Mercury, the Divine Messenger who could soar high and low, and who could 'understand' things and decipher the good from the bad, who could discriminate between the right and the wrong. Thus, the present allegory relates the different levels of human conscious- ness and shows the importance of uplifting experiences through divine inspiration which could be possible when the passional nature of human individua is ready enough to hear its call, forsake its past bondage, and submit to the voice of the Intuition. That call comes from the Moon, when the individual engrossed in exoteric religious practices is ready to hear the call.

The Moon as psyche, or the Spiritual Soul, which is universal pure essence deeply connected with primeval matter as well as with pure spirit, has often been astro- logically represented as the *Hiranyagarbha*, the Bythos, the Great Deep from which everything has finally sprung. In the natal chart, this function is signified by the Fourth House and is also connected with water element. These appellations interpreted macrocosmically and micro- cosmically refer to the very early stage of creative ideation when creativity including generative, preservative and destructive impulses were yet in their latency though already differentiated enough for transformation into objective forms. Even in the constitution of man, the occult science often assigns higher importance to *Buddhi* than to *Atma*, but astrologically one need not enter into this controversy in spite of the fact that one cannot remain oblivious of such a situation. The mysterious nature of the Moon surpassing that of the Sun was well known to the Vedic seers who extolled the Moon in the *Rig Veda* as the *inspirer* of all auspicious thoughts and deeds. One may note here that these ancient sages attached to the Moon the quality of inspirer whereas the Sun could be the active potency, in a way the *Purusha*, who could act and create results. The *Sam Veda* bestowed on the Moon certain attributes which often baffles the scientific knowledge though the occultists have received tremendous enlightenment from the Sam Vedic invocations. The *Sam Veda* stated that the Moon provided light even to the Sun. While invoking Soma as the Great, wise and the hierophant who provided the foundation of varied forms and energised the Shining Ones, gave birth to different sense organs and powers of perception, bestowed the various siddhis and magical powers and gave to Indra who is the centre of manifestation purity and strength of intellect, it stated that Moon filled the Sun with effulgence, glory and fire. The *Sam Veda* assigned higher status to the Moon, for it germinated all herbs and plants and fructified all life-energies while intensifying the poisonous properties of lethal drugs and plants as well. The dual character of the Moon was well known to the ancient seers, the occultists and the astrologers.

While discussing the mysteries of the Moon, H. P. Blavatsky mentioned that the Moon is far older than the earth and further stated that the Moon is the satellite of our earth undeniably but this does not invalidate the theory that she has given to the Earth all but her corpse. It is considered a dead planet only so far as regards her inner principles, that is psychically and spiritually, however absurd the statement may seem. Physically she may be only as a semi-paralysed body. She is, according to Madam Blavatsky, aptly referred to in occultism as the 'Insane Mother', the great sidereal lunatic.[4] She has emphasised the benefic as well the malefic qualities of the Moon. The influences of the Moon are said to be wholly psycho-physiological. ''It is dead, sending out injurious emanations like a corpse. It vampirizes the earth and its inhabitants, so that any one sleeping in its rays suffers, losing some of his life-force. A white cloth is a protection, the rays not passing through it, and the head especially should be thus guarded. It is most powerful when it is full. It throws off particles which we absorb, and is gradually disinte-grating. Where there is snow the moon looks like a corpse, being unable, through the white snow, to vampirize effectively. Hence snow-covered mountains are free from its bad influences. The moon is phosphores-cent.''[5]

It is further stated that plants which under he Sun's rays are beneficient are maleficient under those of the Moon. Herbs containing poisons are most active when gathered under the Moon's rays. The effect of the Moon, as far as the human individuals are concerned is chiefly *Kama-Manasic* or psycho-physical ; it acts on the psychological brain, or the Brain Mind. · That is why we find that individuals with malefic influence of the Moon very easily get their mind deranged ; mental ailments ranging from insomnia to lunacy result from the adverse effect of this planet. With beneficial influence, the Moon creates imaginative mind, great intelligence, sharp

---

4. H. P. Blavatasky, *The Secret Doctrine*, Ib. P. 204, Vol. I
5. H. P. Blavatsky, *The Secret Doctine*, Ib. Vol. V., P. 535

memory, and often gives a healing touch and 'green hand'. It has often been emphasized that the Lunar magnetism genarates life, preserves and destroys it, psychically as well as physically. Because of its influence on the astral world and on the spirits of diverse kinds, the Moon is said to be the friend of the sorcerers and the foe of the unwary. "From the archaic aeons and the later times of the witches of Thessaly, down to some of the present Tantrikas of Bengal, her nature and properties have been known to every occultist, but have remained a closed book for physicists". For the mental health of an individual, the Moon is as important if not more as the ascendant is for the physical health.

In order to understand the influence of Moon on human consciousness, it is enlightening to examine the Puranic representation of the chariot of Moon, the King Soma. This representation does not refer to the inherent qualities of the planet, but it depicts the area of its activities. Specially for the purpose of regulating the impact of this planet, an understanding of this symbol is very useful. According to the Puranas, the chariot of Soma has three wheels and is drawn by ten horses of the whiteness of Jasmine, five on the righthalf of the yoke and five on the left. Anyone even with superficial knowledge of the Hindu philosophy would not find it far-fetched to associate 'whiteness' with purity and the five horses on different sides of the yoke as the five sense-organs of knowledge and five of action. The three wheels are the three Attributes, the *Gunas*, namely, *Sattwa* (harmony), *Rajas* (activity), and *Tamas* (inertia), but the same can also represent the three functions of regeneration (*Brahma's* function in cosmogony), preservation (*Vishnu* Principle) and Dissolution (*Mahesh* Aspect). The king on the chariot is Soma, the

Buddhi, or the Spiritual Soul of the person. While examining this symbology, it would be helpful to recall that Mercury, *Budha,* is a kind of link between the material, the lower or the psycho-physical vesture of the individual, and his Atma–Buddhi–Manas or the higher triad. Mercury, the Intelligence, links the two. The experiences of the world derived by the various sense and action organs filtering through the sieve of Intelligence enable the individual to establish his relationship with the external as well as his subjective world which if properly integrated with his Higher Being represented by the Trinity–Atma : Buddhi–Manas—could enable him to strive effectively for Liberation. *Manas* is represented by Mercury, which indicated a well balanced between Sun *(Atma),* Moon *(Buddhi)* and *Mercury* (Manas) relationship is necessary for a well coordinated personality. Such a relationship for efficient direction from the Moon can be possible if all the sense organs related to knowledge and action are well coordinated so that they do not struggle to run in condradictory directions, which would upset the charioteer.

Moreover, it has also to be reckoned that in the flight from the known to the Unknown, at every stage, whether of regeneration, preservation or dissolution, the guidance is necessary from the Spiritual Soul, Buddhi, the Moon. In actual horoscopy, it is necessary to examine the relationship of the Moon with other planets so as to find out the strength or the weaknesses of the individual's various sheaths, or his *Koshas* related to different planets, and the disposition of the Moon. Having considered the quality of the soul incarnating under the specific conditions under review, the quality of its nature, or of its consiousness, should be studied. His weaknesses as disclosed by the disposition of the

Moon, and its fetters as indicated by its relationship with different planets; and tendencies of his knowledge organs and action organs having been already examined, the individual should carefully take his whole personality in his hand and curb the unwanted propensities and encourage the growth of those which are hindered. Thus organised, the ten horses could be well directed which when linked with the direction of the charioteer, the Spiritual Soul, would enable the Integral Yoga to be achieved.

For astrological prognostications, the association of the Moon with the Ascendant is very important for harmonisation of the physical propensities with Intelligence of the individual concerned. There is a kind of physico—psychological synchronisation : the ·individual gets the necessary energy for what he desires to do whilst what his heart wishes to achieve is fully supported by physical capabilities. As a matter of fact, wherever the Moon is placed it would radiate that specific aspect of one's life brilliantly. But from this rule itself one will have to be very chary with the Moon in the Sixth and the Eighth Houses. In the sixth, the Moon is liable to result in the person being short-lived, ignorant, suffering from stomach ache, and having the possibility of humiliation. As a matter of fact, the sixth being the house related to enemies, thieves, cuts and wounds on the body, disappointments, miseries, sorrows, debts, illness, sinful deeds and so on, the radiance of the Moon in this position will result in nefarious results of the planet so much so that the person would find the period very disturbing. In the Eighth House as well the Moon does not give rise to favourable results : the person suffers from many diseases and his longevity is at stake. The Moon's placement in the Tenth House would lead to changeability in his professional career but he could have supreme adaptability to every situation he is confronted with. In the Fourth House, the Moon is in its natural habitat ; there the Intelligence of the individual could be sharp soaring over the depth and the height of his personality. The mind of such a person could have unrestricted possibility depending upon the sign of the zodiac and the planetary aspects and relationships to express the inner faculties : his latent unconsciousness would have immeasurable depth which given the favourable disposition of other planets could produce large amount of precious jewels.

But, it has to be noted that the lunar intelligence is pure white, that is completely neutral. It is the sensitivity to identify itself with any aspect of manifestation to derive the inner wisdom latent in it. It is necessary for successful life of the individual that the planet is supported by others. That is why it is emphasized that the Moon must be flanked on either side by some planets to make it effective, unless it is located in a quadrant when this requirement is not insisted. The Moon without any support of a planet (other then the Sun) on its either side results in *Kemdruma Yoga* which makes the person dirty, sorrowful, engaged in unrighteous deeds, poor, dependent, a rough person and a swindler. In fact, this placement of the Moon makes the individual unhappy. In essence, it implies that the Inner State of the Being is ineffective and dormant. When there are planets on either side of the Moon, the combination known as *Dhrudhura* makes the native bountiful, blessed with much wealth and conveyances. If there are planets excepting the Sun in the Second House from the Moon, *Sunpha* is caused which leads to self-earned property and makes the native a king, a ruler or his equal, intelligent, and wealthy with good reputation. When there are planets in the Twelfth from the Moon, *Anapha* is formed, which bestows to the native well-formed organs, majestic appearance, good reputation, makes him polite, generous, self-respecting, fond of dress and desirous of pleasure. But the texts say that a person with such a combination in his later life goes for renunciation. and austerity.

One of the most auspicious combinations with the Moon is formed if benefics that is Mercury, Venus and Jupiter are situated in the Sixth, Seventh and the Eighth from it. It is said that even if these planets are in the Sixth, Seventh, or the Eighth, or in two of these houses, or all of them only in one of these houses, in any of these combination, the yoga known as *Adhi* is formed. Commenting on this combination, Dr. B. V. Raman stated that the situation when one of these planets in full strength be in any one of these houses, the person would become a leader ; if there are two, he will be a minister, and if there are three, he will occupy a more eminent situation in life. If all the three benefics, devoid of strength, are in the three signs as mentioned earlier, then also this yoga is said to operate though the influence of this combination in such a situation may be feeble. Adhi Yoga is considered as a Raja Yoga or almost its equal, The reader would have by now realised that the strong reflection of the benefics in unison with the Pure Intelligence of the person could be highly productive of good results. Because of the grace of "universal pure essence", it would alter the very quality of life of the native. In usual parlance, it is said that "Adhi Yoga would bestow much happiness to the person and would make him polite, trustworthy, he would have conditions

which would be very enjoyable and happy, the surroundings would be luxurious and affluent ; the person would
inflict defeats on his enemies, and will be healthy enjoying a long life."[6]

Connected with Jupiter, the Moon has certain special
combinations which have often led the astrologers to
consider their results very carefully. As a matter of fact,
the relationship between Jupiter and the Moon in every
situation must be treated in a special way. Even when
Jupiter is a partner in the formation of *Adhi Yoga,* the
single Jupiter in the Sixth or the Eighth position from
the Moon forms *Sakat Yoga* which is an inauspicious
combination whilst the Moon in opposition with Jupiter,
that is, placed in the Seventh House from it leads to the
formation of a very auspicious *Gaja Keshari Yoga.* If
Jupiter is in a kendra from the Moon, the combination
goes under the name of Gajkeshari, whilst the Moon in
the Twelfth, Sixth, or Eighth from Jupiter gives rise to
Sataka Yoga. Jataka Parijatam defines *Sakat Yoga* differently. It states that if Jupiter occupying the Sixth or
the Eighth Bhava from the Moon be elsewhere than in a
kendra in respect of the Ascendant, the resulting *yoga* is
termed *Sakat.* The result of *Sakat Yoga* is said to be
infrequent impediment in the fortunate occurrences : the
person born in this yoga will often become unfortunate
and may again regain what he once lost. He will be a
very ordinary and insignificant man in the world. He
will attain much mental grief that is inevitable and will
be exceedingly unhappy. The Moon in a kendra position
to Jupiter brings on *Kesari* yoga under which the person
born will destroy like a lion, all his enemies. He will

6. B. V. Raman, *Three Hundred Important Combinations,*
Bangalore. P. 37

speak loftily or nobly in an assembly. He will be passio-
nate and emotional in his endeavour. He will be long-
lived, highly renowned and exceedingly intelligent. He
will conquer everything by his own valour. It is also
indicated that the Moon's placement in Kendra from the
Ascendant nullifies the occurrence of *Sakat Yoga ;* it is
also found that the combination does not necessarily make
the native poor and wretched and the degree of poverty
and misfortune if any, would be nominal. Esoterically,
the relationship between the Moon and Jupiter need not
have much influence on riches and wealth, but actually
on the psychological understanding of the problems of
life ; they should affect the approach to life, in other
words on the philosophy of life of the native. When
rituals and exoteric observances predominate and come
in conflict with inner understanding or the esoteric
wisdom, there could be severe psychological stress
which should be the outcome of *Sakat Yoga* but under
powerful support from intelligence (Mercury) and percep-
tion(Venus) as in *Adhi Yoga* even if Jupiter is in a
situation as to form *Sakat Yoga,* the adverse psychological
wrong judgement and involvement in outer religions
could be well modulated and brought in harmony with
higher inner wisdom conducive to balance in life.

Varahamihira has mentioned a combination which is
very interesting in the present context. When Jupiter,
Moon and the Ascendant are aspected by Saturn, and
Jupiter occupies the Ninth House, then according to
Varahamihira, the person born in the Rajayoga will
become a holy illustrious founder of a system of
philosophy. This combination stresses the annihilating
effect of Saturn. When the interest of the individual in
rituals and outer religious practices has ended, the I-ness
of the native is destroyed by humiliating and other

painful experiences of life, and when all regenerative
potential is annihilated, the individual would experience
or would begin to perceive the formless reality. Under
such a condition, the experience born out of sorrow and
pain, arouse the Spiritual Soul to its consciousness and
the person becomes an honest student of the Inner
Reality.

It is the Sun which reveals the inner life of the
individual. Many concealed aspects of one's life, often
buried under the debris of past *karmas* and indicating
the so-called eternal soul's growth status and the possibility of the development of the spiritual qualities can be
indicated only by the disposition of the Sun. This planet
is not only the *Atma* of the universe, it is the very core
of one's being, and it is the ultimate destiny towards
which all events in life are geered. The Sun is the fire
that burns within every individual in order to make him
what he is ; actually it is the solar energy which activises
all other planets. Therefore the lasting worth of an
individual depends upon the disposition of the Sun. In
this regard, there are three things which are very important for consideration : the Sun does not receive anything
from any other planet, rather the disposition of other
planets is conditioned by the energy imparted by the
Sun to them ; the strength of the Sun as indicated by its
placement in the various signs of the zodiac as well as in
the Fixed Stars, the *Nakshatras*, even and the house in
which it is placed would be very important ; and thirdly,
the relationship of the Sun with Saturn and Rahu/Ketu
showing the karmic impediments faced by the Sun would
be significant in assessing the importance of the Sun in
any horoscope. In order to comprehend the nature and
significance of the Sun in any one's life it would be
helpful if we could at first have an idea of the real

attributes of the Sun itself and what it signifies in the wider context.

The Sun has been given the appellation of *Shivswarupam* and *Maya-athitham*. The scriptures have associated the Sun with Daksha Prajapati whose daughter Aditi in marriage with Kashyapa Prajapati begot 12 *Adityas* or the suns. Obviously the Daksha as well as other Prajapatis were mighty Creative Intelligences who have been engaged in manifesting this universe. It is said that there is the universal perpetual motion which never ceases never slackens nor increases its speed not even during the interludes between the pralayas, or "nights of Brhamas", but goes on like a mill set in motion, whether it has anything to grind or not : this perpetual motion governs the laws of nature, and it is this motion which is Force, ever generating its electricity, which is life. The Sun is that symbolic representation of the Cosmic Energy which is the very life of this solar system and various Prajapatis had been manifested to assist this process. The various offspring of the Prajapatis and the different kinds of marriages they performed all represent this creative process. This Life Process contains within itself the aspect of Time which shows objectification of the subjective or the latent life force. The Lord Shiva is the embodiment of the Perpetual Presence of the Life Force containing within itself the regenerative, preservative, and the capability of dissolution. This aspect of Shiva is well represented by the Sun who gives rise to Time, who provides the energy for every entity within its (solar) system, and pervades all over its manifestation. The appellation *Shivaswarupam* in this way seems apt in order to suggest that every entity on this earth owes its existence to the Sun in whom it lives, moves and dissolves. The very life energy ensouling the

entity not only preserves it but also *directs it* to its goal,
which explains the great importance of the Sun in every
one's horoscope.

The attribute *Mayaatitham* signifying beyond the
influence of *Maya*, illusion, ignorance, shows that nothing which is not real could exists in the Sun. If we recall
that the Sun is considered a malefic, then for this very
reason it would not allow anything to happen which
is not according to its plan : all such spurious incidents
and factors will be eliminated from life as they would be
creating illusion or unreality. They would be intensifying
the veil of *Maya* which the Sun cannot allow to exist.
Under the main period of Sun, the inner glory shines
forth ; or if those divine potentialities which make the
individual divine-like are shrouded by several element
of ignorance, *avidya*, during the period of the Sun those
elements will be eliminated even if it may appear as
misfortune, or difficulties during the life span.

The Sun is said to have married *Sanjna*, a daughter
of *Viswa Karma*. The latter is the creator of the universe,
and the architect of Gods. A female is primarily the
passive creative potential ; she as *Sanjna*, is the embodiment of form. The universal perpetual motion,
which is ever generating electricity, which is life
itself, will necessarily be in an ethereal form incapable
of merging or uniting with anything which
is of the same ethereal quality unless it is
attached to something concrete. Realizing that the
Sun's rays were too severe for her (in another version of
the story, this condition of *Sanjna* is not explicitly
mentioned) she wanted to visit her parents and
meanwhile her shadow, *Chhaya*, bearing her exact
semblance, she made attendant on him (the Sun).
During the course of their stay together, that is of

Chhaya and the Sun, the latter uniting with her begot two sons, namely, *Savarni* and *Sani* and one daughter named *Tapan*. The Sun lived happily with Chhaya so much so that his real wife *Sanjna* on her return to live with her husband was not allowed entry. Disappointed, she assumed the form of a mare to roam around. Realizing the real state of affairs, the Sun also assumed the form of a horse and followed her to soothe her, after which uniting with her he produced the two Kumars— the Ashvins, the ever young celestial doctors. From this, it can be observed that the Sun is able to produce only in association with lower forms of manifestation. Astrologically, it is well recognised that the Sun does not feel happy in the company of its equals : it always shows its creative faculties when concrete tasks are assigned to it. This is not a planet for pure subjective *Samadhi,* contemplation but, for any intellectual, original, and highly effective results there is no other planet equal to the Sun. The Sun and Consciousness both being on purely subjective plane of existence require something concrete for their fructification : either consciousness has to be linked with some objective entity which necessarily has to be shadowy, elusive, in order to enable life ensouling it ; or consciousness as well life-energy both must be in the form of passive (mare) and positive (horse) form of energy in order to produce creative entities. The Sun in any horoscope requires some concrete material support, such as that of Mercury, to show its creative potential.

An important attribute of the Sun is that it can function on different levels of existence with equal ease and effectiveness. The Sun is represented seated in a chariot drawn by seven horses or a horse with seven heads : the chariot has only one wheel and the great

serpent *Nag* who had provided the resting ground for
Vishnu while he was on the *Kshira sagar*, is also related
to the movement of the Sun. The seven horses of the
chariot represent the inner radiations from the Sun. The
planet in its real state is the Invisible Creative Power, its
visible counterpart is the Sun whose number in scriptures
as *Adityas* is given as twelve (the 12 zodiacs?) but in some
occult literature mention has been made of seven states
of consciousness connected with Sushumna, Harikesh,
Vishvakarman, Visvatryachas, Sannaddha, Sarvavasu.
Svaraj : the Sushumna is recognised as the ray which
is active in energising the Moon and is very much
associated with the yoga disciplines performed by the
sages. It is also said that Vishvakarma, the father-in-law
of the Sun when knew of the Sun's effect on his wife
Sanjna who could not cope up with his tremendous
effulgence, cut him to his (Sun's) one eighth part and
the remaining parts fell to the earth to form the discus
of Vishnu, the trident of Siva, the weapon of Kubera,
the lance of Karttikeya and the weapons of other gods.
Thus, the Sun we see is merely a very limited effulgence
of the real Sun, the various means with which other
planets achieve their success are mere fragments of the
Sun-God, There is septenary principle inherent in the
operation of the solar rays. The seven *koshas* or sheaths
of the human being, the seven lokas, or the planes of
existence, the seven planets (including the Sun) all take
their energy and power from the Real Solar Deity. It is
therefore of prime importance that the strength and the
status of an individual is assessed on the basis of the
power and the disposition of the Sun. If the Sun is
well disposed in the natal chart, the person concerned, in
spite of difficulties and trials on the path of his pilgrimage would ascend to the heights signified. Otherwise,

all the well placed planets without the suitable placement of the Sun would be ineffective. In such an
assessment, it has to be assumed that the Sun is not
necessarily a material planet : it is primarily concerned
with the Glory of the Supreme, the Primeval Potential, If
it operates on the material, physical plane it would make
the person glorified king, head of the state and so on ;
working on the psychic plane, it would bestow on the
person immense capability of achieving *siddies* ; on the
spiritual level it would produce great saints and sages
all beaming with the inner glow of the Sun. It is the
ray of the Inner Sun which vivifies the individual and the
level of his operation ; on the expression of the solar
power, the expansion and growth of the individual is
dependent, otherwise other planets might temporarily
give some achievements but not lasting ones. Any
higher achievement in life, whether it is a physical
achievement of acquiring domain over human beings, or
over the intellectual world or it is merging with the
Divine as evident from Initiatory rites in Mystery Schools,
all these can be predicted only on the basis of the basic
foundation laid by the Sun.

In everyday life, the importance of the Sun is to
determine the status,—social, official and spiritual—of
the person concerned. When the Sun is in different signs
of the zodiac, the level of the manifestation of the solar
rays in one's life is assessed on that basis. In Aries,
the Sun's rays would be devastating depending on where
the Sun is placed. If it is the sixth house, the enemies
of the person would be completely vanquished, but it is
difficult to assess the possibility of the development of
his latent faculties. In the Eighth House, such a placement may make the person long-lived, but what about
the possibility of acquiring hidden legacies ? Such a

powerful Sun in these houses may not be very helpful for occult achievements unless other relevant combinations are present, but for the destruction of material obstacles it would be highly helpful. In the Ascendant, the Sun in Aries could make the individual very glorified, full of highly spiritual values. His status in life, both materially and spiritually would be quite high. In the fifth house, as far children are concerned, a powerful Sun is not highly beneficial but for intellectual attainments it would be very proficient. The Sun on the meridian is a special situation under which condition the individual would always aspire and often be near the centre of the seat of the power.

For spirituality, the association of the Sun with Ketu is highly proficient, specially if the real elimination of the Ego and complete humanitarianism based on the Vedantic philosophy are desired. Such a person is not so much fond of rituals, or in spurious philosophy but he would go to the very root of spiritualism and by identifying his personal consciousness with the object of experience, he would perceive the truth or falsehood of the thing concerned. With Jupiter, this result is not expected. Firstly, there is always a possibility that Jupiter might be combust, and secondly if it is not combust, then also it would lead to the destruction of exoteric philosophy and belief in the efficacy of ritualism of religion. Naturally therefore the conjunction of Sun and Jupiter is not very desirable. A special yoga occurs if the Sun is in combination with Mercury which leads to high intellectualism in the person who could bring forth surprisingly original ideas and approaches to various problems of the life. But with Venus, the combination would be destructive to all the happy experiences of life. The person because of extreme subjectivity and

identification with the highest divine in man would not
be able to enjoy the physical side of life. But with Mars,
if the latter is not combust, the Sun would be in its
highest element : there would be immense courage and
enthusiasm for the expression of the innermost goodness
and feelings : such man could be a martyr, he could be a
dauntless explorer, he would be able to bear any amount
of trouble and tribulations for achieving any result. But
with the Moon, the Sun is not in very good shape : the
Moon is good to reflect the glory of the Sun, but in
association with it, the Sun will make, the person a
dried heart.

In fact, for assessing the quality of a chart the
Ascendant, Moon and the Sun could enable the astrologer to get to the root of the person's life : the quest of
his soul could be prognosticated on the assessment of
the nature of the Sun ; the quality of his heart and
Buddhi would be known by the placement of the Moon ;
and the general assessment of his material and physical
pilgrimage would depend upon his Ascendant. All these
are very important in the pursuit of self-knowledge and
astrology is useful very much only when the individual
is vitally interested in the deeper aspects of his life. On
the basis of such an understanding he could eradicate
many of his unwanted proclivities and develop the
faculties which are in nascent stage but having the
possibility of much development in the present incarnation.

JUPITER : THE SUSTAINER

The touch of disappointment which may very often accompany the benefic effects of Jupiter has generally been overlooked by many casual students of astrology. Undoubtedly, this planet has been acclaimed the greatest benefic of the astrological hierarchy, but empirical results of the Jovian influence when critically examined does not *always* sustain the prognostication. The classical texts have laid considerable importance on this planet for the welfare and prosperity of humanity, and the astrologers have habitually been accepting the dictum almost as a matter of course. One however discerns some reservations from Dr. B. V. Raman, the erudite editor of *The Astrological Magazine*, who despite his acceptance of this planet as "a first-rate benefic" has not been oblivious of the streak of encumbrance caused under its impact. While indicating the influence of Jupiterian cycles on mundane astrology, Dr. Raman has on several occasions indicated the devastating effects of this planet. For example, once Dr. Raman mentioned that the first and the second Jupiterian cycles in the history of the United States of America involved the country in bloody warfare and he also gave several explanations for such occurrences. The point to ponder in this connection is not the explanations so much as the causation of unhappiness under the exceptional effect of peace-loving, fortune giving Deva Guru, the preceptor of gods. An understanding of the basic influence of Jupiter could reveal the function of Guru of Gods so as to take the most effective guidance from this planetary Intelligence.

Generally speaking, everyone expects Jupiter to bestow happiness when placed under favourable conditions and to ward off difficulties when adverse influences prevail. The best placement of Jupiter is said to be in the Ninth House and if that happens to be the sign of Sagittarius, it is even better. It means that the best influence of Jupiter should be present for the Aries ascendants, and specially when Jupiter is in the Ninth House. The Ascendant and the Fifth House are also considered very favourable placements for this planet. In the Tenth House, Jupiter has shown very auspicious results. But, unless one is concerned only with the superficial results of this planet one would discover certain traits of it even in its benefic positions which may be very revealing.

The priest of the *Devas*, the gods, has certainly considerable impact on arousing spirituality and righteousness in the heart of the native, and under favourable conjuncture it is prone to confer untold and immeasurable wealth, renown and power. But to expect such results under all conditions may be wrong. What is sometimes found is that the favourable results expected under the influence of Jupiter are radically different and the native is put to untold misery. This point is generally not accepted by common astrologers and they sidetrack the issue by adducing many special explanations for the event. In order to make astrology a helpful guide for the individual's life-course, it is necessary to understand the basic impulse imparted by Jupiter so that in all cases, whether it produces wealth and power, or poverty and mental tension, one could get a feel of what the planet is trying to do for the native.

Jupiter is mentioned in the *Rig Veda* by the name of Brihaspati and Brahmanspati which are synonymous. These are names of a deity in whom the action of the worshipper of the gods is personified ; he is the suppliant, the sacrificer, and the priest who intercedes with gods on behalf of men and protects mankind against the wicked. The priesthood of Jupiter has been overplayed. As the "purohita" or the family priest he is not only expected to know the family tradition and its social responsibilities, but also the highest ethics and religious duties. So the impact of Jupiter must produce the welfare of the person concerned from the longer standpoint. This relegates the importance of material welfare and worldly achievements to an unimportant place. Jupiter is chiefly guided by the ultimate goal of the person which would lie in the establishment of some viable linkage with gods, the spiritual hierarchy, or the celestial Intelligences. The way to this spiritual objective is not always pleasant and not necessarily through affluence. If the growing soul needs wealth, status, and renown for its maturity and disenchantment, Jupiter may bestow these to it but when the soul is already matured, the rituals performed under Jupiter would be of very limited significance. It is for this reason that the Jovian impact becomes enigmatic unless the same is related to the soul's growth.

Under the impact of Jupiter, the religious tendencies are of the exoteric nature : the individual may read scriptures, perform long duration *poojas,* worship, and he deeply interested in external manifestations of religion. He would be regularly present at temples and churches, to him deities are very much personified gods ever ready to forgive the worshipper and capable of removing all the impediments from his path. Jupiter is primarily the

planet concerned with exotericism as a result of which
one surmises that it is linked with form side of life. The
external world is the domain of Jupiter. And no one
would like to destroy what belongs to it, so Jupiter
should like to maintain and nourish the form side of life.

As a *Deva Guru*, the preceptor of gods, one should
expect Jupiter to provide the same type of impulses that
the gods are expected to do. It is certainly God's Grace
which can produce every thing, and Jupiter in many
ways is considered the chalice through which the God's
Grace flows to the world, but the primary function of
Jupiter as that of Gods is preservation of the existing
order. Jupiter maintains tradition ; it is extremely resis-
tant to any kind of change ; it pays obeisance to the
aged and the learned. The gods also involve themselves
in preserving the order 'created' by Brahma. As a
nourisher, Jupiter would not assist the death of any
person ; even if the person has to die under the influence of this planet, such persons would linger on for
a long period before he finally succumbs to death. If
some one has good health, and some other planetary
influence is inclined to create difficulties to it by intro
ducing germs of disease, Jupiter would reinforce health
globules so that the existing health could be maintained.
If some one has already acquired wealth and good position, and some planetary influence tends to unsettle
him, Jupiter would endeavour to protect his affluence
and status. But whether by itself Jupiter could augment
wealth, increase the status, or give rise to renown is a
question on which more critical study is required to be
done.

Being primarily concerned with exoteric knowledge,
Jupiter would fail to satisfy those who having toiled
in religosity for a long period desire to acquire inner

truth of the matter. The allegory of Tara's seduction by the Moon clearly shows that the disciple of esoteric religion could not be held in externals for a long time : he would at the slightest signal from the Buddhi, Inner Illumination, would be willing to forsake the exoteric religion. The involvement with externals necessarily leads to inner disappointment but it could persist only till the opportunity for esoteric learning does not arise.

A transformation of one's real nature can however be foretold under the impact of Jupiter. Specially if Jupiter is powerfully posited in a horoscope, as in Sagittarius, or Pisces connected with the Ninth House, there is a strong possibility of the individual radically transforming his life in the present incarnation itself. The symbology of Sagittarius representing body of a horse with a human head points to the transformation of the animal nature in man to a human quality. It implied not an expansion of the existing traits but a mutation. This happens when Jupiter is powerful. Under that impulse an upward impulse is imparted to the individual. This transformation would involve change in one's psychology and the resulting adaptation to newer ways of life. Such an adaptation cantnot be expected to be always very pleasant. That explains disappointment with Jupiter, but that also suggests that the benefic planets may give rise to unpleasant results.

The ancient seers had recognised that the real deity to whom the obeisance was offered was the power behind the planet. The *Vedas* did not explicitly made the difference because probably they were assuming that the people were already praying to the regent of the planet rather than to the planet itself. This anthropomorphic appellation becomes quite clear for example when it is said "He with his seed spreads forth beyond another's

seed, whomever Brahmnaspati takes for his friend".
With the favour granted by the Regent of the planet,
that is, when the Brahmanspati adds his creative power,
in his seed, to that of the sacrificer, the latter's creative
power increases manifold. The seed in man is capable
of unlimited expansion. Under the Jovian influence this
expansion is luxuriant. Even when the growth is
intended to be of the type of mutation, radically different
from the exoteric side but enabling the inner faculties
to come forth luxuriantly, the operation is effectively
carried out. Keeping in view the luxuriant growth of
this kind, the latter scriptures gave the name of Niti-
Ghosha to the car of Brahmanspati which was said
to be drawn by eight pale horses. Here the reference
to eight pale horses is to the eight perfections, the
siddhis. These accomplishments are the superhuman
powers of becoming as small as an atom, power of assuming excessive lightness at will, power of obtaining anything at one's will, to develop irresistible will, the power
of increasing one's size according to one's will, power
of superiority, power to subjugate anyone to one's
authority; and the power to control and suppress one's
passions. These accomplishments can be possible, to
some extent, under the influence of Jupiter specially if
the person is born under Cancer Ascendant and Jupiter
is placed in the Sixth House. But, generally speaking,
Jupiter, unless other planetary support is given to it,
would increase the hostility of the people against the
native if it is located in the Sixth House.

Astrologically, Jupiter has tremendous auspicious
power to bestow by its beneficial aspect. In Ascendant,
it is aspecting the fifth, seventh, and the ninth houses
whereby there would be an element of contentment and
a sense of fulfilment. In the Fourth House, the individual

would be very magnanimous and would always consider his sufferings and troubles of much less importance than the goodness he can show to others. Jupiter in the Fifth House is not considered good for progeny but for general creative and educational activities this placement is very satisfactory. In the Seventh House, Jupiter makes the person very sociable and the women are very much fascinated by him, but his marital life is not very idealistic. Great uneasiness prevails and the personal life of the person reveals deep rooted disappointment with life. Outwardly such a person could not be singled out as a frustrated one, but he would not be considering himself fortunate though he might even receive legacies and much wealth. Twelfth House Jupiter is good only far psychic development ; such persons are generally hankering after the unknown and dreaming of the possibilities which might have taken place but did not, or which would take place only in the future. Whatever house receives the beneficial aspect of Jupiter, that house in the chart thrives very well.

Among the various combinations that are associated with Jupiter, one recalls, *Gaja Keshari* and *Adhi* yogas connected with the Moon which are auspicious and *Sakat Yoga* which is inauspicious, but the most important combination relating to Jupiter is *Hamsa Yoga*. It is one of the combinations under the special *Panchamaha-purusha yogas*. These are formed when any of the five planets excepting the Sun and the Moon, Mercury, Venus, Mars, Jupiter or Saturn in power *e.g.,* in exaltation or in its own sign is placed in a quadrant from the Ascendant or the Moon. *Hamsa Yoga* is formed if Jupiter is in a quadrant identical with its own sign that is Sagittarius or Pisces, or in Cancer where it gets exalted. This combination is possible only in respect of common and the movable signs, the assumption being that the Ascendant is also counted as a quadrant. Persons born with this combination have "a red mouth and a prominent nose ; their legs are well formed, they have the voice and the phlegm of the swan ; their limbs are fair ; such persons have a beautiful wife ; their own personality is very charming and attractive ; they have every comfort of life at their command ; they are intent on acquiring a knowledg of sacred scriptures and they are devoted to meritorious deeds". In short, the persons born under *Hamsa Yoga* are special favourites of gods.

In conclusion, one can affirm that the vitality of the person with strong Jupiter posited in a favourable conjuncture is considerably strengthened ; he gets special nourishment from celestial powers and his health and prosperity are well protected. Born in Hamsa Yoga, the person would be very lucky, but in *Sakat Yoga* there would be much hardship for him. An important characteristic of Jupiter is that it strengthens the qualities of other planets, rather than creating the result by itself.

SATURN : THE RESTRAINER

Saturn is the most powerful malefic planet. Among the four malefics, namely, the Sun, Mars, Rahu and Saturn, the role of the last one is unique. Its action is intensely decisive. Rahu is malignant with deep impact in colouring the psyche of the individual. His entire psychological structure, the *samskara* as the Hindus call it, is so much debased that all the spiritual tendencies are almost annihilated. The sway of materiality becomes outstanding. This impact is distinctly different from that of Saturn. The latter may create misery, helplessness, utter dismay, turn success into disappointment, gold into dust ; nonetheless, the deep-rooted spirituality in the sense of unity with One Life Universal is never abandoned. Mars is malefic in the sense that its destructive radiation which burns all dross in life is a direct impact of the planet. Suddenly it destroys. The benefic influence of this planet by way of bestowing wealth, status, courage, and magnetic personality cannot be overlooked. The radiation of Mars penetrates the physical and the psychological dimensions of the person leaving almost untouched the higher realms of his being. It is basically a profoundly honest planet. The individual under its impact does not suffer from hypocrisy, deceit, or play foul. His action is straight and forthright. Saturn does not act that way. Its impact is deep-rooted. Its impact is indirectly achieved. Instead of giving courage and strength, it destroys egotism and I-ness. It makes the individual almost helpless. The results of this planet are so deceptive and unpredictable that one is not able to visualise correctly the changes it is going to produce and the way it is going to act. Even compared to the Sun among the malefics, Saturn is very different. The inclusion of the Sun among the malefics is for certain special reasons which are not comparable to any other malefic. The Sun does not destroy the ego of the individual, but it always, whether in a positive or a negative way, accentuates the personality. The action of the Sun is decisive and the after-effect of it almost secondary. The Sun is royalty, a planet of status and the planet whose influence vivifies the relationship of the individual with the centre of the being, which is also the centre of the Universal Life. Saturn acts differently. Its apparent effect is secondary whereas the after-effects are much more lasting. It does not establish the link with the centre, the ego, rather it destroys the same making the individual bereft of all his glory and all his moorings. Thus one finds that the role of Saturn is not only difficult to prognosticate but also very indirect and much enduring. It is indeed the most powerful malefic of the planetary hierarchy.

The ancient seers variously described the characteristics of Saturn. Some compared it with *Yama*, the God of Death, whereas others described it as the worshipper of *Yama* which for the present purpose is only a difference of superficial nature. Saturn has been related to wilderness, burial places and even to dilapidated buildings. Some texts have even related it to the sacrificial fires, remedies for restoring life, and sovereignty over all. Such peculiarities of the planet do not enable the student to investigate the basic nature of the planetary hierarchy, and the spirit energizing this planet.

For this purpose, one has to dive deeper in the mythologies. It is said that the birth of Saturn is a mystery and the descriptions given of it are very elusive. One of the wives of the Sun finding the consortship to this ever-active planet engaged in life-giving process to this cosmos, very arduous and not finding any relief to herself, created a *mayavic* or an illusory replica of herself and placed it to officiate for her while she herself went for a holiday. During this period, from the contact of this shadowy creature with the Mighty Sun was born Saturn at the time of sunset in the asterism of Revati. Swami Dayanand is inclined to interpret this asterism, which finds a place in the *Vedas*, to mean "wise policy". The significance of this interpretation cannot be easily explained unless one considers that the good or the bad effect of this planet is a 'wise policy' from some inner consideration. Being connected with Revati which is the end portion of the signs of the zodiac and the last of all the 27 asterism, and with Pisces which is a watery sign representing the feet of the Heavenly Man, the *Kala Purusha*, Saturn's birth indicates several special features of deeper predictive significance.

Saturn is said to be a son of the Sun by his illusory wife *Chhaya*, meaning 'shadow' which suggests that the planet represents an interaction of the highest principle in cosmos as well as in man, and the world of illusion, shadow or materiality. Even the Greek mythology mentions Kronos, another name of Saturn, as the youngest son of Uranus (Heaven) and Ge (Earth). Here, Uranus symbolising the heaven stands for the highest principle in cosmic manifestation, and Ge, the Earth, as the most material level of manifestation. Naturally, therefore, the effect of Saturn should be the outcome of the conflict born out of materiality, the shadowy wife of the Sun, *Chhaya,* and the Divine Principle of One Universal Life, the Fohat, the Original Source represented as Justice, Harmony, Truth, the Life-Essence. During the period, of Saturn, whether in its malefic aspect or the benefic effect, the much described turmoil and troubles of the individuals arise as a result of the churning of these two polarised forces. The seeming disappointment, failures and frustrations arise due to the Universal Force of Harmony and Justice. In the ignorance of the Divine Laws, one fails to appreciate the benign, long-run, influence of the planet. When the centre of attention of the individual is directed to material attainments and material prosperity, power-position-affluence and the rest of it, Saturn would dissolve all these in order to arouse the interest of the individual in deeper aspects of life. Saturn is not interested in disappointment just for the sake of disappointment; it is result-ward oriented. The churning takes place in order to make the individual contemplative, thoughful, so that on the viewless wings of the thinking principle by concentrating it and directing the same towards the Original Source, the individual could set his feet on the path of righteousness and the path of withdrāwal—the *Nvritti Marg.*

The tradition of Saturn being born in the asterism of Revati, the last portion of Pisces, a sign representing the Great Deep, the Bythos, from which end another vibration of Manavantric Evolutionary Force begins to radiate finds its echo even in the Jewish thought. The Messiah seems to be coming in manifestation "at the conjunction of Saturn and Jupiter in the sign Pisces". In this sign, especially along with the most benefic planet Jupiter, the sting of Saturn is completely neutralised ; his energy for saving the world from entering the deeper layers of materiality is absolutely free and well directed. At such a position, Saturn is ready to enter Aries, the sign of its debilitation suggesting the Messiah as willing to bear the Cross of Golgotha. Apart from the fact that water is another name of the Great Deep, the Primordial Waters of Space or Chaos, it is also related to the celestial Virgin Mother, or Matter, of the visible universe. The Twelfth House of the horoscope where the feet of the *Kala Purusha,* the Heavenly Man, rest, is also the area of the World Beyond, the World of the Dead, the Lokas of *Yama.* An understanding of these references unveils a deeper aspect of Saturn : it is never destructive *per se.* Being a Messiah, a reference reinforced by the belief that Saturn's Spirit or Regent is Mikael or Michael, who is the Christian conqueror of the devil; Kiyum or the God Kivan worshipped by the Jews in the wilderness ; and belief among the Occidental occultists that Saturn, Shiva, and Jehovah were the Same Spirit. Saturn can never be the energy or radiation destroying the human individual by creating a sense of "wilderness" in his psyche. Such great Spiritual Beings or the Celestial Intelligences, whatever their level of manifestatipn, exist to save mankind. They could never pour merciless cruelty on poor human mortals. After bearing the cross of Calvary, Jesus ascended the Heaven ; after Shiva destroyed the Devil (in man), a fresh and purer life manifests ; on the completion of gruesome torture of *sadesati*, the period of $7\frac{1}{2}$ years during which years Saturn transits the Twelfth, the First and the Second Houses from the Moon sign in the natal chart, the individual is given his reward for the endurance when the planet enters the Third House from the Moon sign. That is why, it is said that the Lord Shiva although a destroyer is actually a recreator of all things in perfect wisdom. The recreative energy released from the suffering caused by Saturn is for building a new world in perfect wisdom. Every individual having passed the unsettling period of Saturn knows the soothing reward and tremendous energy he inherits for leading a new life. The fire that burns the dross to purify the gold cannot be considered destructive though in essence it precisely does the same. It could be compared with the medium of the artists, with their chisel and hammer which carve out the beautiful form slumbering within the uncut virgin stone.

Saturn is generally represented as a very old man with a sickel in his hand. The Romans thought him a god of sowing or seedcorn ; Saturn is said to have offered for sacrifice his only begotten son to his father. He is also considered as the king of the golden age and the decrepit old man. Varahamihira described Saturn as dark in form, black in colour, *tamasic* in nature (*i.e.* with proclivity for inertia in action) being disposed towards inactivity, and has assigned to Saturn places where rubbish heaps are stored. Saturn according to him, is related to rags, hillocks, mountains and forests. Similar descriptions have also been given by other Indian seers, all of whom reveal one common and outstanding feature of the planet, namely, that it stands for endless and Immovable Duration, without beginning, without end, beyond time and beyond space. It would be pertinent to enquire as to the reason for the suffering of the individual under the impact of the planet of Duration, Timelessness. It is often observed that the effect of Saturn is so acute and devastating that no amount of propitiation ordinarily mitigates the trouble aroused by Saturn. The outward agent causing the trouble is just a means, the real cause lying deep in the past, in the antiquity of bygone lives and the consequence is the strengthening of confidence and emergence of the archetype already set out for the individual. The past karmic sins raise their head under the period of Saturn to be eliminated permanently. Distortions of limbs, loss of money and status, death of the only son or the most beloved partner, exile in an unknown foreign land, and seemingly unmerited ignomy and humiliation are caused by Saturn because in the time-scale of cosmic manifestation the discordant notes must be harmonised and the past karmic debts completely paid off. When such purging of past discordant deeds takes place, the individual has already forgotton the incident but Time has kept a detailed record of the same to counteract the force thereby generated. That is why Saturn produces the countervailing forces in due time. The cycle of birth, growth and destruction completes the chain of causation. Time knows neither beginning nor end. The hillocks and mountains symbolise eternity, where change does not take place. The decrepit old man is one who has withered and has grown in wisdom. The heap of rubbish is the symbol of the end of the creation which in fact is like the burial ground where the rubbish of mortal child is destroyed. All these are related to Time, Karma, and Infinitude. When the individual action in complete unity, in totality, is exposed to Eternity, a new and radical transformation takes place in the individual where egotism, materiality and the sense of fulfilment vanish like darkness to light. That is one reason why Saturn is said to eat his own son : materiality born out of illusion is sacrificed in the light of Eternal Wisdom. For this reason, Saturn gives renunciation, spirituality, and loneliness in life.

Once Dr. B. V. Raman stated that Saturn in spite of its being a natural malefic is a sustainer and whatever developments occur under this planet last for a long time.[1] Such characteristics of Saturn would take the student to the core of the effect of the planet and it would even explain why Saturn is considered a "planet of democracy". That which is ephemeral, transitory, gives rise to birth, growth, and dissolution, in short, manifestation in Time ; that which is Timeless lies in the bosom of *Yama*, Eternity, Great Deep, where the characteristics of this ephemeral world would not sustain. There only those elements of the being are sustained which are of primordial nature. The hierarchical stratification of the society considered as aristocracy, oligarchy, and so on rests in the time dimension where evolution of the society is taking place. Under democracy, the differences which arise or are caused by the time-effect of manifestation are eliminated, and therefore as every soul or monad in essence, in its primordial nature, is a fragment of Divinity, there is no consideration of levels of the beings there. Every one is the same. It is for this reason that democracy as it is at present understood, does not have smooth evolutionary process of unfoldment : it could be effective only in the realm of *Yama*, where death equalises all ; only when karmic differences arising during several incarnations are completely worked out, the democratic ideal could bring out the golden kingdom. It is for such abstract Timeless existence under the sway of Saturn that it is said that he loved mankind so much that he placed no mortal king or prince to rule over them but placed "spirits and genii of a divine nature more excellent than that of man". Only the spirits and genii are beyond the working of *karmic* principles because they have already become a part of eternal nature. Thus the impact of Saturn even

---

1. B. V. Raman, *The Astrological Magazine*, Bangalore, March, 1977.

during the mortal existence of an individual, whether for the particular being or for the society, is to bring out those qualities of the entity which are of eternal nature. That is to say that the impact of Saturn is more enduring than others : Saturn thus may become "a sustainer and whatever developments occur under his auspices they last for a long time" ; the enduring qualities of the individual are the qualities of perseverence, fortitude, courage, endurance etc. The lasting impact of Saturn is because Saturn is the God of Boundless Time, the Eternity.

One of the *Pancha Mahapurusha Yoga,* namely *Sasa Yoga* occurs if Saturn occupies exaltation, *moolatrikona* or his own house placed in a quadrant. The person born in this combination, according to *Jataka Parijatam,* may be a "king, a minister, or a general haunting woods and mountains ; he would be cruel hearted, and would even deceive in his eager pursuit of metallurgy ; he is bountiful ; he has wrathful eyes ; he is spirited ; he is loving and devoted to his mother ; he is brave ; he has dark form ; lives for 70 years. He is a voluptuary and inclined to play the parmour with the objects of his guilty love". One wonders whether these qualities deserve the qualification of greatness ! There is much dross given in this description though one has to recognise that these are basic urges which activate every materialitstically ambitious man ; he wants to acquire money and wealth even if they are gained by unscrupulous means ; he wants licentious sex life even at the risk of violating the social and moral codes of behaviour ; he wants to wander around the world in a spirit of adventure, and he wants to be famous. For these tendencies, when Saturn is in one of its exceptional combinations, should it be given such a great significance ? What is important

21

in this combination is that the planet of Timelessness completely captivates the core of one's being : *Lagna*, that is, the Ascendant which is the core of one's being, the Fourth House which is emotion, the Seventh House which stands for sociability and partnership, and the Tenth House standing for one's *Karma* in this life, are so much made "karmaless" under this combination that it almost becomes an aspect of *Kaivalya*, the Ultimate Liberated Stage of which Patanjali's *Yoga Sutra* speaks so much ; the Eternal Reality begins to motivate the individual rather than his being drawn towards the attractions of worldly existence. Varahamihira has indicated *digambara sanyasis*, who go around the world naked, as produced under the influence of Saturn. The philosophy which repudiates the significance of materiality, the illusions or *Maya* of manifestation, would not attach any significance to wealth, power, dress, status, or even knowledge. Naga sanyasis are the highly evolved occultists who have been assigned the responsibilities for sustaining the fire of True Knowledge and Wisdom during the period of Manavantric dissolution and creation. Saturn connected with Capricorn and Aquarius is related to the Dragon of Wisdom which leads us to think that the true awareness of Reality is possible when Saturn occupies a quadrant in strength. Probably that is the reason for assigning such a high significance to the *Pancha Mahapurusha Yogas* in the life history of an incarnating ego.

It is not without significance that almost all ascetic combinations are caused by special relationship with Saturn. Ordinarily one should have thought of Jupiter and the Sun as more powerful in this regard. But in actual reality, it is not so. Due to the special repercussions whereby the timelessness of consciousness is aroused in the perceptive principle of the individual, there is the sowing of the seed for attaining Nirvanic heights. It is only when the individual has ceased to sow fresh karmic seeds, good or bad, that he is qualified to aspire for Liberation. In the process of purging out the sediments of past *karmas* and to free the individual for receiving the pure light of spirituality, one has to pass through the pangs of sorrow. The allegory that Saturn killed his only son and ate his own progeny has the suggestion that the bondage of *Karma* which arises as a result of one's action or creativity, which astrologically refers to the Fifth House activity, can be overcome only under the influence of Saturn. Saturn is not good for the Fifth House, which implies that this planet does not very much encourage the formation of fresh *karmas*, under Saturn their binding influence on the individual is minimal.

Powerful association of Saturn with the Fifth House, Ninth House, Tenth House, the Moon and Ascendant would be conducive to real asceticism. In the case of Swami Ramakrishna Paramahamsa, Saturn was in the Ninth House from the Ascendant, the Moon and the Sun thus completely annihilating the serpent of past *karma* from raising its head to engage him in further bondage. In the case of Swami Vivekanand, Saturn was in the Tenth House from the Ascendant, in the Ninth House from the Sun and it was located with the Moon in Virgo. Virgo is the sign containing within itself all kinds of *siddhis*, accomplishments in *yoga*, and produces much sufferings, while Sagittarius qualifies the individual for transformation of his psychic nature. As such Vivekanand was born with the mission for asceticism, developing his spiritual powers, complete stoppage of the activities of mental involvement with matter and to work for the destiny of his Soul. Unless the individual consciousness represented by the Ascendant and the Moon is completely freed from the bondage of time, which is sorrow and creation, and his nature is made crystalline so that the external objects are reflected in it without any distortion, and unless the individual has attained *karma-lessness* signified by the cessation of compulsive actions of the Fifth, Ninth, and the Tenth House, the spiritual heights attained by the yogi would be of a lower order. Only by soaring to the realm of Timelessness, Eternity, the Kingdom of Yama, the secrets of Life and Death can be comprehended and the sorrow inherent in the manifested world eliminated.

The way to Supreme Bliss lies through Golgotha. Only by bearing the cross of sorrow and frustration, disappointments and failures could one aspire to scale such glorious heights. The blessings of Saturn lie in destroying the compulsive forces of past *karmas* so that the individual could be free from materialistic bondage inherent in the act of manifestation. Because Saturn does not succumb to any opposition in his endeavours, he is considered the most powerful malefic, but his malefic influence is to unveil Truth and Reality, freedom from illusion, and to liberate the spirit of the individual into the sphere of Timelessness. This awareness or wisdom is symbolised by age and wrinkles on one's forehead ; this freedom of spirit liberates the individual from social and moral codes of behaviour and class stratifications ; the universalism gives true asceticism. Whatever the apparent sorrow and frustration, Saturn, astrologically, is the agent of the Mighty Liberating Force which unveils a little of Timelessness and latent Reality of the Being.

RAHU : THE PLANET OF KARMIC RETRIBUTION

An old adage that nothing but the good and evil deeds committed by a human being follow him after his death like a shadow is truly applicable to Rahu. It is known as a *chhayagraha*, a shadowy planet, which in fact is a subjective planet which must get a material or objective base for its concretisation. A careful study of this planet would show how much of the past haunts a person in his present life.

The importance of Rahu is no less than that of Ascendant and in almost all significant prognostication of lasting nature, a reference to Rahu is inevitable. For this very reason, from the Vedas to Puranas and epics, this planet has been applauded in glowing terms. Mention has been made of the physical form of the planet as if it were a mountain of lamp-black with an expansive body and a tail, having crown on his head and a mouth which looked terrible. *Shrimad Bhagavat Purana* assigned it throat and neck for its dwelling but also indicated that it moved like the lunar mansions, the *nakshatras*, but some 10,000 yojanas below the Sun in space. In the Bhisma Parva of the *Mahabharata*, the diameter, circumference and width of Rahu were said to be 12,000 yojanas, 36,000 yojanas and 6,000 yojanas. The mythological stories of Rahu devouring the Sun and the Moon at the time of eclipses also assigned to it more power than the mighty planets. From these, one could clearly infer that the ancient seers did not neglect this shadowy planet like our Western astrologers who do not take the shadowy planets of Rahu and Ketu into account for predictive purposes. No one can absolve his past : whether the good deeds done in the past, or the mischiefs precipitated at that time could completely abandon the individual in his present life. Rahu's power of inflicting its effect is so colossal that even the Sun and the Moon have to accept their helplessness to this shadowy planet. It is indeed very significant that Rahu is not only for bestowing the mischief but also material affluence could be expected from this planet. That is why it is said to have a crown over his head.

All astrologers are aware of the great significance attached to the *Kala-Sarpa yoga*. According to this combination, if all the planets in a chart are hemmed between Rahu and Ketu, the efficacy of other planetary combinations are considerably reduced. This combination is a great enigma. But no one so far has ventured to deny the power of this combination. In essence this planetary combination suggests that the person in his past lives had been trying to play with lives of other people in such a manner that their opportunities which they should have legitimately and normally enjoyed, were denied by him and their life was made miserable. As a result of this karmic fault, the cosmic plan decrees that the fate of the same type should befall this precipitator so that he learns the lesson of not denying help and guidance to others.

Rahu is a portion of Eternity which during the period of manifestation enables the Divine nector to get enmessed in matter. The serpent specially when it is swallowing its own tail is represented as a symbol of

Eternity but in the mythologies when serpent is made the seat of Vishnu on which he reclines in *Kshirasagar* it is Eternity rolled out into time dimension, namely past, present and the future. A portion of it under Ketu is forward looking while Rahu is intimately linked with the past projecting itself into the present. This is one of the reasons why the afflictions of Rahu are generally the consequences of past lives. When Rahu is associated with the Moon, it considerably darkens the qualities of the luminary and makes it function as a projection of the past experiences. Some of the past traits of character that a person carries are expressed as phobias, epilepsy, maniac depression, suicidal proclivities, apprehension of sexual inadequacy and a feeling of inferiority. These characteristics of personal psychological structure resist medication almost in an imperceptible manner are strongly linked with the Moon which happens to be related in a special way with Rahu. When such a relationship is noted, it is logical to expect that the individual would require great sympathetic considero-ration in showing that the past germ sprouting in the present psyche should be eliminated with great diligence. Saturn, Mars and Rahu are all intimately connected with past *karmas*, but the last one shows it in a special way. The first two present conditions in an objective manner, something outside the person which he has inevitably to confront and tackle, whereas the last one, that is, Rahu being a part of the Eternity makes the psychological structure of the person itself so much coloured by the past tendencies that the escape from them becomes almost impossible. It can be dissolved only by relegating the compulsions of the *sanskaras*, in-built psychological tendencies, completely in the past. It has been rightly stated that phobias developed in childhood as a result of past karma, plague one all through life. Wrong mental habits of previous lives dig deep grooves in the consciousness of the person that it would be seemingly impossible for him to get complete hold over his thinking. This feature of Rahu was indicated in astrological terms as follows : with Rahu-Moon association in intellectual signs there could be normally a razor-sharp intellect but the person would be lacking in the ability to understand and appreciate other people's emotions. In earthy signs, Rahu-Moon conjunction or opposition leads to a tremendous lust for either earning money or achieving power. In fiery signs there is dissatisfaction with everything and everybody that life becomes unbearable. These are some of the symptoms of Rahu carrying the past tendencies in the present day conditions.

It is very surprising to note that Rahu's capacity to do harm or to help is considerably diminished when it is alone. For example, Rahu's influence on the fifth house is very bad even if it is alone there, but associate it with Mercury in the fifth house, it would be almost impossible to expect a child born to him. Associate Rahu with Sun in the ninth house and danger to father becomes great. Rahu is the curse of the past lives and if it is associated with the good influences flowing from the past, it inevitably diminishes the same. If the curse is added with other curses which the individual has to bear, it only increases the intensity of the same.

Rahu is considered as shadow ; *chhaya* which devours the Sun and the Moon and makes them ineffective in shedding light which is their natural property. This characteristic is predominantly evident when we examine the effect of Rahu in association with several planets. The Sun and the Moon are incapacitated to a

great extent in association with Rahu. Jupiter in association with Rahu produced *Chandal yoga* which signifies
the complete pollution of the benefic effects of Jupiter.
In association with Mercury and Venus, Rahu spoils the
pure quality of thinking principle and sometimes even
affects the mind so much that the person may get perverted thoughts. Venus when affected by Rahu will not
enable the normal expression of love and beauty ; many
of the sexual aberrations result from such afflictions. On
the other hand, Rahu finds considerable amount of
affinity with Saturn of which he is said to take the
temperament. Surprisingly with Mars, in its lower
material aspect, Rahu could be destructive. Rahu and
Mars in the seventh are sure to destroy the marital
happiness and the individual would find it almost
impossible to have the pleasures of a married home.

    Rahu is of *tamasic vritti*. Tamas stands for inertia,
but it also suggests darkness. As a result of this characteristic Rahu is well attuned to providing those things
and circumstances which induce the psyche of the person
towards sloth, indolence, and ease. The condition under
which this sloth is produced, is not so important as the
fact that the afflicted house must show that the individual is considerably attracted towards taking life without
much serious initiative and thought regarding that aspect
which is afflicted by Rahu. If Rahu afflicted the second
house, there could be speech difficulty, but the person
would not seriously consider that as an impediment. In
the fourth house, he may be unsettled about his family
matters ; house and such other things may be always
changing, but the individual would not consider such a
loss as very serious. Those whose fifth house destroys
the possibility of children as a result of Rahu's affliction,
they do not feel that as a curse. Thus, the afflictions

of Rahu having affected the mind and the psyche of the person and inducing him to take pleasure in non-clean aspects of life do not let him feel the pang of this impurity to the same extent as any other person not afflicted by it would feel.

Though Rahu under certain conditions bestow spiritual attainments, it is primarily a planet of material gains. This creates a situation which requires special attention. In order to arouse the spiritual feelings, Rahu at first immerses the person in material affluence. In case Rahu is in the tenth house there is every possibility of the individual acquiring much money in life. Dr. Rajendra Prasad and Dr. Rabindranath Tagore had Rahu in the tenth house and both of them had abundance of money but were not able to get themselves immersed in that. They had money but their heart was not in money. As a karmic result of past detachment and good deeds they were given abundance of material affluence but their destiny made them feel that money was not supreme. Wherever Rahu is placed, the pleasures of that house it would not enable the person to enjoy. In some cases it could be due to physical inability, in others due to psychological and family estrictions, whilsts in many other instances, it is due to the sense of detachment which makes the person turn away their mind from the material affluence. In this sense, under proper conditions, Rahu makes the person look heaven-ward even when there is plenty of money. The detach-ment it gives is not necessarily born out of deprivation but because of some psychological orientation.

Rahu itself is downward looking which implies that whatever the final result, it would always be concerned with things of the world. Umbrella, *chowrie* and kingdom are outstanding symbols of things material. Rahu does not wish to involve itself in things of culture, sophisti-cation, philosophy. Its chief preoccupation is attainment of certain results, good or not-so-good but in the realm of thought. Wherever he is, Rahu would look downward and associate himself with those who are below his status.

An interesting feature of Rahu is his strong desire to do things which are not sanctified by well established legal or social practices. In the marriage he would like to go outside his social circle, in his profession he would do things which are non-conventional and considered not desirable, he would be interested in games and pastimes which are looked down upon, his creative activities will be in the area which is non-respectful. Rahu takes great delight in acting in a manner which provokes people and breaks the well established social code ; it does things surreptitiously, it has intrigues with wicked females, it has intrigues with unscrupulous diplomates, it can maintain clandestine links with government officers. Anything unrespectful, unlawful, not-desirable, not above board, Rahu will take great delight in performing.

In order to know the enigmatic nature of Rahu, one has to study its ramifications in many unusual dimensions. Rahu is considered a serpent which by itself is a very mysterious symbol. Associated with the serpent fire which is the seat of immense occult power, Rahu is a very powerful planet. The effect of Rahu cannot ·be nullified by the counteraction of any other planet. Belonging to the same family of *Ananta-Nag* on which reclines the Lord Vishnu in his outward manifestative function, Rahu is the bestower and support of material riches. The hidden occult power of this serpent is so great that whosoever performed meditation on it, he gets much enlightenment and the knowledge of the hidden. It is said that the sage Garg propitiated the Anant-Nag

and got the knowledge of the planets enabling him to
know the past, present and the future of the universe.

Parasara is of the opinion that the exaltation sign
of Rahu is Taurus, his Mool-Trikona Cancer and Virgo his
own sign. Essential implication of this relationship is
that Rahu is at his best when he is actively engaged in
creative activities for wordly development (Taurus). He
is very happy when he has to link the dizzy heights of
spirituality and dismal depth of materiality (cancer).
Virgo standing for nature's latent powers is said to be
the sign for Rahu in the sense that the planet is most
natural when the individual under its influence is seriously
concerned about developing his inner strength and
deeper understanding of his real Self. Vaidyanath Dikshita
in his treatise *Jataka Parijatam* has recorded Aquarius as
its Moola-Trikona sign and Gemini as the sign of exaltation, while maintaining that Virgo is its own sign. Apparently there seems to be some discrepancy between the
two views but a little closer examination would dissolve
the controversy. Gemini is as much a sign of physical
creativity as Taurus with the only difference that the
latter is the potential of creativity whilst the former is
already engaged in the creative functions. Essentially
Rahu is potential, however for the man of the world the
potential has to be articulated to make it meaningful.
Aqaurius is of water-*tattwa* ; it is a vehicle for carrying
the water of life in which process the entity is spiritualised. Cancer is the link between the spiritual heights
and material depths for the purpose of uplifting the latter
to the former status. Rahu also has the function of
transforming the materiality of the person in a hard way
to the spirituality of his nature. For this similarity
between Saturn and Rahu, there is a general statement
that Rahu functions like Saturn. Considered this way,

there is not much difference between the various statements regarding the relationship of Rahu with different
signs of the zodiac.

Rahu is basically a symbol of dissatisfaction. It is
supremely an earthly planet concerned purely with selfish
enjoyment. In seeking his own object of enjoyment, it
pays little heed to the needs, feelings and comforts of
the other party. From the standpoint of basic urges in
human beings, it is connected with *Artha* (material
wealth) and *Kama* (human desire). From these, one
could see that of Rahu at whatever level it operates
would be from the standpoint of the self. During the
course of evolution at times, it becomes necessary to
strengthen the various sheaths in order to gain experience
so that the inner being understands itself. In this
process, Rahu has an important role to play. It looks
material-ward and as such it has to intensify the urgency
of its own requirements. But being an inevitable part
of Ketu it necessarily arouses a feeling of not wanting
the things and experiences attained. Rahu is not dissatisfaction in the sense that it has the insatiable urge to
indulge, but it arouses the feeling that the desires satisfied in the worldly way do not touch the inner-most
basic urge of the person. Often it is an unspecified
urge, sometimes attempted to be fulfilled by one means,
and at others by another but in all these endeavours,
there is some vague urge chasing and driving the individual to an unknown direction which ultimately may lead
him to spiritual detachment.

It is interesting to note that Rahu is immensely beneficial in *Upachaya Houses*, that is, in 3rd, 6th, 10th and
11th Houses. This situation produces an enigma. 3rd
and 6th Houses are generally considered bad houses in
the sense that some kind of obstruction arises due to

these houses but from a different standpoint these are very significant houses. The Third is linked with valour and courage of the *Kala Purusha* as a result of which the manifestation in spite of insurmountable difficulties takes place. It is this willing undertaking of arduous responsibilities that the *Kala Purusha* is able to fulfil an important assignment bestowed on Him by the Divine. Similarly from this house, besides hardships and difficulties, initiative, courage, valour and the capacity to undertake difficult responsibilities are signified. Rahu is precisely the planet which invisibly enables the individual to discharge the Divine assignment of completing certain tasks. Whatever other difficulties and hardships the individual may have to face in life as a result of the disposition of other planets, if Rahu is in the Third House, none of them could in any significant manner hinder the individual from achieving his goal.

The Sixth House is also no less significant. Generally speaking, it signifies enemy, theft, ill-fame and servitude but deeper implications of this house lead one to get a glimpse of the hidden powers which could be tapped for the advantage of the individual. For those who endeavour to acquire *siddhis*, or the occult perfections, they have to depend very much upon the disposition of this house. The planets which are linked with vital manifestative processes will have significant effects in this House. Rahu is one such planet. Here also the effect of Rahu is in clearing the debris which impede the cosmic purpose to fructify. The will of the Individual must prevail if Rahu is in the Sixth. It is one of the most powerful placements for Rahu because here it is at the acme of its power and importance in the hierarchy of manifestative agencies.

In 10th and 11th Houses, Rahu is able to bestow to

the individual much material reward. Those who are interested in their occult progress would not very much relish the gift of material affluence but the ordinary individuals to whom power, position and material riches measure the success of life would find this planet helping them very much. Such persons could not be expected to be scrupulous of the means they employ to gain their objectives. Often they would be coming in contact with persons who are not very desirable and are ordinarily persons of lower category, but by any means they would be able to get what they wanted.

About Rahu, one could note that the First, Second, Fourth, Fifth, Seventh, Eighth, Ninth and Twelfth Houses are not considered very auspicious. These are the houses which have considerable significance on the growth and fructification of the good deeds of the individual. There would be general gloom and frustration if Rahu is in the first house, impeded creative faculties in the second, unhappy family environment in the fourth, denial of progeny in the fifth, lack of married life in the seventh, malignant diseases in the eighth, distorted and dismal philosophy of life in the ninth and absence of the pleasure of bed in the twelfth. These are some of the general effects but the true significance of these denials will have to be analysed in relation to what they finally lead to. The association of other planets, and the countervailing forces generated by different planets overcoming the radiation of Rahu will have to be taken into account for actual assessment of the effect but essentially Rahu could be considered as a spiritualising planet which bestows material riches and comforts in order to make the individual dissatisfied so that finally his gare is turned upward.

KETU : THE PLANET OF SPIRITUAL HUMILIATION

Ketu is inevitably opposed to Rahu which has already been described as a spiritualising planet. In fact, Rahu and Ketu are parts of the same unity. Taken together they are agents for spiritualising the world of manifestation, but the manner in which they produce the effect is different from each other. Rahu acts through the physical realm of materiality, whereas Ketu works through the psychological structure of the being. Ketu creates a turmoil and sets the mind of the person into deep thinking which finally comes out with certain enlightening results. Generally speaking, Ketu initiates the thinking activities with the experience of some dissatisfaction, at times of the precocious variety. In case Ketu happens to influence the person at an early age, his hair may turn grey, visage old-age type, socially left isolated and psychologically engaged in brooding activities. Ketu must activate the thinking of the individual to show that his own efforts are very insignificant in achieving the fruits of the world and this sense of insignificance makes him feel small which finally links him to the universal consciousness. Thus he achieves the moral and spiritual victory rarely possible for an ordinary human individual. In this way, one could discover streaks of contradictions in Ketu which is not available in any other planet.

Three outstanding characteristics of Ketu that need special notice are (i) his greater power than the visible

Sun and the visible Moon which are obscured by no other ray than the shadow of Ketu (along with that of Rahu), (ii) his immense power over soul represented by the Sun and the psyche consisting of the triple aspect of the individual namely mind, heart and emotion represented by the Moon and, (iii) his capacity to induce the individual towards the path of Liberation which may lead him to Initiations and such other achievements. Having the power to influence the psyche and the soul of the person concerned, Ketu arranges events in such an order that the consciousness of the man transcends the material considerations and he approaches the portals of spirituality and comes nearer the Occult Hierarchy; he becomes thereby really spiritualised, and detached.

Rahu and Ketu taken together represent the Serpent Fire, the occult energy coiled round the base of the spine which when energised might lead to the unification of the individual consciousness of person with that of the Universal Deity. On the differentiation between two planets, Rahu became the direction, the head, the urge for attaining this kind of universal unification whilst Ketu became the tail, the coil, the potential which finally enables the individual to gain the unification.

Being part of a very mystic symbol, it is difficult to explain the various characteristics of Ketu. Serpent is a symbol of soul's evolution, it is an emblem of procreation, and it represents the High Initiates of the Occult Hierarchy. In each of these aspects, Ketu plays an important role. The process by which the soul's liberation from its mortal coil is achieved is signified by this shadowy planet. Ancient scriptures, besides several others, have given it the name of *Adrishtaroopas*, *i.e.* the form of which is invisible, and *Sankaram*, the God of Liberation. The way Ketu operates is actually invisible in the sense that one cannot know the process of its operation but the effect is certainly unmistaken and sure. In the fifth house, the house of creativity, Ketu does not encourage 'visible' creation in the form of children, but on the invisible plane, such as philosophic thought, development of psychic faculties and such other qualities of the individual, Ketu operates very effectively. Whatever strengthens the possibility of Liberation, Ketu encourages the individual to acquire that whilst that which makes him involved in the world of materiality is denied to the person.

It is very suggestive that Ketu has been assigned a star on its head and has been given a tail as its body. Working behind this symbology is the idea of the great splendour contained in this shadowy planet. In the lowest form of the reptile which has the power to degrade even the celestial beings to the world of matter and in the chain of births and deaths, Ketu has his extension implying that even in our worst levels of existence Ketu has his sway but is always directed towards the star at his head. It is a significator of the great status among the hierophants who initiated the neophytes into secret mysteries of the world and expounded the most abstruse esoteric philosophy to his students. About these mystery religions very little is known but under the influence of Ketu these mysteries are revealed directly to the individual. As such, Ketu is a great teacher as well. Ketu connects the earth and the sky. But in this linkage is concealed the great suffering the individual may have to undergo in order to reach the higher levels of knowledge, or the sublime heights of spirituality. Those who try to scale this height could have this urge as well as success on this path only when

Ketu is favourably inclined towards him. To such aspirants there will be plenty of trials and tribulations, sorrows and frustration but the end is the glorious freedom of the open sky and free air. Ketu is the *karaka*, the causative force, for religion, pilgrimage, mendicancy, *kapalika* (a kind of mendicant carrying a human skull in his hand symbolising the end of the human existence), sooth-saying, sublime knowledge, psychic power, strange deeds, Saiva School of Philosophy, cave dwelling, name and fame, ornaments of alloys, diseases like leprosy, wisdom attained due to suffering, and Liberation. Each of these qualities of Ketu deserves deep contemplation in order to discover its true nature, however, essentially they are all spiritual in character.

Much uncertainty exists regarding the effect of Ketu in various houses. Actual effect of the planet would depend upon the disposition of this planet and other accompanying conditions, but some broad indications could however be indicated here. The following is a brief description of what Ketu may do in the twelve houses.

In the First House, Ketu bestows an unusual aura by which the individual is distinguished in some way or the other from other persons. The personality traits of the individual having Ketu in ascendant would be distinct carrying the special imprint of his inner uniqueness. At certain levels of development, it would appear as pride and at other levels it will be the extreme degree of humility. A queer feature of this situation is that the individual prospers well in adversity but he cannot enjoy affluence. There is inner dissatisfaction in him. He feels that there is a mission for him to fulfil. Such a person feels that he should be a channel for something new, something grand and satisfying. Failing to achieve his aspirations, he feels dejected, unhappy, exhausted and often likes committing suicide.

The Second House Ketu gives profound learning though the course of education may not necessarily be smooth and uninterrupted. He is ambitious and feels that he is destined to create a new world for which he is prepared to give up his personal happiness. The individual will not be affluent. His throat may be affected but he will feel a sense of mystery in life and an immensity which overshadows man. Such a man will not be charmed by wealth and luxury but anything providing enlightenment to him will be highly appreciated.

In the Third House, Ketu gives outstanding courage which leads him to achieve marvels even in hostile environment. Such individuals are very active on inner planes. He can be a formidable rival who can use uncommon deceptive tactics to achieve his goal. He will be self-reliant, ambitious, perseverent, and capable of putting enormous effort towards his desired object. Under such a placement of Ketu, the individual may be capable of unusual achievements and his glory in the world of matter as well as in the world of thought could be substantial. But those who wish to have only glory should not wish such a placement of Ketu because even at the height of his glory he would not be interested in his own personal satisfaction but would be eager to know whether he has been useful to anyone else.

In the Fourth House, Ketu gives a restless spirit. The individual feels at home in a new fairy land of his own ; he can dwell in a world created by himself. Sometimes it is a world full of denizens of the invisible world, sometimes it is a world conquered by oneself. Imagination of the individual is great and its flight very wide. It is immaterial as to what is he ; he may be a doctor, painter, poet or anything else, but he will be a man of imagination and his uniqueness will be based on his originality. He would find peace and serenity in the realm of higher world of imagination and in oneness of life. As far as material prosperity is concerned, Ketu's placement in the Fourth House is not helpful, but in the realm of imagination, its influence is superb. He would be capable of transmuting his personal love and affection into universal love and compassion.

Ketu in the Fifth House gives special type of creativity. The individual may have only a few children at all, but somehow or the other his creativity in the realm of matter or spirit would be enormous. This would give him great pleasure, may be affluence as well. When Ketu is posited in the Fifth House, great occultists are born, some of whom may see the future like an open book. But, it is not possible to have that level of occultists always. In such circumstances, the individual may have perverted intellect capable of great argumentative capacity and thereby inducing and encouraging others to non-conventional activities, not always approved by the authorities. Generally speaking, the individual with Ketu in the Fifth House wants to build a new social order.

Intense spirituality arises due to Ketu in the Sixth House. Such individuals could go to the very root of the cosmic power. They could fathom the utmost limit or the very edge of the cosmic veil. They are capable of great spiritual upliftment; they may be Initiated in various Mystery Schools. The Great Lord Buddha was born with Ketu in his Sixth House which happened to be Sagittarius and was aspected by Jupiter from his Tenth House. But, if Ketu functions on lower levels it is capable of making the person fanatic and dictatorial.

The Moghul Emperor Aurangzeb is an example of such a Ketu : he had Aquarius ascendant, but Ketu was powerfully aspected by the third aspect of Saturn from his Fourth House where the Moon was also posited. The fanaticism and his religious bigotism are well known.

The Seventh House is not a good house for the placement of Ketu. In this position Rahu becomes placed in the Ascendant which by no means is a very desirable situation particularly for material comfort and conveniences. But Ketu in the Seventh House is worse. It makes the individual incapable of establishing any firm relationship with any individual ; the marital life of the person becomes unfortunate. The instability is so great that the adjustment problem between the partners becomes difficult ; Ketu in the Seventh House often makes the partners intolerant. Sex life of the person concerned, whether the male or the female, is not of a moral order, and the person fails to discipline his or her biological urges which become more unmanageable because of psychological stress.

In the Eighth House, Ketu creates unusual unhappiness. The impact of this placement is unpredictable. Generally speaking, this situation may lead to sexual perversions and much secret alliances but in favourable situations when the true nature of Ketu is able to operate, it may bestow much occult power, revelations of many occult truths, and immense capability of drawing upon the hidden powers of nature. Such persons can make their imprint on the human society in a significant way.

Ketu in the Ninth House will always make the man attain a position at the helm of affairs particularly in the field of religion, philosophy and spirituality. By itself,

Ketu will be concerned with intensity of thought concerning the humanity and their betterment, but whether it would be merely philosophical and theoretical or it would be deeply religious full of compassion and milk of human kindness depends upon other influences being exercised on it. Under this combination, the individuals concerned are able to acquire an extensive expanse of non-traditional view on life. Such persons may even be supported and assisted by loyal friends and disciples. It is a stage in life when there is some marked change in the psyche inducing the individual to move from materialism to spirituality.

Ketu in the Tenth House makes the individual suffer for the actions of his past life. He endures much hardship; he has to work harder than the rest of his fellows but he does not receive commensurate rewards by way of worldly position and status. Such persons often work for an ideal and even die for an ideal.

The Eleventh House is the house of illusion, *Maya*. Here, Ketu gives a life of disillusionment and the person suffers from poverty, chastity, and austerity. In return he sometimes gets the privilege of discipleship of some great beings which completely revolutionises his life and he achieves the ideal of renunciation. His worldly bondage is thereby considerably reduced.

The Twelfth House Ketu gives austerity and worldly dissatisfaction but in the end there is a possibility of his getting redemption, Liberation. This is the best house for the planet where its spiritual influence is the most satisfying and the individual enjoys lasting peace and security in the after-death world.

To sum up, one can see that Ketu is a highly occult planet whose whole endeavour is to spiritualise the individual in very many ways. It provides the vehicle

necessary for the spiritual downpour of divine energy. It
enables the individual to attain closer relationship with
occult mystery schools which may ultimately enable him
to enter higher levels of Initiation.   How this training is
imparted is mysteriously connected with the placement
of this planet in different signs of the zodiac and in the
different houses in a horoscope.

DEBILITATION CANCELLATION RAJAYOGA
(Neechabhanga Rajayoga)

Neechabhanga Rajayoga based on the cancellation of debilitation of planets is one of the most enigmatic kingly combinations whose efficacy has been widely acknowledged but the rationale of the same has not yet been thoroughly investigated. The yoga has been variously described. Generally speaking, it has been said to occur when a planet occupies his debilitation position, and (*a*) if the lord of the debilitation sign, or the lord of its exaltation sign, that is the seventh sign from where it is posited, occupies a quadrant position from the ascendant or the Moon, or (*b*) if the lord of that debilitation sign occupies its own house or the sign of its exaltation, or a quadrant, or (*c*) if the lord of that debilitation sign aspects the debilited planet. As a result of this combination, the person having the said yoga would be highly venerated and would be very religious minded. This ready and rough summary giving in essence the gist of various descriptions given in different text books may serve as a rule of the thumb, but for any investigative study one will have to go deeper.

The classical texts are not very unanimous regarding the different requirements for the applicability of this yoga. *Jataka Parijata* gives a combination in its chapter on Rajayoga which states that "if at a birth a planet be in its depression and if the lord of the sign occupied by the same or the lord of its exaltation sign be in a quadrant (*kendra*) position in respect of the Moon's place or the ascendant, the person born will be a king and a just ruler". The actual translation of Sanskrit could also imply that the king under this combination could be religious and a kind emperor. This interpretation of the text should suggest that a king with this combination could be an overlord having sway over several other kings and he himself would be of religious temperament. In the following *sloka* itself, the author gives another interesting combination which is quite relevant in case one desires to examine the matter in detail. The sloka states that "if the lord of the *Navamsa* occupied by a depressed planet at a birth be in a *kendra* (quadrant) or *trine* position and if the ascendant be a moveable sign or if the lord of the ascendant be in a *Navamsa* owned by a moveable sign, the person will be a king or will possess great power". Such a *sloka* occurs even in *Saravali*. From these two *slokas*, one infers that the planet in depression does not remain such an inauspicious planet, if certain counterbalancing conditions prevail.

Mantreswara has given a much more elaborate description of *Neechabhanga* Raja yoga and brought out certain combinations which are not ordinarily considered as such. Their inclusion in this category however brings out some significant characteristics of this yoga. He states that "if at a birth, a planet is in its depression and if the lord of that sign or that of the planet's exaltation sign is in a *kendra* (quadrant) position with respect to the Moon's place or the ascendant, the person born will be a king and a just ruler". This sloka in *Phaladeepika* is identical with that in *Jataka Parijata* and the effect also is stated the same, namely, *dharmic* and *chakravarti* about which reference has already been made earlier. But here the text has suggested the possibility of including the lord of the sign where the planet is depressed also in the category of planets causing the yoga. Mantreswara further details that the yoga occurs when the planet is in depression, if the lord of that depression sign and the lord of the planet's exaltation sign are in *kendra* position mutually; the combination will produce a king who will become an emperor respected by all other kings. One has to note here that the causation of this yoga is attributed to the lords of the depression and the exaltation signs being in mutually central position as distinguished from being like that in relation to the ascendant or the Moon position. The effect is also slightly different though not in any significant manner. The famous author further states that a planet in depression but aspected by the lord of that sign should make the person a ruler of the earth and famous, but goes on further to suggest that there was uncertainty about the person becoming a foremost king unless the depressed planet was in an auspicious house, that is, in a house other than sixth, eighth, or the twelfth. This rider has added another significant condition. The causation of the combination is greatly vitiated by a depressed planet occupying an inauspicious house. From this one should conclude that the benefic effect of this yoga should be expected only when the depression does not occur in the sixth, eighth or the twelfth sign. This is a condition requiring emphasis.

Mantreswara gives two other conditions. He states them to be (a) a planet occupying its depression sign but its or the lord of the planet's exaltation sign being in a *kendra* position in relation to the ascendant or the lunar position, (b) a planet being in depression but the lord of its depression sign as well as that of the planet's exaltation sign, or at least one of them being in a kendra. As a result of these conditions, the learned author states that the native could be an emperor, endowed with full riches, virtually disposed, respected by other kings, mighty, famous, and affluent ; in the latter combination the emperor thus produced would be saluted by other kings as well.

These elaborate conditions suggest that the *Neechabhanga Rajayoga* as is generally understood is only one aspect of the various types of auspicious yogas associated with depressed planets. Synthesizing the various combinations indicated above, Sri Subrahmanya Sastri summarised the five types of *Neechabhanga Rajayoga* to be as follows :

(i) The lord of the depression sign or the planet that is exalted in that sign is in a kendra position from the ascendant or the Moon,

(ii) the lord of the depression sign and the lord of the exaltation sign of the depressed planet are mutually in kendra position,

(iii) the planet in depression is aspected by the lord of that sign,

(iv) the lord of the depression sign or the lord of the exaltation sign of the depressed planet is in *kendra* from the ascendant or the Moon, and

(v) the planet in depression is in kendra in respect to the ascendant or the Moon.

From these, one could find that the *Neechabhanga Rajayoga* is necessarily a combination relating the depressed planet to the lords of that sign in which the planet is depressed, and the lord of the sign Seventh from it (that is, the lord of its exaltation sign) and their placements radiating benefic rays to the ascendant, the Moon or to the depressed planet itself. This is the essential or the root condition giving the effect signified by the combination. One conclusion to be deduced from it is that a planet in depression by itself is not so bad in case it gets significant counterbalancing radiations. The most significant counterbalancing radiation comes from the planets posited in the Seventh sign from itself, or from the lord of the Seventh sign from itself, or from the lord of the sign of depression itself, and these planets should have auspicious positions connected with the ascendant, the Moon, or the sign of depression itself.

Applying this principle of *Neechabhanga Rajayoga,* one could see that all planets are not equally affected by this combination. For example, Mars and Jupiter in depression do not require any special conditions according to the tenets of this yoga to produce *Neechabhanga.* In the case of Jupiter being in the depression sign, the planet had to be in Capricorn as a result of which the lord of Cancer being the Moon would always be in *kendra* from itself. Similarly, Mars in depression being in Cancer requires the Moon to be in *kendra* from itself. These cannot be considerd as coveted combinations. The very fact that Jupiter is depressed in a chart should enable materiality to grow having some amount of religious aroma around that activity and acquisition. Similarly, depression of Mars spoils its higher qualities engrossing the planet in its earthly nature.

Let us take the case of the Sun and the Moon. The Sun depressed in Libra should require Mars and/or Venus to be favourably posited in relation to ascendant and/or the Moon. The very fact that the Sun has been in depression suggests that the moral fibre of the person is loose and his will-power greatly reduced. To compensate these, the great valour and ambition of Mars could be effective in some manner. The arrogance and wickedness of the depressed Sun could also be reduced if Venus is in exaltation or in its auspicious nature which could affect the very being of the person or his psyche. Under conditions of depression, the Moon would be in Scorpio. Some of the effects of this placement has been stated to be "immoral, obstinate, unhappy, agitated, sterility, abortion, malicious, cruel". In case Mars is in centre in relation to the Moon, it would not be directly aspecting the Moon only when it is located Fourth from it but in that case also it shall impart considerable strength to it. In case Venus is in the stipulated position with the Moon, the adverse effect of the Moon, could be greatly reduced. In this manner one finds that the counterbalancing of the malefic influences of the depressed planet could be attributed to be the main basis of the special effects of *Neechabhanga Rajayoga*.

In the case of Mercury, its depression sign is Pisces but it lords over its exaltation sign Virgo as well. So a favourable disposition of Jupiter in relation to the Moon should bestow the required yoga but in that case there is strong possibility of *Gajakesari Yoga* being present. In case of Venus being in depression, one has to take note of the fact that Jupiter and Mercury could provide the countervailing radiations. Venus in Virgo bestows the qualities of "petty-mindedness, licentious and unscrupulous disposition, unhappy, and illicit love". Such narrowness of disposition could be removed by favourable disposition of Jupiter and Mercury.

The most serious complication arises from Saturn. Here also the planet in depression requires favourable support from Venus and Mars. When Saturn is in depression, that is in Aries, it is said to produce such men who are "idiotic, wanderer, insincere, peevish,

resentful, cruel, fraudulent, immoral, boastful, quarrelsome, gloomy, mischievous, perverse, and of misunderstanding nature''. These suggest that the nature of the
person under Saturn's depression could be crude lacking
any refinement. Such a nature could be modified only
with some benefic influence. Venus in favourable disposition could provide the qualities of refinement in
nature and Mars, the radiation to dispel gloom and
depression. In these cases also, the benefic effect flows
from the counterbalancing radiations.

The above examples show that *Neechabhanga Raja-
Yoga* is a short-cut method of indicating the effects of
certain combinations producing special conditions. As
a result of this suggestion, one may very legitimately
enquire whether the depression of a planet in a particular
house/bhava is of any special significance. In case the
depression occurs in the Eighth House tenanted by Mars
implying Sagittarius as the ascendant, and if the Moon
is in Capricorn and Saturn in Libra, can this combination
be as effective as depressed Venus in the Eighth House
with Jupiter in the Sxth House and the Moon in the
Twelfth House? The mutual aspect of Saturn and Mars
in the former case having full aspect of Saturn on the
ascendant could never be considered a good combination
in spite of the fact that *Neechabhanga Rajayoga* is
technically present. Even if Venus is debilitated in the
Twelfth House and the ascendant is Libra where the
Moon and the Sun are placed together, while Venus and
Mercury in close association are in the Twelfth House,
and Jupiter in debilitation is in the Fourth House, one
begins to wonder whether the combination could be
considered really good. In the case of Venus being
placed in the Eighth House in debilitation with Jupiter
in the Fifth House and the Moon in the Eleventh House

there is technically *Neechabhanga Rajayoga* but the result in the two cases would be different. In both these cases, there may be considerable amount of wealth, but it leaves many things to be desired. So it is true that the debilitation of Venus being counterbalanced would restore much of the shortcomings with regard to material affluence but there are other colourings which would depend upon the nature and placement of the counterbalancing planets.

If one examines some important charts having this combination of affluence one may begin to see the enigmatic character of this yoga. In *Notable Horoscopes,* B. V. Raman gives a chart without giving the identification details of the person, in which case Capricorn is the ascendant, Rahu and Saturn are in Aries, the Moon in Virgo and in Libra are placed the rest of the six planets namely, the Sun, Jupiter, Mercury, Ketu, Mars and Venus. In this chart, Saturn in debilitation in the Fourth House in Aries and Venus in Libra in the Tenth House (weekly) fulfilling the necessary conditions for *Neechabhanga* combination should give affluence to the person concerned. Again, the Sun is debilitated in Libra in the Tenth House whilst Mars, the lord of the sign of Saturn's debilitation as well as the lord of the Sun's exaltation, both, is in centre (kendra) position from the ascendant. Thus, *Neechabhanga Rajayoga* is fully applicable in this case. But, the native had suffered poverty, low social position and mental frustration. The chart has sufficient evidence for such frustrations ; the presence of this kingly combination of *Neechabhanga* has failed to bestow affluence to him. If this kingly combination which has been so highly spoken of in classical texts depends for its fructification on other accompanying conditions which have not been clearly spelt out, the students must take note of this lacuna very clearly.

In another chart of a person born in New Delhi on 23/24 October 1954 at 2–30 a.m. the *Neechabhanga Raja yoga* is very explicit as it is seen from the planetary positions : Ascendant Leo, the Moon in Virgo, Mercury, Saturn and the Sun in Libra, Venus in Scorpio, Rahu in Sagittarius, and Mars in its exaltation sign Capricorn whilst Jupiter is in Cancer. In this chart, Jupiter is exalted and so is Mars, but the Sun, the ascendant lord, however is debilitated in the Third House, which incidentally is said to be a good house for the Sun. Libra also contains Saturn in exaltation but it is placed with the Sun in debilitation. The Lord of Libra, that is Venus being in Scorpio is in central position in respect of the ascendant. The native had the Sun main period at the time of birth, and the period of Mars has pasaed without any significant improvement in his material welfare. In this case one hoped that the Jupiterian influence might raise his material status, otherwise this kingly combination may not be of much use. In this case what one can conclude is that depression of a planet does not necessarily destroy the house in which it is posited. If the combination is fulfilled, then the malefic effect of the debilitated planet is nullified. In this manner, the combination refers more to the nullification of the evil, rather than fructification of the positive good.

The above conclusion is strengthened if we examine another chart which is as follows : Ascendant Scorpio, Mars in Ascendant ; Jupiter in Aquarius, the Moon and Rahu in Pisces ; Saturn and Ketu in Virgo ; the Sun, Mercury and Venus in Libra, where the Sun is debilitated whilst the lord of its exaltation sign is in ascendant itself and in strength. In this case the Sun is debilitated

23

in the Twelfth House whilst Mars the ruler of the Sixth
House and ascendant as well is in Ascendant itself thus
fulfilling the condition for this *yoga*. The effect of
this combination may be noticeable by the fact that the
native has got a good central government service though
that could even be explained by the fact that the Tenth
House lord the Sun is having the full aspect of Jupiter,
the lord of the Fifth House and the Sun being associated
with Mercury and Venus, the two important benefics.
Nonetheless, the popular belief that *Neechabhanga Raja
yoga* is a combination far outstanding and astounding
wealth and money is not adequately justified in this case
also. All the affluent acquisitions of this native could
be explained by other combinations. In such a case, it
becomes irrelevant to give undue importance to this
kingly combination. One thing however to be noted in
the present case is that the native has initiative which
ordinarily should have been absent due to the debilitation of the Sun and it can be explained by the counterbalancing impetus given by the presence of Mars in the
ascendant. The effect of this kingly combination can
very legitimately be considered merely as counterbalancing factor rather than associating it with kingship
unless by that word the self-generated egotistic feeling
is suggested but in that case it should be considered
the effect of the Sun rather than of any othe condition.

Let us consider the possibility of *Neechabhanga
Rajayoga* resulting from the debilitation of the Moon. In
this context, one could examine the following combi-
nation. Ascendant Aries with the Sun, Mercury and
Venus in this sign ; Ketu in Taurus, Mars in Leo, the
Moon and Rahu in Scorpio the sign of the Moon's
debilitation, Jupiter in Sagittarius along with Saturn.
This chart belongs to a government official who rose

from an ordinary position to a very affluent condition finally ending with an United Nations' assignment. In this chart, the debilitation of the Moon is counterbalanced by Venus, the lord of the Second and the Seventh Houses placed with the lord of the Fifth House in ascendant itself and that also in association with the Sun which is posited there in its exaltation sign. In this case, Mars also considerably strengthened the horoscope. Temperamentally the debilitation of the Moon has caused much personal dissatisfaction to the native but Mars the lord of the Moon's debilitation sign posited in *kendra* from it has given considerable positive creativity to the native.

Debilitation of the Moon with *Neechabhanga Rajayoga* by the quadrant position of Venus in relation to the ascendant is evident even in the case of Albert Einstein. In his chart, Gemini is the ascendant, Ketu is in Cancer, the Moon in Scorpio, Mars and Rahu in Capricorn, Jupiter in Aquarius, and in Pisces there are the Sun, Mercury, Venus and Saturn. Commenting upon this chart, the erudite Indian astrologer Dr. B. V. Raman once mentioned that "Lagnadhipati, that is the lord of the Ascendant subject to *Neechabhanga* in the Tenth House by Venus who in turn has caused Malavya Yoga, (the yoga formed by the exaltation or ownership of a quadrant position by Venus) clearly reveals that Einstein was undoubtedly one of the greatest intellect mankind has ever produced". Einstein never showed the effects of the debilitation of the Moon but in his psyche the exaltation of Venus was very prominent. Furthermore, it is said that Venus in Pisces gives "wit, tact, learning, popularity, righteousness, ingenuity, modesty, refineness, power, respect, and pleasure seeking". The *Neechabhanga* has been able to eliminate some of the adverse effects caused by the Sixth placement of the Moon but besides counterbalancing the adverse effects of the Moon's debilitation, other qualities of Einstein could be explained on account of the presence of several other auspicious combinations.

From the above, one is inclined to infer that *Neechabhanga Rajayoga* need not be rated as high as to provide the very basis of kingship or even much wealth and affluence. Such conditions in life require many other auspicious combinations to exist. The primary role of this *Yoga* is in counterbalancing the adverse effects of the debilitated planet. In doing so, the nature of the planets affected by the combination and the houses of their placements are important. The technical effect as stated in the classical text-books should only be taken to mean that the student should be careful in assessing the effect of debilitated planets. The term *'chakravarti nripa'* that is, over-lord, should only imply that under suitable conditions this combination is likely to give much benefic effect by eliminating the adverse effects of the debilitation.

An important aspect of astrology is the calculation of timing for the occurrence of an event. The *Neechabhanga Rajayoga* is the result of several combinations of different planets. In such a case, it becomes difficult to specify the particular planet causing the yoga and as such it becomes difficult to maintain that a specific result may follow under the influence of a predetermined planet so that during the main or the sub-period of that planet the resulting event could be predicted. The planet depressed in the chart is one of the planets forming importantly the yoga under consideration ; it cannot be considered or conclusively affirmed that its adverse nature is completely eliminated. The counterbalancing

radiation occurs as a result of *kendra* or quadrant
position of different planets according to their position
in relation to the ascendant or the Moon. The nature of
the planets counterbalancing the effect of the debilitated
planet also enters in an important manner in deciding
the effect. The combinations taking place in relation to
the Moon should give rise to a different result than those
occurring in relation to the ascendant. The classical
text books are silent about these points. Empirical
researches have not so far been very enlightening. For
these reasons, one feels inclined as not to assign a
tremendously high position to this combination : it is
merely an indicator of the depressed planet getting radically modified in case the radiations of counterbalancing
planets are adequate to overcome the effects produced
by the debilitation. To expect the native to obtain the
position of kingship or even a high status in life without
taking other factors into account may be unrealistic.

SAKATA YOGA
Sixth–Eighth Relationship between Moon and Jupiter

Sakata Yoga has been variously described in astrological treatises. According to Varahamihira, Sakata Yoga signifies the placement of all planets in the First and the Seventh Houses, as a result of which the person concerned will gain his livelihood by driving a cart, will be sickly and cursed with a bad wife. In *Jataka Parijatam* Sakata Yoga is stated to occur when Jupiter occupies the Sixth or the Eighth Bhava from the Moon elsewhere than in the quadrant in respect to the Ascendant. It further states that the person born in the Sakata Yoga even if he is from a royal family, becomes indigent and in consequence of the trouble and fatigue falling to his lot, he is always distressed and becomes an object of aversion to the king. Mantreswara in *Phaladeepika* has mentioned that the Moon in the 12th, 8th, or 6th from Jupiter causes Sakata, but if the Moon be in a quadrant from the Ascendant, there is no Sakata. He indicates that the person born in the Sakata Yoga will often become unfortunate and may again regain what he once lost. He will be very ordinary and insignificant man in the world. He will attain much mental grief that is inevitable and will be exceedingly unhappy. Another text indicates that the person afflicted by Sakata Yoga will have decline in his fortune but he will again graciously retrieve his entire fortune ; he will be very

renowned but shunned, will take refuge in sinful acts
and would be intensely unhappy. The various authorities
have laid down different criteria for the affliction of the
Sakata Yoga. Summarising the various features of this
Yoga, Dr. B. V. Raman defined the Yoga as the Moon in
the Twelfth, Sixth, or Eighth from Jupiter as a result of
which the native loses fortune but may regain it. The
native will be ordinary and insignificant ; he will suffer
from poverty, privation and misery. He will be stubborn
and hated by relatives. Commenting on this Yoga, Dr.
Raman remarked that there was difference of opinion as
regards the definition of this Yoga. The great Parasara
and Varahamihira say that when all the planets are in the
First and Seventh, Sakata is caused. But Dr. Raman has
cited some eminent astrologers as expressing their doubts
with regard to this definition, specially the rationale of
the planets in the Seventh not being very clear. On the
contrary the definition limiting the placement of the
Moon to the Twelfth, Sixth or the Eighth from Jupiter
seemed logical and reasonable in as much as the Yoga
was generated by the Moon occupying the three
Dusthanas or evil houses from the greatest benefic
Jupiter thus obstructing the free flow of fortune. But
this approach to Sakata Yoga has some limitations which
will be seen later on.

Essentially, the Sakata Yoga is a relationship
between Jupiter and the Moon. When these two planets
are situated as sixth-eighth to each other, the Sakata
Yoga takes place. When one of the planets atleast is
exalted or is in its own sign, the intensity of the
affliction is greatly reduced. The placement of any of
these planets in a quadrant, that is, in any of the central
houses namely the first, fourth, seventh, or the tenth
nullifies the affliction. This placement is said to absolve

the planets from their malefic effects. Such controversial statements one may find at various places but the important point for pondering in this connection is the possibility of nullifying any planetary effect at all, or to accept that the combined influence of several forces will affect the individual in a radically different way.

One should, at the very beginning, recognise that the sixth-eighth position of the Moon from Jupiter is not a very uncommon position. The very fact that the Moon traverses all the signs of the zodiac during the course of its monthly sojourn atleast once suggests that for about five to seven days in the month, the Moon could easily form the combination considered under the Sakata Yoga. Therefore, roughly speaking, atleast one-fifth of the humanity must suffer from it. From this, one is liable to infer that such a common place combination need not be very important or exceptional to take a note of, or it may be merely highlighting certain universal tendencies under which the humanity evolves. Whatever the philosophical implications of the combination, we shall begin by considering some of the implications of the yoga.

One of the considerations relating to this yoga is that the combination affects more like a 'general influence' affecting the entire life of the person showing some inherent inbuilt feature of the person's psychological and physiological constitution rather than merely the mere bestowal of any special misery, indigence, loss of prestige, humiliation or fall from grace. Sakata yoga could therefore be taken as a general precondition for the prognostication of the welfare of the person. The possibility of disgraceful or the so-called unlucky events occurring in any one's life may be related to several factors and not only to one. As far as Sakata Yoga is concerned, there may be a feeling of *occasional*

experience of physical or psychological vitality being
sapped out. As this combination is found to be present in
many eminent persons like Jawaharlal Nehru, the Nizam of
Hyderabad, Sri Aurobindo, Shivaji the Great, it should
be reasonable to infer that the combination does not
necessarily mar the horoscope in every way. The presence
of Sakata Yoga does not *necessarily* mar the supreme
excellence or otherwise of the horoscope, rather it adds
one more dimension to it which should be taken into
account while studying the nature of various planets in
relation to the life of the person concerned.

While considering the impact of Sakata Yoga, it is
useful to recall that the Moon is closely connected with
this combination and so is Jupiter, both of which have
been assigned special significance in exoteric as well as
in esoteric philosophy. The Moon represents the Great
Passive Principle of the universe, which ultimately in
association with *Maya,* the Great Creative Illusion,
enabled the cosmic ideation to take place. It is either
the seat of the Primordial Matter or is the Primordial
Matter itself depending upon the level at which this
planet, or the deity represented by this planet is considered. The Moon is considered both the efficient and
the material cause of the visible universe, the essence
from which all created things are produced and into
which they will at one stage of the manifestation of the
solar system, be absorbed. As far as the life of the
individual is concerned, the Moon is considered very
vital, significant next only to the Ascendant. The seed
for the development of various talents, as well as the
possibility for attaining material and spiritual heights
must be contained in the Moon if the possibility has any
chance for its fructification.

In *Uttar Kalamrita*, mention has been made, besides other aspects of the Moon, to relate this planet to *Buddhi* (intelligence), *Nidra* (sleep), *Stri* (Female), *Lavana* (Salt), *Madhu Prasad* (Sweet Blessings, or Honey), and *Minadya jalaja* (Fish and other water-born creatures). From these, the discerning students may visualise the Moon as having close association with the Passive Creative Principle (Buddhi), but it may be in its latency as suggested by the word *Nidra* (Sleep) which is itself a passive state of the individual Females also represent the same kind of Passive Principle. Salt is a very esoteric symbology ; it can merge itself completely and be invisibly assimilated in water (an active principle of life), yet it would preserve its special quality (of saltiness) so that under suitable conditions (*e.g.* after evaporation of water as a result of heat), it can revive its pristine nature. The Moon was known to the ancient seers as the main source of man's life which represented the efficient and the material cause of his manifestation. The creative qualities of man namely the *Buddhi*, the field where such possibilities can fructify (*Stri*), the special features of man, *.i.e*, his individuality (*Lavana*), the sweetness experienced by great mendicants and Higher Beings (*Madhu Prasad*), and the various material attainments and auspicious results of man's efforts (*Minadya jalaja*) are very rightfully ascribed to the Moon. Any affliction of this planet would certainly disturb the individual's physico-psychological balance.

The Moon, the Mind, is in fact, the crystallization of that principle in man which is, on higher planes, represented by the Sun. The Moon is the reflection of the Sun. Whatever the nature of the Moon, it is primarily a shadow, and it has no reality in the sense the Sun is so. Atma in man, represented by the Sun, is an undecaying,

unchangeable, principle, though its pristine quality
can be veiled under certain conditions. The veiling in a
horoscope is indicated by the planetary disposition in
various signs of the zodiac and the different *Bhavas*, or
the House-divisions. The position of the Sun is also,
and in an important way, a significator of it. The veiling
would suggest the special purpose for which the particular incarnation of the individual has taken place. This
subject is very long and intricate but here, it may be
relevant to emphasize that the Moon reveals what special
lessons the individual has to learn in any particular incarnation. The effect of the Moon is basically on the
psychic and the psychological planes. In Sakata Yoga,
the Moon plays an important part, on the psychic and
the psychological planes. The effects of Sakata Yoga
do not take place merely during the directional periods
of these two planets, namely the Moon and Jupiter,
rather the influence of this combination is felt throughout
the life span of the individual. The physical and mundane
effects of the combination either flow from the impulses
aroused in the psychical vesture of the individual, or the
physical conditions are oriented in such a way as to
influence the psychic—and psychological make up of the
person.

As far as Jupiter is concerned, it has a different kind
of radiation, and its influence is qualitatively different.
It is God's Grace, the spring wind which provides
suitable conditions for the growth and development of
all the faculties latent in an individual. The special
significance of Jupiter among the Planetary Hierarchy
has been implied in many mythologies connected with
the planet. Generally speaking, many astrologers both
amateurs and professionals, are apt to attribute all
the auspicious and desired effects on the life on an

individual to this planet, which is eulogising it much more than what it deserves. Irrespective of the quality and the nature of the desired objects, one expects Jupiter to bestow all that one desires in life: money, children, status, renown, health, longevity and so on. But in actual life, which has been time and again empirically confirmed is that the effects of Jupiter are a little different from the expected ones, though the planet may be helpful in fructifying all that is latent in an individual. Dr. B. V. Raman considered Jupiter as ''the first rate benefic of the solar system'', whilst H. P. Blavatsky stated that to be ''merely the personification of that immutable Cyclic Law which arrests the downward tendency''. The benefic effects of Jupiter can therefore be considered as the power that arrest materialisation of the individual and they emphasize the rhythmic occurrences of the events. That which arrests materialisation does not always give results very satisfying to the wordly and the material expectations. The most significant effect of Jupiter is related to its fructifying effect which also implies the most favourable condition for the growth and expansion of desirable virtues and qualities. In the Vedic literature, the guiding spirit or the deity of Jupiter has been called Brahamanaspati. He is worshipped as 'He with his seed spreads forth beyond another's seed, whomsoever Brahmanaspati takes for his friend'; 'His children and his children's children grow in strength whomsoever Brahmanaspati takes for his friend'. From such hymns one deduces that the Vedic seers envisaged the planet Jupiter to be related to the fructifier of the seeds, and the bestower of progeny for several generations. Jupiter could be considered the influence which helps creation and generation.

One interpretation of *Taraka–Maya* caused by the Moon impregnating *Tara*, the wife of Jupiter from which act Mercury was born is that the birth of Intelligence (Manas, Mercury), which has been the embodiment of Mind-Principle in the human beings, is the outcome of the union between the Passive Principle (wife) of Jupiter and the seed (impregnation) by the Moon. In exoteric astrology, favourable disposition of the Moon (seed) and Jupiter (fructifying agency) both are essential for the material welfare of the individual. In studying the characteristics and effects of Sakata Yoga, the basic nature of the Moon and Jupiter as well as the relationship between the two require to be kept in the foreground. Their sixth-eighth relationship is primarily concerned with impeding the growth and development, that is, with the spreading of the seed, or the Germ. of the manifestation : Jupiter will endanger the growth, development and fructification, whilst the Moon will endanger the basic, inherent quality, the seed.

The basic feature of Sakata Yoga consists in the relative position of the Moon and Jupiter. The sixth and the eighth houses are very mysterious ; any interpretation of their effects is generally based on their superficial considerations. As a matter of fact, it should be recognised that both these houses constitute important aspects of the Original Substance, not material, in kind but of the nature of "Principles", or of the nature of primeval spirit; these houses link the human individual with his innermost karmic relationships going back to the very beginning. The sixth house is generally said to represent disease, obstacles, enemies, dissipation, indebtedness, mental worry, etc. For those who are on the *Nvritti Marg*, the Path of Withdrawal, the house signifies the power or the control

over various *siddhies,* attainments of or domination
over the Nature's subtler forces. Limiting oneself to
everyday explanation of the various houses, one finds
Uttarakalamrita emphasizing intense mental anguish and
material deprivation as important aspects of the sixth
house ; but here, a very unusual characteristic of the
house has also been mentioned. The house is said to
represent "a fall from a boat". In this connection, it is
worth its while to recall that the sign Gemini is symbolised by a man and a female in sexual embrace, sitting in
a boat. The boat is a means of movement on water
which itself is a symbol of the manifestative process of
life. This symbol repeated again in the sixth house
(sixth sign is again connected with Mercury which owns
the Gemini as well as Virgo) suggests another aspect of
the *Cycle of the Necessity,* or the Manifestative Process.
The material-ward movement of the Ego, at this stage, is
upset ; a new direction in one's evolutino becomes
imminent. A benefic at this house will provide vital
impulses for the upsetting process. As Jupiter is considered the first rate benefic and the Moon is another
benefic of the same system and intimately connected
with the very Germ of Life, the Mind Principle, it would
be logical to infer that the placement of one of these as
sixth from the other would give a new impulse to life.
But, would this impulse be pleasant to the individual
concerned ? Not necessarily. While studying the impact
of this combination, sometimes it is noticed that
disease, and obstacles, and indebtedness become instru
ments for giving a new direction, both karmic and otherwise, to life. Difficulties, diseases, etc., arise in order
to clear the past karmic debts and to give a new insight
in the Life Process so that the Ego adopts a new way of
life.

The eighth house which also is involved in this combination is also a 'mystery house', a 'hidden house'. It signifies the hidden sides of one's life, like death (or longevity), witchcraft, loss of money or unintentional receipt of other's money. It has been stated that the eighth house represents longevity, secret organs, death legacies and gifts, unearned wealth, cause of death,' wills, digrace and degradation, the place and surroundings of death, defeat or insult, sorrow, blame, servants and impediments. Obviously, any benefic planet placed eighth from any significator, or any other planet, would greatly exaggerate the difficulties met by the same in its fruition. From another standpoint, the eighth house signifies a radical transformation from the material to the spirit-ward turn of events. How would it take place is itself a mystery, a secret, which the Divine Power wields in each case distinctly different from every other case. The eighth house signifies vailed mystery of life. It may be induced in many different ways. The radical change could occur by an accident, some material deprivation, deep sorrow or humiliation, karmic retribution or purging out of old karmic debts as some would call it, or even by unfolding of one's inner, veiled spiritual perception or by the fortuitious meeting with highly evolved souls. It is not possible to know how the transformation would be induced but the fact of transformation can be observed after the initial push, and then, at that stage it sometimes is possible to link the cause for the same with the eighth house disposition in a horoscope. In studying the sixth-eighth house relationship between the Moon and Jupiter, this aspect of the horoscope becomes very significant.

Applying these general principles to the analysis of Sakata Yoga, one finds that the Moon is important for the individual in many way : in fact, the Moon is Mind, the Essence or the very core of one's being. Jupiter being the creative influence, the deity which enables the seed of his friends to spread beyond another's, or who helps the children of his friends to grow in strength, would be greatly detrimental for the expression and growth of the individual's creative faculties if placed in adverse relationships with the Moon. Under such circumstances, the usual life pattern, specially the approach to life, connected with thinking principle or the very consciousness itself would be greatly upset signifying the fall from the boat which necessarily is a period of great mental anguish and serious mental readjustment and physical resettlement. When the benefic influence of fructifying Jupiter is distorted, the possibility of the flowering of the material germ would be thwarted. While Jupiter placed sixth from the Moon arouses churning in mind, a turmoil in the mental world, the Moon placed eighth from Jupiter creates almost similar conditions in the generative and protective power of the first rate benefic of the solar system. As a result of this placement, the mysterious link with the protective deity, Jupiter, is snapped which is a kind of death-like experience, leading to great isolation and loneliness when the need for some help because of the turmoil in the mind, is very great. The Moon being an important constituent of this combination produces a rhythmic alteration based on its changing phases, which in the case under consideration need not necessarily be connected with its fortnightly rhythm. This approach to rhytmic alteration in the effect of the Moon explains to some extent the rhythmic impact indicated under the Sakata Yoga. For this reason, one expects periodic difficulties confronting the individual under this combination.

Under this situation, there would be several jolts in life
forcing the individual to consider the problems of life
facing him very seriously and from a radically different
standpoint. There would be material deprivations, social
obloquy and drying up of helpful and friendly support.
Because these influences do not aim at penury, disgrace,
or loss of strength *for their own sake* but in order to
induce a different way of life, such impulses continue
till the required change is attained. This condition
induces loss and retrieval of the position lost, again to
lose the same and to retrieve it so that there is complete
indifference to those material attachments. The circu-
larity is repeated till the mind is completely disentangled
from the old moorings.

These influences are amply demonstrated if one is
careful about the various horoscopes coming to the
attention of the astrologer. For an examination of this
combination, one should recall that it is not a poorman's
yoga, nor of an ordinary person. Eminent persons in
different walks of life can only have Sakata Yoga. In
that sense, one could even label this combination as
one leading to eminence in some areas though psychologically the impact may be distressing. Take for example,
Shivaji the Great who had Sakata Yoga in his chart. He
was decidedly one of the greatest patriots produced on
the Indian soil, and his chivalry and presence of mind
knew no bounds. In his case, the Moon was in Virgo
while Ascendant was Leo, and Jupiter with Sun was in
Aquarius which resulted in the Sakata Yoga. He also had
Adhi Yoga with Jupiter in the sixth, Mercury in the
seventh and Venus in the eighth from the Moon. The
mental anguish and suffering of the kind he had experienced in his life was not mitigated by Adhi Yoga but the
great radical transformation or the strengthening of

spirituality both for his own life and for the country
through him could be made possible only on account of
the Sakata Yoga in his chart.   The tremendous strength
enjoyed by the Moon has not reduced the impact of this
yoga·   As a matter of fact, from the present standpoint,
it could be said that the strength of the Moon in fact
has increased the intensity of the Sakata Yoga. It is well
known to his biographers as well as to almost every
Indian, the unexpected stoppages of protective and helpful forces along with periodic upsettings which marked
his life, but they were all for a noble purpose.   Shivaji's
life from his Ego's standpoint was a great trial ; for him
the spiritual unfolding and the religious mission were
regularly tested by periodic deprivations, obstacles,
humiliations and great personal loneliness.   In fact, the
Sakata Yoga in his case was intended to purify the gold
in him.

Take another example of Yogi Aurobindo. Here is an
example of Sakata Yoga in its highly significant spiritual
conditions : Jupiter in cancer ascendant, and the Moon
with Saturn in Sagittarius signifying an ideal exchange
as well.   The creative and generative capacity of Jupiter
was greatly impeded on the physical plane, while the
Sakata Yoga, after creating a radical transformation in
his life, after material 'setbacks' such as resignation
from the Indian Civil Service and imprisonment, aroused
in him his latent spiritual powers, the *Kundalini Sakti* or
the Serpent Fire, which endowed him with a clear spiritual
perception.   Periodic changes in his life are outstand-
ingly obvious ; brilliant scholar plunging into political
activity for about ten years suddenly turning to *Yogic
Sadhana* that is Spiritual Meditation for spiritual contemplation which also implied his shutting up of automatic
generative impulses (Jupiterian influence) and unifying

his physical consciousness with the Source of Life and Light exemplifying the effect of the Sakata Yoga. His international renown, and death, both occurred in Jupiter main period. From this one is apt to think that the heart wrenching Initiatory experiences must have taken place during the period when he was completely severed from any other supporting influence (signified by Jupiter) making him stand completely on his own, on the support and strength of his own understanding and intelligence (the Moon effect).

One can even cite the example of Jawaharlal Nehru who also had Sakata Yoga in his horoscope. In many ways, his is a chart complementary to Yogi Aurobindo's. The Moon, instead of Jupiter, is in his ascendant which is Cancer, while Jupiter is in Sixth House from the Moon, which also happened to be Sagittarius, his own house. Undoubtedly, Pandit Nehru was a great mind, but whether he was able to express all that he wanted in his life or not is a mute question. Here one is not only thinking of his masterly command over English literature, but of all other aspects of life's unfoldment. He had plenty of impediments in his life ; he suffered from several limitations ; he had the British Government itself as his enemy, but he was placed at the helm of India and he enjoyed tremendous international renown and influence. The effect of all these, including the Chinese attack on India which broke his very backbone, was to induce him towards greater, and inner insight into God's plan. In personal life he could be consi-dered a failure in several ways, but from his soul's point of view, there had been a tremendous transformation in his life. Periodic influx of loss—physical and psycho-logical, great sense of inner loneliness, mental isolation and expansion of psychological and spiritual perecption

characterised his life. These are the typical influences
which the Sakata Yoga creates in any one's life.

The above analysis leads us to think that the Sakata
Yoga is a very uncommon combination of two first
class benefic planets. The effect of this yoga is experienced throughout the span of life. It provides the
general conditions under which the life evolves in this
world. The deeper examination of the placement of the
two involved planets in this combination shows that the
individual is put under the influence of this yoga when
he is inwardly ready for spiritual transformation.
When the individual is ready for some spiritual unfoldment, he has to undergo certain deprivations. Only at
the sacrifice of material comfort can one expect to
progress on the path of spirituality. The individual has
to experience some hard realities of life before he could
experience the spiritual delight. The obstacles, difficulties, deprivations, and such other conditions face him
in order to restrict his growth on the material plane.
These upsettings necessarily create mental anguish, and
a feeling of isolation, loneliness, deprivation of all
expansive factors around oneself. From these conditions
a new consciousness has to arise. As the new life
requires constant hammering before this understanding
is concretised, it is necessary to have the experiences
repeated several times before it is firmly established in
the individual. Therefore periodicity becomes an important characteristic of Sakata Yoga. This yoga should
not be confused with such other planetary combinations
which are connected with penury and indigence. It is
a planetary combination under which two of the most
important benefics of the solar system try to induce a
new transformation moving the individual to a deeper
understanding of the purpose of creation and the role of

the individual in the realm of cosmic manifestation. For such an experience to occur, one does not have to be internationally known and very popular, or to suffer from abject poverty and humiliation, but even in an ordinary way in one's everyday living, the Sakata Yoga can bring about the radical spiritual transformation in its own way at its own limited or proper level.

PLANETARY RETROGRESSION

Simply stated a retrograde planet is one which is moving in an orbit in the direction opposite to that of the earth in its revolution around the Sun, but from the ancient days, this subject of astrological retrogression has baffled the seers of the subject. A planet in retrogression is, from every point of view, radically different from that in its direct motion. The difference lies not only in the intensity of the effect but also in the nature of its influence. The subject therefore remained lively both for the ancient seers as well as for the modern astrologers.

Many aspects of the question of retrogression have to be considered by serious students. The *Suryasiddhanta* refers to eight kinds of motions of a planet namely, (i) *vakra*—retrograde, (ii) *anuvakra*—somewhat retrograde, (iii) *kutila*—traverse, (iv) *manda*—slow, (v) *mandatara*—very slow, (vi) *sama*—even, (vii) *seeghra*—swift, and (viii) *seeghra-tara*—very swift. All these are however not considered retrograde proper because many of them refer only to the rate of the progress. Generally, the first three may be considered as retrograde, but Varaha Mihira considered only the first two, namely *vakra* and *anuvakra* as retrograde. In fact, it would be interesting to consider the planets as living entities and the rate of progression an expression of their relationship with the sign of the zodiac to which they are moving or from which they are receding. These motions in fact result from the specific relationship between the planet and the Sun : these motions result when a planet is at a particular distance from the Sun.

In solving the manifold complexities of human psychology, the retrograde planets make very substantial contribution. But the classical astrologers have approached the problem very differently. The usual view that a retrograde planet if it happens to be a debilitated one, gives the effect of an exalted planet is widely held. So are other suggestions *e.g.* the planets in retrogression change their very nature thus a retrograde Jupiter may give the effect of a malefic planet. Mantreswara has observed that a retrograde planet not only possesses strength but produces the effects similar to those of exaltation even though such a planet is debilitated or occupy an inimical place. Kalyanvarma stated that retrograde benefics confer political power while retrograde malefics cause sorrow and aimless wanderings. *Bhavartha Ratnakara* indicates that malefics cause good effects by being in retrograde motion. Summarising the various views on the subject, B. Suryanarayan Rao gave the following :

(a)   Benefics in retrogression bestow kingdom and malefics in the same position cause sorrow, and make one an exile,

(b)   When a planet is retrograde, its effects are similar to those of its exaltation, though posited in an inimical place or debilitated place,

(c)   When a planet is retrograde, it is said to possess strength or when its rays are full,

(d)   A benefic in retrogression gives good effects,

(e)   A planet is strong when retrograde provided it is not in its depression sign. The classical works say that a planet in debilitation will not be competent to do good and more so a planet in association with such debilitated planets.

A careful examination of various views on retrogression shows that the question is still an open one and final conclusions have not yet been established. When confronted with such a situation in a horoscope, the student has to take an overall view of the chart and consider the significance of retrogression. Often one finds that the result is not on the traditional lines of suggestions. For this reason one could probably ponder over some unorthodox views on the subject and apply them in an experimental manner.

The first point we wish to make here is somewhat of a controversial nature but the reader should take it as an hypothesis and test the validity of the conclusion according to his own experience. We feel that the ancient seers have been very skeptical in approaching the subject. In *Uttarakalamrita*, it is stated that when a planet is retrograde in its motion, its strength is similar to that in his exaltation. If a planet is conjoint with a retrograde planet, its strength is half a Rupa. If a planet is retrograde in its exaltation house, it gets only its strength of debilitation, that is almost nil. If a planet is retrograde in its debilitation house, its strength is similar to that in its exaltation. Thus we find the text suggesting radical changes in the nature of the planet when it is in its retrogression. From this it appears that the effect of a retrograde planet will have to be considered differently from the usual rules of planetary effects its normal exaltation does not yield the same result whilst the nature of the planet in debilitation also gets modified. Conjunction with other retrograde planets also changes the effect of the associating planet. When details of these combinations and characteristics with regard to different planets in retrogression are examined, the text draws almost a blank. The rationale of the conclusions is also not easily available.

Some clarification of the changing strength of a retrograde planet is given in a cryptic form in *Phaladeepika* when it stated that even if a planet is in its debilitation or in *neecha amsa* but retrograde and full of benefic rays, it should be considered strong. Like the Moon, whether the planet is exalted, is in its own sign or even in a friendly house, if its rays have been combust, it is weak. It is in fact important to note that the rays ultimately constitute the means by which the individual is affected and as such it is important to understand the nature of radiation caused by any planet whether in direct motion or in retrogression. The nature and significance of retrogression is important in a secondary manner.

Secondly one must examine whether the nature of a retrograde planet itself is changed under the changed direction of its motion or it remains as before and the peculiarity of the effect is caused due to the angular relationship between the earth, the Sun and the planet under question as a result of which the radiation belt is affected and a different kind of magnetic field is created. Considered in this way it is clear that the planet in retrogression does not get any inherent change in its characteristics. It creates merely an occular illusion. The planets by themselves are quite normal and natural in their motion. What makes them different is the view from the earth. This illusion appears so because of the angular relationship between the Sun, the earth and the planet concerned. Generally speaking, Mars, Jupiter, and Saturn appear retrograde when they are in the Sixth, Seventh and the Eighth Houses from the Sun. They tend to become retrograde when they are in the Fifth House and resume direct motion on arrival in the Ninth House. Regarding Venus and Mercury this rule does not apply ; it is not possible to conclude about their retrogression in general terms.

This being so, to consider that the retrograde planets change their nature radically would be illogical. It is merely the reflection and refraction of their inherent rays through the cosmic particles of different kinds and influenced by the different signs of the zodiac and stellar constellations or *nakshatras* that they finally affect the individuals. The impact of retrograde Saturn in Aries, his debilitation sign, cannot be the same as that of Saturn in direct motion in Libra, his exaltation sign. No matter how high an authority for this kind of deduction is quoted, the fact that a retrograde planet which is debilitated, cannot be the same as when in exaltation need not be disputed. As such, the astrological vibrations of such situations must be interpreted with care and understanding. This completely changes the usual line of approach. This complexity has certainly led to various abstruse statements appearing in different scriptures and predictions of the effect of retrograde planets becoming highly baffling.

In order to predict the astrological influence of the retrograde planet, one must take into account (*a*) the inherent or the basic nature of the planet in retrogression, (*b*) *Rasi* or the zodiacal sign in which the retrogression occurs, (*c*) the house or the *Bhava* in which the retrograde planet is posited, (*d*) the relationship between the retrograde planet and others, specially with other retrograde planets if any, and (*f*) the basic *guna*, that is, *sattwic* (harmonious), *rajasic* (action oriented), or *tamasic* (inclined to be in inertia) nature of the horoscope, that is the basic nature of the individual. In short, the retrogression changes the nature of the influence generated by it due to its special circumstances. The basic nature of the planet remains the same while its location in various houses and signs gives certain special characteristics to it. The planet tends to give the effect of the preceding house or the sign whilst it has a tendency to be mysteriously related to the sign next house or the sign where the planet is posited. Such a situation will create a special situation for the planet. Considered this way, the anomaly and confusion aroused due to exaltation of the planet giving the effect of debilitation and *vice versa* and such other special features of the retrograde planets might get solved. On this line of inquiry, let us see pragmatically whether any special feature of the horoscope becomes clear and whether the principle here enunciated works out in actual life correctly.

Let us consider a chart having Leo ascendant, the Moon in Virgo, Rahu in Libra, Saturn (Retrograde) in Sagittarius, and Jupiter (Retrograde) in Capricorn, Ketu in Aries, Venus and Mars in Gemini, Sun and Mercury in Cancer. It belongs to a very successful lawyer who rose without any support and merely by the dint of his own efforts to the highest level in the district town where he earned fabulously both money and renown. He had absolutely no enemy in his personal life and instances have been there to show that even those who were against him for some reason or the other sooner or later turned out to be his friends and well-wishers. He got six sons and three daughters all of whom were well placed. He built several houses and had been a landed aristocrat as well. As a student, he was renowned to be a very good student but he did not obtain any good degree of high level; he was a linguist, a deep student of literature, philosophy and occult sciences but he did not publish any book though he had a few articles published in legal journals. Now, let us examine how the retrograde Saturn and Jupiter in fifth and sixth Houses have behaved !

Summarising the effect of Saturn in the Fifth House, Dr. B. V. Raman stated in his *Hindu Predictive Astrology* that it would make the person narrow minded, insignificant, no children, perverted views, tale teller, royal displeasure, troubled life, clear minded. As a matter of fact, none of these characteristics applies to the native whereas if we examine Saturn's characteristics in the Fourth House, we find the results much more agreeable. Professor Raman stated that Saturn in the Fourth House gives dangers to mother if with the Moon, unhappy, sudden losses, colic pain, narrow minded, miserable, crafty, estates encumbered, good thinker, good patrimony, success in foreign countries, political disfavour, licentious, interrupted education. Many of these attributes are true in the case of the native (though all of them may not be considered so). What is more important is that the native felt a sense of loneliness, he had many houses but he did not feel at home anywhere. He had very little comfort of mother though he was extremely attached to her. The third aspect of Saturn in this case should have fallen on the Seventh House where it should naturally operate if it is considered posited in the Fifth House where Saturn is actually so. But the native in actual life was very fortunate as far as *Kalatrabhava*, or the house of married bliss is concerned. If we consider Saturn aspecting the Third House considered backward from the Fifth House because he is now moving towards the Fourth (*i.e.* in the opposite direction) House, one could find some interesting conclusions appropriately applicable in the present case. For example, the individual had unqualified success in whatever pursuit he engaged himself. The backward tenth aspect of Saturn being on the Eighth House also gave him good longevity. On the above empirical evidence, one is inclined to infer that the position of a retrograde planet in a House or a sign is intended to indicate its basic characteristics, that is, whether the planet is functioning as benefic or malefic whilst its location for the predictive purposes should be considered as 'tending towards' the previous house and the effect is expected as if the planet was located in the previous house. As the retrograde planet has changed the direction of its motion, its aspects should be considered backward. It could also be considered as if the planet is reluctant to affect the next house.

Applying these rules for the interpretation of the effect of Jupiter, we may see their validity a little more clearly. In the above chart, Jupiter is retrograde in Capricorn which forms the Sixth House of the horoscope. By its position in Capricorn, there is some kind of *Neechabhanga* (cancellation of debilitation) Raja Yoga, but more important task in the present context is to examine whether Jupiter gives the effect of his location in the Sixth or of the Fifth House. Again, we find Dr. Raman summarising the effect of Jupiter in the Fifth House by stating that Jupiter's effect in this house would be "broad eyes, statesmanly ability, good insight, high position, intelligent, skilful in trade, obedient children, pure-hearted, a leader". These attributes are very correct in the case of the native. His children considered him almost godlike; about the purity of his motives, it is true that like Tulsidas he felt that he had more faults than those whom the general public accused to be sinners. Such a saintly man to the core of-his heart is difficult to find.   About his being a leader, it may be stated that he was never a politician but whenever any impartial arbitration was needed and whenever any person wanted any personal advice, he was always considered better than anyone else in the locality for such a help.

Against this, let us see what Dr. Raman says about the effect of Jupiter in the Sixth House.   He states that such a placement makes the native "obscure, unlucky, troubled, many cousins and grandsons, dyspeptic, much jocularity, witty, unsuccessful, intelligent and foeless". It would be far-fetched to consider the native unsuccessful ; He was never jocular either.   He cannot be considered obscure, unlucky in the usual sense, and generally speaking he was not troubled.   He never had any cousin, he had no uncle, no brother, no sister. Obviously, in this chart, the effect of Jupiter is more akin to its being in the Fifth House rather than in the Sixth.   By this special disposition of retrogression the native has escaped the ill-effect of Jupiter, (the *karaka* of *putra-sthana* or of the Fifth House posited in the Fifth House itself) this is a singular feature of the horoscope. Jupiter has escaped the adverse effect of nullifying the children's welfare as it is said to be the usual effect of Jupiter itself being in the Fifth House.   But Jupiter did not give the adverse effect of its placement in the Sixth House either. The retrogression of Jupiter in the present case very well exemplifies the principles on retrogression enunciated earlier.

Another example which we may take up is illustrative of a more complex situation.   It belongs to a lady who is no more. She had Piscian Jupiter as the ascendant, Rahu is in Capricorn, Sun, and Mercury in Aquarius, Jupiter

in Pisces, Venus in Aries, the Moon in Taurus, Saturn in
retrogression in Gemini, Mars in retrogression along
with Ketu in Cancer. She had a loving husband, several
children, some of whom died early, she did have some
abortions. She died of a malignant undiagnosed disease
relating to marrow, blood and bones. She was a
madhyayu—bestowed with only middle duration of longevity ; she died in her fifties. If we consider that the lord
of the ascendant Jupiter is in strength and hemmed
between two benefics, and posited second from the Sun,
we should ordinarily expect the native to be *sattwic*,
religiously inclined, harmonious, person with occasional
fits of depression mainly due to the placement of Saturn
in the Seventh House, and aspecting the Ascendant lord.
But it was merely a superficial, if at all, characteristic of
the situation. Saturn in the Seventh House is expected to
give 'more than one wife, enterprising, sickly, colic pain,
deafness, diplomatic, unhappy marriage, ambitious,
political success, travelling, dependent, dissimulator,
foreign honours, deputation''. None of these can be
considered in any real sense applicable to the person.
Her married life by all worldly standards had been happy
but what was significant to note in her case was the
deep urge for debauchery which for some unknown
reason could not fructify in actual life. She had a few
children but she also had abortions which can clearly be
considered as the result of the hind-sight of retrograde
Saturn as well as of Mars on the Fifth House, the former
located in the Seventh House and the latter in the
Eighth. She died a *sumangali* that is, while her husband
was alive which completely belies the effect of Saturn
and Mars in the Seventh and the Eighth Houses respectively. This may, as a matter of fact, suggest that the
retrograde planets almost become blank as far as the

House in which they are posited. Their effect must be predicted either by relating them to the former or their reluctance to be in the latter house ; their placement in the former House is more realistic.

Such examples can be multiplied. But one realistic conclusion that could be drawn from such examples would be that the retrograde planets considered pragmatically may appear misleading and unorthodox to traditional astrologers, if one begins to consider such planets on the lines indicated above. Theoretically, the traditional astrologers would very strongly differ from the above approach, but in actual life, the retrograde planets would operate on some such lines as indicated above. In fact, the retrograde planets have distinct differences in their physical and psychological effects than they would produce in their normal situation. There would be several events in life which could be explained by associating a retrograde planet with the previous house while absolving it of any benefic or malefic characteristics which could have been expected of them due to their placement in those Houses. Their aspects should be considered hind-ward. Retrograde planets occur in a chart due to certain deep-rooted karmic factors reaching out from past incarnations, such that their results would often belie normal and obvious predictions.

PLANETARY COMBUSTION

Empirical investigation into the horoscopic influence of planetary combustion due to their proximity to the Sun reveals that the commonly held traditional view suggesting complete destruction of the main characteristics of the combust planet is not born by facts. Proximity of the Moon, Venus, and Jupiter to the Sun destroys much of their special features, while Saturn and Rahu radically affect the Sun itself. Mercury is never combust. Martian priximity lends added strength to the Sun.

The Sun as the soul of the universe provides sustenance for the human individual as well as for every other life form on this globe. Once Dr. B. V. Raman gave three main reasons for the supreme importance of this planet in astrological predictions, specially when it is in combustion, association or conjunction with other planets. Firstly, he stated that the Sun is the centre and the controlling force of the entire solar system. Gravitationally, it holds all the planets in their respective places. Their actual motions in orbit result from a balance between the Sun's attraction and their original motions in space. Secondly, the Sun is a star, only one near enough to us. This has many implications which need much serious study. In order to know the occult significance of the Sun assigning it the central regal status amongst our planetary system, one will have to find out the distinctive features of the Sun. Thirdly, Dr. Raman emphasized that the Sun is the source of all the power, heat and life on earth. The Sun's rays act upon watery surfaces and water is converted into vapour; vapour is condensed by cold blasts of wind and falls as rain; rain sustains vegetation and vegetation nourishes man.

Evidently, the role of all other planets is subordinate to the status of the Sun. The radiation of the Sun is much more important than that of any other planet. In actual operation how these interactions express themselves is not easy to decipher. The complexity is considerably increased if these planets, as well as the Sun are not considered mere physical entities. The ancient seers considered them as *devas*— the shining gods or beneficient powers of the celestial hierarchy. The *Rigveda* referred to the relationship between the Sun and other manifestations of the solar influences represented as Indra, Mitra, Varuna, Vayu, Agni, Yama etc. This showed that the central planet, namely, the Sun was not to be assumed merely as a physical entity radiating specialised influences through differing aspects of its own being and through other planetary hierarchies officiating for it at different levels of manifestation in order to effect this terrestrial plane of existence. The Sun is to be considered as a living entity, scintillating with enormous energy, radiating influences which are beneficient for human beings as well as for the devas angels and other celestial beings.

When the solar influences are considered this way, many interesting questions deserve our attention. The astrological theory that the proximity of certain planets with the Sun completely annihilates their basic characteristics seems an illogical one. If the Sun is the central controlling force of the entire solar system, and if it is the bestower of all the power, heat and life on this globe, then why should it operate in such a manner as to destroy the natural propensities of certain planets? Astrologically, conjunction, association and aspects are acknowledged relationships which exist between different planets. Depending upon special characteristics of the various planets, the resulting influences are accordingly modified. On the same analogy, why should combustion not be considered merely a variant of the general theory of planetary association? This is the crux over which all students of astrology must ponder. As the astrological savants are agreed on the fact of solar combustion, there must be a radical difference between the nature of the Sun and other planets. Mercury is said to be an exception. But, if the solar heat and the brilliance of its rays cause the combustion, why should there be an exception to Mercury? The argument that the distance of Mercury is always within a narrow margin to the position of the Sun is not a complete and a satisfactory answer. One is apt to think that the gravitational pull of the solar orb while exerting certain physical influences giving motion to different planets and direction to them on their orbit, the Sun also influences them in such a way as to impart certain special characteristics to their nature due to their closeness.

For example, we have been told that the preceptors who advised the royalty on ethical matters, should not freely and closely mix with the kings, but should keep their distance. There is much meaning in this kind of advice. Jupiter and Venus are said to be preceptors, the former of *Devas*, the gods, and the latter of *Asuras*, the non-gods, so their code of behaviour, if some special reasons were there for this code, should regulate them even in their relationship with the Sun, the king of the planetary hierarchy. In the case of combustion of the planets, we find Jupiter and Venus are combust in an important manner.

Before we dwell on the nature of different planets, let us examine the question of combustion itself and the way it differs from other planetary relationships. Given the latitude of the Sun, if a planet is within a range of 5°, it is considered completely combust; the range extending upto 10° makes it partially so, but in the case of planets being more than 15° away, it is said to be free from this affliction. The exactitude of the dividing line as in the case of the sign of the zodiac or in Navamsa divisions is not so important in the present context as the angular distance. Nearer the location of the Sun, greater the combustion, whilst the planets beyond the specific limit is completely free from such an affliction. This situation is analogous to a total eclipse. When the intervening planet, for example, the Moon in the case of the solar eclipse, or the earth in the case of the lunar eclipse, begins to approach the planet, the influence begins to be felt till it completely veils (eclipses) the planet and thereby inhibits its radiations to flow freely in the direction of the eclipsing planet till it is gradually freed.

A significant difference between this phenomenon and the combustion is that the approaching planet itself is affected in the latter case. The point for comparison is the intensity of combustion which depends upon the proximity of the planet and the Sun. As the proximity is the deciding factor, one would, for the time being, ignore the influence of the zodiac where the occurrence takes place, or in the lunar constellation where it happens. The combustion is primarily a relationship between the Sun and the planets and as such, where it occurs is not so important except for deciding the affliction of the houses owned and governed by the combust planets.

The combustion does not affect all the planets in the same manner. Mercury is an important exception. But, the birth on the New Moon day, which is an obvious example of the proximity of the Sun and the Moon, is treated in a singular way ; the power and the potential of the Moon is much reduced by the occurrence. The reflecting medium must be away from the reflected image in order to give good results. Venus is an important victim as far as the expression of its own qualities is concerned. In the case of Alexander the Great, Dr. B. V. Raman calculated the position of the Sun as 123° 35′ whilst that of Venus is 126° 20′, the Ascendant being 19° 31′, which is a clear illustration of combustion in the Fifth House of Venus. Consequently, the Venusian characteristics of sensuous pleasures, as well as the possibility of good academic career, were absent to this great man. But the association of Venus and the Sun gave him much glory and renown. According to Dr. Raman, Venus sub-period in Mercury main period was of outstanding importance to Alexander the Great. It was during this period that he led his army into India and conquered the Punjab, the goal of his life's mission·

In the chart of Sri Adi Sankaracharya, Ascendant 99° 22′, the Sun is at 8° 12′, Venus at 3° and Mercury 24° 6′. Here also Venus is combust. The obvious result was the negation of worldly pleasures ; the spotless purity of Adi Sankaracharya is ideal. But it was from the influence of (combust) venus that he derived almost the divine sublimation of his vital energy ; the planet also bestowed on him the finest musical composition and penetrating insight into human character. Even otherwise, his triumphant tour of the country commenced

in Venus sub-period in the main period of Jupiter.
According to B. V. Raman, Sri Sankaracharya though
donning ascetic robes, enjoyed all the paraphernalia of
royalty.   Apparently, Venus reflected some of its
characteristics through the Sun. In the case of Sri
Ramanujacharya, another saint of India, he had Ascendant at 102° 2', the Sun at 11° 32', Venus at 16° 36' and
Mercury at 24° 42' ; discussing the combination,
Dr. B. V. Raman stated that Venus occupying *Karma-
sthana* with *Atmakaraka* Sun suggests that making
Bhakti (devotion) as the pivot of religion was one of the
most important point in the life-work of Ramanuja. On
the same authority, it is on record that Ramanujacharya
did not find in his wife that ready sympathy and compli-
ance to his own wishes he expected of her. He took
advantage of an invitation from his father-in-law to send
away his wife and immediately assumed *sanyasa*. In
this way, one finds that the mundane sphere of Venusian
activity got almost annihilated whilst it led him to
sanyasa (asceticism) which is the very antithesis of
Venus.   The discovery and consecration of the temple
at Melkote took place in Venus Main period and Saturn
sub-period while during the same Venus period,
Ramanujacharya was prosecuted by the Chola King
Kulottunga.

  Another example of combust verus was that of Marie
Antoinette who was prosecuted in her 38th year at the
altar of Liberty. Her ascendant at 74° 1', the Sun at
201° and Venus at 202° is a perfect illustration of
combustion. Her education was faulty but she was
always, almost from her very childhood in the midst of
court intrigues. She was married at the tender age of 13
years, in Venus sub-period of Rahu main period, and
was suddenly thrown in the midst of the most corrupt

and licentious court in "the Europe of that most dis-
solute age". Venus and the Sun have shown here their
influence in a very emphatic manner ; the former forced
upon her the negation of even ordinary marital felicity
though Venus was located in its own house. Her married
life was wretched ; her husband suffered from "some
sort of impotence" ; she was abandoned even "at the
door of her bridal chamber" on the very first night of her
marriage. Such unfortunate conditions with *swakshetri*
(the lord of the house located in the house itself) Venus
along with the benefic Moon would be unthinkable unless the nature of Venus was completely changed, not
merely annihilated as generally said to be the effect of
its combustion with the Sun.

The empirical study of Jupiter-Sun conjunction,
or combustion, is also not less rewarding. Chengiz
Khan, Hyder Ali, and Aurobindo Ghose had their Jupiter
within less than 10° of the Sun. The former two, namely
Chengiz Khan and Hyder Ali had their Jupiter within 1°
of the Sun, while in the case of Aurobindo Ghose
Jupiter was about 9° apart and both Jupiter and the Sun
were in different houses. In the case of Chengiz Khan,
ascendant Cancer, there were six planets in his Third
House ; the Sun 169° 23', Mars 179° 38', Mercury 154°
33', Jupiter 170°, Venus 155° 24', and Saturn 174° 18'.
Of these, the most afflicted ones are Jupiter and Saturn.
About Saturn, we shall come back later. The combustion
of Jupiter played devastation in his life. Jupiter aspected
his Seventh, Ninth, and Eleventh Houses. None of the
Jupiterian influence on these Houses had been noticed
favourably in his case. It was Mars and Saturn in the
Third House along with Venusian association in that
House which played the most significant part. The
pleasure of a happy family life, benediction of righteous

religious duties and the harmonious (*sattwic*) means of livelihood could never be associated with this greatest conqueror, wanderer, and the most brutal murderer of the world. No one could think that God's Grace poured over him.

Hyder Ali also had six planets together in Scorpio and in his Second House, his ascendant being Libra. In his case, the Sun 237° 24', the Moon 227° 47', Mars 222° 5', Mercury 216° 42', Jupiter 238° 12' and Saturn 235° 58' were together of which the Sun and Jupiter were within 2° of each other. Whatever the merit of the horoscope, the combustion of Jupiter annihilated all the finer religious feelings in him. His Tenth House is aspected only by Jupiter and Venus, but the historians testify the absence of Jupiterian qualities from his Tenth House.

When we consider Aurobindo Ghose, there could be an opinion suggesting his spiritual eminence due to the placement of the Sun, Mercury and Venus together in Leo which was his Second House. The most favourable placement of Jupiter in the ascendant, and in his exaltation sign in association with Mars, a friendly chaste planet who has *neechabhanga* (cancelled debilitation) as well, in a different person, would have bestowed the native with children, family life and much ritualistic and ceremonial religious life. Instead, Aurobindo's life was that of a revolutionary—throwing bombs (Mars) in nationalistic and righteous cause (Jupiter)—both in in the mundane as well as in spiritual realms ; his spiritual path was that of sharp and penetrating intellect, formidable but persuasive, poetic and sensitive, though highly individualistic. One does not find the classical impact of Jupiter, as it is ordinarily believed, in his case. From these examples, one could conclude that Jupiter is also likely to get combust which in this case implied the absence of Jovian impact.

When we come to Saturn and Rahu, we find that the Sun itself shows a sort of weakness in their close association. Some important examples of the Sun-Saturn conjunction are in the charts of Madhav Rao S. Golwalkar, Sri Krishnaraja Wadiar IV, Tippu Sultan, Hyder Ali and Gautam Buddha. Of these, the most helpless Saturn had been that of Gautam Buddha. In this case, Saturn had been debilitated and his nature was very much influenced by close proximity of Mars while Venus was also in the same sign. Nonetheless, one could find that Saturn had been ineffective, though it did have its impact to some extent. Saturn, the planet of concretisation and democratisation, connected with *sudras* and *malechchas* (foreigners) placed in his Tenth House, enabled his Sun (Jupiter and Venus as well) to be projected through Saturn which gave Buddhism a berth among the non-Brahmanical fold and in overseas communities. The powerful Sun, exalted in the Tenth House with full aspect of the Moon made him temendously important, religious, philanthropic but the rays of his eminence could shine only through the veil of Saturn, that is, primarily in traditionally non-Brahmanical and overseas communities or in foreign countries.

The example of Golwalkar is also very interesting. Saturn is powerfully posited in its own House in close proximity with the Sun who is not without weakness. Venus is combust in the same way, as we have discussed earlier, but Saturn gave him obstacles and delays in all his activities. The influence of the Sun could not make him shine brightly: even now, many persons do not view his *Sangh* (the R.S.S. organisation) very positively. He was a bachelor with no family life : his

Fourth House affliction is significant. And his financial position could not be considered happy. The Saturnine influence could not be annihilated in his case either, rather Saturn played hostile role to the Sun.

It is generally felt that in the Sun-Saturn conjunction, Saturn does not lose its characteristics but a struggle takes place between the two in which the former is much weakened and has to work through the overall veil of Saturn as a result of which the rays of the Sun get much blackened.

Like Saturn, Rahu, the dragon's head, which always threatens the Sun to devour it is never combust by the Sun, rather it radically affects the Sun's influence. Though a kind of spirituality is always associated with Rahu, it gives the spirituality of the ascetic rather than of the holy order of the kind of Vivekananda. If not capable of bestowing this kind of spirituality, it tends to make the person a profligate. The radiation of the Sun is markedly of a different character. When the Sun is afflicted by the combustion of Rahu, its regal splendour is denied and the latter becomes subservient to the former adding to itself whatever energy the Sun had acquired.

Such examples are found in the case of Nathuram Godse (ascendant 79° 16', the Sun 36° 41', Rahu 37° 17' and Mercury 45° 39'), H. G. Wells (ascendant 273° 16', the Sun 157° 52', and Ranu 162° 15'), Karl Marx (ascendant 302° 56', the Sun 24° 18', the Moon 24° 8', and Rahu 18° 39') and Shri Chaitanya (ascendant 184° 24', the Sun 323° 52', Rahu 328° 10'). In the case of Godse, the Sun, the lord of the Third House, posited in the Twelfth House with Mercury and Rahu did not only direct his courage towards his own end, but even the direction of his valour was perverted. About H. G. Wells it could be said that the righteous character denoted by the Sun in the Ninth House aspected by Jupiter and Mars was absent. His father was a very ordinary man but what is more important is the unbridled sex life of the great author. It showed his immense psychological instability, lack of inner strength, and confidence, and tension of the infested brain. He had no ethical code in the religious sense. This arose from the affliction of the Sun with Rahu. He even got into difficulties with ecclesiastical authorities. Karl Marx born on a solar eclipse day, had both his Sun and Moon seriously afflicted by Rahu thus making his thinking and ideals perverted. The affliction sapped his moral vitality completely which enabled him to propound the most upsetting theories of social organisation and human morals ; he worked so hard as to ruin his personal health almost beyond repair. His Sun placed in the Third House is fully aspected by Jupiter in Sagittarius, his own sign, and by Saturn from Aquarius which also happened to be the ascendant, but the nature of initiative, courage and strength of Karl Marx was directed towards the destruction of the Sun representing the royalty, the elite class, and the traditional respectability. Marx did not have any regard for the social prestige and status of individuals ; he was himself so much psychologically tortured and mentally insecure that his personal family life was almost a wreck. He became famous which was more due to Rahu rather than due to the Sun. Jupiterian aspect on Rahu turned his efforts into patronage to factory workers (ruled by Saturn) but the main purpose of this patronage was to pervert the existing social organisations, arouse licentiousness among the underdogs and to destroy gods and divinities. These are the tendencies where Rahu is more powerful than the

Sun. Under the influence of the Sun posited in the
Third House and in his exaltation sign aspected by
Jupiter from its own sign, Marx should have struggled
to uphold the established social hierarchy. Obviously,
the Sun is powerless in combusting Rahu, rather the
association of Rahu with it contaminates its influence
and destroys its natural tendencies.

In the case of Sri Chaitanya, the apostle of devotion
and the embodiment of self-surrender, the affliction of
the Sun with Rahu within less than 5° gave entirely a
different character to this great spiritual sage. He was
born on a lunar eclipse day when Saturn and Mars aspected the Moon but the Sun was unsullied by any malefic
aspect, or for that matter by any planet excepting the
Moon, but it was almost conjunct with Rahu. The
result: his father (related to the Sun) died early in his
life ; he became a *sanyasi*, an ascetic, at the age of 25
years of age (that is, he renounced all those aspects of
life which are related to Venus – his ascendant lord, and
thus abandoned everything intended for self, represented
by the Sun), and he associated himself with "all the
lowly, the outcast and the poor ; he ate, sang and prayed
with them" which signified the acme of Rahu's influence
on the Sun. These examples show the helplessness of
the Sun under the threatening radiation of the Dragon's
head the Rahu.

Mars has special influence when in conjunction or
combustion with the Sun. Commenting upon the horoscope of Emperor Nero, who had *vargottama* Mars, the
Sun and Saturn, besides *vargottama* ascendant, Dr. B.V.
Raman has stated that "the Sun and Mars are the
planets for power and when they are so powerful, it is
no wonder that Nero revelled with childish delight in the
consciousness of absolute power". In the case of Nero,

the Sun being 267° 30' and Mars 271° 2' which were
within 5° though in different signs of the zodiac, the
influence of Mars which was in the Second, the House
of Speech, was not destroyed, rather the tremendous
strength imparted to his vocal chord and melodious
voice bestowed by Venus posited in that house made
him the most famous musician both in Rome and Greece;
he even valued his musical talent more than his regal
status· In his case, the Sun did not subdue the Martian
characteristics, rather the closeness of the *Vargottama*
Sun which also happened to be in the *Vargottama* ascen-
dent, made him tremendously proud. A similar trait was
discernible even in the case of Chengiz Khan whose
Third House contained six planets including the Sun
(169° 23'), and Mars (179° 38'). The proximity of Mars
to the Sun made the latter which was already spoilt by
other associations much more ruthless than Chengiz
Khan would have been otherwise. Mars and the Sun
are of the same *tattwas*, the elements, which rainforced
each other adding considerable strength to the chart
and immense potentiality for the expression of the vital
energy latent in the individual.

From the above, it could be seen that the combustion
of various planets with the Sun is neither an unmitigated
evil, nor does it completely destroy the special characteristics of the other combust planets. In the case of the
Moon, this relationship spoils the sensitivity of the
person· Combust Venus destroys the marital felicity.
Jupiter conjunct with the Sun is bad for conventional
religious and ritualistic orientation of the person. Saturn
debases the Sun by deflecting the solar radiation towards
outcasts and foreigners. Rahu leads to perversions and
unrespectful behaviour. Mars adds to the energy of the
Sun. It would indeed be erroneous to assume that the

combustion of different planets uniformly 'burns out'
their characteristics.   Why such differing results are
observed according to the nature of different planets is
a complex subject.   The complexity of the situation can
be resolved only when these planets are regarded as
living *devas* with special responsibilities to discharge
and when combustion viewed merely as a special case of
association.

TRANSITS

All the planets are ever on move. Even if the knowledge of their position and the disposition of their influences at the time of the birth of the individual are accurately obtained, they cannot be the conclusive basis for well considered astrological prognostications. As these planets are dynamic force centres ever scintillat ing with highly charged magnetic energy thus creating a widespread electro-magnetic field, the nature of which are ever changing according to the changes in the position of these planets in the firmament. In order to apprehend the stellar repercussions on everyday life of the individual and on his environment and his society, merely an assessment of the radical planetary positions at birth is not adequate rather the changing state of the cosmic field in relation to their radical position will have to be studied. Planets at the time of the birth provide the basic nature, the latent potential, of the individual but its fructification depends upon the main period of the planet ruling at a given age of the person, as well as on the general radiation disseminated at that period. The natal chart shows the receptivity of human individual, the planetary direction at any period of his life indicates which of his qualities is likely to develop, and the transiting planetary disposition indicates whether the existing cosmic forces are agreeable to the growth and development of those qualities. This is a unique contribution of the Hindu

astrology on whose careful delineation depends the
revelation of the periodicity in any one's life.

The planetary Direction is worked out on the basis
of the Moon's position in the natal chart.   Once this
position is accurately worked out, subsequent planetary
rulerships can be determined according to a given order
of sequence where each planet is assigned certain
number of years which are not identical for every planet.
The Sun has been assigned 6 years in a cycle of 120
years, the Moon 10 years, Mars 7 years, Rahu 18 years,
Jupiter 16 years, Saturn 19 years, Mercury 17 years,
Ketu 7 years, Venus 20 years; the sequence of the planetary rulership following this very order.   The initial point
of the first zodiac that is, Aries, or the beginning of the
first lunar asterism namely Ashwini commences with the
rulership of Ketu and this rulership ends with every
nakshatra that is after every *13° 20'* of the zodiacal sign.
From *13° 20'* in Aries begins the rulership of Venus and
so on ; but though the span of first *13° 20'* in Aries
would only obtain 7 years of the rulership of Ketu, the
next *13° 20'* would obtain 20 years of Venus. The
general condition during a period would be linked with
the general disposition of the ruling planet.

In the Hindu system of prediction, the influence of
transiting planets is considered no less important than
the radical planetary disposition but there is a special
method of working out the effect of the ransiting planets.
It is primarily studied under the system which is popularly
known as *Gochar-phalam*, meaning the effect of the
movement of the planets. The effect of transiting planets
does not depend merely upon the changes of their place
since the birth time of the individual, but it requires
firstly, the determination of its quality of influence, and
secondly, the intensity of its effect.   Even if a planet is

basically an auspicious one, there is a possibility that the
transiting effect of it may not be so. For example, Jupiter
which is considered the first rate benefic of the planetary
hierarchy fails to help the native if in transit it is in the
Moon sign of the radical chart. Similarly, a malefic
planet does not always harm the person. Saturn as well as
Rahu, both are dreaded planets, but if they are in third
house from the Moon sign in transit, they bestow much
material advantages. It is not only the angular relation
from the Moon or any specific planet that determines the
goodness or adverse nature of these planets ; each of the
situation where the planet is likely to create some
favourable effect must be free of obstructive impediments. There are set rules to find out whether any
benefic planet is suffering such obstructive impediments, technically known as *Vedha*, or not. If a planet
is placed in a favourable combination in the natal chart,
and is having its own ruling period, *and* if it is transiting a
house where it has acquired the nature to bestow goodness and is free of any Vedha, it is decidedly going to
be helpful. The intensity of this helpfulness is calculated
on the basis of *dots and dashes*, which are based on the
distance of the transiting planets from the natal position
of the planets. Certain positions between the planets
are considered helpful which yield dots, whilst the
unfavourable positions are assigned dashes. The number
of dots in a house for any planet shows the intensity of
goodness of the planet. The maximum benefic dots any
planet can acquire are eight in number ; if more than
four dots are obtained, then the planet would do
good, whereas if a planet, though a benefic and placed
in an auspicious relationship, yet if it has secured less
than four benefic dots it would not be very helpful.

The effect of transiting planets is primarily assessed in relation to the Moon sign, but the same can be done even with regard to Ascendant and the Sun. The importance of the Moon sign is mainly for the reason that the general public is still on that level of existence where the Moon's effect is the most prominent. The Moon is intimately connected with mind, under which term we include both the thinking and the feeling principles. Our life is, to a great extent, controlled by the state of our mind. The mineral mercury which symbolised mind is considered solid according to some of its scientific qualities but it is highly fluid like a liquid. It is extremely· susceptible to any change in the external situation. While comparing mind with water, which is often done in occult literature, it should be noted that the mind like water gets easily disturbed by the slightest disturbance or even by the feeblest vibration over its placid surface ; when there is turmoil in the atmosphere, there could be a mighty storm on the sea. Such being the nature of the mind ruled by the Moon, it is quite natural to consider the vibrations of the transiting planets in relation to this planet, that is in relation to the state of the thinking and feeling level of the person on which depends his material well being. The cosmic vibrations arising from the planetary changes alter the state of the psychological and psychic structure of his being and his responses to these changes react on his physical and social relationships and activities.

But, from the larger standpoint, the effect of transiting planets could even be meaningfully considered in relation to Ascendant and the Sun. The Ascendant is the very base of the horoscope implying thereby that the changes affected by any influence to be effective must be in consonance with it. The impact of transiting planets in relation to the Moon is easily perceptible because it is very clearly visible even in an objective way, but the changes occurring in relation with the Ascendant are often deeper and subjective. When studied in relation to the Sun, the effect of the transits is still much more profound but not so obviously felt on the external pattern of life. Each incident in any one's life is ultimately directed towards the fulfilment of the goal set out by the Atma. What that goal is for different persons is very difficult to establish but each event, in the long run, could reveal the central direction in the person's pilgrimage. Therefore, the effect of the various transiting planets becomes important in order to discover the path the central core of the being, the Soul, has been following. The Moon is important for considering the effects of the transiting planets on the imminent changes in the life pattern, on Ascendant for studying the general wellbeing of the person, but such effects in relation to the Sun should be studied to assess the direction in the evolutionary course of the Soul.

The profundity of the impact of the transits depends upon the speed of the movement of the planet in any one house. The slow moving planets have a much enduring effect. Such enduring effects can be unravelled on the basis of the transits of Saturn, Rahu and Jupiter. On an average, Saturn completes its round of the zodiacal cycle in about 29 years and a half thus traversing a sign of the zodiac in about two and a half year. The period taken for the same is a year and half for Rahu and a year for Jupiter. As a result of such long duration of stay in one house division by these planets, their influence on the life of the person is quite lasting. These planets can be examined in order to find out long term impacts. The Moon on the other hand takes only $2\frac{1}{2}$

days. Mars transits a sign generally for about 45 days. The Sun takes a month whilst Mercury and Venus complete their journey in a house roughly in about two to three weeks time. For lasting results, one has to examine slow moving planets, whereas for short duration effects, fast moving planets need to be studied.

The basic nature of the impact made by the various planets on the same lines as in directional astrology. The inherent nature of the planets would be the same whilst other changes of the superficial type could be there for other reasons. An exalted planet in the radical horoscope, even bad in transit could not be so bad as a debilitated one. The goodness of a planet may be watered down due to the transit position, yet its basic goodness cannot be completely annihilated. Furthermore, every planet has its special method of interaction which also cannot alter. For example, the radiation of Jupiter is intended to expand the qualities of the house where it is located or of the planets which it aspects. The Saturn, on the other hand, specialises in restricting the qualities of the house tenanted or the planets aspected. Mars brings out the hidden characteristics to the surface as a result of which one could expect hidden treasure to be discovered under its impact, or when the wound is infesting the system inwardly, Mars would lead to surgical operation or bursting of the boil. The Moon imparts the life sustaining energy, the sap to the tree of life. Consequently, wherever the Moon is transiting, it would nourish that house. While transiting the house connected with wealth and income, it would make these aspects prosper, but similar would be the influence even when it transits the house of penury, sickness and expenditure, that is these also could get intensified under the lunar influence. Mercury assists the thinking

principle. Being a benefic its general nature is towards
doing good unless otherwise constrained by other
conditions. Venus adds the quality of attachment,
involvement and objective enjoyment of the situation.
Rahu and Ketu are karmic planets which implies that
these planets give an effect because that effect would
dissolve some of the past karmas, good or bad, so that
the future journey of the Soul could be unhindered by
any restricting influence.

The most dreaded transit of Saturn, spoken of by
different names in astrological text books, cannot be
overlooked very easily. Completing its journey round
the zodiacs in slightly less than 30 years, it is approximately for about $2\frac{1}{2}$ years in one house. This position is
repeated almost every thirty years. Being a very powerful planet for creating its impact, this 30 year cycle is of
considerable importance in moulding the life-pattern of
the individual. Saturn is very effective. Whatever its
consequence, good or bad, it has a lasting imprint on
the psyche of the person. For this reasons many a time
people eagerly wait for the favourable conjunction of
Saturn so that they could expect some relief from
their long drawn maladies or receive gifts of luck, whilst
in other cases, they begin propitiating the planet well in
advance of its entry into a sign in order to ward off the
impending misfortune. The yogis also look for special
placements of Saturn so that under its favourable radiation they could hope for advancements in their occult
practices. Of all the situations of Saturn, the period of
$7\frac{1}{2}$ years that is $3 \times 2\frac{1}{2}$ years, considering it to be for $2\frac{1}{2}$
years in every house though in fact due to retrogression
or for other reasons sometimes this duration may slightly
differ, is considered most dreadful when it transits the
12th, 1st and 2nd houses from the Ascendant, Moon or

the Sun. During this period, the individual is thoroughly
shaken. Once a person has passed through this period
of 7½ years he is a new person. His attitude to life,
experiences of the life-forces impinging on a person, and
expectations are never as before. Nothing expected
occurs during this period. During the course of its first
cycle, it destroys the already crystallised thinking pattern.
Monetary conditions and social life are not necessarily
in adverse but they are necessarily visibly changed. If
the conditions are so construed, the individual may
even go overseas, meet new type of people, acquire lasting friendships and even may engage in new job
opportunities. But underneath all these changing
conditions of life, what is of significance is the sense of
disappointment, a kind of disillusionment, no enjoyment
in life and a feeling that life has no attraction of permanent nature to live by. This psychological transformation
is what is induced by Saturn under this placement ; in
order to create this impact it may try many devious
methods which cannot be apprehended before hand.
During the course of the second round of this 7½ years
period, some physical loss occurs. It could be theft,
death, loss, or any serious deprivation which creates
deep rooted impression on the mind as a result of which
the man is never as before. During the third round
effect, the individual may have to prepare himself for the
land of *Yama*, Death God, symbolised for ordinary persons
by Saturn, while for the Yogis, this is the period of
attaining the results of arduous yogic practices.

SATURN

Some indications of the effects of Saturn in different
houses in relations to Ascendant, Moon and the Sun are
given below which will have to be appropriately adapted
according to the point of reference under consideration :

1st House : The feeling of being caged and confined would be predominant. Bereft of friends, feeling disappointed from wife, suffering bad health and general fatigue, the individual would be surrounded by general gloom. Humiliation and bad news, social and professional tension along with denial of legitimate opportunites for one's all round growth and prosperity would characterise the period.

2nd House : Gloom over family affairs, loss of motherly affection, chances of malignant diseases, unpleasant travels, conflict with near and dear ones and curtailment of social life may occur during this period. Dr. B. V. Raman feels that the individual during this period will get wealth from other men but will not enjoy this wealth long.

3rd House : One of the beneficial houses for Saturn. Whenever it occurs there is a significant turn for the better in the life-pattern of the individual. Impediments are removed, long delayed rewards are made available, and the individual begins enjoying his material affluence. Recovery of debts, fresh sources of income, new alignments in life, may take place though there may be some afflictions for the children and lack of interest in creative pursuits.

4th House : Quite unsatisfactory place for Saturn ; it restrains the enemies' activities to a limited extent but considerably augments sorrow and frustrations otherwise. There may occur unwanted change of house or the place of work, professional setback, humiliation in public life and affliction of relatives and ill health to his own self.

5th House : Frustration arising from restrictions imposed on one's creative activities would be severe. Added· to this could be sickness of wife, disapproval from the government, loss of money and failure in one's ambition.

6th House : One of the most helpful placement for Saturn in transit. For the individual concerned, it would be a period of distant vision when the clarity of goal and necessary support for its fulfilment would fill his heart with enthusiasm and initiative.

7th House : Not enjoying the love and affection of one's married wife, there is attraction and involvements with other sources of lusty expression ; family life having gone to rocks, personal life facing (false) allegations and losing personal and paternal wealth, and the individual losing his heart might indulge in unethical behaviour and would have a dirty mind. Association with psychologically evolved persons and interest in esoteric religious and occult practices could develop.

8th House : Persephone has now been taken by Pluto to Hades in due course to return as the expression of Spring. While experiencing the gloom, loss and separation under Saturn in the eighth house, the individual may feel that his life is going to dissolve. There could be professional trouble, public disapproval, family disturbances, loss in speculation, and affliction of children as a result of which there may be mental depression and sorrow and the individual may feel humiliated and crest fallen, but such delays in all matters and failures in all undertakings are preludes to better turn of events. Restrictions on the fruition of the past *karmas* are to teach a lesson of patience and perseverance. An important period for the yogis for their *siddhis*, perfections.

9th House : An important phase in the life of the individual marked by radical change in his mental attitude.

Self centredness, formulation and concretisation
of his personal philosophy would take place ; he
would confront loss of income, denial of friendship
and exasperation at the world receding on all sides.
But he would have victory over his enemies and
smoothening of the path despite psychological
cobwebs being there. A period of great and lasting
spiritual progress.

10th House : The storm is not yet over but the individual has started getting premonitions from the other
world ; suitable adjustments without the knowledge of the individual concerned have begun to
enable him to take advantage of the coming prosperity. Apparently there may be disturbed life, fall
from a high status, estrangement with wife and
change in the existing environment of residence
as well as work, but such occurrences pave the
necessary orientation for the impending psychological change in life.

11th House : The change will fructify and the individual
would climb another ladder of his personal unfoldment and material prosperity. Increased income,
enlargement of social circle, possibility of courtship,
recovery of past debts and asset formation characterise the period. There would be concretisation of
one's philosophy of life in which there may be
greater practicality than imagination and wish fulfilment. A new adaptation to life conditions satisfying the requirements of diminishing physical
energy would take place.

12th House : God's protective forces are temporarily
withdrawn to let the personal proclivities of the
individual have a freer play. Unlees the individual
is spiritually advanced, there could be moral degra-

dation, sorrow arising from loss of wealth and destruction of fixed assets, deterioration of health, theft and several frustrating experiences, but in the case of those who have already aroused their spiritual nature, this could be a period of great spiritual unfoldment. The inner-most content of his psyche could begin to establish a closer control of his psychology and thereby give a new orientation to his life.

JUPITER

The impact of Jupiter is no less significant than that of Saturn. During the course of a year, when Jupiter is transiting a sign so much of benefic radiation is concentrated there that the support provided to that aspects of life is greatly increased. Primarily, the effect of Jupiter is to give protection, induce the various aspects of life to grow towards-their perfection, and make the individual an enlightened being. In order to do so, it has to tend the various dimensions of life in such a manner that the necessary direction is provided to the person. Some of these forces emanating from Jupiter when it is transiting the various houses are given below :

1st House : A very difficult house for the transit of Jupiter. Under the assumption that the quantum of its radiation is so intense in this *bhava* or the house that it gets completely disturbed, one would find that Jupiter in the First House is very devastating. It disturbs the existing environment; it destroys wealth and settled habits and relationships. But all these happen in order to enable the individual to be a chalice for the divine downpour.

2nd House : Extremely good for finance ; possibility of sudden inflow of unexpected wealth and income.

There would be greater renown and professional achievements. But there may be slight sorrow either on account of illness or due to enmity with some-one.

3rd House : Being a house of bad thoughts and of impediments, as it is eighth from the eighth house, Jupiter's transit in the Third House is not good. Shift from one's established place of residence and change in affection also occur during this period.

4th House : A period of considerable psychological un-settlement. There may be unexpected downpour of divine influences as a result of which a radical change in life-pattern will take place. It may be induced by some disease, unnecessary expenditure, change of residence or due to association of some great saint, but the change is the primary effect.

5th House : A great upsurge of mental creativity lead-ing to tremendous feeling of upliftment directing the individual towards his ultimate goal in life is characterised by this position of transiting Jupiter. Increased income, unexpect reward, general prospe-rity and growth of personality are some of the mundane expressions of this transit.

6th House : Paying off the past (karmic) debts is chara-cterised by this transit. Increased enmity, unmerited blasphemy, obstacles, hospitalisation and wrong accusations could occur at this time ; even some increased inflow of income is a possibility. But underneath all these, there would be a feeling of disenchantment. Dr. B.V. Raman has very poetically expressed the situation when he stated that ''the person will be so much afflicted at heart that he will take no delight in the agreeable faces of beautiful women, the music of the peacock and the cuckoo and in houses made pleasant by the frolic of children playing like the young of the deer''.

7th House : The Divine would look into the face so as to arouse the most pleasant experiences of life : company of beautiful women, amiable social life, increased income, gain of friendship and expression of latent faculties would be expected at this period.

8th House : For the persons aspiring after occultism and higher knowledge, Jupiter's transit in the 8th House would increase his interest in yoga, occultism, *tantras* and such other *siddhis* (perfections) but for the man of the world this period is of serious affliction, penury, restrictions, fruitless endeavours, and unexpected blame.

9th House : Triangularity of benefic influences being the main characteristic of Jovian radiation, the planet bestows all the best influences it is capable of when it is transiting the ninth house. Possibilities are that there would be auspicious ceremonies, growth in respectability, expanded opportunities for creative activities, long travels and deeper insight in scriptures.

10th House : Undoubtedly there could be increased enmity, jealousy, debts and theft possibilities, but despite all these, there would be great peace of mind and equanimity in disposition, chances of professional preferment or some activity which brings out the best in the man ; the capacity to advise others would also increase.

11th House : The Jovian radiation to inculcate the feeling of contentment is immensely effective and such radiations occur when it is transiting the eleventh house. Increased income, improvement in status, help from brothers, gain in speculative activities, married happiness and beneficial travels are some of the effects of this transit.

12th House : Not a very pleasant house for Jupiter to be. It imparts here the radiation which would transform all the material attainments into spiritual capabilities. For this reason, there are increased possibilities for illness, penury, failure attempts, loss of property and larger number of enemies, change of environment, but there will also be stirrings in emotional nature and success of in yoga.

MARS

While assessing the effect of Martian transit, it is important to note that it is the vital energy which enables every form of relationship to grow. Under the Martian impulse, the seed breaks through its shell and sprouts through the hard crust of the earth. Third, sixth, tenth and eleventh house transits of Mars are good while others are trying. The following table gives a synoptic view of different transit effects of Mars.

1st House : Unless the individual has sufficient strength to absorb the Martian radiation, the influx of tremendous force under its first house transit might be devastating. In ordinary cases, Mars' transit here would create excess of heat in the body and accident proneness. For average healthy persons, this transit would lead to emotional outbursts, agility, increased anger, difficult adjustment problems with some possibility of wife's illness. Change of house, blood pressure and other ailments connected with hyper-tension could also occur.

2nd House : Much upsetting in the family circles and loss of wealth. The children are liable to suffer from blood oozing ailments, and father will also be suffering from hyper-tension or surgical operations. In the case of painters, an opportune time for painting the fire of hell, and for poets to compose ballads.

3rd House :   Added valour to the individual with enormous amount of challenging and enterprising energy impinging on the person which could enable him to succeed in almost every activity he undertakes. All round success, status increase, challenging initiative, encouragement and patronage for all his activities would certainly make this short period of Martian transit remarkable.

4th House :   Let the individual take precaution that excessive pride does not ruin his opportunities. Misunderstanding and quarrel with superiors, loss of income, estrangement with wife and danger of high blood pressure might occur. For females, this period could lead to separation and even death of husbands.

5th House :   A bad period. Affliction of children, ill-health, sorrow and loss of income are possible events. But there is also a likelihood of developing some new interests in life and students of yoga may progress towards achieving some perfections—siddhis.

6th House :   One of the best transiting houses for Mars when the past efforts get suitable opportunities to fructify. Under the impulse of Mars transiting the sixth house, one could expect solution of long-drawn problems, success in every aspect of life, and betterment in life. For those who are on the path of spiritual unfoldment, this transit provides suitable conditions for important pilgrimages, and they would also be appropriately attuned to receiving messages from the Deva-loka, the world of the gods.

7th House : The relationship with wife gets worse, and personal health of the native is in jeopardy. Even the professional life cannot be peaceful and loss of wealth and death of some family relations could occur.

8th House : Either there would be discharge of blood, surgical operation, bilious ailments, or development of some latent faculties and attainment of occult powers. Generally speaking, one could expect estrangement with friends and relations, loss of money, increased amount of tiresome work, besides personal sickness or accidents.

9th House : Unexpected events may take place and the individual may discover some hidden conspiracy against him. There could be decreased capacity to take up challenging work and the family life may be, to a great extent, disturbed nonetheless the individual will be able to establish link with his higher nature.

10th House : A period of all round vigorous activity, both professionally as well as personally; familywise, the time would be good and the children would do well. One could expect during this period professional preferment, extension of friends' circle, increased renown and general environmental improvement around himself.

11th House : Unexpectedly good influence in all aspects of life ; increased income, unexpected friendships, greater work and social opportunities, revival of old interests and recovery of lost propoerty.

12th House : A period of mixed results, physical depletion of energy, mental tension and difficult adjustment problems, but there could be new service prospects and elimination of enemies. Wife will not be favourably disposed towards the person.

SUN

The solar transits have to be assessed in such a way that the general effects of this solar sojurn is repeated every year for every month. This repetitive nature of the solar transit with precise regularity requires the prognostication to be made very carefully. The essential function of solar transit is to consolidate the experiences and qualities developed during last twelve months. Every month, the sun radiates a specific quality impinging a particular house under which the powers acquired during the year are consolidated. This makes it relevant to what the individual had been undergoing and how his life-course had been flowing. With this general background, one has to recognise that the house in which the Sun is located during the month gets highly surcharged with its energy as a result of which there is much activity relating to that house and to the house which it aspects, that is the seventh house from where it is transiting. The unsettling and the nourishing effects occur with a purpose. The former is done so that the fresh impetus given to the house is properly absorbed, while the latter is done so that the impulses sent to it by other planets are thoroughly assimilated. These effects will have to assessed according to special planetary disposition in each horoscope, but the following are some broad indications of the solar transit.

1st House: The Sun provides enormous amount of vitality in this house as a result of which there is great unsettlement in every aspect of life. The Sun is averse to everything material, so there will be general destruction of material welfare. Even to marital relationship, the Sun in the first house is not helpful. When the individuality of the person is aroused and his spiritual nature enkindled, his attachment to wealth, body pleasures, and sexual entanglements would be completely eliminated. Prior to attainment of that status of unfoldment, these deprivations may appear unpalatable events.

2nd House : In the second house, the Sun would induce fall in income, loss of relations, and greater physical discomfort.

3rd House : The Sun's rays are conducive to produce favourable results in the third house as a result of which there will be improvement in health, removal of obstacles and favour from superiors.

4th House : Change of environment, domestic unhappiness, mental agitation and occasional flashes of eternal truths may occur with the Sun in the Fourth House.

5th House : Fear, affliction of children, bad social relations are the results of Sun's transit in the Fifth.

6th House : Victory over enemies, smoothening of the path of success, and removal of restrictive conditions. Consequently there could be success in undertakings, good health and professional preferment.

7th House : Health of many persons in the family would cause concern, and there could be wearisome travels.

8th House : Danger of accident and illness ; adjustment problems with friends and family relations, quarrelsome attitude, and one may suffer royal displeasure specially because of his sharp tongue.

9th House : Would alienate the native from other associates and induce in him a sense of isolation, and he would feel run down. For those who are materially

27

involved, this transit is not good, but for those who are on occult training, it would be a period of significant expansion of spiritual consciousness.

10th House : Resurgence of pride and efficiency ; the work in accordance with one's destiny would be performed at this time.

11th House : A significant contact is established between the individual and his Divine Protector and there is great downpour of benediction to his life. Consequently, he is able to achieve much of his desired goal, complete many arduous duties and attain a new position with much honour.

12th House : A sense of disappointment will dawn on the individual and he would feel a sense of irreparable loss of everything—status, wealth, honour and sense of direction in life.

MOON, MERCURY AND VENUS

The three benefics, namely, Moon, Mercury and Venus are quick moving planets which change their signs during transits very quickly. The Moon transits a house in $2\frac{1}{2}$ days, Mercury and Venus, if they are not in retrogression, may take about 3–5 weeks which shows that their impact could be considered merely like ripples of the waves : their effects have to be assessed only as short-time impacts. In this movement also they do create good and disadvantageous effects with their transitary radiations but these effects are not lasting. The classical texts have however indicated that these transits are also of certain nature. For a general assessment of their several effects on life these may be taken into account.

The Moon will generally nourish the house which it is transiting but because of the different nature of these houses sometimes these effects appear to be good, bad or indifferent. The Moon produces good effect when it transits the 7th, 1st, 6th, 11th, 10th and 3rd houses if planets other than Mercury do not transit the corresponding vedha places namely 2nd, 5th, 12th, 8th, 4th and the 9th. The planet in its sojourn of the different houses give the effect as follows : (i) dawning of fortune, pleasant feeling, and comfortable living, (ii) loss of wealth, obstacles and run-down feeling, (iii) success and receipt of enjoyable things, (iv) mental disturbance, (v) humility, disease, and sorrow, (vi) wealth, health, and freedom of mind, (vii) optimism, (viii) unexpectedly gloomy days, (ix) fatigue of body, headache and uneasiness, (x) hopeful days, attainment of one's cherished desires, and receipt of favourable news, (xi) joyful company and bright prospects, and (xii) increased expenditure.

Mercury's primary contribution is to make the person think seriously in some given direction. When unpleasant transits occur, the individual may be caught in gloomy and brooding moods whilst under favourable transits there is outward looking optimism and deeply penetrating thought. Mantreswara gives the effect of Mercury in its transit of the 12 houses as follows : (i) loss of wealth, (ii) financial gain, (iii) fear from enemies, (iv) influx of money, (v) quarrel with one's wife and children, (vi) success, (vii) misunderstanding, (viii) acquisition of children, wealth, etc., (ix) impediments, (x) all-round happiness, (xi) prosperity, and (xii) fear of humiliation.

About Venus, it is said that it will confer on the native all kinds of enjoyments in the first house; in the second, there will be financial gain, prosperity in the third house; increase of happiness and friends in the fourth house ;

acquisition of children in the fifth; mishap in the sixth; trouble in the seventh; wealth in the eighth; happiness in the ninth; quarrel in the tenth; safety in the eleventh; and acquisition of money in the twelfth.

RAHU AND KETU

Generally speaking, it is said that Rahu will give the effect of Saturn and Ketu will function as Mars. But this is not the true indication of the situation. In fact, every planet has its own unique nature and we must know it. The basic nature of these two planets is to be important media for karmic retribution. Over the number of lives we have generated much undesirable forces which require to be diffused in order to render them neutral in future. This operation requires much careful adjustment both of the good as well as bad types. The two shadowy planets, namely, Rahu and Ketu have been assigned the task of dissolving those forces during their natal position as well as during their transits. In their characteristic way of introducing their effects surreptitiously with deep impact Rahu resembles Saturn, whilst in its suddenness, Ketu has some similarity with Mars. These characteristics are prominent in transits. These planets always in retrogression have their fundamental influence of producing their effects in the most unusual manner. Wherever these planets are placed during their transits, one must expect that those houses will be activised in the most unusual manner in order to diffuse some of the past karmic forces. They can never be expected to be happy in the first and the second, unless there are reasons to consider otherwise; their effects in third and sixth are very beneficial. Mantreswara has given the effect of Rahu as follows: (i) sickness or death, (ii) loss of wealth, (iii) happiness,

(iv) sorrow, (v) financial loss, (vi) happiness, (vii) loss, (viii) danger to life, (ix) loss, (x) gain, (xi) happiness, and (xii) heavy expenditure.

LUNAR CONSTELLATIONS

The most complex consideration with regard to transits is related to the movement of the different planets through the various lunar constellations. The *nakshatras* are indeed very powerful forces radiating impulses of highly sensitised nature. Any planet coming in contact with them becomes galvanised in a special manner. In order to comprehend the special changes occurring in the effect of different planets, it is necessary to understand the structure of the radiation belt of the lunar mansions. The appended diagram shows the chief characteristics of different *nakshatras*; it shows the forces which are perennially disseminated from these *nakshatras*. Whenever any planet comes within any special kind of radiation zone, it gets significantly influenced by that radiation. The nature of planets at the time of the birth shows the permanent influences which would flow from them. When they come in contact with various *nakshatras* during the course of their transits, they begin to send somewhat altered influence. The actual forces which would affect the individual at any time would be a synthesis of all these. On the basis of this diagram, the student may be able to work out the special nature of transiting planets as they would affect the individual at any time.

Strength and Obstructions

The transiting planets are very effective in producing certain results. For example, the effect of Jupiter while transiting the fifth house from Moon or ascendant invari-

ably preduces some auspicious events in the family.
Saturn transiting over the Sun sign inevitably creates unhappiness from the father's side or profession-wise.
These are some of the features which the students learn
by experience. During such transits, on occasion, the
student finds that the effect does not fructify at all. In
regard to this he has to examine the possibility of the
occurrence of *vedhas* or the presence of obstructing
factors. For every planet which may be radiating helpful
influences there are certain indications of obstructing
conditions. It has been mentioned that the absence of
any planet in some houses corresponding to benefic
houses for the transiting planet is a necessary condition
for the fructification of the effect of the transiting planet.
If any planet is present there, the effect does not take
place. In this connection, it may be noted that no
restrictions are imposed due to the presence of a
planet having father-son relationship. Saturn is the son
of the Sun and Mercury of the Moon, and no *vedha*
occurs between these planets.

The points of *vedhas* for the various planets are given
below. The number in brackets indicate the vedha house.
That is, if a particular planet say, the Sun is expected
to be beneficial in a house denoted by 11, that is the
eleventh sign say from the sign in which Moon is placed
in the radical chart, then, 5 in bracket indicates that
there should be no planet in the fifth sign from the
radical Moon in order to enable fructification of this
beneficial transit effect.

Sun : 11 (5) ; 3 (9) ; 10 (4) ; 6 (12)
Moon : 7 (2) ; 1 (5) ; 6 (12) ; 11 (8) ; 10 (4) ; 3 (9)
Mars : 3 (12) ; 11 (5) ; 6 (9)
Mercury : 2 (5) ; 4 (3) ; 6 (9) ; 8 (1) ; 10 (7) ;
      11 (12)

Jupiter :   2 (12) ; 11 (8) ; 9 (10) ; 5 (4) ; 7 (3)

Venus :   1 (8) ; 2 (7) ; 3 (1) ; 4 (10) ; 5 (9) ; 8 (5) ;
               9 (11) ; 11 (6) ; 12 (3)

Saturn :   3 (12) ; 11 (5) ; 9 (9)

The most difficult calculation is that of the determination of the specific strength in accordance with which
the planets radiate their influences. It is done in accordance with the *Ashtakavarga* system. *Ashtakavarga*
means the eight-fold energy of the planet. The different
kinds of strength thus determined are dependent upon
the placements of the radical planets, that is, the positions
of the planets at the time of the birth, in relationship
with one another. These positions could be ascertained
from the classical works where they are given in detail.
For example, one could see *Phaladeepika* by Mantreswara,
chapter XXIII, or *Hindu Predictive Astrology* by B. V.
Raman, chapter XXVI. Explaining the essential features
of the *Ashtakavarga* system, Mantreswara has stated that
the *ashtakavarga* is the combination of the good and
bad positions of a planet in respect of the seven planets
and the ascendant taken together comprising eight
situations. Rahu and Ketu are left out from this consideration. So it is the combination of the benefic and
malefic dots in a planet's chart with reference to the
positions of the eight planets (that is, including ascendant as one of the same). Addition of all these dots
will give the number of benefic dots for different planets
in different signs. When the number of these dots exceed
4 in any sign for any planet, then that planet, even if
had otherwise, would not create any bad effect rather it
would try to do some good depending upon the number
of dots in excess of four. The highest number of dots
for any planet in any house is eight. On the other hand,
even if a planet is expected to do some good as a result

of its transiting position, it may fail to be effective if the number of dots in that sign is less than four. Thus, the good and bad effects of various planets described above are restricted by the presence of benefic dots for any planet in any sign resulting from the position of radical planets. The planets in transit are, in this way very much restricted in influencing the individual according to the basic quality of his natal chart.

THE LUNAR MANSIONS

The *nakshatras* or the lunar mansions are highly powerful force centres radiating influences which fundamentally affect the relationship between the man and his universe, besides their contributing significantly in the evolutionary process of the universe itself. A detailed esoteric knowledge of these *nakshatras* is possible only to the advanced students of occultism and to the adepts connected with the cosmogenesis, but no astrologer venturing to peep in the mysteries of the stars as they affect the everyday life can afford to neglect their study.

The Hindu astrology is deeply entrenched in the functioning of these *nakshatras* whose origin and growth are inextricably woven in classical mythologies and allegories whose understanding reveals some of the hidden aspects of this highly abstruse subject. The ancient seers of India had a very clear awareness of the vitality and the far-reaching consequences of the lunar mansions even during the pre-Vedic period. For this reason one finds elaborate mention of the *nakshatras* in their present nomenclature in the *Atharva Veda*. Such knowledge existed even among the Chinese, Egyptians and other ancient civilisations. The Chinese knew them under the name of *hsiu*, four of which divided the sky into four quadrants which were known as far back as the 14th Century before the Christ, while the knowledge of the 23 ones mentioned in *Yioch Ling* has been traced back to the 9th Century before the Christ. Even in Mesopotamia, the system of the Lunar Mansions was known to the astrologers. As far as India is concerned, the knowledge of the *nakshatras*, as a part of its occult literature, is estimated to be atleast 25,000 years old. The *Atharva Veda* did not merely contain the complete list of these Fixed Constellations with their current nomenclature but also gave their various associations and relationships with cosmic deities who played their distinctive role in cosmogenesis in which act of manifestation, the *nakshatras* played a vital role. From these descriptions one gets a feeling that the Vedic seers considered the Fixed Constellations as the outer veils of the inner deities, or the Cosmic Intelligences who were actively engaged in cosmic ideation which included both the manifestation of the universes in different phases and the origin and growth of human beings from their most primitive to the highest stage of the emergence of Planetary spirits who being merely of the spiritual nature could consciously perform inter-stellar commutation without any loss of consciousness or being obliged to castaway their 'physical' vestures. This assumption of the Hindu astrology, rather this esoteric knowledge of the relationship between the planetary spirits and the human genesis and growth which formed the bedrock of Indian astrology.

The *nakshatras*, which literally means that which is never destroyed has been considered the most important stage in the step-down process of the Divine Creative Impulse; at one stage of manifestation it is through the vehicles of these Fixed Stars that the Divine Breath for works incessantly as Manavantar. Till the creation lasts, the *nakshatras* constantly radiate the required creative impulse influencing the generation preservation and dissolution of all forms according to the Divine Plan. Commissioning of such a mighty task cannot be made to the blind impact of matter. This fact was well recognised by the Indian seers who always worshipped the Divine Intelligence represented by these stellar constellations with whom they were magnetically linked. Many modern astrologers, specially in the West who have not worked out the rationale of delinking the degree of precession with the signs of the zodiac or with the lunar asterisms show their bewilderment at the predictive significance of their relationship.

In order to appreciate the difference between the two approaches relating to the "fixed" and the "moving" zodiacs, the basic approach of the two schools may be examined. The Hindu astrology is based on a system of 'fixed' zodiac wherein the astrological signs correspond to the astronomical constellation of the same name. The zodiacs under this system start with Aries 0° in the same constellation. As long as the beginning of the lunar asterisms, the signs of the zodiac and the vernal equinox synchronised with one another, no discrepancy between the two schools existed. There was no difference between the 'fixed' zodiacs and the 'moving' ones. As soon as the adjustment due to the gravitational force of the sun and the moon on the earth leading to shift of the equinoxes during successive sidereal years caused by the slow retrograde motion of the equinoctial points along the ecliptic is taken into account the synchronisation of the three was upset. The point of intersection of the celestial horizon and the ecliptic considered as the first point of the zodiac under the 'moving' zodiac shifts by about slightly less than a minute every year. This slow retrograde motion at the equinoctial points along the ecliptic radically alters the relationship between the three. As a result of this change, what was the first point of the third lunar mansion, namely Krittika, a few thousand years ago became the beginning of the last lunar mansion namely the last quarter of Purva Bhadrapada, or the last point of Revati, depending upon the time-gap. But apart from the shift, another difficulty also arises due to the difficulty in fixing the precise degree of the Moon comprising the asterism at birth on the basis of which various astrological calculations including that on the basis of which the rulership of any planet at any given period of the individual's life is determined.

The difference between the sidereal and the tropical zodiacs has drawn considerable attention of the astrologers. The significance of this difference is highlighted by the fact that the whole region defined by the group of stars known as Pleides or *Krittika*, the third lunar mansion, lies wholly in the astronomical constellation of Taurus and not partly in Aries and partly in Taurus as claimed by the sidereal zodiac of the regular size. Another glaring example of the same type occurs with regard to Scorpio. This astronomical constellation has three sub-constellations : the head is known as *Anuradha*, the seventeenth asterism, the heart as *Jyestha*, the eighteenth asterism, while the tail is *Moola*, the nineteenth asterism whereas the Hindu astrologers have *assumed* the nineteenth asterism of *Moola* completely within the area of Sagittarius. On the basis of such spread-outs and taking into account the various magnitudes of *ayanamsa* or the degree of precession, the Hindu astrological asterisms or the *nakshatras* are not identical with the astronomical constellations. Thus, one finds that the Indian approach to the Fixed Stars is not based on the visible constellations ; they are merely symbolic, and the various names given to them or attributes assigned to them are intended to reveal their occult nature. The astrological nomenclature given to them did not necessarily refer to a frame of fixed stars rather they endeavoured to suggest their intrinsic symbolic characteristics.   The antiquity of asterisms along with very exact astronomical knowledge of the ancient seers and the mention of the lunar asterisms in many mythologies and allegories lead us to believe that the Hindus always believed that the deity presiding over a *nakshatra* was the real important influence and *not the astronomical visible stars of the asterism.*

A study of the subject in its cosmogenetic perspective by unravelling the primary characteristics of these *nakshatras* could probably enable the student to comprehend the mysterious relationship between the human individual and the cosmic forces flowing to him through the intermediary of the lunar asterisms. The various propitiatory practices as well as the astrological guidance to diurnal and other mundane activities included under the *Karma Kanda* of the Hindu ethics are based on an understanding of this relationship. As Eliphas Levi, the great Kabbalist, once mentioned that God sows the idea of the Infinite, and the rays of the Sun bring to birth the germs to the Planets, the ancient seers visualised the ever active celestial hosts discharging their divine responsibilities mainly by bringing out the latent destiny of the individuals as well as that of the nations, mother earth, solar system and the cosmos itself according to the Divine Plan. The process of cosmic ideation, the transmission of the Divine Idea to the planetary regents, from them to the terrestrial system and then, to the human individuals could be described only in the language of esotericism as finite similies are unfit to express the abstract and the infinit, the objective ever unable to describe the subjective. For this reason the incomprehensibility of the Vedic hymns in praise of the *nakshatras* led the Puranic scriptures to describe the highly mysterious radiations of the planetary spirits in garbled mythologies but with the possibility of their being deciphered with the aid of appropriate keys to those mystery languages. On the basis of these descriptions, there is a possibility of getting some hints regarding the cosmogenetic expansion of the Heavenly Man so that the subjective and objective relationships at the various stages of macrocosmic and microcosmic or anthropomorphic evolution along with the special mission assigned to *nakshatras* and the zodiacs could be somewhat understood.

The very term *nakshatra* in *Sanskrit* is derived from the root word which signifies that which never decays or dissolves, but it has been interpreted in many ways. H. P. Blavatsky thought it to consist of *naksha* meaning to approach and *tra* to mean to guard which implied that the lunar asterisms were the abode of gods devoted to guarding and guiding the cosmic, solar, and terrestrial evolutions. But the root meaning of the word referred to ''Imperishable'' which made the lunar asterisms the primeval passive principle working eternally for the regeneration and evolution of the universe. This eternal cosmic principle was described in the various *Puranas* in several ways. Essentially however they refer to the *nakshatras* as the twentyseven daughters of Daksha Prajapati. When the various experiments of evolving the human kingdom failed, Brahma, the Progenitor of the Cosmic manifestation created from several parts of his body several Regents, *Devas* and *Asuras,* the gods and demons, and other spiritual beings and bestowed on them specialised functions and energies. From his *Prana*, the Vital Airs, he created *Daksha* (meaning the Expert) and married him to *Prasuti* (meaning procreation) and charged them with the responsibility of programming the system of copulative generation. Over a period of several *Kalpas* of 432 million years each, Daksha Prajapati begot 60 daughters, of which 10 were married to *Dharma* (meaning Righteousness) who held together the creation, 27 daughters were married to the Moon who became responsible for the expansion of consciousness, and 13 daughters were married to Kashyap Prajapati who were assigned the task of racial evolution, and so on. Furthermore, the mythology stressed that the Moon showed special favour to *Rohini nakshatra* as a result of which all the rest complained to their father of this partiality which led the *Daksha* to curse the Moon to die of tuberculosis but on the second consideration he was cursed to gradually weaken to death but again to revive and come back to his full self. In this, one deciphers a close relationship between the Moon and the constellations with a view to propagating the human race. Constellations being of the feminine character, they have the passive creative potential in which the Seed, the Germ, or the active creative essence must be put to incubate and take birth. This preservation and generation of the life seed is expected to be different in each asterism. In carrying out this procreative process, the Moon though attached more to some has to suffer himself. The periodicity of the phases of the Moon which assists the evolution of life on this earth is an act of great sacrifice on the part of the Moon. But the Moon itself is a passive agent with regard to the Sun, because it receives the Ray from the Sun and only that which it has received it can implant. But in doing so, the final result differs due to its association with different asterisms. In all this operation, the area of activity is the human consciousness. Whenever one examines the effect of lunar asterisms, it is necessary that the impact on the psyche of the individual concerned is studied.

The *nakshatras*, each one of them, has unique identities of its own. Difficulties in expressing those special qualities of these asterisms led the ancient seers to describe those qualities in human terms leaving much to the understanding and intuition of the student. The sex differentiation between male and female, the categorisation between seven classes of functional differentiations such as Brahman, Kshatriya, Vaisya, Sudra, Farmer, Outcaste, and Butcher, or between 14 categories of animals, between different types of living entities belonging to different regions such as human, forest dweller, quadruped, aquatic or insect, and finally between the categories of men, gods, and demons are all suggestive to indicate the basic inherent qualities of these asterisms. Whether they primarily impart preservative or germinative impulse determines their sex : many of these *nakshatras*, such as Krittika, Rohini, Mrigashirsha, Aridra, and Punaravasu, excepting Krittika are chiefly generator of those impulses which are clearly the recipient of impulses for further incubation. As it would be seen from the later description, Rohini is related to *Hiranyagarbha*, Mrigashirsha with *Tan Matras*, Aridra with *Mahat* and Punaravasu with *Nada* and *Bindu* all of which require some activising agency in order to be fruitful. On the other hand, Ashwini, Pushya, Ashlesha, Makkha, and Uttara Phalguni being connected with Spiritual magnetism, Differentiation of Life–Energy, Transmigration of Soul, and Siddhis are the chief active impulses which can fructify only when suitable milieu is provided to them. In this way, one finds that the classification of the asterisms, though generally speaking they are primarily passive potential, into sexes refer to their further differentiation between preservative and generative qualities. Those individuals who have, say their Moon or any other planet in a male asterism would find the development of the lunar or the planetary radiation fructifying when they are *actively* involved in their operation. Whatever their circumstances, they should be involved in some positive action, whenever they are inactive, or at the receiving end, their psychology would be depressive. On the other hand, the planets in Rohini or Mrigashirsha would bestow their result as a result of some other agency, they would be happy to receive the reward and preserve and develop whatever is received. When they have to take initiative in order to obtain those qualities, they are unhappy and do not feel very elated.

The categorisation of the asterisms in seven caste groups goes deeper in revealing the inner motivation of the individual. As the asterisms are more powerful than the radiation of the signs of the zodiac, the asterisms must be capable of explaining much better the characteristics of the human groups, which are generally classified as the seven 'rays' of human temperaments. These special temperamental attributes of human beings are considered universal and clairvoyant investigations of C. W. Leadbeater, Earnest Wood, and Geoffrey Hodson have all corroborated to the fact that all living entities can be grouped in seven main types. These types are linked with the septenary channels of life waves. Often attempts are made to relate the seven planets with these seven human temperaments, or with the seven main flows of life-energies. It is probably these seven life currents which are further divided into twentyseven specialised radiations, for which reasons each of these twentyseven channels maintain their original qualities in spite of several modifications they have to undergo in the process. The Ray of Power requiring the individual to be outgoing in the realm of consciousness building new continents of thought and crystallizing new races and social organisations rightly typified by the office of Manus in Hindu and other scriptures is symbolised in this classification by the Kshatriya caste. Whilst the kingly responsibilities take the royalty to conquer new domain and protect its own subjects and express his power, the butcher is no less powerful but in the realm of objective world where he destroys the living organisms in order to take out the usable portion of the same. In essence, that is what the modern scientists charged by the task of experimental enquiries do. In the theo- sophical literature the former is stated to be the First Ray while the latter as the Fifth Ray, without having any reference to the order of preference or priority or prece- dence, but just for identification of the two distinct qualities of the human temperament. The Vaisya commu- nity in the ancient Indian society, under the Manu's system of social organisation, had the charge of preser- vation of the established community and sustaining it by providing the necessary wherewithal for the same. They were the "Trustees" of the community. In essence that is the function of esoteric wisdom, arising out of Buddhic consciousness which give insight into the laws of the universe. That True Wisdom in terms of settled social organisation could best be exemplified by the function of the Vaisya community. The farmers provided the necessary amenities for the preservation and sustenance of the community. The former caste was the custodian of the general organisation of the work whilst the latter had to provide the necessary constituents with which the work of the former could be carried out. In terms of philosophy, if the former could be considered corresponding to the Esoteric Wisdom, the latter would be the Exoteric or the Ritualistic part of the same. In terms of the theosophical classification, the former is the Second Ray and the latter the Sixth Ray. On the same analogy, Sudras are accepted as an important component of the community providing the basic amenities of services for the community while the outcastes were something unassimilated caste in the general body politic. The Third Ray represented here by the Sudras is linked with thought as a component of activity as far as the human constitution is concerned. In the realm of consciousness, everything is activised as a result of the operation of thought, on the same analogy but in a different manner, the temperament which is concerned with fine arts whereby the archetype is crystallized, or by which effort the universal harmony latent in nature is objectified, that temperament is labelled as the Seventh Ray and that could very well be categorised by the function of the outcasts. The function of the Brahmans was to establish (religious) harmony among the various sections of the community. They were not expected to impose their own self or their own opinions on the community ; rather their responsibility was to coordinate the activities of the other classes with a view to unifying them all. That is what the Ray of Harmony, the Fouth Ray of the theosophists, was expected to do. In this way, one could perceive the different asterisms, though stated to belong to certain castes in the ancient Indian body politic, yet suggestive of the basic human temperaments. Understanding of these impulses could reveal the special effects expected of different planets coming under the influence of these asterisms.

On the lines of castes indicated above, other categorisations of the asterisms among different species, temperaments, animal type or the directions in space should be comprehended and appropriately interpreted. These characteristics are very useful for proper integration of diverse forces operating on the individuals themselves through different planets so that contradictions and conflicts of the personality could be properly understood and resolved. More than this, these asterisms also indicate the adjustment problems between different human individuals with whom one comes during the course of one's daily intercourse. A person of the elephant animal type, if married to the lion or tiger type of wife would find adjustment problems quite difficult. A cat and dog relationship may not be as bad as between cat and rat combination. In the same way, god-demon union would inevitably lead to serious discord whilst god-man relationship may be highly harmonious. On the basis of these considerations, the astrologers, to a great extent, determine the marriage compatibility between two individuals. The characteristics of lunar asterisms are given in the following table. It imay give to the student an insight into the nature of the asterisms.

For indicating the various characteristics of the lunar mansions, the classical astrological texts have given many other indications which were mentioned earlier, the asterisms are very basic for astrological predictions; they carry with them some of the primeval impulses which go to the very root of cosmogenesis. In this regard, the relationship between the three Basic Attributes or the three *Gunas* namely, *Sattwa* (Harmony), *Rajas* (Activity) and *Tamas* (Inertia) and the lunar asterisms is very important, and so is their linkage with the four basic human impulses namely, *Dharma* (righteousness, religion), *Artha* (material gain, meaning), *Kama* (passion), and *Moksha* (Liberation) ; the diagram appended gives an indication of these relationships. In order to study the relationship between the various impulses flowing through these asterisms, it is necessary to note that these *Gunas* flow in such a way that the primary flow has the secondary undercurrents of the three and each secondary flow has also the tertiary flow of the three currents within it. So the impact of this spread of the Basic Attributes has to be studied very carefully and much depends upon the understanding of the nature of the *Gunas* and their interplay. The complex nature of this circulatory motion in ring within rings may well be appreciated by the fact that the universal cause of cosmic manifestation, according to the Vedantists being *Maya* or the Great Creative Illusion, is also considered as *Avidya* or Ignorance which in fact for providing various channels for creative differentiation in life exprexes itself as the three Basic Attributes. The *nakshatras* are linked through the *Gunas* to the primeval creative process whereby the one becomes many.

The relationship between the Basic Attributes and the *nakshatras* is not two-dimensional. It is a multi-dimensional relationship pervading the entire spherical universe both in its subjective as well as the objective planes of manifestation. These *nakshatras* are also intimately linked with the four primary motivational impulses, namely *Dharma, Artha, Kama* and *Moksha* which do not arise from the three Basic Attributes *i.e.* the

The Primary Characteristics of the Lunar Asterisms

	Nakshatra	Sex	Caste	Specie	Tempera-mental Cate-gorization	Animal Type	Direction
	1	*2*	*3*	*4*	*5*	*6*	*7*
1.	Ashwini	Male	Vaisya	Horse	God	Quadruped	South
2.	Bharani	,,	Outcaste	Elephant	Man	,,	West
3.	Krittika	Female	Brahman	Goat	Demon	,,	North
4.	Rohini	,,	Sudra	Serpent	Man	,,	East
5.	Mrighashirsha	,,	Farmer	,,	God	Quadruped (2) Human (2)	South
6.	Aridra	,,	Butcher	Dog	Man	Human	West
7.	Punarvasu	,,	Vaisya	Cat	God	Human (3)	North
8.	Pushya	Male	Kshatriya	Goat	,,	Aquatic (1)	East
9.	Ashlesha	,,	Outcaste	Cat	Demon	Aquatic	South
10.	Makha	,,	Sudra	Rat	,,	Forest Dweller	West
11.	Purva-Phalguni	Female	Brahman	,,	Man	,,	North
12.	Uttara-Phalguni	Male	Kshatriya	Cow	,,	Forest Dweller (1) Human (3)	East

No.	Name		Caste	Animal		Category	Direction
13.	Hastha	Female	Vaisya	Buffalo	God	Human	South
14.	Chitra	,,	Farmer	Tiger	Demon	,,	West
15.	Swati	Male	Butcher	Buffalo	God	,,	North
16.	Vishakha	Female	Outcaste	Tiger	Demon	Human (3) Insect (1)	East
17.	Anuradha	,,	Sudra	Deer	God	Insect	South
18.	Jyestha	Male	Farmer	,,	Demon	,,	West
19.	Moola	,,	Butcher	Dog	,,	Human	North
20.	Purva-Ashadha	,,	Brahman	Monkey	Man	Human $(\frac{1}{2})$ Quadruped $(3\frac{1}{2})$	East
21.	Uttara-Ashadha	,,	Kshatriya	Mongoose	,,	Quadruped	South
22.	Shravana	,,	Outcaste	Monkey	,,	Quadruped	North
23.	Dhanishtha	Female	Farmer	Lion	Demon	Aquatic	East
24.	Sat-Bhisag	,,	Butcher	Horse	,,	Human	South
25.	Purva-Bhadrapada	Male	Brahman	Lion	Man	Human (3) Aquatic (1)	West
26.	Uttara-Bhadrapada	Female	Kshatriya	Cow	,,	Aquatic	North
27.	Revati	,,	Sudra	Elephant	God	,,	East

[Numbers in brackets show the number of *padas* of the quadrants of the asterisms belonging to the category of the animal type mentioned.]

Gunas but they arise from entirely a diferent direction and pervade the lunar mansions giving them a new dimension for their functioning. These asterisms have been classified as follows in the four primary impulses:

Categorisation of Lunar Asterisms into Four Primary Motivational Impulses

Dharma	Artha	Kama	Moksha
Ashvini	Bharani	Krittika	Rohini
Pushya	Punaravasu	Aridra	Mrigashirsha
Ashlesha	Makha	Purva-Phalguni	Uttara-Phalguni
Vishakha	Swati	Chitra	Hastha
Anuradha	Jyestha	Moola	Purva-Ashadha
Dhanishta	Sravana	@	Uttara-Ashadha
Sat-Bhisag	Purva-Bhadrapada	Uttara-Bhadrapada	Revati

@ Abhijit was an asterism during the Vedic period and it was presided over by Brahma, the Creator of the Universe, but later on, it was dropped out making the present number of nakshatras as only twenty-seven, which is equal to three times the number of planets.

The Hindu system of astrological prognostication, is in fact an endeavour to reveal the message of the Permanent Spirit or Soul to the transient personality as evident from the labyrinth of planets, zodiacs and the *nakshatras*. The effect of the planet is radically altered according to their location in any sign of the zodiac or in any stellar constellation. The planets vibrate the tune whilst the zodiacs and the nakshatras determine the resonance of the same. The final effect depends upon the sum total of all these influences. An understanding of the nature of all the three is important in order to indicate the various possibilities open to the individual under any specific situation. In order to understand the nature of the *nakshatras* it is necessary to examine them from various angles. A synoptic view of the several characteristics of the different *nakshatras* such as their symbolic representation, presiding deities, primary impulses and impact on the individuals on the evolving side and on the materialising side, on the suggestions of which one could work out greater details of these asterisms is given in a tabular form as an appendix. The symbols used are Indian in character, but there are a large number of these which are universal, such a head of a horse, coral, potter's wheel and so on. The presiding deities could be understood only when the Indian mythologies and scriptures are studied in depth. As far as primary impulses are concerned, one will find that the earlier asterisms are generally concerned with arousing and giving rise to the wherewithal with which evolutionary process could be made possible, such as regenerative potential, primordial light, Hiranyagarbha or the great deep, or *Tan-Matras* or subtile elements and so on. It is on the support of these forces or the factors that the life of the individual is concretised. For the latter, one needs experience, expansion in time and space, acquisition of several supernatural powers and so on. The second set of asterisms are concerned with these activities. And lastly, they will have to energise the forces which would finally dissolve everything and merge all in their ultimate source. The sequence of the *nakshatras* may be studied keeping this evolutionary sequence in the background.

The extension of the asterisms, as indicated earlier, is not related to their actual spread but the later is to be considered only as some sort of physical of the deity or seat of the radiations from these *nakshatras,* the two being linked in some mysterious manner. For astrological purposes, each asterism is assumed to extend over 13° 20' beginning with Aries 0°. Each of these is further sub-divided into four quarters of equal division : every 3° 20' of the asterism is considered a *pada* or a portion. The *nakshatra* is assigned to some planets, whilst each *pada* is also assigned some planetary ownership, the both are not necessarily always the same. These ownerships of the *nakshatras* as well as of their *padas* are indicated in the chart appended. Such complications only make the examination of lunar asterisms very indeterminate, but surprisingly, the sequence of the planetary rulership over the individual at any time which depends upon the position of the Moon at the time of the birth in these asterisms, as well as the sequence and duration of these ownerships are all intimately connected with the asterisms. Furthermore, the planets give effects not necessarily of what is inherent to them but according to the nature of the planets and their disposition due to their ownership of any specific *nakshatra* and their quadrant, where the planet is located in the natal chart. This shows that the student who desires the knowledge of astrology for his practical guidance will have to approach the question of lunar mansions very seriously and care-fully. Only a synthetic study of Hindu scriptures, mythologies, and several other occult texts like *Yoga Sutras*, *Mantra Sastra,* and *Tantric* literature could provide a comprehensive view of the special magnetic radiations of these lunar mansions. The hints so far given in exoteric astrology are merely suggestive of the basic principles on which the cosmic and human evolutions are guided ; on the knowledge of these principles it could however be possible for the individuals to reorient themselves in a more meaningful way and approach life and their everyday problems in order to fulfil their ultimate destiny.

Appendix II

Symbols, Presiding Deities, and Various Impulses of Different Nakshatras

Nakshatras	Symbols/ Presiding Deities	Primary Impulses	CHARACTERISTICS ON THE	
			Evolving Side	Materialistic Side
1	2	3	4	5
1. Ashwini	Head of a horse *Aswini Kumars* : The Celestial Physician	Regenerative Potential	Leadership	Thirst for Sensation
2. Bharani	*Yoni* : The Female Sex organ *Yama* : The God of Death	Preservation of the Germ	Investigation into Occult Laws	Excessive Indulgence in Sex
3. Krittika	Razor *Agni* : The God of Fire	Primordial Light : The latent Active Principle	Dedicated Divine Service	Quarrelsome and Selfish Efforts
4. Rohini	Chariot *Brahma* : The God of Creation	*Hiranyagarbha*, or the Great Deep : The Incubative Potential	Engineering the Divine Power	Social Progress and Love for Wealth
5. Mrigashirsha	Head of a Deer *Soma* : The Moon	*Tan-Mátra* : The Subtile Elements	Intelligence	Egotism : I-ness
6. Aridra	Precious Stone, or a Human Head *Rudra* : The God of Destruction	*Mahat* : The Universal Intelligence	Study of Esoteric Laws	Conflict

		Union of Sound and Divine Consciousness (Nāda + Bindū)	Discipleship	Accentuation of *Kama-Manas*, or of Passional Nature
7. Punara-vasu	Bow; House *Aditi*: "Visible Infinity"			
8. Pushya	A Flower, a Circle or an Arrow *Brihashpati* (Jupiter)	Spiritual Magnetism	Tranquil Mind	Emotional Instability
9. Ashlesha	Serpent *Nagas*: The Serpent God	Differentiation of Life Energy	Initiation in Esoteric Mysteries	Treachery and Immorality
10. Makkha	House or Palanquin *Pitris* (Manes)	Metempsychosis: Transmigration of the Soul	Regal Glamour; Prestigious Office	Servitude
11. Purva-Phalguni	A Couch; A Platform, or Fireplace. *Bhaga*: The God of Fortune	*Trishna*: Thirst for Experience	Conquest and Domination	Debauchery, Gambling and Black Magic
12. Uttara-Phalguni	A Small Bed *Aryaman*: The Wooer	*Siddhis*: The Latent Powers in Man	Ambition	Black Magic
13. Hashta	Palm *Savita*: The Sun	Duration; Time	Public Service	Earning One's Bread anyhow; Penury
14. Chitra	One Pearl *Tvastra*: The Celestial Architect	Space, Dance of Shiva	Urge to Build	Pig in rhe Mud

1	2	3	4	5
15. Swati	Coral *Vayue* : The God of Air	*Akasa* (Sky)	Passion	Pleasure
16. Vishakha	Potter's Wheel *Indra* and *Agni* (The Lord of Gods, and the Gods of Fire)	Psychism	*Tapas* : (Purificatory Austerity)	Experience of Restrictions
17. Anuradha	Lotus Flower *Mitra* (A Sun)	Spirit-Matter Mix	Occult Powers used for Selfish Ends	Depth of Material Whirlpool
18. Jyestha	Ear Ring, Umbrella *Indra* : The Lord of Gods	*Kundalini* : The Serpent Fire	Divine Benediction	Arrogance
19. Moola	Tail of a Lion; Elephant's Goad *Nritta* : A Demon	*Munukshutwa* : The Urge for Liberation	Karmic Nemesis	Cruel ; Possessive
20. Purva-Ashadha	Tusk of an Elephant Water	Reflecting the Divine	God's Grace	Pride
21. Uttara-Ashadha	A Small Cot *Vishwa Deva* : 'Universe as God'	Cosmic Unity	Humility	Self-Centredness
22. Shravana	Ear ; An Arrow *Vishnu* : The Preserver	The Great Silence	Meditational Attention	Obedience

		Radiation of Life Force	Occult Attainment	Deprivation of Material Conveniences
23. Dhanistha	A Musical Drum *Vasus**			
24. Sat-Bhisag	Hundred Flowers *Varuna*: Regent of the Ocean	Maintenance of Law; Nature in Bloom	Blending of Consciousness (in Infinity)	Psychological Pain
25. Purva-Bhadrapada	Sword *Ajaikapada* (One Footed Goat)	Cosmic Stability	Fearlessness	Anguish; Sorrow
26. Uttara-Bhadrapada	Number Two; A Twin *Ahirbudhanya*: (The Serpent of the Deep)	Unveiling of the Wisdom	*Kaivalya* : *Nirvana* : Liberation	Complete Dis-interestedness
27. Revati	A Fish. *Pushan***	Nihil—The Dissolution	Equanimity	Complete Destruction

* A class of Vedic deities related to wealth and auspicious things in life; they are said to be eight in number.

** *Pushan* is a Vedic deity vibrating throughout the sky with primary function of nourishing for which reason he is also known as the "Nourisher".

SOME PRELIMINARY INFORMATION ON HINDU ASTROLOGY

There is nothing esoteric or anything incomprehensible about a natal chart or a horoscope as it is commonly known. The horoscope merely represents the position of various planets at the time of the birth of an individual or the occurrence of an event. The scope of deductions from this basic chart is however very extensive. The event of which a chart is drawn at its commencement can be the moment of impregnation, birth of a baby, beginning of any mundane act, putting specific query to the astrologer, beginning of a new year and so on. The casting of the horoscope at the time of the actualisation of an event enables the Hindu astrology to predict the future in many diverse fields. These areas have generally been classified under genethlialogy, mundane, catarchic or state, and interrogatory or horary astrology. Besides these, the Hindu astrology also deals with medicines and military strategies but these are actually some variations of one of these indicated above.

Under genethlialogy, which is the most popular branch of asrtology, predictions are made regarding human individuals based on the basis of planetary positions at the time of his birth. The general or the mundane astrology deals with the planetary influences as they affect social groups, nations or all humanity *en bloc*. It includes predictions relating to meteorology, seismology, husbandry etc. Catarchic, state or the civic astrology is concerned with the destinies of nations, kings and the rulers. It answered the auspicious or otherwise nature of a chosen moment for the success of a course of action begun in it. The interrogatory or horary astrology provided answers to a client's query based on the planetary situation at the moment of his putting the question or approaching the astrologer. In all these branches of Hindu astrology, the most important requirement for astrological predictions is the knowledge of the stellar position at the time of the event. The horoscope provides this information.

The Horoscope

One need not be intrigued by the format of a horoscope. Essentially, in all forms of representation, whether it is the so called the western system chart, or based on the Hindu astrology, even if it is a regional variation of casting the horoscope, whatever the format it merely represents the planetary position at the time of the birth. It is therefore important to know how the chart represents the planets. In mapping out the sky, it is necessary to begin from a central point in relation to which all other co-ordinates are presented. But, as the sky is not a flat surface, it is a kind of sphere, the determination of the cardinal points becomes difficult. The difficulty is increased by another fact that the depth of the sky is also to be indicated in the horoscope.

Astrology is concerned with the movement of the planets which takes place within a narrow band of the sky : it is called ecliptic. It is defined as the great circle formed by the intersection of the plane of the earth's orbit with the celestial sphere. It is the apparent annual path of the sun in the heaven. This is the path taken up by the various planets as well. The path of the planets is seven to eight degrees above or below the ecliptic. This ecliptic forms the axis for the horoscopic mapping; other portions of the sky are not of any great significance. They are not attempted to be incorporated in the astrological chart.

The ecliptic can be observed and identified by following the movement of the sun. The sun rises in the east, moves to the mid-heaven at noon, sets in the west and traversing the downward circle rises again in the east. The mid-day sun is not always at the zenith (it is at the meridian) though it is the highest point it could reach during the day. The horoscope is concerned with this path of the movement of the sun. Other planets also follow the same path. For identifying the location of planets, the first referal point is the east.

For fixing the other co-ordinates required to specify the positions of the planets, the intersecting points of celestial equator and the path of the ecliptic are noted. These points are not always identical with the east ; the difference arises due to the rotation of the earth. The planets move on the path of the ecliptic. In order to identify their positions on this path, one of the intersecting points known as the vernal equinox is taken as the referal point.

On the path of the ecliptic one can also observe certain groups of stars which do not alter their relative positions. Such stars are spread all over the zodiac. If the entire path of the ecliptic is divided into twelve parts each consisting of thirty degrees, each division is said to correspond to a sign of the zodiac. There are twelve signs of the zodiac. The groups of the stars mentioned above have been classified in twelve units and special names have been given to them. These are the names such as Aries, Taurus, etc., frequently used by the astrologers. Though these groups of the stars comprising different zodiacal signs are not necessarily contained within the thirty degrees assigned to each of them, yet the Hindu astrology assumed them so. When a planet is shown in a sign of the zodiac, it shows its distance from the beginning of the zodiacal sign.

The Hindu astrology also takes into account another set of stars situated much beyond the zodiacs. These stars are divided into 27 groups and are called the *nakshatras*, asterisms, or the Lunar Mansions. Their relative positions also do not change. For predictive purposes, they are much more powerful than the various zodiacal signs. The traditional Hindu astrology preferred showing the planets in these *nakshatras* which also served the same purpose as the signs of the zodiac in identifying the planets from a given co-ordinate in the sky.

Once the beginning of the nakshatras or of the signs of the zodiac in relation to a given position of the planet within it is identified and indicated, by its location vis-a-vis the east point, it could be possible to fix the planetary position in the sky. A horoscope actually does this.

The Hindu astrology assumed for the horoscopic purposes the coincidence of the vernal equinox on the path of the ecliptic, the first point of the zodiacal sign, and the first point of the Lunar Mansions. This assumption is a matter of serious controversy among the various schools of astrology, but for mapping out the planetary positions in the sky, this assumption does not vitiate the predictions in any substantial way provided one knew the existence of this controversial point. For the present, it is no use going into details of this controversy though some of it has already been mentioned in the text of the book under relevant chapters.

While casting the horoscope, it is important to note that the east point rising in the sky and the signs of the zodiac at its zero point (and the commencement of the Lunar Mansions) are not always identical. Therefore a difference has to be recorded. The different systems of casting the horoscope records this difference in different ways and there is no one universally accepted system to do so. This often confuses an amateur.

It has already been mentioned that the east is the ascendant, or the first house in the horoscope. The entire sky is divided into twelve such houses. The mid-heaven is the tenth house, rather the mid-heaven is included in the tenth House. The twelve houses in the horoscope represent the twelve divisions of the sky beginning with east as the first house. But, the twelve divisions of the ecliptic or the twelve signs of the zodiac are different from these houses. The natal chart shows the relationship between these two sets of division. In some types of horoscopic format, the sky with the east as the central referal point known as the ascendant is fixed first and the signs of the zodiac are superimposed on it and the planets are placed therein ; in some other format, the zodiacal signs are predetermined and the ascendant that is the east point is superimposed thereon. In both types of horoscopic castings, the planets are always indicated in the different signs of the zodiac according to their longitudes, that is, their zodiacal degree.

Some Basic Concepts

The celestial equator is the extension of the earth's equator in the sky. The sun crosses it, or seems to cross it, at different times of the year. During the summer months, in the northern hemisphere, the sun moves north of this equator and during the winter months, it is south of it. The movement of the sun is recorded on the path of the ecliptic. Thus there are two points of intersection between the path of the sun and the celestial equator. These two points are called *equinoctial points*. The point of intersection of the celestial equator and the sun's annual path or the ecliptic when the sun is on its way from south to north is called the *vernal equinox*. The vernal equinox is taken as the commencement of the sun's path or of the ecliptic and also the beginning of the celestial equator.

The *sidereal year* is the division of time representing the period required for the earth to complete one revolution around the sun, whereas a *tropical year* is the division of time equal to the interval between one vernal equinox and the next.

The difference between the tropical and the sidereal years occurs due to the annual solar movement itself. As a result of this difference, the *vernal equinox* also moves along the zodiac. A controversy has therefore arisen regarding the beginning of the sign of the zodiac. The Hindu astrology assumed the two as coincident whilst the western system takes the degree of precession of the equinoxes also into account. As a result thereof, one often gets marked differences between the signs of the zodiac in relation to planets and ascendants as referred to in the two systems. This aspect of the problem may presently be suspended and we may proceed further by assuming the vernal equinox as coincident with the first degree of the zodiac beginning with Aries.

The Twelve Horoscopic Divisions

As mentioned earlier, the ecliptic and thereby the entire sky, has been divided into twelve sections each of 30 degree extension and considered as a house division of the horoscope. In astrology, each of these houses is considered significator of certain important aspects of one's life. It is not known how these relationships were established. This relationship, however, holds good both in the western system of prediction and the Hindu system of astrology. The twelve houses have been related to twelve different aspects of life, but in Hindu astrology, each house has been assigned so many un-related things that any approach to rationalise them becomes (almost) impossible. However, it is desirable that the scope of different houses is recognised. In fact, each house has only a few basic keynote indicators but these keynotes themselves have intensive as well as extensive ramification. For example, an individual has his physical existence, his emotional existence, his intellectual existence, his inspirational state and even higher aspects of life. As far as his physical body is concerned, he has his face, eyes, ears, shoulders, chest, stomach, and so on. This is when we consider him as an individual being. When we consider him in his social relationships, we find him connected with his mother, father, mother's brothers, uncles, friends, wife, business colleagues and others. Again we find him with his homeland, as well as with places located far away; he is even connected with forests, rivers, mountains, temples, and so on. When we visualise an individual, we cannot leave any aspect of his relationship on any level of exi-stence. This comprehensive approach to a person's life makes the Hindu astrology astoundingly interesting.

Given below are some important features of different houses :

The First House : It is represented by the eastern part of the horizon where the sun rises. It is linked with the personality of the individual. It represents his facial expression, general health, conduct (deportment), the quantum of energy ensouling him, the purpose of his birth, the inherent impulses and tendencies with which the individual is born.

The Second House : It stands for wealth specially the accumulated treasure, eyes specially the right eye, procreative potential, family relationship specially material uncles and aunts, general intelligence.

The Third House represents prowess, ears and throat, brothers and collaterals, and daring activities. It is the will-force with which one enters the world and proceeds further in carving out the destiny assigned to him.

The Fourth House signifies general comforts, pleasures of comfortable living and tension-free mind, education, chest, mother, transport facilities, and royal favour. It is related to *Hiranyagarbh* or the Great Depth from which the entire creation has been externalised.

The Fifth House is connected with creativity, intellect, education, children, heart and stomach, and the store house of accumulated karma to a great extent. It forms the second angle of the Spiritual Triangle which provides the energy for the existence and continuance of any form of existence on this earth.

The Sixth House creates difficulties, resistance, diseases and enemies. It is connected with naval and the connected region of the stomach ; it is associated with the capacity to control the nature's finer forces thus acquiring what is known in yoga literature as *siddhis* or

supernatural powers. Service conditions are
by this house.

The *Seventh House* represents wife, the cou...
of the personality, the area of activity through whic...
individual satisfies his creative urges. It is that asp...
of life of which the *Bhagwad Gita* speaks of as 'field'
when it discussed the Field (*Kshetra*) and the knower of
the field (*Kshetrajna*). It also signified private parts of
the body, regaining of lost property and business
partnership.

The *Eighth House* signified longevity and matters
relating to death, hidden treasure, foreign travel and
every hidden aspect of the person's life. It is the seat
of the Serpent Fire and the Mystery Schools where secret
Initiations in Divine Mysteries are given.

The *Ninth House* shows the religious proclivities,
ethical conduct, pilgrimages and the blessings of the
Divine Beings. It shows the *prarabdha* or the karma
allocated for fruition in the given birth. It forms the
second angle of the base on which the Spiritual Triangle
stands (the first being the fifth house).

The *Tenth House* is related to destiny of the individual, his role in this world, government, father and
general affluence, success in enterprises, royal favour,
and foreign travel. It is the radiation which marks the
limit of growth and rise of the individual in this world
and the realm in which he would operate.

The *Eleventh House* is known as the house of
income and profit, satisfaction of needs, friendship,
elder brothers and sisters, and receipt of desirable objects.

The *Twelfth House* is related to outgoings of the
life-force, of wealth and therefore it is related to expenditure. It signifies bad health, foreign travel and
residence abroad, prison house, left eye, addiction to

sexual pleasures and drugs. It is linked with that part of the cosmic existence wherein every aspect of life comes to rest and loses its selfhood. It is the realm where the soul rests before embarking upon a new pilgrimage of births and deaths.

The Hindu astrology makes a distinction between the equi-distant house divisions and the *Bhava Kundali*. Mention has already been made as how to prepare the *Bhava Kundali*. The western system of horoscopy gives much importance to this casting. For exact delineation of the effect of any aspect of life, this kind of house division is given importance even in Hindu astrology. Under this type of chart, the different houses do not have the same extension : some are bigger than 30 degrees and some smaller depending upon the latitude of the place and the time of the year of birth. For general purposes, however, the equal size house divisions do serve the objective.

For those who wish to follow up the preparation of the *Bhava Kundali*, they may note that the duration of the day is measured in hours and the midpoint of the day is considered as the noon when the sun is at the meridian: the noon time is taken as the cusp of the tenth house. The distance between the sunrise and the noon, and again between the noon and the sunset are located on the different signs of the zodiac. Now the zodiacal distances of these two sections can be trisected to give the cusp of all the houses from the seventh to the first. These dividing lines could be extended to the other side of the circle to mark the cusps of other houses on the other side of the circle. Dividing each section in two equal parts, one could get what is known as different *Bhavas* meaning aspects of life which may provide a more precise basis for more accurate prognostication relating to different aspects which have been indicated under the various houses of the horoscope. This is however a refinement of the general method of predictions which one may overlook at the first instance.

Casting of the Natal Chart

The determination of the ascendant is the most important step in the casting of the horoscope. An accurate delineation of the ascendant would be required for precise pedictions. In this connection, one may note that the correct timing is the most difficult thing to record : in many cases the birth time is a mere conjecture, or the watch is not very accurate, or the conversion of the time given to their astrological equivalence is beset with many kinds of controversies. In spite of these limitations, one has to proceed very carefully in the determination of the ascendant. An expert astrologer would require much care and attention in completing this task : an amateur or a beginner looking for a rough and ready birth chart on the basis of which he could understand the general planetary influence on him, may follow the method suggested in Preface of this publication (pp. viii and ix) as the first step. As the sun completes its diurnal journey in 24 hours, so having known the birth time following the sunrise, one can roughly indicate the zodiacal sign of the first house. Having fixed the sign of the first house, the signs of all other houses can be fixed accordingly.

As far as other planets are concerned, it may be remembered that Saturn takes 10,759 days or roughly $29\frac{1}{2}$ years to go round the sun, that is, to complete its round of the twelve zodiacal signs. Roughly, therefore, it takes about $2\frac{1}{2}$ years in traversing a single sign of the zodiac but this period can differ depending upon its retrogression which would apply in cases of other planets as well. The period of Jupiter's revolution round the sun being 4332 days or a little less than 12 years, gives it approximately a year in any one sign of the zodiac which can vary depending upon its retrogression as mentioned in the case of Saturn. Rahu and Ketu take approximately 18 years for going through the twelve signs of the zodiac thus remaining for a period of $1\frac{1}{2}$ years in each sign of the zodiac, but their movement is always backwards. Mars complets its journey round the sun in 687 days or about a month and 27 days in each sign. Venus covers all the signs of the zodiac in 225 days thus remaining in one sign only for about 19 days. Mercury revolves round the sun in 88 days. The Moon takes about $2\frac{1}{2}$ days in one sign of the zodiac. The backward working of the positions of quick moving planets becomes difficult but the slow moving ones can lead to fairly accurate position of their locations at any earlier time. If a reader wishes to work out a very tentative horoscope or the location of planets and the sign of the ascendant, these data may be helpful.

Even in such cases, it would be necessary to have a good ephemeris to know the current planetary positions. From the publishers it could be possible to obtain ephemeris of an earlier year at a very nominal price. (Lahiri's Ephemeris published by M. K. Lahiri, Astro-Research Bureau, 17 Brindaban Mullick 1st Lane, Calcutta–700 009 ; they have published the same for all the years following 1875; Lahiris have also published *Table of Ascendants* about which we shall refer shortly. *Raphel* as well as *Die Deutsche* have also published ephemerises which could be readily available in European countries and they are very elaborate.)

For the preparation of a natal chart, the first requirement is to obtain the *local time* of birth. Given the
standard time of an event at a given longitude one could
obtain the difference between the local longitude and
the longitude for which the Standard Time is available.
A time difference of four minutes for every degree of the
difference between the two longitudes has to be
adjusted to the Standard Time. If the longitude is
greater, the time difference has to be added ; if it is
less, it has to be deducted. That gives the local time of
the event.

The second step is to find out the *sidereal time* for
the event. This calculation involved several adjustments
from the sidereal time for the day given in the ephemeris.
But these details are very minor and do not affect the
rough calculations and at the initial stages of the preparation of a natal chart they could be overlooked. They
are however needed when very precise occurrence of an
event is desired. For general purposes, what can be
done is to find out the sidereal time for the noon for a
given day and having considered it equivalent to the
noon time, one is required to deduct the difference
between the noon time and that of the occurrence of the
event if it is in the forenoon ; in case it is in the afternoon the difference has to be added. That is to say,
if the local time of birth is 9 a.m., the difference between
the noon and this time is (—) 3 hours, if it is 3 p.m., the
difference becomes (+) 3 hours. This difference added
to the sidereal time for the noon given in the ephemeris
gives the sidereal time for the event, whether the event
is the birth of an individual or any other occurrence.

The third step is to find out the ascendant for this
sidereal time. The *Table of Ascendants* which is either
appended to some ephemeris or can be separately

obtained for the various latitudes would enable us to get the ascendant. Against the given sidereal time, one can read the ascendant details giving the precise degree of the sign of the zodiac for it. From the same source, and in the same manner one can also obtain the *Right Ascension of the Medium Coli* (R.A.M.C.) which signifies the cusp of the tenth house.

The fourth step is to work out the extent of different houses, that is, the erection of *Bhava Kundali* of which we spoke earlier. Either on the lines suggested above, or according to various other methods suggested in different ephemerises themselves, one could work out the sizes of different houses in the horoscope. But this calculation, as mentioned earlier, is needed for an in-depth study of the chart. The general readers, presently familiarising themselves with astrological problems and different guidelines for prognostication, could do away with it for the time being and revert back to this problem of erection of different houses when they have acquired familiarity with the preliminary details.

The fifth step involves fixing of the planets in different houses. This is comparatively an easy task. The ephemeris gives the location of different planets for certain dates and time. On the basis of these details one can find out the daily motion of the planets. Following the simple arithmetic and the rule of the three, the planetary positions for the given date and time can be worked out. If any planet becomes retrograde on any specific date, that is also generally given in the ephemeris. The reader will have to take special note of such directions of the planetary motion. Having worked out the locational details of the various planets, these details have to be incorporated in the format of the natal chart. This completes the preparation of the natal chart and the reader is ready to proceed with his study of predictive portion of astrology.

Nature of Planets

The Hindu astrology takes into account only nine planets namely Sun, Moon, Mercury, Venus, Mars, Jupiter, Saturn, Rahu and Ketu. The last two are not exactly planets in the usual sense : they do not have any objective existence as other planets have. They are merely the nodes, the points of intersection of the orbit of the moon with the plane of ecliptic. But the Hindu astrology attaches great importance to these points and as such they are considered as important as the planets. On the basis of Hindu astrology, extra-Saturnine planets such as Uranus, Neptune and Pluto are not taken into account.

SUN is the central orb of the solar system and the sustainer of life-force at all the planets. It has been assigned supreme importance in astrological prognostication. The sun is nearly 750 times larger than all the planets put together and its diameter is approximately 110 times that of the earth. It generates its own energy and thereby provides sufficient warmth and vitality to all other planets of the system and all the life subsisting on them. It is the *universal life* which comprises all, ensouling them all within itself. For this reason, it is considered positive, incisive, majestic and the highest principle in everything that exists or can exist on any planet. For human beings, it is considered as his soul, and the inner ruler immortal. The sun is also said to represent the king, royalty, government, and the official status of the individual. Among the metals, it is related to gold and in religion Vedanta.

MOON is considered the queen of the planetary hierarchy, in its operation with regard to the earth, It functions like a mother. The sun represents the positive pole of electrical energy, the father, whereas the moon represents the negative pole and the mother. The moon receives the life-force from the sun, radiates it to the earth, generates the energy required for growth, that is, for change and progress towards the full blossoming of the inner seed of potentialities latent in man. It is like the invisible mind difficult to define but essential for all kinds of growth and development ; it is like water which in association with heat from the sun nourishes and enables the plants to grow and bear fruit. The same relation holds good between the moon and the man. Astrologically, the moon represents the *elan vital*, the vital energy that provides the capacity to grow ; it signifies the mind, mother, house, conveyance, pearl, and silver among the metals. Tranquillity of mind as well as peace and harmony in various human relation-ships and different situations of life are associated with favourable disposition of the moon.

MERCURY signifies duality, polarisation, and intellect which also has duality as its main characteristic. The planet is closest to the sun and takes almost the same time for rotation on its axis as in revolution around the sun. It almost always faces it, and is under the direct influence of the sun but it maintains its own position in such a way that one half of it ever receives the rays of light and heat from the sun whereas the other half ever remains as night without having the chance to see the sun at all. One half of it is very hot having its tempera-ture around 360 degrees centigrade, whilst the other half is as cold as the Arctic region during its severe winter months. But Mercury has no atmosphere. In its astrological influence. Mercury does not have a distinctive personality of its own : it imbibes the features of the planets which is associated with it. It has a dual life. It articulates and expresses brilliantly whatever is put through it. For this reason, not originality of thought but brilliance in expression, supreme quality of adjustment and flexibility, immense capacity to play the opposite (dual) role in anything are the main traits of the planet. Polarisation is its central quality, and its main function is to carry the message of gods to men and of men to gods ; to make the inner, abstruse ideas very intelligible to humankind and comprehend very quickly what others wish to convey. Trade, transport, and diplomacy besides proficiency in languages are special areas of its influence.

VENUS represents the energy that procreates, is sensitive to the finer forces in nature, and perceives the divine purpose in every form of manifestation. It produces harmonious relationships, capacity to enjoy pleasures of life, and bestows artistic nature. In the planetary hierarchy, Venus is considered the teacher of *Asuras*, the no-gods but it is through the Venusian radiation that one receives intuitional flashes. Venus produces unity, and the desire to unite. Astrologically, Venus is connected with men's vital fluid, and it controls the sexual attraction between men and women.

MARS considered as the commander-in-chief of the planetary hierarchy is basically related to blood circulating in the body to keep it warm and alive ; it represents the heat which enables all forms of creation to grow. It is life in the sense that externalisation is its basic nature: whatever is within is brought without under its impulse. Because of its function in assisting the unveiling of the inner content of the entity which is intimately connected with the very expression of the life force, Mars is considered harmonious with the sun. Mars governs the menstrual flow in women. It is impulsiveness, valour, activity that is energy-on-move, accident, fiery speech and so on. Connected with red colour, blood and externalisation of that which lies within, Mars is expected to operate at all levels of existence from the physical to the supreme spiritual. Action is its very nature so idleness is very frustrating to Martian nature.

JUPITER stands for wisdom that comes to men by God's grace. In the planetary hierarchy, it represents the teacher of gods ; for earthly mortals Jupiter is the bestower of blessed living, expansion, God's protection, contemplation and the desire to be on the God's side. Such radiations are not conducive to impulsive action or to an indulgent life, but wherever the Jovian influence pervades, there could be growth and expansion. Protection is a primary quality of this planet, as a result of which Jupiter likes to uphold traditional values, culture, religion, social organisations, political systems and the settled way of life, evolution rather than revolution. It is not so much concerned with innovation as with preservation. Jupiter sustains life and form.

SATURN is a veil over manifestation. It hides the true nature of the thing. It puts a limit .beyond which the expansive urge could not fructify. In life, it manifests as longevity which is another way of revealing the time of death. It puts restrictions and impediments which implies cessation of expansive tendency in all aspects of life. The Hindu tradition identifies Saturn as *Yama*, the God of Death. The burning ghats where dead persons are cremated are the special areas of Saturnine activities and influence. It implies that Saturn dissolves everything to their primeval nature. It is black : it does not accept any external influence.   Renunciation is its nature.   As a corollary, it destroys all material or the unreal forms of existence.   Spiritual   enlightenment   is   the   essential feature of the Saturnine radiation.   Saturn governs iron among the metals.

The Nodes, namely RAHU and KETU are not actually concrete planets rather they are just imperceptible points in the sky, on the path of the ecliptic.   Though invisible they are extremely powerful in their influence. Together they represent the Great Naga with which the ocean was churned by the gods and the no-gods, and the scriptures state that in spite of gods' desire to exclude the demon represented by Rahu and Ketu in unity, they partook a bit of the nectar obtained from the churning operation. When the gods knew it, in their effort to destroy this being they cut it into two but because of the nectar partaken, immortality became an aspect of them though in the physical form they became cut into two.   This allegory has various layers of meaning but for astrological purposes the nodes signify the karmic influences on the individual which could never be destroyed.

These two Nodes are separate, but they represent a unity. Their unity does not destroy the specialised nature of the two.   Rahu has great affinity with material forms of existence and Ketu with spiritual. They churn the life of the individual together with a view to manifesting the Divine Plan meant for him. The eternal law which regulates life on this earth is expressed as the law of Karma.   It enables the individual to enjoy the gifts of life as much as his destiny permitted the same. In the same way, the individual is denied any fruit of his good karma if the karma so decreed. The two Nodes function like the two sentinels of the Lords of Karma in restricting as well as granting the gifts according to this

law. The two nodes therefore form the important axis
around which the entire life of the individual moves. Rahu
immerses the man at first in affluence to lead him later
into frustration, whilst Ketu gives humiliation to arouse
spirituality.

The keynotes of the nine planets can be summarised
as below :

Sun	:	Positive spark of Divine Life.
Moon	:	Receptacle of the Life–Spark.
Mercury	:	Polarisation of the Life–Spark.
Venus	:	Electrical Spark resulting from the pola- risedSpark.
Mars	:	Generation of Electrical Fluid.
Jupiter	:	Distribution of the Divine Benediction : The Divine Power Grid.
Saturn	:	The boundary of the Electro–Magnetic Field of Divine Energy.
Nodes	:	The Law of Divine Manifestation : the Law of Karma.

Assessment of the Planetary Strength

To determine the strength and nature of the planets,
the Hindu astrology has laid down six groups of guidelines. These guidelines are studied under (i) *Rasi* or the
signs of the zodiac, (ii) *Hora,* (iii) *Drekkan,* (iv)
Navamsa, (v) *Dwadasamsa,* and (vi) *Thrisamemsa.* All
these are actually different ways of looking closer at the
planets in the signs of the zodiac.

As we have already seen every sign of the zodiac is
assumed to extend over 30 degrees on the path of the
ecliptic. In the above classifications, this distance is
divided into various sizes for examining the disposition
of the planets. For example, *hora* assumes two division
of the zodiacal sign. Under *drekkan,* the entire 30

degree of the sign are divided into three parts and the location of the planets in such different divisions is considered. Under *navamsa,* the same sign is divided into nine parts each comprising merely $3° 20'$. When the zodiacal sign is divided into twelve parts each consisting of $2° 30'$, it is known as *dwadasamsa.* Under *thrisamamsa* division, the sign of the zodiac is divided into thirty equal parts each of which is equal to one degree each. Obviously, these are different ways of associating the planet with different nuances of the zodiacal radiations. Though all these considerations are important for examining different aspects of one's life, the more important among these are *hora, navamsa,* and *thrisamamsa.* We shall briefly describe these three before we indicate the characteristics of the signs of the zodiac.

Hora : Hora is important in the sense that the active or the passive, the masculine or the feminine tendencies of the planets are revealed by it. Every planet can operate in either way, and it is *hora* classification which would indicate these special features of the planets in any sign of the zodiac. The first half of the odd number zodiacs such as Aries, Gemini, Leo and so on belong to the *hora* of Sun and the second half of that of Moon. On the contrary, the first half of the even number zodiacs such as Taurus, Cancer, Virgo etc., belong to Moon and the second half to Sun. Those planets which fall under the Sun hora arouse active or the masculine propensities of the related planet whilst those under the Moon hora would develop more of the feminine or the receptivity with regard to the characteristics of the planet in that sign of the zodiac and the corresponding house.

Navamsa : Navamsa division reveals the most pronounced affinity of the planetary situation. It indicates the inner nature of the planet. Say, if a planet is in the navamsa of Jupiter, much of its own qualities would become similar to or in harmony with the Jovian proclivities. The navamsa division is worked out on the principle that Aries, Leo and Sagittarius begin their first navamsa division with Aries and the successive navamsas fall seriatim, that is, in 2, 3, 4, and so on signs of the zodiac. The planets ruling these signs are said to govern those navamsas. Taurus, Virgo and Capricorn signs begin their navamsa classification with Capricorn, the tenth sign of the zodiac and proceed seriatim thereafter till we end up with Virgo. The first navamsa of Gemini, Libra and Aquarius begins with Libra and counting the same way they end with Gemini. Cancer, Scorpio and Pisces begin their first navamsa with Cancer and end up with Pisces. The navamsa chart is ordinarily prepared along with the natal chart itself showing the location of the planets in different signs of the zodiac, and therefrom their navamsa positions are derived and shown in their respective navamsa signs separately. As the navamsa determination may be slightly tedious to work out on the basis of above guidelines, the following table is given to help in readily fixing the navamsa division of any sign of the zodiac which could facilitate the navamsa placement of the planet if its degree in any sign of the zodiac is known.

Thrisamamsa : This division is important to indicate the nature of each degree of the zodiacal sign. Each of these radiates special qualities and the disposition of the planet should be considered accordingly when any one of these is placed at any specific degree of the sign. We have seen earlier that each planet shows certain

Navamsa Sign and their Lords for Different Planetary Positions

Sign	1st 0°0' to 3°20'	2nd 3°20' to 6°40'	3rd 6°40' to 10°0'	4th 10°0' to 13°20'	5th 13°20' to 16°40'	6th 16°40' to 20°0'	7th 20°0' to 23°20'	8th 23°20' to 26°40'	9th 26°40' to 30°00'
0 Aries	0 Mars	1 Venus	2 Mercury	3 Moon	4 Sun	5 Mercury	6 Venus	7 Mars	8 Jupiter
1 Taurus	9 Saturn	10 Saturn	11 Jupiter	0 Mars	1 Venus	2 Mercury	3 Moon	4 Sun	5 Mercury
2 Gemini	6 Venus	7 Mars	8 Jupiter	9 Saturn	10 Saturn	11 Jupiter	0 Mars	1 Venus	2 Mercury
3 Cancer	3 Moon	4 Sun	5 Mercury	6 Venus	7 Mars	8 Jupiter	9 Saturn	10 Saturn	11 Jupiter
4 Leo	0 Mars	1 Venus	2 Mercury	3 Moon	4 Sun	5 Mercury	6 Venus	7 Mars	8 Jupiter
5 Virgo	9 Saturn	10 Saturn	11 Jupiter	0 Mars	1 Venus	2 Mercury	3 Moon	4 Sun	5 Mercury
6 Libra	6 Venus	7 Mars	8 Jupiter	9 Saturn	10 Saturn	11 Jupiter	0 Mars	1 Venus	2 Mercury
7 Scorpio	3 Moon	4 Sun	5 Mercury	6 Venus	7 Mars	8 Jupiter	9 Saturn	10 Saturn	11 Jupiter
8 Sagittarius	0 Mars	1 Venus	2 Mercury	3 Moon	4 Sun	5 Mercury	6 Venus	7 Mars	8 Jupiter
9 Capricorn	9 Saturn	10 Saturn	11 Jupiter	0 Mars	1 Venus	2 Mercury	3 Moon	4 Sun	5 Mercury
10 Aquarius	6 Venus	7 Mars	8 Jupiter	9 Saturn	10 Saturn	11 Jupiter	0 Mars	1 Venus	2 Mercury
11 Pisces	3 Moon	4 Sun	5 Mercury	6 Venus	7 Mars	8 Jupiter	9 Saturn	10 Saturn	11 Jupiter

specialised manifestative principle in nature. Those
principles should again be taken into account in relation
to the operation of different planets in order to see the
level at which they would function. In odd signs, the
first five degrees of the sign are governed by Mars, the
next five by Saturn, the subsequent eight by Jupiter,
followed by seven degrees owned by Mercury and the
last five by Venus. In the even number signs of the
zodiac, the order is reversed. That is, the first five
degrees of these signs are governed by Venus, followed
by Mercury governing its next seven degrees, the following eight degrees are ruled by Jupiter, the subsequent
five degrees by Saturn, and the last five degrees by Mars.

The Signs of the Zodiac

ARIES is the first sign representing the unborn
(unmanifest) potential chafing to externalise itself.
TAURUS is the procreative potential desiring self-expression and seeking security. GEMINI is duality, polarisation and birth of intellectual perception. CANCER
provides pliability, emotion and the quality of sympathetic appreciation. LEO represents creativity, the
articulation of Divine Nature in man; it is objectified
Divine Power. VIRGO contains within itself the nature's
finer forces which contain ideals and perfections; it is
that energy which suffers for the growth and fruition of
a child's desire. Ordinarily, Virgo arouses conscience
and suffering for a noble cause. LIBRA is balance, the
mid-position where immersion in materiality ceases and
spiritual awakening begins. SCORPIO is the pit, the
hidden recess of the earth where the Serpent Fire or the
latent powers in man are hidden awaiting arousal.
Unless one is careful, much dangerous and destructive
possibilities come out of radiations of this sign of the
zodiac. SAGITTARIUS is the centaur representing

transformation of the beast into a humanbeing ; under its impulse the base nature is changed into noble qualities. This transformation however bestows much turmoil, challenge, confrontation and wanderings into various realms of spirituality. CAPRICORN is active involvement of the individual in the process of universalisation of the human energy. It involves much hardships and sufferings. Under this impulse, consciousness begins to be linked with thought currents and inspirational vibrations from higher realms of existence and the powers that govern the universe. Under AQUARIUS, the turmoil in one's individual life is immensely increased and the individual begins working according to the Divine Plan and annihilating his personal ego. PISCES is the cessation of all worldly efforts ; it is the final merging of the individual with the universal. It gives much peace and comforts.

Relationship Between the Zodiac and the Planets

There is an intimate relationship between the various signs of the zodiac and the planets. This is expressed by way of rulership, exaltation and debilitation. The following table gives a synoptic view of this relationship:

Planets	Rulership	Exaltation	Debilitation
Sun	Leo	Aries (10°)	Libra (10°)
Moon	Cancer	Taurus (3°)	Scorpio (3°)
Mercury	Gemini, Virgo	Virgo (15°)	Pisces (15°)
Venus	Taurus, Libra	Pisces (27°)	Virgo (27°)
Mars	Aries, Scorpio	Capricorn (28°)	Cancer (23°)
Jupiter	Sagittarius, Pisces	Cancer (5°)	Capricorn (5°)
Saturn	Capricorn, Aquarius	Libra (20°)	Aries (20°)
Rahu +	Virgo	Taurus	Scorpio
Ketu +	Pisces	Scorpio	Taurus

(+) There is no unanimity about the relationship between the nodes and the zodiacal signs ; here the most commonly held view is indicated.

The above table indicates the inherent relationship between different planets and the signs of the zodiac, but due to their location in any horoscope their relationship is *temporarily* altered. Planets located in 2nd, 3rd, 4th, 10th, 11th, and 12th houses are considered temporary friends. Likewise, those placed in 5th, 6th, 7th, 8th, and 9th are reckoned as temporary enemies.

Aspects of the Planets

A special feature of the planets is known as *aspects*, which imply casting of their glances. All planets cast their direct glance or aspect on the seventh house from where they are placed. Thus, a planet located in Aries will cast direct aspect on Libra which happens to be seventh from Aries ; similarly, a planet posited in the zodiacal sign Gemini will directly aspect Sagittarius. Besides the seventh aspect, some planets have special aspects. Mars, Jupiter, and Saturn enjoy this special privilege. Mars casts fourth and eighth aspects besides its usual seventh aspect. It implies that if Mars is posited say in Taurus, it would directly aspect Scorpio which happens to be seventh from Taurus but it would also aspect Leo which is fourth from Taurus, and Sagittarius which is eighth from Taurus. Jupiter casts fifth and ninth aspects besides the usual seventh ; Saturn aspects third and tenth houses directly besides the usual seventh.

The planets also possess side glance which implies not direct aspect but partial ones. It is said that they cast even half, three-quarters and a quarter glances. The intensity of the power to influence any specific house as a result of the planetary aspect is related to the intensity of the aspect : the direct glance has the full effect whilst the half aspect will have half effect and so on. The

following table shows the oblique aspects of different
planets.

The Intensity of Planetary Aspects

Planets	Full Aspect	Three-Quarters Aspect	Half Aspect	Quarter Aspect
Sun	7	4, 8	5, 9	3, 10
Moon	7	4, 8	5, 9	3, 10
Mercury	7	4, 8	5, 9	3, 10
Venus	7	4, 8	5, 9	3, 10
Mars	4, 7, 8	—	5, 9	3, 10
Jupiter	5, 7, 9	4, 8	—	3, 10
Saturn	3, 7, 10	4, 8	5, 9	—
Rahu	5, 7, 9, 12	2, 10	3, 4, 6, 8	—
Ketu	5, 7, 9, 12	2, 10	3, 4, 6, 8	—

Nakshatras

Beyond the zodiacs, there are Lunar Mansions, the
asterisms or the *nakshatras* which surround the earth the
same way as the zodiacs but from a much distant horizon
and exerting much powerful influence. The Hindu
astrology assumes the first point of the asterisms which
are 27 in number, the beginning of the zodiacs and the
vernal equinox as coincident. Details of these asterisms
are already given in the chapter dealing with the Lunar
Mansions. But, here, it requires to be mentioned because
the nakshatras play a decisive role in determining the
periodicity of the rulership of a planet at any moment of
time in the life of an individual. It is the exact degree
of the moon in any nakshatra which fixes the rulership
of various planets.

The name of the individual is also expected to be
based on these nakshatras though at the present time
this practice is not generally followed. The auspicious
time for commencing any important activity is also fixed
on the basis of these nakshatras.

Five Steps for Predictions

For working out the details of the effect of any planet, there are five important steps.

First, the nature of the planets, that is, their inherent radiations, must be carefully considered.

Second, the strength of the planets has to be worked out. For this purpose, the various calculations and considerations already mentioned earlier are important.

Third, the final view on planetary influences in any chart requires a good understanding of astrological principles. The various sections of the book attempt to indicate some of these principles on the basis of which one should be able to approach predictive astrology in a meaningful way.

Fourth, the time when the significator of an event in the life of the person would be effective and fructify is worked out on the basis of the rulership of the planet at any specific period of time. For this purpose, it is necessary to calculate the main period and the sub-period of different planets ; these are generally known as *maha-dasa, dasa,* and *antar-dasa* of different planets in Hindu astrology. This is a special feature of the Hindu astrology and we shall presently indicate how this can be worked out.

Fifth, for the fruition of any result the transits of different planets in different houses and in various signs of the zodiac are important. Mention of it has already been made in detail in the chapter on *Transits.* There is however another method known as *Varsha phala,* that is, the annual results of the planets which are worked out on the basis of what is generally known as *Annual Solar Return.* It is related to the return of the sun to its exact degree as at the time of birth and working out other planetary details for this solar return time : the horoscope thus cast as supplemented by the natal chart is expected to indicate the various important events that may occur during the year.

Periodicity of the Planetary Rulership

The delineation of the periodicity of the ruling time of any planet is worked out on the basis of the exact degree of the moon. The asterism in which the moon is posited will have predominance in the life of the indrvidual, but the planet owning that asterism will also have precedence over all other planets. Each asterism is governed by a planet. The moon at the time of the birth will give rise to the rulership of the planet that owns the asterism. There are many systems for the working out of the different planetary rulership for this purpose. The Vimshottri and the Ashtottari systems of planetary periodicity are more common but the former is the most popular one and the most effective system. We shall here indicate the method of working out the periodicity of the planets based on this system.

Under this system, that is under *Vimshottri Mahadasa Padatti*, when the moon at the time of the birth is in Krittika, Uttar Phalguni, or Uttar Ashadha, it gives the main period of Sun ruling at the time of the birth. Similarly, under Rohini, Hastha, and Shravana, it is the Moon's main period ; under Mrigashirsha, Chittra and Dhanistha, it is Mars' main period. Similarly, Aridra, Swati, and Satabhisag give rise to Rahu's rulership; Punarvasu, Vishakha and Uttara Bhadrapada Saturn's, Ashlesha, Jyestha, and Revati lead to Mercury; under Makkha, Moola and Ashwini, the main period of Ketu begins. If the Moon at the time of birth is in Purva Phalguni, Purva Ashadha or in Bharani, then the main period of Venus is at the commencement of one's life.

Under Vimshottri, the total time allotted to different planets is 120 years ; during this period all the planets complete one round of their rulership. This period is divided as follows: Sun 6 years ; Moon 10 years ; Mars 7 years ; Rahu 18 years ; Jupiter 16 years ; Saturn 19 years Mercury 17 years ; Ketu 7 years, and Venus 20 years. The cycle of rulership of different planets follows the same sequence. That is, the period of Moon's rulership always follows that of the Sun, that of Mars follows that of Moon and so on.

When the Moon is not at the beginning of an asterism, its placement and the determination of the planetary rulership have to be worked out carefully. Assuming the Moon's position at the time of the birth is in Krittika giving rise to the rulership of the Sun as 6 years, one has to work out how much of this period has elapsed if the Moon has already proceeded farther in the asterism. If it has traversed half the nakshatra, it will be assumed that half of the period of Sun's rulership is over. For this calculation, one has to take into account the fact that the extension of any nakshatra is of 13° 20', and on the basis of the position of the Moon in this parameter, the simple arithmetical calculations of proportionate relationship between the nakshatra traversed and the rulership period already completed could be applied. But in this calculation, however, it is to be remembered that the extent of every nakshatra is the same extending over 13° 20' of the zodiac, but the rulership period of different planets differs from one another. Therefore, if the ruling planet is Jupiter and the nakshatra is Punarvasu and the Moon has traversed half of it, the remaining period of the planetary rulership of Jupiter would be eight years though there is no difference between the size of extension of Punarvasu ruled by Jupiter (16 years) and Krittika ruled by Sun (6 years). No matter where the planetary rulership begins, the sequence of planetary rulerships remains the same, that is Mars will always follow Moon, Rahu will follow Mars and so on. And, also if the beginning of a planet lasts only for a few years depending upon the location of the Moon in any specific nakshatra, the following planets will have their full period of rulership. The balance uncovered by the first planet would be covered towards the end of the cycle.

An easier method of working out the period of the planetary rulership is to refer to the table which gives the balance of planetary rulership at the time of the birth depending upon the degree of the Moon in different signs of the zodiac. This, in fact, is a table derived from the basic guidelines indicated above. An abridged table on the basis of which by simple arithmetical calculation on the basis of the rule of the three, the detailed period of rulership and the balance at birth for intervening degrees can be worked out, is given below for ready reference :

For working out the sub-period in the main-period of a planet, we have to remember that each planet begins its rulership with the sub-period of the same planet. That is to say, the Sun's main-period would have at the beginning the sub-period of Sun itself. To work out the sub-period of a planet during the main rule of a planet, the easiest method is to multiply the duration of the rulership of the two planets ; the last digit of the product should be multiplied by 3 to give the number of days whilst the other digits coming before the last digit would give (without multiplying it with any number) the number of months for the sub-period of the intervening planet. To illustrate, if one had to find out the sub-period of

Balance of Vimshottri Dasa by Different Degrees
of the Moon

Longi-tude of Moon		Moon in Aries, Leo and Sagittarius	Moon in Taurus, Virgo, and Capricorn	Moon in Gemini, Libra and Aquarius		Moon in Cancer, Scorpio, and Pisces
		y m d	y m d	y m d		y m d
0° 0'	Ketu	7 0 0	Sun 4 6 0	Mars 3 6 0	Jupi.	4 0 0
3° 20'		5 3 0	3 0 0	1 9 0	Sat.	19 0 0
6° 40'		3 6 0	1 6 0	Rahu 18 0 0		14 3 0
10° 00'		1 9 0	Moon 10 0 0	13 6 0		9 6 0
13° 20'	Venus	20 0 0	7 6 0	9 0 0		4 9 0
16° 40'		15 0 0	5 0 0	4 6 0	Merc.	17 0 0
19° 00'		11 6 0	3 3 0	1 4 6		14 0 9
20° 00'		10 0 0	2 6 0	Jupi. 16 0 0		12 9 0
23° 20'		5 0 0	Mars 7 0 0	12 0 0		8 6 0
26° 40'	Sun	6 0 0	5 3 0	8 0 0		4 3 0
30° 00'		4 6 0	3 6 0	4 0 0		0 0 0

Jupiter in Mars main period of rulership, we may proceed as follows ; Mars' main period of rule is 7 years, and that of Jupiter is 16 years. By multiplying 7 with 16, we get 112. The last digit is 2 in this product which when multiplied by 3 gives 6 which becomes the number of days, whilst 11 which were the digits before 2 which was multiplied by 3, give the number of months. The sub-period of Jupiter in Mars main period thus works out to be 11 months 6 days.

A problem will arise regarding the fixing of the ruling sub-planet if some period from the total period of rulership of a planet has already elapsed. For example, if half the period of Jupiter has already elapsed, that is, if 8 years of Jupiter's main period of rulership is over, then, whose sub-period would start ? This will have to be worked out by calculating the sub-periods as if from the very beginning, and then locating the planet appearing at the beginning of the ninth year in the main period of Jupiter's period of lordship. At the end of 7 years 10 months 12 days Ketu's sub-period would have ended, therefore of the 2 years 8 months of the Venus sub-period only 2 years 6 months 12 days remains as balance at the commencement of the 9th year of Jupiter's rule.

For pin-pointing any predicted event more precisely, the *antaram*, also known as inter-period within the sub-period of a planetary rulership is worked out on the same principle. The same arithmetical principle of the rule of the three would yield the result keeping in view that every planet allows the following planetary rulership to begin with its own. That is to say that Mars main period would have Mars' sub-period as the first sub-period, but when Mars is having the sub-period of Jupiter, Jupiter will allow only Jupiter's inter-period or the sub-sub-period to follow its sub-period at the first instance. Thus after 1 year 5 months 15 days of period of the Martian main-dasa, when Jupiter's sub-period begins for 11 months 6 days, this sub-period will have the first sub-sub-period of Jupiter itself followed by Saturn's sub-sub-period and so on. The sequence of planetary lordship will always remain the same.

To find out the duration of a sub-sub-period of a planet, one has to multiply, in the short-cut method of calculation, the periods of rulership of *all the three* planets concerned. That is, to find out the sub-sub-period of Saturn in the sub-period of Jupiter in the main-period of Mars, one has to multiply $(19 \times 16 \times 7)$ which is equal to 2527 This product has to be divided by 40 which gives the number of days of the required sub-period of the planet concerned, which in the present case would be equal to 2 months 8 days 4 hours 12 minutes.

Astrology an Occult Art

Having worked out such detailed calculations, the Hindu astrology expects that the astrologers would endeavour to have an intuitive sensitivity to the working of the God's Plan of manifestation and perfection of men on the basis of the Law of Karma and applying the astrological guidelines envision the future awaiting for the man concerned. The ancient seers thought that this could be possible only if the individual astrologer lived a pure life and attained occult perfections known as *siddhis*. That is why astrology was considered an occult art, and it was given out to the world as occult knowledge in the mysteries of nature. Till that position of perfection is attained, the student of astrology may begin with whatever exoteric astrology is available to him in general treatises wherein many general astrological predictive principles are enumerated without clarifying their rationale.

SELECT BIBLIOGRAPHY

Ayer, V.A.K., *Everyday Astrology,* Taraporewala, Bombay, 1958

Behari, Bepin and Madhuri, *Introduction to Esoteric Astrology,* Sagar Publications, New Delhi, 1997

Defouw, Hart, and Robert Svaboda, *Light on Life,* Penguin, London, 1996

Ojha, Gopesh Kumar, *Hindu Predictive Astrology,* Taraporewala, Bombay, 1972

Raman, B.V., *Hindu Predictive Astrology,* Raman Publications, Bangalore, 1970

Other Astrological Books by Bepin Behari

A Study in Astrological Occultism, I.B.H. Prakashan, Bangalore, 1983

Myths and Symbols of Vedic Astrology, Morson Publishing Co., Utah, USA, 1990

Fundamentals of Vedic Astrology, Morson Publishing Co., Utah, USA, 1992

Planets in Signs and Houses, Morson Publishing Co., Utah, USA, 1993

Phalit Jyotish Mein Grahon Ke Phala (Hindi), Ranjan Publications, New Delhi, 1997

Esoteric Principles of Vedic Astrology : A Treatise on Advance Predictive Techniques, Ranjan Publications, New Delhi, 1997

Astrological Exploration of the Soul, Author, Delhi, 1997

Astrological Biographies, Seventeen Examples of Predictive Insight, Motilal Banarsidass, Delhi, 1998

Astrology Simplified, Sterling Paperbook, New Delhi, 1999

Phalit Jyotish Mein Janma-Lagna Ke Phala (Hindi), Ranjan Publications, New Delhi, 1999

INDEX

[This cross reference is intended to assist those readers who wish to pursue study of any related subject.]